DOMINANCE THROUGH DIVISION

The governance of Japan presents a puzzle: it is a democracy yet is dominated by a single party that wins almost all elections. Stranger still, the Liberal Democratic Party (LDP) and its policies are not particularly popular with voters. How has this situation arisen, and how is it sustained? Amy Catalinac argues that when politicians compete in electoral districts with discernible voter groups, they can make allocations of central government resources contingent on how groups vote. Using a wealth of quantitative and qualitative data spanning 1980–2014, Catalinac shows that LDP politicians have been doing just that, leveraging their dominance to make groups *compete* for resources. *Dominance Through Division* sheds new light on why the LDP has remained in power for so long, why opposition parties are weak, and why policy preferences do not always align with vote choice. It also explains why Japan's 1994 electoral reform has had limited impact.

Amy Catalinac is an associate professor of politics at New York University. She received her PhD from Harvard University, where she is also a faculty associate at the Program on US–Japan Relations. Amy has held appointments at Princeton University, Harvard University, and Australian National University. She is an editor at the *Journal of Politics*, the author of *Electoral Reform and National Security in Japan: From Pork to Foreign Policy* (Cambridge University Press, 2016), and has published articles in *American Political Science Review, World Politics, Journal of Politics, Comparative Political Studies, Electoral Studies*, and other journals. She is the recipient of prizes awarded by the *American Political Science Association* and *Midwest Political Science Association*. Amy is a cofounder and organizer of the Japanese Politics Online Seminar Series.

POLITICAL ECONOMY OF INSTITUTIONS AND DECISIONS

Series Editors

Jeffry Frieden, *Harvard University*
John Patty, *Emory University*
Elizabeth Maggie Penn, *Emory University*

Founding Editors

James E. Alt, *Harvard University*
Douglass C. North, *Washington University of St. Louis*

Other books in the series

Faisal Ahmed, *Conquests and Rents: A Political Economy of Dictatorship and Violence in Muslim Societies*
Alberto Alesina and Howard Rosenthal, *Partisan Politics, Divided Government and the Economy*
Lee J. Alston, Thrainn Eggertsson and Douglass C. North, eds., *Empirical Studies in Institutional Change*
Lee J. Alston and Joseph P. Ferrie, *Southern Paternalism and the Rise of the American Welfare State: Economics, Politics, and Institutions, 1865–1965*
James E. Alt and Kenneth Shepsle, eds., *Perspectives on Positive Political Economy*
Josephine T. Andrews, *When Majorities Fail: The Russian Parliament, 1990–1993*
Pamela Ban, Ju Yeon Park and Hye Young You, *Hearings on the Hill: The Politics of Informing Congress*
Jeffrey S. Banks and Eric A. Hanushek, eds., *Modern Political Economy: Old Topics, New Directions*
Yoram Barzel, *Economic Analysis of Property Rights*, 2nd edition
Yoram Barzel, *A Theory of the State: Economic Rights, Legal Rights, and the Scope of the State*
Robert Bates, *Beyond the Miracle of the Market: The Political Economy of Agrarian Development in Kenya*
Jenna Bednar, *The Robust Federation: Principles of Design*
Adam Bonica and Maya Sen, *The Judicial Tug of War: How Lawyers, Politicians, and Ideological Incentives Shape the American Judiciary*
Charles M. Cameron, *Veto Bargaining: Presidents and the Politics of Negative Power*
Erin Baggott Carter and Brett L. Carter, *Propaganda in Autocracies: Institutions, Information, and the Politics of Belief*
Kelly H. Chang, *Appointing Central Bankers: The Politics of Monetary Policy in the United States and the European Monetary Union*
Tom S. Clark, *The Supreme Court: An Analytical History of Constitutional Decision Making*
Mark Copelovitch and David A. Singer, *Banks on the Brink: Global Capital, Securities Markets, and the Political Roots of Financial Crises*

Peter Cowhey and Mathew McCubbins, eds., *Structure and Policy in Japan and the United States: An Institutionalist Approach*
Gary W. Cox, *The Efficient Secret: The Cabinet and the Development of Political Parties in Victorian England*
Gary W. Cox, *Making Votes Count: Strategic Coordination in the World's Electoral System*
Gary W. Cox, *Marketing Sovereign Promises: Monopoly Brokerage and the Growth of the English State*
Gary W. Cox and Jonathan N. Katz, *Elbridge Gerry's Salamander: The Electoral Consequences of the Reapportionment Revolution*
Adam Dean, *Opening Up by Cracking Down: Labor Repression and Trade Liberalization in Democratic Developing Countries*
Tine De Moore, *The Dilemma of the Commoners: Understanding the Use of Common-Pool Resources in Long-Term Perspective*
Adam Dean, *From Conflict to Coalition: Profit-Sharing Institutions and the Political Economy of Trade*
Mark Dincecco, *Political Transformations and Public Finances: Europe, 1650–1913*
Mark Dincecco and Massimiliano Gaetano Onorato, *From Warfare to Wealth: The Military Origins of Urban Prosperity in Europe*
Raymond M. Duch and Randolph T. Stevenson, *The Economic Vote: How Political and Economic Institutions Condition Election Results*
Jean Ensminger, *Making a Market: The Institutional Transformation of an African Society*
David Epstein and Sharyn O'Halloran, *Delegating Powers: A Transaction Cost Politics Approach to Policy Making under Separate Powers*
Kathryn Firmin-Sellers, *The Transformation of Property Rights in the Gold Coast: An Empirical Study Applying Rational Choice Theory*
Sean Gailmard, *Agents of Empire: English Imperial Governance and the Making of American Political Institutions*
Clark C. Gibson, *Politicians and Poachers: The Political Economy of Wildlife Policy in Africa*
Daniel W. Gingerich, *Political Institutions and Party-Directed Corruption in South America*
Avner Greif, *Institutions and the Path to the Modern Economy: Lessons from Medieval Trade*
Jeffrey D. Grynaviski, *Partisan Bonds: Political Reputations and Legislative Accountability*
Stephen Haber, Armando Razo and Noel Maurer, *The Politics of Property Rights: Political Instability, Credible Commitments, and Economic Growth in Mexico, 1876–1929*
Ron Harris, *Industrializing English Law: Entrepreneurship and Business Organization, 1720–1844*
Anna L. Harvey, *Votes Without Leverage: Women in American Electoral Politics, 1920–1970*
Seth J. Hill, *Frustrated Majorities: How Issue Intensity Enables Smaller Groups of Voters to Get What They Want*
Shigeo Hirano and James M. Snyder, Jr., *Primary Elections in the United States*

Murray Horn, *The Political Economy of Public Administration: Institutional Choice in the Public Sector*
John D. Huber, *Rationalizing Parliament: Legislative Institutions and Party Politics in France* Jack Knight, Institutions and Social Conflict
Sean Ingham, *Rule of Multiple Majorities: A New Theory of Popular Control*
John E. Jackson, Jacek Klich and Krystyna Poznanska, *The Political Economy of Poland's Transition: New Firms and Reform Governments*
Jack Knight, *Institutions and Social Conflict*
Michael Laver and Kenneth Shepsle, eds., *Cabinet Ministers and Parliamentary Government*
Michael Laver and Kenneth Shepsle, eds., *Making and Breaking Governments: Cabinets and Legislatures in Parliamentary Democracies*
Michael Laver and Kenneth Shepsle, eds., *Cabinet Ministers and Parliamentary Government*
Margaret Levi, *Consent, Dissent, and Patriotism*
Brian Levy and Pablo T. Spiller, eds., *Regulations, Institutions, and Commitment: Comparative Studies of Telecommunications*
Leif Lewin, Ideology and Strategy: *A Century of Swedish Politics (English Edition)*
Gary Libecap, *Contracting for Property Rights*
John Londregan, *Legislative Institutions and Ideology in Chile*
Arthur Lupia and Mathew D. McCubbins, *The Democratic Dilemma: Can Citizens Learn What They Need to Know?*
C. Mantzavinos, *Individuals, Institutions, and Markets*
Mathew D. McCubbins and Terry Sullivan, eds., *Congress: Structure and Policy*
Anne Meng, *Constraining Dictatorship: From Personalized Rule to Institutionalized Regimes*
Gary J. Miller, *Above Politics: Bureaucratic Discretion and Credible Commitment*
Gary J. Miller, *Managerial Dilemmas: The Political Economy of Hierarchy*
Ilia Murtazashvili, *The Political Economy of the American Frontier*
Monika Nalepa, *After Authoritarianism: Transitional Justice and Democratic Stability*
Douglass C. North, *Institutions, Institutional Change, and Economic Performance*
Elinor Ostrom, *Governing the Commons: The Evolution of Institutions for Collective Action*
Sonal S. Pandya, *Trading Spaces: Foreign Direct Investment Regulation, 1970–2000*
John W. Patty and Elizabeth Maggie Penn, *Social Choice and Legitimacy*
Daniel N. Posner, *Institutions and Ethnic Politics in Africa*
J. Mark Ramseyer, *Odd Markets in Japanese History: Law and Economic Growth*
J. Mark Ramseyer and Frances Rosenbluth, *The Politics of Oligarchy: Institutional Choice in Imperial Japan*
Stephanie J. Rickard, *Spending to Win: Political Institutions, Economic Geography, and Government Subsidies*
Jean-Laurent Rosenthal, *The Fruits of Revolution: Property Rights, Litigation, and French Agriculture, 1700–1860*

Michael L. Ross, *Timber Booms and Institutional Breakdown in Southeast Asia*
Meredith Rolfe, *Voter Turnout: A Social Theory of Political Participation*
Shanker Satyanath, *Globalization, Politics, and Financial Turmoil: Asia's Banking Crisis*
Alberto Simpser, *Why Governments and Parties Manipulate Elections: Theory, Practice, and Implications*
Norman Schofield, *Architects of Political Change: Constitutional Quandaries and Social Choice Theory*
Norman Schofield and Itai Sened, *Multiparty Democracy: Elections and Legislative Politics*
Alastair Smith, *Election Timing*
Pablo T. Spiller and Mariano Tommasi, *The Institutional Foundations of Public Policy in Argentina: A Transactions Cost Approach*
David Stasavage, *Public Debt and the Birth of the Democratic State: France and Great Britain, 1688–1789*
Charles Stewart III, *Budget Reform Politics: The Design of the Appropriations Process in the House of Representatives, 1865–1921*
George Tsebelis and Jeannette Money, *Bicameralism*
Georg Vanberg, *The Politics of Constitutional Review in Germany*
Nicolas van de Walle, *African Economies and the Politics of Permanent Crisis, 1979–1999*
Stefanie Walter, *Financial Crises and the Politics of Macroeconomic Adjustments*
John Waterbury, *Exposed to Innumerable Delusions: Public Enterprise and State Power in Egypt, India, Mexico, and Turkey*
David L. Weimer, ed., *The Political Economy of Property Rights Institutional Change and Credibility in the Reform of Centrally Planned Economies*

DOMINANCE THROUGH DIVISION

Group-Based Clientelism in Japan

AMY CATALINAC

New York University

CAMBRIDGE UNIVERSITY PRESS

CAMBRIDGE
UNIVERSITY PRESS

Shaftesbury Road, Cambridge CB2 8EA, United Kingdom

One Liberty Plaza, 20th Floor, New York, NY 10006, USA

477 Williamstown Road, Port Melbourne, VIC 3207, Australia

314–321, 3rd Floor, Plot 3, Splendor Forum, Jasola District Centre,
New Delhi – 110025, India

103 Penang Road, #05–06/07, Visioncrest Commercial, Singapore 238467

Cambridge University Press is part of Cambridge University Press & Assessment, a department of the University of Cambridge.

We share the University's mission to contribute to society through the pursuit of education, learning and research at the highest international levels of excellence.

www.cambridge.org
Information on this title: www.cambridge.org/9781009588508

DOI: 10.1017/9781009588522

© Amy Catalinac 2025

This publication is in copyright. Subject to statutory exception and to the provisions of relevant collective licensing agreements, no reproduction of any part may take place without the written permission of Cambridge University Press & Assessment.

When citing this work, please include a reference to the
DOI 10.1017/9781009588522

First published 2025

A catalogue record for this publication is available from the British Library

A Cataloging-in-Publication data record for this book is available from the Library of Congress

ISBN 978-1-009-58850-8 Hardback
ISBN 978-1-009-58853-9 Paperback

Cambridge University Press & Assessment has no responsibility for the persistence or accuracy of URLs for external or third-party internet websites referred to in this publication and does not guarantee that any content on such websites is, or will remain, accurate or appropriate.

For my children, Elizabeth and Arthur

Contents

List of Figures		page xv
List of Tables		xvii
Acknowledgments		xxi

1	Introduction		1
	1.1	Theory in Brief	4
	1.2	Empirics in Brief	11
	1.3	Contributions to Japanese Politics in Brief	19
2	The Enduring Success of Japan's Liberal Democratic Party		24
	2.1	Victorious under Different Electoral Systems	28
		2.1.1 SNTV-MMD, 1958–1993	29
		2.1.2 MMM, 1994–2021	34
		2.1.3 Untouched by Post-2012 Party System Transformation	49
	2.2	Eclipsing Other Parties in Support	51
	2.3	Electoral Institutions Advantage the LDP?	54
	2.4	LDP's Policies Are More Popular?	60
	2.5	Distributive Politics?	65
	2.6	How This Book Contributes	70
3	A Theory of Group-Based Clientelism		73
	3.1	What Is Clientelism?	76
	3.2	Problem of Contingency	80
	3.3	Shifting the Target of the Exchange from Individual to Group	84
	3.4	Political Institutions Are Key	91
	3.5	Contributions	100
		3.5.1 Bringing Institutions Back	101
		3.5.2 New Ideas about the Role of Brokers	103
		3.5.3 Clientelism Occurring at High Levels of Development	105
		3.5.4 Democracy Is Undermined, But by Club Goods	106
4	Second Prize Is a Set of Steak Knives		108
	4.1	The Tournament Theory	112

	4.2 Tournaments in Many Electoral Districts	120
	4.3 Hypotheses	124
	4.4 Implications	127
	4.4.1 Raising the Costs of Voting for the Opposition	127
	4.4.2 Policy Positions Matter Little to Incumbent Reelection	129
	4.4.3 Money Flows to Core Supporters	129
	4.4.4 All Groups Are Subject to the Same Competition	133
	4.4.5 Resource Allocations Take Place after Elections	134
	4.4.6 Asymmetry in Group Size Matters	135
5	Perfect Storm Conditions for Tournaments in Japan	137
	5.1 Observing Support	140
	5.1.1 How Votes Are Counted	143
	5.1.2 How the Level at Which Support Is Discernible Varies	145
	5.2 Delivering Goods	147
	5.2.1 Vertical Fiscal Imbalance in Japan	148
	5.2.2 Municipalities Depend on Central Government Transfers	152
	5.2.3 National Treasury Disbursements	155
	5.2.4 Impact of Decentralization	161
	5.3 Fewer Tournament-Possible Districts over Time	163
	5.4 Election Outcomes Differ in Tournament-Possible Districts	168
6	How Politicians Tie Money to Electoral Support	173
	6.1 Empirical Strategy	175
	6.1.1 Data	176
	6.1.2 Variables	178
	6.2 Within Districts, Money Follows Support	180
	6.2.1 Before Electoral Reform, 1980–1993	184
	6.2.2 Competing Explanations and Placebo Tests, 1980–1993	188
	6.2.3 After Electoral Reform, 1996–2014	195
	6.2.4 Competing Explanations and Placebo Tests, 1996–2014	198
	6.2.5 LDP Winners Double Down after 2009 Election	203
	6.3 A Convex Relationship between Support and Transfers	206
	6.4 Evidence of the Theory's Microfoundations	210
	6.4.1 LDP Politicians Influence NTD Allocations	211
	6.4.2 Voters Are Aware of This Strategy	222
	6.5 Where Prior Research Went Wrong	228
7	Which Electoral Districts Get More Money	233
	7.1 Empirical Strategy	239
	7.1.1 Variables	239
	7.1.2 Potential Confounders	241
	7.2 Asymmetric Electoral Districts Receive More Money	246
	7.2.1 Comparing Electoral Districts in the Same Election	248

Contents

	7.2.2 Comparing Electoral Districts over Time	251
	7.2.3 Japan's 1994 Electoral Reform as a Quasiexperiment	257
7.3	Asymmetric Electoral Districts Exhibit Less Support	263
7.4	Reconciling Puzzles in Prior Work	269
8	How Tournaments Impact Decisions to Vote	272
8.1	Empirical Strategy	275
	8.1.1 Variables	276
	8.1.2 Potential Confounders	278
8.2	Concentrating Votes on a Single LDP Winner Increases Turnout	283
	8.2.1 Before Electoral Reform, 1980–1993	287
	8.2.2 Competing Explanations and Placebo Tests	290
	8.2.3 After Electoral Reform, 1996–2014	294
	8.2.4 Competing Explanations and Placebo Tests	297
8.3	A Convex Relationship between Vote Concentration and Turnout	299
8.4	Impact of Competitiveness Depends on Vote Concentration	301
	8.4.1 Competing Explanations	307
8.5	Takeaways for Japanese Politics	309
9	Conclusion	311
9.1	Questions for Future Work	315
Appendix A		321
A.1 Supplementary Tables for Chapter 2		322
A.2 Notes on Data Collection, Chapters 6–8		324
A.3 Supplementary Material for Chapter 6		328
A.4 Supplementary Material for Chapter 7		335
A.5 Supplementary Material for Chapter 8		342
References		345
Index		363

Figures

2.1	Tree depicting the transformation of Japan's party system, 1955–2018	page 50
2.2	Public support for LDP and second most-supported party, 1980–2020 (Jiji Survey Data)	52
5.1	Number of municipalities per electoral district, 1980–2014	147
5.2	Tax revenue by tier of government, 1980–2015	148
5.3	Expenditure by tier of government, 1980–2015	149
5.4	Municipal spending by purpose, 1980–2015	150
5.5	Municipal spending by type, 1980–2015	151
5.6	Revenue structure of local governments, 1980–2015	152
5.7	Share of electoral districts in Japan's Lower House elections (1980–2014) in which tournaments are not possible	166
5.8	Share of all voters subject to a tournament in Japan's Lower House elections, 1980–2014	168
6.1	The relationship between rank and transfers is convex, 1980–2014	208
6.2	The relationship between rank and transfers is convex, 1980–1993	209
6.3	The relationship between rank and transfers is convex, 1996–2014	210
6.4	LDP candidates in tournament-possible districts include more discussion of pork-barreling in their manifestos, 1986–2009	219
7.1	A plot of the concentration of voting population per electoral district for tournament-possible districts with LDP winners, 1980–2014	247
7.2	This plots the concentration of voting population ($HI_{d,t}$) in districts prior to Japan's electoral reform in 1993 (on the left) and in districts after reform (on the right)	268

List of Figures

8.1 The relationship between rank and turnout is convex, 1980–2014 — 300
8.2 Average marginal effect of Margin$_{d,t}$, with 95% confidence intervals, at different levels of Rank(Single LDP Winner VS$_{m,t}$) — 306
A.1 Tree depicting the transformation of Japan's party system, 1955–2018 (Japanese names) — 322
A.2 Key to the English and Japanese names of parties represented by numbers in Figures 2.1 and A.1 — 323

Tables

2.1	Seats and votes captured by major parties in elections, 1958–1993	*page* 30
2.2	Seats and votes captured by major parties in elections, 1996–2009	35
2.3	Seats and votes captured by major parties in elections, 2012–2021	43
5.1	Share of electoral districts not meeting the conditions for a tournament, 1980–2014	164
5.2	Tournament-possible districts have higher support for LDP candidates and higher turnout, 1980–2014	169
6.1	Within electoral districts, municipalities exhibiting higher support for LDP winner(s) received more transfers after elections, 1980–2014	182
6.2	Within electoral districts, municipalities exhibiting higher support for LDP winner(s) received more transfers after elections, 1980–1993	185
6.3	Increases in support within the same municipality translate into increases in the amount of transfers received, 1980–1993	187
6.4	Within electoral districts, the amount of transfers municipalities receive is not determined by support for senior LDP winners, non-LDP winners, or losing LDP candidates, 1980–1993	190
6.5	Municipalities that slip in support are penalized with fewer transfers after elections, 1983–1993	194
6.6	Within electoral districts, municipalities exhibiting higher support for LDP winners received more transfers after elections, 1996–2014 (excluding 2009)	196
6.7	Within electoral districts, municipalities exhibiting higher support for LDP losers did not receive more transfers after elections, 1996–2014 (excluding 2009)	199

List of Tables

6.8	In electoral districts without LDP winners in elections, 1996–2014 (excluding 2009), LDP-aligned independents distributed transfers in accordance with support, but New Frontier Party and Democratic Party of Japan winners did not	202
6.9	Within electoral districts in 2009, municipalities exhibiting higher support for DPJ winners did not receive more transfers, but municipalities exhibiting higher support for LDP winners did	205
6.10	Survey respondents who live in tournament-possible districts and who say they like LDP policies are more likely to vote for LDP candidates	226
6.11	Among those who voted for an LDP candidate, being in a tournament-possible district is negatively associated with liking LDP policies	227
7.1	Across districts with LDP winners, greater asymmetry in municipality size is associated with receiving more transfers after elections, 1980–2014	249
7.2	Across electoral districts with LDP winners, greater heterogeneity in municipality size is associated with receiving more transfers after elections, 1980–1993	253
7.3	Across electoral districts with LDP winners, greater heterogeneity in municipality size is associated with receiving more transfers after elections, 1996–2014	255
7.4	Increases in district-level asymmetry are associated with increases in postelection transfers, 1996	260
7.5	Across districts, greater heterogeneity in municipality size is associated with less support for the LDP in elections, 1980–2014	266
8.1	Municipalities that concentrate votes on a single LDP winner have higher turnout in elections, 1980–2014	284
8.2	Municipalities that concentrate more votes on a single LDP winner have higher turnout in elections, 1980–1993	288
8.3	Increases in voting concentration within the same municipality are associated with increases in turnout, 1980–1993	289
8.4	Municipalities delivering more votes to the LDP per se do not have higher turnout in elections, 1980–1993	292
8.5	Municipalities that concentrate more votes on a single LDP winner have higher turnout in elections, 1996–2014	296

List of Tables

8.6	Municipalities concentrating more votes on losing LDP candidates and DPJ winners do not have higher turnout in elections, 1996–2014	298
8.7	Increases in competitiveness impact turnout differently, depending on how supportive municipalities are for their LDP winners, 1980–2014	304
8.8	The finding that increases in competitiveness impact turnout differently, depending on how supportive municipalities are for their LDP winners, is robust to alternative explanations	308
A.1	Descriptive statistics for variables used in Chapter 6	328
A.2	Table 6.2, with alternative controls	329
A.3	Table 6.4, with alternative specifications of electoral support	330
A.4	A municipality's postelection transfer allocation as a cubic function of its position in a ranking constructed on the basis of support, 1980–2014	331
A.5	A municipality's postelection transfer allocation as a cubic function of its position in a ranking constructed on the basis of support, 1980–1993	332
A.6	A municipality's postelection transfer allocation as a cubic function of its position in a ranking constructed on the basis of support, 1996–2014	333
A.7	Relationship between support and transfers across districts is negative and statistically insignificant in the absence of district-level controls, 1980–2014	334
A.8	Descriptive statistics for variables used in Chapter 7	335
A.9	Table 7.1, with alternative indicators for strength of LDP support	336
A.10	Table 7.1, with no controls for strength of support for the LDP	337
A.11	Table 7.2, with an alternative indicator for strength of LDP support	338
A.12	Table 7.2, with an alternative indicator for strength of LDP support	339
A.13	Table 7.5, on the sample of electoral districts from the prereform period, 1980–1993	340
A.14	Table 7.5, on the sample of electoral districts from the postreform period, 1996–2014	341
A.15	Descriptive statistics for variables used in Chapter 8	342
A.16	Turnout as a cubic function of the degree to which a municipality concentrated votes on a single LDP winner, 1980–2014	343

Acknowledgments

As with all manuscripts of this length, I have many people to thank. Working with Bruce Bueno de Mesquita and Alastair Smith early on in my time at New York University made me profoundly interested in the concept of tournaments and whether they could account for the pronounced disconnect I observed in the politics of Japan, in which many people appeared to have feelings toward the Liberal Democratic Party that ranged from lukewarm to negative; yet those feelings proved sufficient to stave off almost all serious threats to the party's hold on power. I learned so much from working with them, about both theory and empirics, and enjoyed the experience very much. Without the work that we did together, I would not have embarked on this lengthier study.

Without the dedicated assistance of Shiro Kuriwaki, the data upon which this manuscript is based would never have become so clean and complete. We spent many hours trying to get this dataset just right, which meant managing the copious (indeed thousands) of changes in municipal and electoral district boundaries that took place during the thirty-five-year period that I wanted to study. I remain enormously grateful for the care, conscientiousness, and patience Shiro demonstrated while working with me. I also want to thank Tatsuya Koyama and Ivan Aleksandrov for assistance with figures, data, and code and Kenneth McElwain, Kuni Nemoto, Dias Akhmetbekov, Fukumoto Kentaro, Yusaku Horiuchi, Cristina Mac Gregor Vanegas, and Dan Smith for assistance with data. Maia Halle deserves credit for the beautiful and informative party trees included in Chapter 2.

An earlier version of this manuscript was presented at a book workshop in the fall of 2022 hosted by the politics department at New York University. This was attended by a distinguished set of scholars of comparative politics and the politics of Japan: Gary Cox, Phillip Lipscy, Patti Maclachlan, Noah Nathan, Len Schoppa, and Dan Smith. I am so grateful to these scholars for reading what in hindsight I can say was a very

Acknowledgments

early draft and providing me with pages of feedback on every single chapter. The manuscript is so much better for this conference. It is also better for the comments and suggestions of Susan J. Pharr, who continues to offer all manner of support for her former students. I also wish to thank Jeff Frieden, John Patty, and Maggie Penn, the editors of the Political Economy of Institutions and Decisions Series at Cambridge, for reading the manuscript and being so enthusiastic about it being part of their series. I am also grateful for the comments and suggestions of the anonymous reviewers, whose feedback helped shape the book what it became.

Parts of the manuscript were presented at workshops and seminar series in the United States, Japan, and New Zealand. In particular, I presented chapters at the University of Southern California, Victoria University of Wellington, the University of Tokyo, Musashi University, Stony Brook University, Temple University, Yale University, and Princeton University. I want to extend a heartfelt thank you to all the scholars who invited me, took the time to host me during my visits, and provided me with thoughtful feedback on my work. These scholars include Saori Katada, Gabrielle Cheung, Stephen Levine, Fiona Barker, Kenneth McElwain, Kuniaki Nemoto, Charles McClean, Helen Milner, Lucia Motolinia, Stephanie Rickard, Steven Wilkinson, Ana de la O, Michael Peress, Adam Ziegfeld, Jessica Stanton, Taishi Muraoka, and Jim Raymo. Paper-length versions of the argument and empirics were also presented at the American Political Science Association, Midwest Political Science Association, Southern Political Science Association, Asia Polmeth, Visions in Political Methodology, and the Japanese Society for Quantitative Political Science. At these conferences, I received exceptional feedback from dedicated discussants Jean Hong, Alicia Cooperman, Guillermo Rosas, Matthew Simonson, and Nishimura Tsubasa and also from Junko Kato, Herbert Kitschelt, Kosuke Imai, Megumi Naoi, Yukari Iwanami, Kentaro Fukumoto, Yusaku Horiuchi, Yuki Shiraito, Masaaki Higashijima, Hidekuni Washida and Jiajia Zhou.

I have now been conducting research on Japanese politics for close to twenty years. There are so many people who work *in* Japanese politics, for members of parliament, the bureaucracy, and for the LDP itself, to whom I am grateful. These people welcome me with open hearts whenever I travel to Japan and have provided me with an unrelenting stream of encouragement, introductions, and time over the years. It was very hard to work on this manuscript when I could not travel to Japan due to COVID-19. I am so grateful to these individuals and to other friends in Japan who helped me with all manner of inquiries when I was finally able to visit again. I also want to thank the friends with whom I am delighted

Acknowledgments

to run the Japanese Politics Online Seminar Series: Christina Davis, Shinju Fujihira, Yusaku Horiuchi, Saori Katada, Phillip Lipscy, and Dan Smith. I will also remain forever grateful for the support of Dolly Ibanez and Elainy Rodriguez Martinez.

My biggest thanks go to my family: in particular, my husband Arthur and my children Elizabeth and Arthur. Frankly speaking, completing this manuscript took a lot from me, and they were all very patient as the weeks of working on it stretched on and on. Every day, I am reminded in countless ways how lucky I am to have them: my biggest cheerleaders. I also want to thank my parents, Steve Catalinac and Beth Inglis, for taking me to Japan when I was young, and for encouraging my interest in it, both then and now.

I

Introduction

Political science has become a broad discipline. This book takes it back to a question present at its founding and central to its purpose: How do incumbent political parties in democracies seek to stay in power? Because incumbent parties have control over central government resources, this question often boils down to asking how they seek to use the resources under their control to ward off electoral challenges and prolong their reign. While much ink has been spilled on such an old question, the central contention of this book is that there is more to be done. We do not know *enough* about what democratically elected incumbent parties do in office to try to lay the groundwork for their victory in subsequent elections. As a result, we cannot assess what consequences this laying of the groundwork has for the quality of political competition we observe.

This book breaks new ground in three ways. The first is *theoretical*. It offers a theory for how incumbent parties in a democracy can harness central government resources in ways that increase their chances of winning the next election. Put simply, the theory holds that under a certain configuration of political institutions, politicians in the ruling party will be able to increase the number of votes won by dividing their electorates up into groups of voters and making it clear that the amount of central government resources groups receive will be a function of their voting behavior. The second part of the theory, which draws on prior work, holds that when the ruling party is *dominant*, in the sense that there is low uncertainty over whether it will win the next election, its members will be able to make groups compete for resources. By making it clear that the amount of resources groups receive after elections will be a function of how much support they gave the incumbent in the election, with a very large resource allocation awaiting the group that gave the incumbent the most support, incumbents can convert voting into a competition over which groups are the most electorally supportive. In this competition, politicians have *voters* compete for *their* favor, rather than the other way around. Thus, a key implication is that competition plays a bigger role in the election of dominant parties than we realized. However, this competition is not of a *democratic* nature, in which politicians vie for the favor of voters, but of a decidedly *undemocratic* nature, in which voters are having to vie for the favor of the politician.

Critically, whether politicians are able to do this is conditional upon a certain configuration of political institutions. These institutions are *electoral*, but they do not pertain to the electoral *system* under which votes are converted into seats. Instead, they pertain to how the *electoral districts* in which candidates run for office are *configured*, relative to the lower-tier administrative entities to which central government resources can be delivered. A key takeaway is that the electoral strategy envisaged by the theory is not limited to any particular electoral system. It is possible under different electoral systems, so long as the electoral districts used to select members of parliament are configured in a way that satisfies the theory's requirements.

The book also breaks new ground *methodologically*. It offers a blueprint for how researchers interested in examining whether an incumbent party in their country of interest is adopting this strategy should go about doing so. First, a deep dive into the country's political institutions is required, to ascertain whether electoral districts meeting these conditions exist and if so, how many and which ones. This involves the aggregation of different types of information, not readily available in existing datasets, concerning how national elections are administered and votes are counted, how the country is organized at the subnational level, and how those two features interact with each other. If there are electoral districts meeting these conditions, the second task is to gather data at the level of the lower-tier administrative entity located within these districts. This data should encompass voting behavior, resource allocations, and any confounding variables with the potential to influence the relationship between voting behavior and resource allocations. Once gathered, researchers should leverage deep case knowledge of the country in question to devise and implement stringent tests of the theory. To be most effective, these tests should be designed to pit the expectations of the theory against those of rival theories, ideally rival theories germane to the country in question.

The testing process should not be limited to quantitative tests. If incumbent party members are pursuing the electoral strategy described in this book, then we should be able to observe evidence of it in the statistical analyses of government spending and voting behavior that I recommend. But we should also be able to observe evidence of it in other facets of their behavior and in the political system they have helped shape. We

Introduction

should observe particular types of people seeking to enter politics under the party's label. We should observe party members devoting a disproportionate amount of time to activities that help them implement this strategy, which can include lending their support to informal institutions set up to facilitate it. We should observe evidence of their pursuit of this strategy in their dealings with voters and central government bureaucrats. We may even observe, as we do in this book, popular fiction reflecting politicians' use of this strategy. Bringing different types of evidence to bear on this question will help assuage concerns that the relationships observed in the statistical analyses are products of factors orthogonal to the theory.

Finally, the book breaks new ground *substantively*. The subtlety of the information needed to assess whether the conditions for the theory hold, and the comprehensiveness of data that must be gathered to implement rigorous tests of it, mean that I have limited this book's evaluation of it to a single case: Japan's Liberal Democratic Party (LDP). The results of my tests, which lend strong support to the theory, enable me to shed new light on the question of why the governance of Japan, the world's fourth-largest economy and a democracy since 1947, has been dominated by the LDP for the near duration of that party's existence. The LDP's electoral successes are unparalleled in the democratic world. Of the twenty-two Lower House elections held since the party's formation in 1955, the LDP has won a plurality in twenty-one, a majority in fourteen, and in excess of 60% of seats in seven.[1] This extraordinary electoral record, in a parliamentary democracy in which the party controlling the Lower House elects the prime minister, has put the LDP at the helm of the government of Japan for all but four of the past sixty-nine years.

Unsurprisingly, political scientists have tried to explain this puzzle. They have crafted compelling explanations centered on the advantages conferred on the LDP by the electoral system, the popularity of its policy positions, and its use of government resources to cultivate and nurture core supporters, respectively. However, the combination of real-world events and scholarly work has, over time, chipped away at the explanatory power of these accounts. One explanation holds that if we observe LDP victories *today*, under current electoral rules, it must be because the party's policies are superior to the opposition's (Krauss and Pekkanen 2010; Rosenbluth and Thies 2010). However, since 2012 the LDP has managed some of its largest seat majorities ever, yet repeated attempts to ascertain the popularity of its policy platforms reveal that they are

---

[1] As this book was going to press, a snap election was held on October 27, 2024. This is not included in this tally.

among the *least* popular, not the most popular (Eshima et al. N.D.; Horiuchi, Smith and Yamamoto 2020). Another explanation attributes LDP victories to a concerted effort to steer government resources toward core supporters, who vote for the party because they have no guarantee they would be able to receive similar favors from another party (Ramseyer and Rosenbluth 1993). Despite the accumulation of qualitative evidence bolstering this, repeated attempts to verify it with statistical analyses of money and votes have either revealed *no* relationship between the two or a relationship that runs in the *opposite* direction: Places that deliver *fewer* votes for the party get rewarded with *more* money (McMichael 2018; Hirano 2011; Saito 2010; Horiuchi and Saito 2003; Reed 2001).

Ultimately, my use of Japan as a laboratory in which to test the theory enables me to offer an original account of LDP dominance. While the *account* is original, several of its *key inputs*, including municipality and electoral district size, the fiscal relationship between tiers of government in Japan, and the share of subsidies in the government's budget, are not (Scheiner 2006; Saito 2010; Hirose 1993; Reed 1986). Prior work recognized the importance of these inputs, but the theory in *this book* helps us see how they work, both together and in tandem with other, previously *unnoticed* inputs, to put LDP politicians in a position where they are able to vanquish their opponents, election after election, minimizing the impact of variables that tend to bring about changes of government in other countries, such as economic downturns, policy mishaps, or revelations of corruption and incompetence. We are left with a much firmer grip on the puzzle of single-party dominance in Japan. We are also left with new explanations for numerous other facets of Japanese politics, such as why the LDP is factionalized, why its politicians form both programmatic and particularistic linkages with voters, why these politicians structure their campaign mobilization the way they do, why these politicians are drawn from a relatively narrow set of former occupations, and – perhaps most importantly – why Japan's 1994 electoral reform was insufficient to usher in a competitive, two-party system with regular alternations in power.

1.1 THEORY IN BRIEF

The book's theory is in two parts. First, I make the case that when politicians are running for office in electoral districts divisible into groups of voters, from whom levels of electoral support are discernible and to whom central government resources are targetable, they will have the tools to pull those groups into a clientelistic exchange, in which the amount of money groups receive after elections is tied to how they voted.

I call this group-based clientelism (GBC). Fleshing out this claim and its implications is the subject of Chapter 3.

Scholars of comparative politics will be familiar with the large literature on clientelism that has cropped up in the past two decades, ignited by seminal works in the mid 2000s (Stokes 2005; Kitschelt and Wilkinson 2007).[2] Clientelism is a mode of distribution that occurs when a politician is able to tie the distribution of a valued good to a person's voting behavior. By ties, I mean that the good is conferred on the understanding that the politician will receive a vote in return, and if it becomes apparent that she is not, will not, or did not, the good is withdrawn. Clientelistic exchanges, at least how they have traditionally been conceived, embody contingency: The distribution of goods is made contingent on how someone votes. Contingency demarcates clientelistic exchanges from nonclientelistic exchanges. A nonclientelistic mode of distribution is when a politician distributes goods in the hope they turn into votes but does not make their distribution *contingent* on votes in the same way. Reflecting the sheer volume of work on clientelism, the *Annual Review of Political Science* has seen fit to publish not one but three articles surveying developments in the field in recent years (Hicken and Nathan 2020; Mares and Young 2016; Hicken 2011).[3]

The first part of my theory, which holds that under the right conditions, politicians can pursue GBC, extends the clientelism literature in several new directions. First, it offers a solution to the *problem of contingency*, widely recognized as plaguing virtually all modern-day studies of clientelism. What is this problem? In a clientelistic exchange, a politician seeks to buy votes with goods; she is exchanging goods for votes. Such an exchange is not simultaneous; typically, there is a delay between when a voter receives the good from the politician and when she casts her vote. This delay would matter less if the politician could verify that the voter cast her ballot correctly (for her). But a hallmark of democracy is that voters enjoy the right to vote *in secret*. The secret ballot prevents the politician from discerning how any voter she has given goods to votes (Mares 2015). The fact that the politician cannot verify whether the individuals she is attempting to buy votes from followed through on

---

[2] For an introduction to work on clientelism, see Golden and Nazrullaeva (2023); Aspinall et al. (2022); Ravanilla, Haim and Hicken (2022); Cruz (2019); Larreguy, Marshall and Querubín (2016); Nichter (2018); Bussell (2019); Kuo (2018); Diaz-Cayeros, Estévez and Magaloni (2016); Holland and Palmer-Rubin (2015); Gans-Morse, Mazzuca and Nichter (2014); Weitz-Shapiro (2014); Stokes et al. (2013); Hicken (2011); Chandra (2007); Stokes (2007); Medina and Stokes (2007); Magaloni (2006); Wantchekon (2003); Piattoni et al. (2001); and Scott (1972).
[3] Four, if Golden and Min (2013) which covers distributive politics more generally, is counted.

their promises and voted for her gives those individuals the opportunity to defect, where defection means taking the good and voting for someone else. So long as the politician receives a *modicum* of votes in a locale, a voter will always be able to credibly claim that *she* supplied one of those votes, and the politician will not know the difference.

Given that the buying and selling of votes is troubling from the perspective of democratic integrity, and the secret ballot protects voters from being pulled into them, readers may be thinking: What is the problem, exactly? The problem is not for the *voters* in these exchanges but for the *scholars* studying them. One of the reasons clientelism emerged as a central topic of concern for scholars of comparative politics is because of the threat it poses *to democracy*: It is thought to undermine voter autonomy, constrain voter choice, and pervert the functioning of elections as a means of holding politicians accountable for their actions (Stokes et al. 2013). But by definition, democratic institutions make it unlikely that politicians can rely on such exchanges to win. There are simply too many opportunities for defection. Given this, attempts to buy votes should be rare, and we should observe politicians investing in alternative, *non*clientelistic modes of distribution. Yet the clientelism literature tells us that they are not rare. They are in fact a fixture of politics in *many* democracies. In this way, the fact that politicians cannot make goods *truly contingent* on votes (because they cannot observe individual votes) yet still devote an inordinate amount of time to attempting to buy votes emerges as a *problem* for the literature.

Recent work proposes solutions. One is to assume that politicians *know* that this electoral strategy is not fail-safe and will lead to leakage, in the sense that not everyone a politician tries to buy votes from will follow through and vote for the politician. But politicians *anticipate* those defections and factor them into their strategy by increasing the number of people they target with vote buying (Hicken and Nathan 2020). A different solution is to view the buying of votes as a practice politicians feel compelled to do to burnish their credentials as defender of a certain type of voter or protector of a certain set of interests (Aspinall et al. 2022; Golden and Nazrullaeva 2023). Together, these solutions essentially say: It does not matter that politicians cannot make their exchanges truly contingent, so scholars are better off setting this fact aside and exploring the numerous other purposes clientelistic practices might be serving.

GBC offers an alternative solution to the contingency problem. It posits that when politicians run for office in electoral districts that are divisible into groups of voters, from whom levels of electoral support are discernible and to whom central government resources are targetable, they will prefer to form clientelistic relationships with these groups, not with individual voters. The reason is simple: When vote tallies are reported at the level of a group within a politician's electoral district, such as a municipality or precinct, this is the level at which clientelistic exchanges are *enforceable*. After elections, all a politician has to do is consult publicly available vote tallies to discern which group gave them the most electoral support, met a certain target, or exceeded the level of support it gave the politician in a previous election. Once discerned, these levels of support can be used to determine each group's resource allocation.

While the other solutions to the contingency problem just referenced recommend a *jettisoning* of contingency, my solution says the opposite: It proposes *reinstating* contingency as the hallmark of a clientelistic exchange. It says that being able to *enforce* a clientelistic exchange, by discerning whether the other side is holding up their end of the bargain, is so important that, whenever possible, politicians will shift the clientelistic exchange up a notch, to the level at which it is enforceable. The theory helps us see that one reason clientelism-like practices are so ubiquitous, even in settings with the secret ballot, could be because politicians are trying to buy electoral support from *groups*, not votes from individuals. If this is the case, there are profound implications for the subgenres of clientelism literature that address the role played by brokers in helping politicians carry out their exchanges, the potential for economic development to put a dent in clientelism, and the threat to democracy posed by resources deliverable to groups (otherwise known as club goods, or pork-barrel politics), respectively. These implications are all spelled out in Chapter 3.

GBC extends the clientelism literature in a second direction, also. I am not the first to notice the potential of disaggregated vote counts to politicians seeking to win election and reelection (Rueda 2017; Larreguy, Marshall and Querubín 2016; Medina and Stokes 2007; Kitschelt and Wilkinson 2007; Schwartz 1987). However, my theory helps us see that it is not disaggregated vote counts per se, but the degree to which those disaggregated vote counts *map onto* subnational jurisdictions to which central government resources are deliverable, and are *contained* within a single electoral district, that determine their potential to be pulled into clientelistic exchanges with a politician. Disaggregated vote counts are far less useful to a politician when they do not line up with the subnational jurisdictions to which central government resources are deliverable. This happens when, for example, subnational jurisdictions are so large that they are either coterminous with the boundaries of a single electoral district or have more than one electoral district nested within them. In both of these cases, a politician might be able to see where her support came from in the electoral district, and perhaps even at a fine-grained level, but she will not have the capacity to steer government resources toward those areas. In the former instance, she can only steer resources to the electoral district as a whole. In the latter, because her electoral district is one of several within a larger jurisdiction to which central government resources are deliverable, she lacks the capacity to steer resources to her *own* electoral district, let alone to the corners within it that supported her the most.

To my knowledge, this feature of a democracy's political institutions, what I call "overlap," has not been the subject of concerted theorizing or analyses. One reason for this may be because of an early consensus that emerged in the clientelism literature, which was that political institutions could not explain why the politicians in some countries formed clientelistic linkages with voters while the politicians in others did not (Kitschelt and Wilkinson 2007; Mueller 2007). While the political institutions these scholars examined may have had little bearing on the clientelistic practices they observed, I contend that the way electoral districts are *configured*, relative to the lower-tier administrative entities to which government resources are deliverable, is a political institution that is likely to have a larger impact, essentially determining the viability and appeal of GBC. If this is the case, then by extension, reconfiguring a country's electoral districts or rethinking the substance or structure of subnational governance could go a long way toward eradicating GBC. Future research should follow the blueprint offered in this book to classify countries as to whether or not the institutional conditions for GBC hold and in countries (or electoral districts) in which they do, examine whether or not politicians are pursuing it.

The second part of my theory addresses the nuts and bolts of *how*, exactly, a politician can go about tying a group's resource allocation to its electoral support. This is the subject of Chapter 4. There are several ways this can be done. I focus on one particular way, which is available to the politicians in a dominant party. This part of the theory is drawn from the formal models presented in a series of studies that ought to be credited for introducing what I call the "tournament theory" to political science (Smith, Bueno de Mesquita and LaGatta 2017; Smith and Bueno de Mesquita 2019, 2012). Instead of reproducing the formal models in this work, Chapter 4 concentrates on fleshing out several of their implications in the most intuitive way possible, so that the advantages tournaments offer politicians and the mechanics of how they can be conducted in different settings can be better understood by political scientists. One of the goals of the book is to help lay the theoretical and empirical groundwork upon which researchers can devote serious

1.1 Theory in Brief

attention to the possibility that tournaments are being used by politicians in their countries of interest, both in the electoral sphere and beyond.

In a nutshell, the tournament theory holds that when there is low uncertainty over which party is going to win the next election, politicians in that party will be able to win the most votes, conditional on resources delivered, by pitting the groups in their electoral districts against each other in a competition for resources. In such a competition, a "tournament," the politician lets it be known that groups will be ranked according to their loyalty in the most recent election and prizes, in the form of resource allocations, will be awarded on the basis of rank. By making it clear that the highest-ranked group will receive a very large prize, the politician encourages groups with a chance of attaining this position to compete for it. This drives up the politician's support in groups that are quite supportive of her, creating neck-and-neck competition for first place. Neck-and-neck competition, in turn, creates a situation in which a group's ranking can hinge on a handful of votes. When a handful of votes stands between a high rank and a lower one, and a significant increase or decrease in resources awaits any change in rank, voters have a reason to set aside whatever personal feelings they may harbor toward the politician and her policies and think primarily about the amount of influence their vote wields over their group's prize.

When resource allocations are structured in this manner, voters in groups that are usually quite supportive of the incumbent (and thus, stand to gain a lot of resources if they continue to be supportive) may actually *prefer* the opposition and its policies but will draw the line at using *their votes* to elect them. Instead, these will reason that, given the incumbent's reelection is so likely, they are better off using their vote to make sure their group maintains its high level of resources after the election. In this way, tournaments work by making the costs of voting for anyone other than the incumbent unpalatable for a sizeable share of the electorate. Many voters may want someone else elected, but they want that person elected with *other people's votes*. Thus, when incumbents are using tournaments, it will be very hard for the opposition parties to make headway. No matter how popular their policy platforms are with ordinary voters, they will find it extraordinarily difficult to defray the costs of voting for them, which have been imposed on voters by the incumbent.

Early work on clientelism raised the possibility that politicians could form clientelistic exchanges with groups, in addition to forming them with individual voters (Kitschelt and Wilkinson 2007). Today, however, 95% of studies of clientelism conceive of it as a relationship politicians form with individual voters (Hicken and Nathan 2020). One reason for the near-exclusive focus on the individual as the target of a clientelistic exchange is likely because whenever politicians have group-level benefits to allocate, a collection action problem emerges within each group (Morton 1991). While every member of the group benefits from the group being awarded the good, members also know that the amount of influence they personally wield over whether or not their group wins it is negligible. When a group's voting behavior is the heuristic used to award goods, for example, then each individual contributes a single vote. Thus, individuals have incentives to free ride on the efforts of other group members, where free riding means sitting out the election, and deciding *not* to contribute to collective efforts to secure the good. Thus, a politician who shifts the target of the clientelistic exchange from individual to group may just be kicking the can down the road in terms of problems: She solves one (she cannot enforce the exchange) but introduces another (the collective action problem).

Critically, while the other forms of GBC mentioned in Chapter 4 might have this problem, tournaments do not. As I have explained, in a tournament, resource allocations decline in a step-wise manner, with the steepest stairs at the very top of the staircase. By structuring resources this way, the incumbent is able to *reach inside groups* to solve the collective action problem. Because a very large payoff awaits the group deemed most supportive, groups will compete for that position, which magnifies the amount of influence group members have over whether or not their group wins it. Whereas group members are not pivotal to the outcome of the election (everyone knows the incumbent is likely to win), they have been *made pivotal* over the size of the prize their group wins. From the perspective of the incumbent, this is the beauty of a tournament: The resource allocations *themselves* motivate group members to contribute to collective efforts to secure the good for the group.

As the articles introducing the tournament theory make clear, tournaments are likely to have profound implications for the political system. The incumbent in a dominant party knows that her positions on policy issues or her conduct in office matter less than her ability to carve up government resources into bite-sized chunks of different sizes that can be channeled to groups in the form of prizes. So long as she can keep this up, she will be able to stave off most threats to her reelection, whether they originate in dissatisfaction with her policies or the rise of reform-minded opposition parties. Tournaments also mean that after elections, the tournament-reliant politician will be able to point to her vote tallies as evidence of her numerous supporters in the electoral district, who, she can plausibly argue, have given her a mandate to enact policies on their behalf. Importantly, however, this masks the fact that many of those people voted for her not because they like her *policies*, but because they were afraid that, in the likely event that she won, their group would be penalized with fewer resources after the election, on the grounds that it was found to be insufficiently loyal.

1.2 EMPIRICS IN BRIEF

The testing ground for the theory is Japan. Given that Japan has a dominant party (the LDP), I posit that of all possible forms of GBC, LDP politicians will use a tournament. Catalinac, Bueno de Mesquita and Smith (2020) began the process of examining whether LDP politicians conduct tournaments. In that article, we offered reasons to believe LDP politicians use tournaments and conducted tests of that proposition with data on geographically targetable government spending and voting behavior in the 1980–2000 period. This book extends that study in the following ways. First, it leverages a nuanced understanding of the rules surrounding the drawing up of electoral districts and the intricacies of subnational governance in Japan to classify the universe of electoral districts used in the twelve Lower House elections held between 1980 and 2014 in terms of whether or not they are "tournament-possible." Armed with this information, it compares electoral outcomes in tournament-possible and tournament-impossible districts and finds that the former have higher support for LDP candidates and higher turnout, respectively. This lends support to the claim that tournaments help LDP politicians win elections. Next, it brings a host of new evidence to bear on the question of whether tournaments are being conducted *within* tournament-possible districts. This new evidence comes in the form of additional theoretical implications tested, additional tests conducted, additional Lower House elections examined, and qualitative data to evaluate the likelihood that the relationships observed in the statistical analyses could be a product of factors orthogonal to the theory.

As I explained, the theory holds that dominant party members will be able to conduct tournaments when they are competing in electoral districts divisible into groups of voters, from whom levels of electoral support are discernible and to whom central government resources are targetable. In Chapter 5, I explain that in Japan, votes are counted and reported at the level of the municipality, and municipalities are also administrative entities to which central government resources can be delivered. Of the various types of transfers that flow from central government to municipalities each year, allocations of "national treasury disbursements" (NTD) are decided at the discretion of central government bureaucrats. In 2015, this fund allocated 15,282.2 billion yen, which amounts to approximately $113 billion USD. Numerous studies

Introduction

make the case that NTD is susceptible to influence by LDP politicians. Municipalities, for their part, can be cities, towns, villages, or special wards. Japan's electoral laws stipulate that where possible, electoral districts used to select Members of the Lower House, the country's more powerful legislative body, must respect the boundaries of existing administrative entities. This means that they have to be drawn *around* the boundaries of municipalities.

Together, these features of Japan's political system mean that the conditions for a tournament are satisfied in some electoral districts, but not in others. In a nutshell, when there is a relatively *small* number of electoral districts and a relatively *large* number of municipalities, electoral districts tend to satisfy these conditions. These electoral districts are divisible into multiple municipalities, all of which are perfectly contained within a single electoral district. In contrast, when electoral districts are smaller (meaning, there are more of them) and municipalities are bigger (meaning, there are fewer of them), more electoral districts do not meet these conditions. These electoral districts either consist of a single municipality, have large shares of voters residing in municipalities whose borders extend beyond the borders of a single electoral district ("split municipalities"), or are nested within much-larger municipalities, whose boundaries contain several electoral districts.

The empirical focus of the book is Lower House elections, 1980–2014. Between 1980 and 1994, Japan's Lower House used approximately 130 electoral districts to elect its members, and there were more than 3,300 municipalities. During this period, I found that the conditions for tournaments were satisfied in 91% of electoral districts (Table 5.1). In 1994, Japan reformed its electoral system. The 129 (multiseat) electoral districts that existed in the 1993 election become 300 (single-seat) electoral districts in the 1996 election. This decreased the number of electoral districts in which tournaments were possible. In the 1996, 2000, and 2003 elections, tournaments were possible in about 73% of electoral districts. Then, in the mid 2000s, municipal mergers took place, which reduced the number of municipalities to around 1,700. This increased the number of electoral districts with large shares of their voters residing in split municipalities. In the 2005 election, tournaments were possible in about 62% of electoral districts. In the last three elections in my sample, in 2009, 2012, and 2014, respectively, the number of electoral districts with split municipalities increased further, as urbanization made larger cities even bigger. This culminated in a situation in which tournaments were possible in about 50% of electoral districts.

After establishing that electoral districts vary in terms of whether the conditions for a tournament are satisfied, I conduct a simple comparison

1.2 Empirics in Brief

of election outcomes across the two types of districts. If LDP politicians are using tournaments in tournament-possible districts and a different electoral strategy altogether in tournament-impossible districts, then leaving aside the question of what that latter strategy is, we are likely to observe qualitatively different election outcomes across the two types of districts. Evidence of qualitatively different election outcomes bolsters my claim that LDP politicians use a distinct electoral strategy in tournament-possible districts. This is exactly what we find: Controlling for other differences across electoral districts, we find that tournament-possible districts produce higher vote shares for LDP candidates and higher turnout, respectively. Given my claim is that tournaments help LDP politicians win elections, the direction of the difference in outcomes, with LDP politicians doing *better* in tournament-possible districts, also accords with the theory's expectations.

In Chapters 6–8, I move to the question of whether tournaments are being conducted within tournament-possible districts. I leverage a comprehensive new dataset on the universe of Japanese municipalities that existed between 1980 and 2014 to conduct rigorous tests of the hypotheses offered in Chapter 4. In Chapter 6, I examine whether the relationship between electoral support and resource allocations within (tournament-possible) districts is consistent with a tournament. I construct variables capturing the amount of electoral support each municipality gave its LDP winner(s) in the twelve Lower House elections in my sample, as well as ranked versions of these variables, which capture where each municipality stood in a ranked ordering of municipalities in the same electoral district in the same election. Using a variety of regression specifications, which control for potential confounders at the level of the municipality, include the lagged dependent variable, and employ one- and two-way fixed effects, I find that a municipality's per capita NTD allocation in the years following Lower House elections is indeed a function of its position in this rank ordering.

Next, I divide the sample up into elections before and after Japan's 1994 electoral reform, which redrew the boundaries of electoral districts and changed the electoral system under which candidates are competing. Dividing up the sample enables me to conduct more-rigorous tests that pit the tournament theory against rival theories tailored to the specifics of each period. My results show that, both before and after the 1994 reform, the amount of money municipalities receive after Lower House elections is a function of their relative levels of support for the LDP candidates who won the election, including LDP-aligned independent candidates who were admitted to the party after clinching victory. In contrast, the amount of money municipalities receive after elections is *not* a function

Introduction

of support for LDP candidates who lost the election; nor is it a function of support for candidates from other parties who won the election. Similarly, the amount of money municipalities receive after elections is not a function of support for senior LDP winners only. Additional tests show that it is unlikely that these results can be explained by certain municipalities having special ties to their LDP incumbents, such that they are exempted from the tournament. It is similarly unlikely that my results are explained by the inclusion of electoral districts with "dominant municipalities," defined as municipalities in which more than 80% of the district's voters reside.

As I explained in Section 1.1, the tournament theory has specific expectations about the *shape* of the relationship between electoral support and resource allocations to municipalities within electoral districts. The theory expects that if LDP politicians are having municipalities *compete* for resources, they will design resource allocations such that the amounts municipalities are competing over are larger at higher ranks. Offering a very large prize for first place is what galvanizes voters in municipalities that are ordinarily quite supportive of the politician to reason that, because the incumbent is very likely to win, they may as well use their votes to make sure their group wins as many resources as possible after the election. Consistent with this, the tests in Chapter 6 suggest that the relationship between electoral support and resource allocations within (tournament-possible) districts is *convex*, not linear. Specifically, municipalities that manage to increase their position at the top of the ranking receive a lot more money after the election than municipalities that manage an equivalent increase in ranking at the middle or bottom of the ranking. This is a critical piece of evidence that helps distinguish between a situation in which LDP politicians are steering resources toward municipalities that are supportive, perhaps even blithely, and a situation in which they are having those municipalities *compete* for resources.

Having established that the direction and shape of relationship between electoral support and resource allocations within (tournament-possible) districts is consistent with the theory's expectations, the second part of Chapter 6 attempts to assuage concerns that these relationships are better explained by factors orthogonal to the theory by fleshing out the theory's underlying assumptions about LDP politicians and voters and presenting evidence of these. One key assumption is that LDP politicians are capable of influencing annual allocations of NTD, which are decided upon by bureaucrats. A vast literature in Japanese politics suggests that this assumption is warranted. I supplement the findings of this literature, some of which is older, with more recent material, including anecdotes reported in the news media, interviews with politicians, analyses of the

1.2 *Empirics in Brief*

promises made in LDP candidate election manifestos, and case studies of how individual LDP politicians structure their vote-mobilization efforts. I consider whether it is plausible that rank-and-file LDP politicians possess the kind of connections to bureaucrats that would enable them to make resource allocations a function of electoral support, and I conclude that both informal institutions within the party (factions) and background characteristics of LDP politicians (many are former bureaucrats or local politicians) likely help with this.

A second key assumption is that there is awareness in the electorate that resource allocations are a function of electoral support. I explain that LDP politicians are unlikely to make what they are doing explicit due to the implied threat to democratic integrity. While they may be more frank about the competitive nature of resource distribution when dealing with the local politicians they rely on for help with vote mobilization, this frankness is unlikely to extend to their everyday dealings with constituents. Nevertheless, we can point to indirect evidence that suggests there is at least a modicum of awareness in the electorate. For example, LDP candidates write campaign manifestos, which are replete with statements alluding to the fact that they are the very best person to serve as a pipeline between the national treasury and municipalities in their electoral districts. Some of these manifestos tout their backgrounds as central government bureaucrats as evidence of their connections in this area, while others include lists of the amounts of money they have secured for their constituents and the names of projects they have provided. These manifestos are distributed to all registered voters at the time of elections, and survey data reveal that sizeable shares of voters report seeing the manifestos of the candidates running in their electoral districts. In addition, popular fiction in Japan depicts the life of an LDP politician, who makes the amounts of money municipalities receive conditional on how much electoral support they provide, and survey data reveals that relatively large shares of the Japanese public support increased spending on public works.

A central implication of the theory is that in electoral districts in which LDP politicians use tournaments, voters in municipalities that are highly supportive of this politician will be less likely to vote on policy grounds. Ideally, we would be able to evaluate this hypothesis with survey data, but this difficult because such data rarely includes identifiers linking survey respondent to electoral district and/or municipality. However, using the results of a survey conducted in the 2012 election, I present evidence that people who voted for the LDP in tournament-possible districts are *less* likely, relative to their peers who voted for the LDP in tournament-impossible districts, to report liking LDP policies. This is evidence, albeit from a survey conducted in a single election, that people voting for the LDP in tournament-possible districts use different heuristics to decide who to vote for than their counterparts voting for the LDP in tournament-impossible districts, and those different heuristics are consistent with the theory.

In Section 1.1, I explained that a convex relationship between electoral support and resource allocations within electoral districts helps to distinguish my hypothesis, which is that LDP politicians make municipalities compete for resources, from a rival hypothesis, which holds that LDP politicians steer resources toward supportive municipalities. Another piece of evidence that helps distinguish a tournament from a simpler, reward-the-supporter logic is if resource allocations *across* electoral districts were found to be a function of the degree of asymmetry in municipality size. Evaluating this is the subject of Chapter 7.

Why does asymmetry in municipality size matter? As I explain, the tournament theory expects that the total amount of money incumbents have to offer to entice the groups in their electoral districts to compete against each other will be a function of the *ease* with which tournaments are administered. Put simply, when groups are similarly sized, politicians can induce competition with a relatively small prize. When groups are asymmetrically sized, in contrast, a larger prize is needed. This is because when groups are asymmetrically sized, voters will not know how the incumbent plans to *compare* the level of support exhibited by such differently sized groups. Different ways of comparing groups can yield different rankings for the same set of vote totals when groups are asymmetrically sized. This complicates voters' ability to gauge the extent of influence their vote wields over their group's prize. All else equal, the theory expects that this will lower the incentives of voters to support the incumbent in "asymmetric" electoral districts. It further expects that LDP politicians will *anticipate* this lowering of support and try to offset it with a larger prize. However, because politicians generally prefer to minimize the amount of government resources that must be used for prizes, they may not deliver a prize large enough to totally offset the lowered propensity to support them in these districts. The implication is that asymmetric districts are likely to exhibit less support, even as they receive larger prizes.

In Chapter 7, I conduct a range of tests to try to isolate the independent impact of what amounts to a new variable in political science research: the relative sizes of the subnational jurisdictions within a given electoral district. First, I comb the literature for alternative reasons why resource allocations can be expected to vary across electoral districts. Focusing on the Japanese politics literature, this yields variables such as

1.2 Empirics in Brief

the degree to which electoral districts are malapportioned, the raw number of subnational jurisdictions in the electoral district (this determines the number of local politicians the district has), the seniority of the LDP politicians representing the district, among others. I operationalize all of these variables with my data. Then, I use a range of regression specifications, including a quasi-experiment leveraging the fact that the same municipality was plucked from one electoral district in the 1993 election and placed in another electoral district for the 1996 election, to show that electoral districts characterized by greater asymmetry in municipality size receive systematically larger resource allocations after elections. In spite of these larger resource allocations, these electoral districts tend to (although, not always) exhibit *lower* levels of support.

Chapter 7 shows that the pattern of spending across electoral districts is the reverse of what happens within electoral districts. Within electoral districts, places (municipalities) that exhibit more support for the LDP receive more resources. But across electoral districts, places (electoral districts) that exhibit more support for the LDP receive *fewer* resources. If we had examined resource allocations within electoral districts only, extant theories would have led us to conclude that politicians were targeting "core supporters" (Cox and McCubbins 1986). If we had examined resource allocations across electoral districts only, extant theories would have led us to conclude that politicians were targeting either "swing voters" or those least likely to vote for them (Stokes 2005; Dixit and Londregan 1996). The tournament theory helps us make sense of these different patterns: Critically, politicians are not *targeting* one type of voter at one level and another type of voter at another level. A third variable, the relative sizes of the groups into which votes are arranged, is exercising an independent and previously unnoticed impact on the baseline level of electoral support politicians are likely to enjoy, and through that impact on support, changing the amount of resources they have to deliver to win.

In Chapter 8, I look for evidence of tournaments in voter decisions to turn out. The theory expects that decisions to vote will hinge on *where* in the ranking a given municipality is expected to end up. As I have explained, by proposing a very large prize for first place, incumbents can elicit neck-and-neck competition for this position. Among municipalities with a chance of attaining it, neck-and-neck competition means that a single vote can end up wielding considerable influence over where in the ranking a voter's municipality ends up, and consequently, the amount of resources it receives. This is not the case among municipalities that are less supportive. While voters in these municipalities can still increase the size of the prize awarded to their municipality by achieving an increase in rank, the fact that large prizes do not await increases in rank at the middle or bottom of the ranking means that neck-and-neck competition for those ranks is less likely to materialize. As such, rankings at the middle or bottom of the ranking do not hinge on individual votes in the same way. All else equal, then, the theory expects that voters will be systematically more likely to go to the polls in municipalities projected to place highly in the ranking than municipalities not projected to place highly. It further expects that the same convexity we observed in the relationship between electoral support and resource allocations within electoral districts, presented in Chapter 6, will also be evident in the relationship between electoral support and turnout.

Chapter 8 implements three sets of tests that examine whether the motivation to vote differs systematically according to where in the ranking a municipality is projected to end up. I operationalize new variables capturing the degree to which a municipality concentrates its votes on a single LDP winner. Using these, I first examine whether, within (tournament-possible) districts in the same election, turnout increases as municipalities concentrate larger shares of votes cast on a single LDP winner. Using a host of specifications that control for confounders at the level of the municipality, include two-way fixed effects, and pit the predictions of the tournament theory against rival theories specific to each electoral system, I find that they do. Next, I examine the shape of the relationship between concentrating votes on a single LDP winner and turnout. I find evidence that it is convex, not linear. My results show that among municipalities that are *already* concentrating a great deal of voters on a single LDP winner, further increases in vote concentration bring about even *larger* increases in turnout.

By comparing turnout rates between municipalities in the same district-year, these first and second sets of tests hold constant the effect of all variables influencing turnout at that level. My third test leverages variation across electoral districts in the degree to which races are projected to be *competitive* to further evaluate whether the motivation to vote differs according to a municipality's projected position in the ranking. While the literature leads us to expect that projections of competitiveness increase turnout everywhere, the tournament theory suggests that such projections will have a *smaller* impact, all else equal, on turnout in municipalities projected to place highly. This is because in these municipalities, motivations to vote are primarily driven by voters' desire to realize the largest prize possible for their municipality. As such, the theory expects that turnout will be significantly less affected by situational elements of any given election, such as closeness. My results, which are robust to rival theories, show that this is indeed the case.

1.3 CONTRIBUTIONS TO JAPANESE POLITICS IN BRIEF

As this summary of the book's empirics has made clear, the book sheds new light on a range of questions of interest to scholars and observers of Japanese politics. Its six main takeaways can be summarized as follows. First, in a relatively large subset of electoral districts used in Lower House elections, LDP politicians have been winning elections by making the receipt of valued central government resources contingent on repeated displays of electoral loyalty. In this subset of electoral districts, evidence suggests that LDP politicians elicit the help of central government bureaucrats to calibrate resource allocations to municipalities in ways that give the voters who live in those municipalities reason to try to influence how much money their municipality is awarded. Voters exercise this influence by turning out and voting for the LDP politician. Because of the way resources are allocated within these electoral districts, the implication is that voters are deincentivized to vote in accordance with their policy preferences. Importantly, however, the costs of voting according to one's policy preferences are not imposed on voters in a *uniform* fashion. Because voters in municipalities that are ordinarily quite supportive of the LDP politician stand to lose the *most*, in terms of resources, by voting for anyone other than her, those voters shoulder particularly large costs in order to vote on the basis of their policy preferences.

Second, my finding that LDP politicians win elections by making the receipt of valued central government resources contingent on repeated displays of electoral loyalty may come as a surprise to scholars who collected similar data and made use of similar empirical tests to investigate the relationship between money and votes in Japan (McMichael 2018; Hirano 2011; Saito 2010; Horiuchi and Saito 2003; Reed 2001). As I explain in Chapters 6 and 7, these studies either found *no* relationship between the electoral support entities such as prefectures, electoral districts, and municipalities delivered to the LDP and the amount of resources the entity received after elections, or a relationship that appeared to run in the *opposite* direction to that presumed in canonical work on LDP dominance, which rests on the idea that a central component of the party's electoral prowess was its ability to steer resources toward core supporters. The fact that *multiple* studies were conducted, and mixed conclusions were reached, occasionally within the *same* study, may have contributed to a perception among Japanese politics scholars that there was not much to be found. Either distributive politics played less of a role in LDP election victories than we thought, or it played a role, but the resource being exchanged for votes was not something out in the open, in the sense of being collectible by scholars, but something more insidious, hidden from public view.

Introduction

In Chapter 6, I use the logic of the tournament theory to explain why prior studies yielded conclusions that are so different from mine. As I alluded to above, tournaments are conducted by relatively *autonomous* LDP politicians, who face variation in the number and size of municipalities in their respective electoral districts. Variation in the number and size of the municipalities within each electoral district creates variation across electoral districts in the total amount of money LDP politicians must offer to entice municipalities to compete against each other. LDP politicians facing a set of municipalities that are relatively evenly sized can realize competition with less (money) than their counterparts facing a set of municipalities that are unevenly sized. To uncover the relationship between money and votes, then, it is critical to compare the electoral support delivered and money received by municipalities in the same district after the same election. This is a point not appreciated in prior work, which did not have the tournament theory upon which to draw.

My analyses suggest that the main reason prior studies did not reveal evidence that LDP politicians were using central government resources to buy votes is because they did not limit their comparison to municipalities within the same electoral district. Instead, they took all municipalities in a given election and adopted regression specifications that amounted to asking whether, generally speaking, municipalities with higher levels of electoral support for the party received more resources. Their specifications also tended to include votes cast for *losing* LDP candidates in the operationalization of support for the LDP. As I explain, however, the tournament theory expects that LDP losers will not conduct tournaments. They find it difficult to create the perception that allocations to one's municipality are on a knife edge the way their counterparts who win their seats are able to do. I present evidence that conceptualizing electoral support in this way, and not limiting the comparison to municipalities in the same electoral district, risks misconstruing the relationship between money and votes in Japan and likely contributed to the mixed findings of prior work.

Third, in another subset of electoral districts, LDP politicians cannot conduct tournaments. Importantly, this has nothing to do with the characteristics of the voters who reside in these districts. Instead, it is solely a function of how the *boundaries* of that particular electoral district are drawn, relative to the municipalities within it. Until 1994, LDP politicians could conduct tournaments in 91% of the electoral districts used in Lower House elections. After 1994, the share dropped to around 72% of electoral districts, after which it dropped further, to around 50% of electoral districts as of 2014, the last election in my sample. In this way, the theory helps us see that the redrawing of electoral districts that

1.3 Contributions to Japanese Politics in Brief

accompanied electoral reform in 1994 and the municipal amalgamations that occurred between 2002 and 2006 created two distinct sets of LDP politicians. Some LDP politicians use tournaments to get elected. These politicians present voters with campaign manifestos touting their ability to secure targetable government resources for their constituents. They receive relatively high levels of support in these electoral districts and usually win. Other LDP politicians *cannot* use tournaments to get elected. These politicians present voters with manifestos staking out positions on programmatic issues of concern to cross-cutting groups of voters. They face tougher races than their counterparts in tournament-possible districts, in the sense that their vote shares are lower and they are more likely to lose.

Fourth, the book presents suggestive evidence, which future research should subject to greater empirical scrutiny, that this bifurcation in LDP politicians' electoral strategies, a consequence of how their electoral district is configured, has consequences for the degree of congruence between policy preferences and vote choice. This provides an explanation for the puzzle of why many Japanese voters do not seem to vote in line with their policy preferences. As Chapter 2 explains, experiments that set out to measure the relative popularity of the policy platforms offered by parties contesting Japan's last three Lower House elections yielded the conclusion that the LDP's was among the least popular (Eshima et al. N.D.; Horiuchi, Smith and Yamamoto 2020). As the authors note, people report liking the opposition's policies a great deal more than the LDP's, but when they go the polls, they vote for the LDP. The main claim of this book, which is that a large share of Japan's electorate risks incurring costs in voting for the opposition, so are dissuaded from doing so, can account for this disconnect. As I have explained, the costs voters would incur in voting for the opposition are greatest in municipalities in tournament-possible districts that are ordinarily quite supportive of their LDP incumbent. In these municipalities, what voters are doing is entirely rational: They are not incentivized to vote on policy grounds, so they do not. Future research should investigate whether the degree of congruence between policy preferences and vote choice is lowest in these municipalities.

Fifth, there is now a large stream of research documenting the effects of Japan's 1994 electoral reform (Goplerud and Smith 2023; Smith 2016; Catalinac 2015, 2016, 2018; Rosenbluth and Thies 2010; Estevez-Abe 2008; Krauss and Pekkanen 2010). There are several unresolved questions in this literature. One is why programmatic policy competition increased after reform and was accompanied by other changes such as the strengthening of party leaders at the expense of backbenchers, yet promises to secure government spending for projects in one's electoral district remain a fixture of electoral competition. A second question is why a two-party system accompanied by regular, or even occasional, changes in government has been so hard to realize. A third question is what explains the mix of electoral strategies LDP politicians use, with some relying on old-fashioned "vote mobilization" techniques, in which personal support organizations (koenkai) are cultivated and staff are hired to make phone calls to a carefully maintained list of supporters during campaigns, while others embrace more modern "vote chasing" strategies, which involve using the LDP's brand, its programmatic policies, and the face of its leader to attract independent voters (Koellner 2009).

To date, virtually all research on Japan's electoral reform has focused on elucidating its effects on intraparty competition. As I explain in Chapter 2, the introduction of Japan's version of a mixed-member electoral system, mixed-member majoritarian (MMM), entailed the elimination of multimember districts (MMDs) and the introduction of single-seat districts (SSDs). Under the former electoral system, voters had a single vote, and LDP politicians had to compete against other LDP politicians for those votes. After reform, LDP politicians are the sole representatives in their electoral districts. A rich theoretical literature in political science shows that when politicians from the same party are forced to compete against other, they have to come up with reasons why voters should vote for them over their co-partisans, and this can lead to intense particularism, as politicians use government resources to build personal bailiwicks (Crisp et al. 2021; Myerson 1993; Carey and Shugart 1995). As such, prior work on Japan's 1994 reform posited that the elimination of intraparty competition would lead to less particularism, the centralization of power in the hands of the party leader, and even a recalibrating of politician's relationships with the bureaucracy.

This book uncovers another way in which Japan's 1994 electoral reform influenced politics in Japan. In addition to removing intraparty competition, it also created more tournament-impossible districts. Thus, the changes in party politics and campaigning after reform likely had *two* causes: One was the elimination of intraparty competition, but the other was the increased share of tournament-impossible districts. This provides an explanation for why pork-barrel–related promises did not disappear from LDP candidate manifestos after 1994, and why old-fashioned vote-mobilization techniques coexist with more modern ones in present-day Japan. Theories rooted in intraparty competition do not have explanations for this, whereas this book does. This book also offers a new explanation for why Japan's 1994 electoral reform was not sufficient to untether the LDP from the hands of power. Ultimately, the party's

1.3 Contributions to Japanese Politics in Brief

ability to wield its control over central government resources in ways that make it costly for large shares of the electorate to vote for anyone other than them means that unless the opposition parties can find a way to defray those costs, it will remain difficult for them to secure control of government.

Sixth, and finally, the book offers a new answer to the question of what might cause the LDP to *lose* its control of government. The empirical analyses in Chapter 5 show that the party is most vulnerable in tournament-impossible districts, in the sense that its candidates do worse and are less likely to win. Thus, as these electoral districts increase as a share of the total, so will the party's vulnerability. In addition to the redrawing of electoral districts that accompanied electoral reform and municipal mergers, respectively, urbanization has necessitated the creation of more of these districts over time. While urbanization is typically discussed as a process that results in the creation of a distinct set of voters with distinct preferences (or is caused by the creation of such voters, which happens first), this book shows that it produces another effect: making it less likely that electoral districts will be comprised of multiple units at which electoral support is discernible and resources targetable. As the share of tournament-impossible districts increases, the LDP will develop new electoral strategies for these districts. Indeed, it is already doing so. However, it will attempt to strike a balance between electoral strategies that "work" for its politicians in those electoral districts and electoral strategies that "work" for its politicians in tournament-possible districts. Its ability to continue to develop such strategies, and allow both sets of politicians to deploy them to maximal effect, will determine its chances of staying in power.

2

The Enduring Success of Japan's Liberal Democratic Party

Today, Japan is the world's fourth-largest economy and a close ally of the United States. Yet its politics are highly anomalous: It is a democracy in which one party wins nearly every election. This party, the Liberal Democratic Party (LDP), has won pluralities in all but one of the twenty-two elections to Japan's Lower House that have been held since the party's formation in 1955.[1] In fourteen of these elections, the LDP's plurality was a majority, meaning it exceeded 50% of seats. In seven of them, its seat share exceeded 60%. While the *non*democratic world furnishes plenty of examples of ruling parties that are never out of power, the democratic world does not. This extraordinary string of electoral victories, with only one real loss in sixty-nine years, in an institutional setting in which the party controlling a majority in the Lower House elects the prime minister, has given the LDP a degree of influence over the lives of Japan's 126 million inhabitants that exceeds that of any other democratically elected political party, including the longstanding governing parties of Sweden, Italy, Israel, Mexico, and Botswana, to which the LDP has been compared.

While this string of election victories would raise eyebrows in any democracy, it is even more stunning when one recalls that the electoral system used to select Lower House members was reformed in early 1994, when the LDP found itself out of government for the first time. As I explain below, the LDP's first stint as the opposition was triggered by a split in its ranks, which saw some of its lawmakers supporting a nonconfidence motion sponsored by the opposition and leaving the party. While the party managed to retain its plurality in the election held in 1993, its seat share dipped just low enough to see the longstanding opposition parties team up with the new parties created by LDP defectors to form the first non-LDP government since 1955. This government, an eight-party

---

[1] As this book was going to press, a snap election was held on October 27, 2024. This is not included in this tally.

coalition, set its sights on reforming the electoral system, on the grounds that the system in place since 1947 had by then been deemed conducive to single-party dominance. A new system was chosen with a view to maximizing the probability that elections would feature programmatic duels between two large parties, each with a shot at controlling government. Despite its enactment in 1994, today, thirty years after the reform was passed, the LDP appears as dominant as it has always been and no such second party exists. If anything, election outcomes in recent years are reminiscent of the first few elections of the party's existence, with seat shares in the mid–late fifties (2021) and sixties (2012, 2014, and 2017).

By now, it is obvious that we can add Japan's 1994 electoral reform to the list of near-cataclysmic changes the LDP has weathered successfully. Others consist of the transformation to Japan's society and economy wrought by its rise from occupied, defeated power in the late 1940s to the world's second-largest economy in the late 1960s, and then the nearly three decades of anemic economic growth and deflation it has experienced since the 1990s. These changes generated pressures from which politics was not immune: The collapse of the traditional opposition in the 1990s was followed by a period in which programmatic competition between the LDP and a second party, the Democratic Party of Japan (DPJ), came to fruition. Then, the election of the second-ever non-LDP government in 2009 eventually culminated in defections from the ruling DPJ, which kicked off further changes in the party system, as new parties formed, the LDP returned to power, and the new parties reconstituted themselves. The LDP has also survived revelations of corruption and incompetence, with policy mistakes including overlooking evidence that North Korean agents were disappearing people off Japanese beaches, failing to ensure that adequate safeguards were in place at nuclear reactors, misplacing millions of pension records, failing to devise measures to stem the rapid aging of society, and failing to address the root causes of Japan's prolonged economic malaise, among others. Despite each revelation leading to a pronounced souring of opinion against the party, none have been sufficient to dislodge it from power, and many have had near-imperceptible impacts on election results. Why? Why has the LDP managed to stay so aloof from changes wrought by shifts in Japan's economic power and international influence, party system reconstitution, corruption, policy missteps, and electoral reform?

As I explained in Chapter 1, this book tackles a question of general interest: how political parties seek to stay in power. It offers a theory, also of general interest, which holds that under the right institutional conditions, governing parties will be able to make the distribution of central government resources to groups of voters conditional on how those groups vote. While *how*, exactly, governing parties seek to tie resources to electoral support will vary, I argue that when there is a dominant party, this party will be able to leverage resources in a manner that makes it extraordinarily difficult for certain groups of voters to cast their votes for anyone else. This restricts the freedom of voters to vote for whoever they like and weakens the capacity of elections to function as a transmission belt for voter preferences. Having a dominant party, Japan presents a nice laboratory in which the theory can be tested. However, Japan is far more than "just" a laboratory: Its politics present a puzzle of great substantive importance, and concerted attempts to explain puzzles have the potential to yield theoretical insights that can reorient scholarship on the form and functioning of democracy toward new lines of inquiry.

With these aims in mind, the purpose of this chapter is twofold. First, I flesh out the substantive puzzle that motivates this research. I present data on the outcomes of every Lower House election the LDP has fought since its inception in 1955. To make sense of these outcomes, I explain how the electoral systems Japan has used during this time convert votes cast for parties into seats for those parties. I describe the circumstances surrounding the two elections that saw the formation of non-LDP governments, in 1993 and 2009, respectively, and chronicle how, after the LDP regained control of government in 2012, it went on win a streak of elections, in both the Lower and Upper Houses. It is fair to say that this streak was unanticipated by scholars.

Because election outcomes are the product of an electoral *system*, which determines how votes are converted into seats, they are by no means a pure indicator of the relative strengths of different parties. Therefore, I supplement data on election results with data on the share of respondents who said they supported each party in nationally representative surveys conducted monthly since 1980. If anything, the support rates gleaned from survey data paint an even more dire picture of Japan's opposition than that painted by the election results. The impression one gets from looking at support rates is that even *chronicling* other parties and their movements, as I do in this chapter, may risk overstating their significance in contemporary Japanese politics.

Next, I move to the explanations scholars have offered for why the LDP is so dominant. Being at the helm of the world's second (and now fourth-) largest economy for sixty-nine years, the literature on the party and its staying power through bumpy economic performance, money politics scandals, policy missteps, institutional reforms, national security challenges, and inept leadership, is immense. Nevertheless, we can distil three categories of explanations. One emphasizes *structural features* of the two electoral systems Japan has used and explains how those structural features translated into advantages for the LDP and disadvantages for the opposition, respectively. Essentially, this category of explanations takes it as a given that a modicum of Japanese voters will vote LDP, without probing their reasons for doing so, and explicates how, under different electoral systems, that modicum of votes was sufficient to secure seat majorities for the party. The other two categories of explanations probe the reasons why a voter might vote for the LDP. One, which I use the umbrella label of *programmatic politics* to describe, holds that voters vote for the LDP because they prefer its policy positions, ideological orientation, leaders, or reputation for competence over the alternatives. The other category, which I call *distributive politics*, boils down to the idea that the LDP uses its access to government resources to bestow benefits on select constituents. Because there is no guarantee that those constituents will get the same benefits under an alternative governing party, they continue voting for the LDP. This second category of explanations hold that an "I'll scratch your back, if you scratch mine" relationship between the LDP and select constituents explains the party's success.

As will be obvious, the theory offered in this book falls squarely into the distributive politics camp. In its emphasis on features of Japan's *institutional setting* that make group-based clientelism (GBC) possible, it draws on pioneering work by Scheiner (2006). Its expectation that dominant parties will have incentives to make the allocation of resources a *competition* has much in common with the argument in Saito (2010), but it is able to present a more complete picture of competitive resource allocations that accounts for why that study's results were not entirely consistent with its claims. Below, I explain that distributive politics explanations appeared most persuasive when applied to elections prior to 1994. While not necessarily *crafted* to pertain to this period only, after Japan's electoral reform, elections began to feature programmatic competition and promises of particularism declined. As such, scholars stopped considering the possibility that distributive explanations could account for LDP victories. Instead, they restricted their gaze to programmatic explanations. However, just as distributive politics explanations fell out of favor, programmatic politics explanations have been dealt a major blow by recent work showing that the LDP has the least popular policy platform of any party (Eshima et al. N.D.; Horiuchi, Smith and Yamamoto 2018). If elections are fought on programmatic grounds and the LDP wins every time, then the LDP must have the most *popular* policies, not the least popular. If it has the least popular, then programmatic policies may not be dominating voter calculus to the degree we thought they were.

Ultimately, the theory and evidence in this book suggests that it was premature to assume that the rise of programmatic policy competition after electoral reform meant that distributive politics had been put on the back burner. We know from seminal work in comparative politics that parties can connect with voters on both programmatic and distributive grounds (Kitschelt and Singer 2018; Kitschelt and Kselman 2013; Magaloni, Diaz-Cayeros and Estévez 2007). They can be what is called a "diversified linkage party." The findings in this book corroborate that this is exactly what the LDP is. Furthermore, the theory helps us see *why* the LDP is a diversified linkage party. It is a diversified linkage party because LDP politicians cannot pursue an electoral strategy of GBC and tournaments when their electoral districts are *not* divisible into groups of voters, at which electoral support is discernible and government resources deliverable. While these conditions were met in more than 90% of electoral districts prior to 1994, Chapter 5 shows that the electoral reform, the municipal mergers that took place in the mid 2000s, and urbanization required the creation of many electoral districts where these conditions are *not* met. In these electoral districts, theory and evidence suggest that LDP politicians have little choice but to try to connect with voters on programmatic grounds. In contrast, their counterparts in electoral districts where the conditions *are* met can rely on distributive politics to win. This leads to a bifurcated ruling party, with some members embracing distributive politics, and others trying to craft policies that appeal to the median voter.

2.1 VICTORIOUS UNDER DIFFERENT ELECTORAL SYSTEMS

The LDP was formed on November 15, 1955 from the amalgamation of two conservative parties, the Liberal Party and the Democratic Party. These parties had emerged from a series of mergers and splits in the conservative camp that had begun during the Allied Occupation (1945–1951) and continued thereafter. A merger had been on the cards ever since the February 1955 Lower House election had returned a plurality – but not a *majority* – for the Democrats, which put them in charge of a minority government. The previous Liberal-led government had run into problems as a minority government. After protracted negotiations, in which a critical issue was who would be designated as the leader of the amalgamated party, a merger in the socialist camp finally galvanized the conservatives to set aside their differences and join forces (Kohno 1997a).

What kind of setting was this party operating in? Chapter IV of the Japanese constitution, promulgated in 1947 under the Allied Occupation, stipulates that Japan's legislature is comprised of two Houses, the House of Representatives (or Lower House) and the House of Councilors (or Upper House). Both Houses have the authority to elect the prime minister,

2.1 Victorious under Different Electoral Systems

authorize budgets, and conclude treaties with foreign powers, but in the event the opinion of the Houses differ, the Lower House prevails. Its members serve terms of four years, but the prime minister is permitted to dissolve the House and call for an election at any time. Upper House members, on the other hand, serve terms of six years, with elections held for half the House's members every three years. To become law, bills have to pass both Houses, but in the event a bill is rejected (or ignored for a period of sixty days) by the Upper House, it can still become law if, upon being sent back to the Lower House, two-thirds of Members agree. The Lower House is thus the more powerful House and the group with a majority in it controls government. The 1955 merger gave the newly formed LDP 63.8% of Lower House seats (298 out of 467) and 46% of Upper House seats (115 out of 250), enabling it to comfortably elect its preferred candidate as the prime minister.

2.1.1 SNTV-MMD, 1958–1993

To provide a sense of how dominant the LDP let us begin with election results. Table 2.1 presents data on the performance of the LDP and other major parties in the thirteen Lower House elections held between 1958 and 1993. The numbers in bold are the share of seats won by each party in each election. The number in parentheses underneath this is the share of valid votes cast that were won by each party. In this period, the Lower House used an electoral system called "single non-transferable vote in multimember districts" (or SNTV-MMD) to elect between 467 and 512 Members. Under this system, the country was divided into between 118 and 130 multimember districts. Each district elected between two and six candidates, with the vast majority electing either three (32% of districts), four (27%), or five (33%) candidates.[2] Voters cast a single vote, meaning that they wrote down the name of one preferred candidate. The M candidates with the largest vote tallies won, where M refers to the number of seats available in the district (the district magnitude).

In these thirteen elections, Table 2.1 shows that the LDP secured majorities in nine elections and more than 60% of seats in three. Its seat shares were often more than twice that of the second-largest party, the Japan Socialist Party (JSP), with the remainder divided amongst three smaller opposition parties: the Democratic Socialist Party (DSP), the Komeito, and Japan Communist Party (JCP). With a few exceptions, the LDP's seat share exhibited a declining trend over this period, but so did the seat share of the second-largest party (JSP). The most serious

---

[2] There was one electoral district that elected a single winner. It was abolished in 1990.

Table 2.1 *Share of seats (in bold) and votes (in parentheses) captured by major parties in Japan's Lower House elections, 1958–1993.*

	1958	1960	1963	1967	1969	1972	1976	1979	1980	1983	1986	1990	1993
LDP	**61.5** (57.8)	**63.3** (57.6)	**60.6** (54.7)	**57.0** (48.8)	**59.2** (47.6)	**55.2** (46.9)	**48.7** (41.8)	**48.5** (44.6)	**55.6** (47.9)	**48.9** (45.8)	**58.6** (49.4)	**53.7** (46.1)	**43.6** (36.6)
JSP	**35.5** (32.8)	**31.0** (27.6)	**30.8** (29.0)	**28.8** (27.9)	**18.5** (21.4)	**24.0** (21.9)	**24.1** (20.7)	**20.9** (19.7)	**20.9** (19.3)	**21.9** (19.5)	**16.6** (17.2)	**26.6** (24.4)	**13.7** (15.4)
DSP		**3.7** (8.8)	**4.9** (7.4)	**6.2** (7.4)	**6.4** (7.7)	**3.9** (7.0)	**5.7** (6.3)	**6.8** (6.8)	**6.3** (6.6)	**7.4** (7.3)	**5.1** (6.4)	**2.7** (4.8)	**2.9** (3.5)
Kōmeitō				**5.1** (5.4)	**9.7** (10.9)	**5.9** (8.5)	**10.8** (10.9)	**11.2** (9.8)	**6.5** (9.0)	**11.4** (10.1)	**10.9** (9.4)	**8.8** (8.0)	**10.0** (8.1)
JCP	**0.2** (2.5)	**0.6** (2.9)	**1.1** (4.0)	**1.0** (4.8)	**2.9** (6.8)	**7.7** (10.5)	**3.3** (10.4)	**7.6** (10.4)	**5.7** (9.8)	**5.1** (9.3)	**5.1** (8.8)	**3.1** (8.0)	**2.9** (7.7)
NLC							**3.3** (4.2)	**0.8** (3.0)	**2.3** (3.0)	**1.6** (2.3)	**1.2** (1.8)		
Shinsei													**10.8** (10.1)
Sakigake													**2.5** (2.6)
JNP													**6.8** (8.0)
Other	**2.8** (6.9)	**1.4** (3.1)	**2.6** (4.9)	**1.9** (5.7)	**3.3** (5.6)	**3.3** (5.2)	**4.1** (5.7)	**4.2** (5.7)	**2.7** (2.6)	**3.7** (5.7)	**2.5** (7.0)	**5.1** (8.7)	**6.8** (8.0)
Total seats	467	467	467	486	486	491	511	511	511	511	512	512	511

This table was compiled from data provided by Susan J. Pharr, Ministry of Internal Affairs and Communications reports, as well as Reed et al. (2013) and Curtis (1999).

LDP is Liberal Democratic Party; JSP is Japan Socialist Party; DSP is Democratic Socialist Party; JCP is Japan Communist Party; Shinsei is Japan Renewal Party; and JNP is Japan New Party. Other includes the Socialist Democratic Federation (SDF, 1979–1993).

2.1 Victorious under Different Electoral Systems

challenge – perhaps better described as a wrinkle – emerged in 1976, when a handful of LDP legislators left the LDP and formed a new party, the New Liberal Club (NLC), in protest of a corruption scandal that implicated the LDP's Prime Minister Tanaka Kakuei. In the five House of Representatives (HOR) elections contested by the NLC, the LDP's seat shares dipped below 50% in three. However, it was able to make up a governing majority by admitting conservative-inclined independents into the party after the election and soliciting the support of NLC lawmakers on key pieces of legislation (Reed 2009; Nam 1977). In a pattern that would repeat itself in subsequent years, the NLC eventually disbanded and its members rejoined the LDP in the wake of the 1986 election, which saw the LDP increase its share of seats by almost 10% above the 1983 election.

Five years later, in June 1993, a more serious wrinkle emerged. The JSP submitted a motion of no confidence in LDP Prime Minister Miyazawa Kiichi, which passed when a group of LDP lawmakers decided to vote for it. In response, Prime Minister Miyazawa Kiichi dissolved the Lower House. In the election held in August, the LDP managed 43.6% of seats. This was still more than three times the seat share of the second-largest party, the Socialists, who captured only 13.7%. However, the gap between that number of seats (223) and the number needed for a majority (256) created an opening the opposition was able to exploit. The election had been contested by three new parties, two of which were comprised of the forty-six former LDP lawmakers who had defected after the passage of the no-confidence motion. These parties, the Japan Renewal Party (Shinseito), Sakigake, and Japan New Party (JNP), appear in the final rows of Table 2.1. After votes were counted, these new parties, plus four older opposition parties, had just enough seats between them to form the first non-LDP government in thirty-eight years (Desposato and Scheiner 2008; Otake 1996).

Even though the 1993 election resulted in a non-LDP government, a postmortem revealed that this election was similar to previous elections in that by and large, incumbents were reelected (Curtis 1999, 69). The decline in the LDP's seat share between 1990 and 1993 can be attributed to the fact that LDP incumbents who had built up their careers within the confines of the party were now running from *other* parties. While the LDP fielded candidates in place of these defectors, some of whom were former Diet Members who had lost the 1990 election, voters did not vote for those candidates in large enough numbers to give the party a governing majority. To account for this election result, then, it makes more sense to ask why a sizeable number of LDP legislators sided with the Socialists in their attempt to bring down the government.

While the stated reasons had to do with Prime Minister Miyazawa's foot-dragging on the issue of electoral reform, positions on this issue had become connected to a battle over the leadership of the party (Kato 1998; Cox and Rosenbluth 1995; Otake 1996). The previous year, disagreement over who would lead the LDP's largest faction led to its splintering as those on the losing side left the faction. It was this group of lawmakers who sided with the Socialists on the no-confidence motion. While these lawmakers might have had more reason to support electoral reform than the average LDP lawmaker, leadership tussles that threatened the party's hold on power were nothing new. In 1955, one had almost derailed the merger. In 1980, a similar tussle had also led to a Socialist-sponsored no-confidence motion, which a group of LDP lawmakers, unhappy over the party's selection of leader, had abstained from voting on. In contrast to what happened in 1993, however, in 1980 the disgruntled LDP lawmakers had decided to stay in the party and work out their problems, rather than leave (Curtis 1999).

Unsurprisingly, one of the most prominent items on the new non-LDP government's agenda, which parties in the coalition had campaigned on during the 1993 election, was electoral reform. By 1993, Japan's SNTV-MMD electoral system had come to be blamed for a variety of ills. As I explain below, one of those ills was creating the conditions believed to be conducive to single-party dominance (Otake 1996; Cox and Niou 1994). After a period of negotiation, the system introduced, which is still in use as of the time of writing, is called mixed-member majoritarian (MMM). It is comprised of two electoral "tiers" that overlay each other. Voters cast a single vote in each tier, for a total of two votes each.

One tier is comprised of single-seat-districts (SSDs). Initially, there were 300 SSDs, but this number has been reduced over time and is 289 today. In one's SSD, voters cast a single vote for their preferred SSD candidate and the candidate capturing the most votes wins the seat. In the second tier, closed-list proportional representation (PR) is used. The country is partitioned into eleven PR blocs, each of which is made up of one or more prefecture.[3] Initially, district magnitudes varied from six in the smallest bloc to 33 in the most populous bloc. Nowadays, they range from six to 29. Whereas a total of 200 members entered the Lower House via the PR tier in the 1996 election, this number was reduced to 180 in 1999 and is 176 today. In each bloc, parties present voters with lists of candidates, the order of which is fixed prior to the election and unalterable by voters, and voters select one of these lists (Reed and Thies 2001). Votes cast for the parties in each bloc are converted into seats for those

---

[3] Japan's administrative setting is described in greater detail in Chapter 5.

2.1 Victorious under Different Electoral Systems

parties according to the divisor-based method, d'Hondt (Catalinac and Motolinia 2021b).

Under MMM, the results in each tier are independent from each other, meaning that the total number of seats a party wins is the sum of the number of seats it wins in both tiers.[4] The fact that every SSD counts (in the sense of adding to a party's seat share), combined with the fact that there is larger number of SSDs than PR seats (initially, 300 to 200), led to expectations that MMM would foster a party system characterized by two large parties and a handful of smaller ones (Rosenbluth and Thies 2010; Bawn and Thies 2003). Because only one candidate can be successful in an SSD, it was thought that SSDs would become duels between candidates of two larger parties (Catalinac 2018; Cox 1990; Downs 1957). Because votes are converted into seats in a relatively proportional manner under PR, it was thought that competition in the PR blocs would feature those two larger parties, plus a few more (Cox and Schoppa 2002).

It took several years for Japan's party system to conform to these predictions. After the electoral reform legislation passed both Houses in March 1994, disagreements between the coalition partners began surfacing. Taking a page from the Socialists' playbook, LDP politicians waited for the right opportunity to exploit those disagreements. They did not have to wait long: In April, another spat between the coalition partners led to the Socialists leaving the coalition, immediately after they had thrown their support behind the coalition's candidate for the prime minister in the Diet. Two months later, the LDP announced its plans to submit a no-confidence motion in the new government. In response, the new prime minister, Hata Tsutomu, resigned. The LDP then proposed a coalition between the Socialists and another disaffected coalition member, the Sakigake. On June 29, the plan was realized when the Socialists' leader won a Lower House vote called to elect a new prime minister, over the candidate put forward by the non-LDP governing coalition. The LDP thus found itself back in government in a coalition with a party it had fought against for nearly half a century, on the one hand, and a party comprised of former members who had caused its loss of government the year prior, on the other (Curtis 1999).

The remaining members of the non-LDP coalition included older opposition parties that had existed since the 1960s (the DSP and Komeito) and two of the three parties that had been formed the previous

---

[4] Note that this distinguishes MMM from the other type of mixed-member system, mixed-member proportional (MMP). Under MMP, the total number of seats a party wins is derived solely from the share of votes it wins in the PR tier. This gives parties incentives to chase PR votes and assign relatively little importance to winning SSDs (Catalinac and Motolinia 2021a; Krauss, Nemoto and Pekkanen 2012).

year (JNP and Japan Renewal Party). Following the inauguration of the LDP–JSP–Sakigake governing coalition, these parties entered into talks to create a single opposition party that they hoped would be able to challenge the LDP in the next Lower House election, which had to take place by July 1997. Under MMM, mounting a serious challenge to a governing party requires fielding enough candidates capable of placing first in their respective SSDs, in addition to winning PR votes. To this end, the New Frontier Party (NFP) was launched in December 1994. Both the LDP and the NFP concentrated on building consensuses within their parties over which candidate should run in each SSD and how the order of candidates on the eleven PR lists would be decided. The LDP tended to have more than one viable contender in rural SSDs and few viable contenders in urban SSDs; the NFP tended to have the reverse (Reed 1995).

2.1.2 MMM, 1994–2021

Table 2.2 displays data on the performance of the LDP and other major parties in the first five HOR elections following the 1994 reform. Each cell reports a party's total share of seats won in that election in bold, at the top. Below this are two subcolumns, one containing information about the party's performance in the PR tier (left subcolumn) and the other containing information about the party's performance in the SSD tier (right subcolumn). In the left subcolumn, the figure in bold is the share of PR seats won, while the figure below that is the share of PR votes won. In the right subcolumn, the figure in bold is the share of SSDs won, while the figure below that is the share of SSD votes won.

In the first election held under the new system, in 1996, the LDP captured 47.8% of HOR seats. The second-largest party, the NFP, captured 31.2% of seats. While the NFP's share was considerably smaller than that captured by the LDP, it was larger than the share captured by the second-largest party in the last few elections held under the old electoral system. On this basis, the 1996 results suggested that Japan was on its way toward becoming a system characterized by competition between two large parties and several smaller ones. Importantly, the losers of the 1996 election were the LDP's coalition partners. The Socialists, which had renamed themselves the Social Democratic Party (SDP), had already seen their seat share decline from 27.5% in the 1990 election to 13.7% in the 1993 election. This was thought to be partly due to the arrival of the three new parties described above. However, in 1996, its seat share dropped even further, to a mere 3%. Despite fielding candidates in 43 SSDs, it only won four. The Sakigake went from 2.5% of seats in the 1993 election to only 0.4% (two SSDs and zero PR seats) in 1996. After the

Table 2.2 Share of seats (in bold) and votes (in parentheses) captured by major parties in Japan's Lower House elections, 1996–2009. Under the total share of seats won, the numbers on the left pertain to seats and votes in the proportional representation tier, while those on the right pertain to seats and votes in the single-seat district tier.

	1996	2000	2003	2005	2009
LDP	**47.8**	**48.5**	**49.4**	**61.7**	**24.8**
	35.0 56.3	31.1 59.0	38.3 56.0	42.8 73.0	30.6 21.3
	(32.8) (38.6)	(28.3) (41.0)	(35.0) (43.9)	(38.2) (47.8)	(26.7) (38.7)
Sakigake	**0.4**				
	0.0 0.7				
	(1.1) (1.3)				
NFP	**31.2**				
	30.0 32.0				
	(28.0) (28.0)				
Conservative		**1.5**			
		0.0 2.3			
		(0.4) (2.0)			
Liberal		**4.6**	**1.3**		
		10.0 1.3			
		(11.0) (3.4)			
	3.0	**4.0**			
		8.3 1.3	2.8 0.3		
		(9.4) (2.9)	(5.1) (2.9)		
SDP				**1.5**	**1.5**
	5.5 1.3			3.3 0.3	2.2 1.0
	(6.4) (2.2)			(5.5) (1.5)	(4.3) (2.0)

(continued)

Table 2.2 (continued)

	1996		2000		2003		2005		2009	
DPJ	**10.4**		**26.3**		**36.9**		**23.5**		**64.2**	
	17.5	5.7	26.1	26.7	40.0	35.0	33.9	17.3	48.3	73.7
	(16.1)	(10.6)	(25.2)	(27.6)	(37.4)	(36.7)	(31.0)	(36.4)	(42.2)	(47.4)
Komeito			**6.3**		**7.1**		**6.5**		**4.4**	
			13.3	2.3	13.9	3.0	12.8	2.7	11.7	0.0
			(13.0)	(2.0)	(14.8)	(1.5)	(13.3)	(1.4)	(11.5)	(1.1)
	5.2		**4.2**		**1.9**		**1.9**		**1.9**	
JCP	12.0	0.7	11.1	0.0	5.0	0.0	5.0	0.0	5.0	0.0
	(13.1)	(12.6)	(11.2)	(12.1)	(7.8)	(8.1)	(7.3)	(7.3)	(7.0)	(4.2)
Your party									**1.0**	
									1.7	0.7
									(4.3)	(0.9)
Other	**2.0**		**4.6**		**3.4**		**4.9**		**2.2**	
	0.0	3.3	0.0	7.1	0.0	5.7	2.2	6.7	0.5	3.3
	(2.5)	(6.7)	(1.5)	(9.0)	(0.0)	(6.9)	(4.7)	(5.6)	(4.0)	(5.7)
Total	500		480		480		480		480	
	200	300	180	300	180	300	180	300	180	300

The total share of seats won by each party appears in bold above each bar. Below this, the party's seat share in the PR (left) and SSD (right) tier appears, also in bold. Below that, in parentheses, is the share of votes the party won in the PR (left) and SSD (right) tier. DPJ is Democratic Party of Japan; NFP is New Frontier Party; and SDP is Social Democratic Party of Japan (the Japan Socialist Party renamed). Other includes minor parties and Independents.

2.1 Victorious under Different Electoral Systems

election, the LDP decided to keep these parties in the coalition, albeit with no Cabinet portfolios, but began casting around for alternative coalition partners.

Like all large parties in the history of Japanese politics, the NFP was plagued with dissension. In 1997, twelve NFP members abandoned collective efforts to fashion the party into a second majority-seeking party and decided to rejoin the LDP. With these new members, the LDP was able to reclaim its Lower House majority. After a period of internal conflict, the NFP eventually fell apart at the end of 1997 when its leader, former LDP heavyweight Ozawa Ichiro, announced he was leaving. Ozawa formed a new party, the Liberal Party. In April 1998, other former NFP members announced that they were joining the DPJ. Created by Socialist and Sakigake politicians unhappy with their leaders' decisions to ally with the LDP, the DPJ had been the third-highest vote-getter in the 1996 election. It had captured 10.4% of seats and among these, seventeen SSDs. With the influx of new members, the DPJ, which refounded itself in the process, became the largest opposition party in the Lower House. It would hold this honor until 2016, when further upheaval in the party system would lead to its disintegration.

Another hint that a two-party system was emerging in the wake of electoral reform came in the 1998 Upper House election. In Upper House elections, a share of members are elected in a nationwide district according to PR, while another share are elected in prefecture-wide districts according to SNTV-MMD. By virtue of the staggered nature of Upper House elections, in which one half of its Members are up for reelection every three years, some of the prefecture-wide electoral districts are single-seat districts (Nemoto and Shugart 2013). Between Lower House elections, then, both the PR tier and SSDs in Upper House elections function as a bellwether for how the LDP might fare in a Lower House election against whatever opposition party is the next-most-popular. Despite having only just refounded itself (or perhaps because of the publicity it gained from doing so), the DPJ performed unexpectedly well in the 1998 Upper House election, winning only one fewer seat in the PR tier than the LDP. For its part, the LDP found itself without the majority necessary to secure smooth passage of its bills through the Upper House. Part of the explanation for the LDP's relatively poor performance in this election was thought to be the 14% increase in turnout: Analysts suggested that the stagnation in Japan's economy energized nonhabitual voters to turn out and express their dissatisfaction with the LDP (Curtis 1999, 207–9).

The 1998 Upper House election left the LDP in a situation where, despite having regained its Lower House majority and unshackled itself from unpopular coalition partners, it now needed an alternative source of support to ensure the passage of government-sponsored legislation in the second chamber. In January 1999, the LDP entered into a coalition with Ozawa's party, the Liberals. Later that year, it convinced another smaller party, the Komeito, to join this coalition. The Komeito had contested elections since 1965, but decided to merge itself into the NFP upon that party's formation in 1994. After the NFP's disintegration in 1997, the Komeito reemerged as an autonomous party. It had performed unexpectedly well in the 1998 Upper House election, garnering 13.8% of votes in the PR tier. After the formation of this coalition, the Liberals proved an unreliable ally: In April 2000, half of their members left the coalition while the other half stayed, under a different moniker (the Conservatives) (Curtis 1999). The Komeito, on the other hand, has proved to be a reliable ally and has been the LDP's coalition partner ever since (Catalinac and Motolinia 2021*a*; Liff and Maeda 2019).

As Table 2.2 shows, in the next election, held in 2000, the LDP held its ground, winning 48.5% of seats to the DPJ's 26.5%. Together with the PR seats won by its coalition partner, the Komeito, the LDP was able to maintain its seat majority. After this election, the Conservative Party disbanded, with its members joining the LDP. The Liberal Party also disbanded, with its members joining the DPJ. A year later, the LDP elected a new leader, Koizumi Junichiro, whose Cabinet boasted unheard-of approval ratings (in the eighties) at the time of its inauguration in 2001.[5] Despite Koizumi being a great deal more popular than any of the LDP's former leaders, including Mori Yoshiro, who was supported by only 17% of Japanese voters at the time of the 2000 election, the results of the 2003 election were similar to those of 2000. While the LDP's seat share increased slightly to 49.4%, the DPJ's seat share jumped by more than 10 percentage points. Whereas it only captured 80 SSDs in 2000, by 2003, its tally had reached 105 SSDs. It also won more PR seats than the LDP.

The LDP's lukewarm results in 2003 were followed, just two years later, by a landslide victory in the 2005 election. The party managed 61.7% of seats, its best electoral performance since 1960. The DPJ's seat share, on the other hand, was reduced to 23.5%. Patterson and Maeda (2007)'s analyses suggest that these results stemmed from a nationwide swing in favor of the LDP, which came at the expense of the DPJ. The vote share of the average LDP SSD candidate increased by 3% relative to 2003, while that of the average DPJ SSD candidate decreased by 3%. In an electoral system comprised of SSDs with two serious competitors,

---

[5] The data on Cabinet approval and party approval referenced in this book come from the NHK Broadcasting Culture Research Institute, available at: www.nhk.or.jp/bunken/research/yoron/political/2018.html.

2.1 Victorious under Different Electoral Systems

anything that can give one party's candidates an edge over the other's is likely to result in the former's victory. The LDP managed to win sixty-one more SSDs in 2005 than it did in 2003, while the DPJ lost sixty-two (Patterson and Maeda 2007). While I discuss the party's strategy in this election in more detail below, suffice to say that it encompassed a conscious effort to orient the party toward urban voters (and away from rural ones). The 2005 election showed that the LDP had lost votes in rural SSDs and gained them in urban ones. This had the effect of swinging an unprecedented number of urban SSDs its way and flattening out its support base across the country (Maeda 2010; Reed, Scheiner and Thies 2012).

Four years after the LDP won its largest-ever Lower House majority (in 2005), it was served up its first-ever Lower House defeat (in 2009). What happened in the intervening years? In September 2006, Koizumi's second term as party leader ended and he declined to run for a third. In his place, the party chose Abe Shinzo. The ensuing three years were a downward spiral. Abe's popularity suffered when the government's Social Insurance Agency was discovered to have lost 50 million pension records and he agreed to readmit former LDP politicians who had opposed the party's signature platform in the 2005 election (postal privatization) but won reelection in 2005 without the party's endorsement (Reed, Scheiner and Thies 2012). By the July 2007 Upper House election, public support for his Cabinet had halved. The LDP managed only 37 of the 121 seats up for grabs, while the DPJ captured 60 (Pempel 2010, 251). For the first time since its formation, the LDP was no longer the largest party in the Upper House. In September 2007, Abe resigned and party members selected Fukuda Yasuo. A year later, Fukuda also resigned, after sinking approval rates. Party members then threw their support behind Aso Taro, whose support rates started off lower than the former two prime ministers and followed an even-worse trajectory.

If the 2005 election showed that party leaders with a favorable public image are assets for candidates trying to place first in their SSDs, the 2009 election showed how serious of a liability an unpopular leader can be. By early 2009, Aso's support rate was in the single digits. The global financial crisis had led to a contraction in Japan's GDP and an increase in unemployment. Scandals involving Cabinet Ministers, a relatively regular occurrence in Japanese politics, appeared particularly galling in this context. Yet LDP lawmakers struggled to replace Aso (Arase 2010). At the same time, the DPJ's performance in the Upper House election the year before had knitted together previously divided groups in the party and focused the minds of lawmakers on presenting the DPJ as a unified party that posed a viable alternative to the LDP (Konishi 2009). In July 2009, public support for the DPJ exceeded that of the LDP for the first time ever, in the same month that Prime Minister Aso dissolved the House and called for new elections. Having waited until the very end of the term of Lower House Members, presumably in the hope that something might happen to boost the party's popularity, Aso had little choice.

Held on August 30, 2009, the election was disastrous for the LDP. Table 2.2 shows that its seat share dropped to 24.8%, while the DPJ's increased to 64.2%, the largest share of seats a party has ever obtained in a Lower House election in Japan. Having obtained 219 SSDs in 2005, the LDP managed only 64 in 2009. The DPJ, in contrast, captured only 52 SSDs in 2005 but walked away with 221 SSDs in 2009. All told, 60% of LDP incumbents (184 in total) lost their seats, many of whom were senior, experienced lawmakers (Maeda 2010; Pempel 2010).

Analyses revealed that the DPJ's landslide stemmed from a nationwide swing away from the LDP and toward the DPJ, just like the 2005 election, which had seen the reverse. Whereas in 2005, the LDP's SSD vote share was 47.8% and the DPJ's was 36.4%, in 2009, the parties had switched places: The LDP was at 38.7% and the DPJ was at 47.4%. According to Maeda (2010), the swing toward the DPJ impacted SSDs in a relatively uniform fashion, regardless of whether they were rural or urban, represented by an LDP heavyweight or inexperienced newcomer. His analyses revealed that SSDs that had experienced greater shifts in PR vote shares *to* the LDP between 2003 and 2005 saw greater shifts *away* from the party between 2005 and 2009. He interprets this as evidence that the LDP had been able to attract floating voters in 2005 but lost them in 2009. McElwain (2012), too, identifies this election as a turning point. Whereas LDP incumbents used to be able to rely on personal characteristics such as experience to insulate themselves from dips in their party's popularity, his analyses showed that by 2009, this was no longer working. While the LDP lost votes in all types of SSDs, the decline was noticeably larger in urban ones. The fact that rural voters turned to the DPJ was also a product of a concerted strategy of that party's leaders to appeal to them (Kushida and Lipscy 2013).

After its 2009 landslide, the DPJ found itself dependent on two parties to pass bills in the Upper House. The DPJ Prime Minister Hatoyama Yukio brought them on board as part of a coalition government. Just like the LDP-led administrations of the preceding three years, the years from September 2009 to December 2012 saw three DPJ prime ministers. Like their LDP predecessors, each kicked off their administrations with decent approval ratings: in the seventies (in the case of Hatoyama Yukio, 2009–2010), sixties (in the case of Kan Naoto, 2010–2011), and fifties (in the case of Noda Yoshihiko, 2011–2012). But before long, each saw their

2.1 Victorious under Different Electoral Systems

approval sink to the twenties or tens and for the most part, languish there (Pekkanen and Reed 2013). Hatoyama's, for example, dropped from a high of 71% immediately after his Cabinet's inauguration to just 17% by May 2010. In a manner reminiscent of their LDP predecessors, initial declines could be traced to an occurrence that called into question their judgement or gave the impression they were mismanaging a situation, but once the decline had begun, it proved difficult to reverse.

In the early 1990s, defections from the LDP showed that prime ministers are not immune to challenges from within. Recalcitrant DPJ members took criticism of their leader to a new level (Nyblade 2013). Barely a year after the inauguration of the first non-LDP government in fifteen years, and the first non-LDP government to rest on an undisputed electoral mandate, DPJ members declared they were opposed to an increase in the consumption tax, which their newly minted prime minister had announced was needed. While this had not been part of the DPJ's 2009 election manifesto, Prime Minister Kan Naoto argued that it was necessary to reign in spiraling public debt and put the nation's finances on a healthier footing. Japan's society was aging, he argued, which meant it needed to plan for a future in which a smaller workforce would be able to support the pension and health-care needs of a much-older population.

On the heels of this public disagreement, the DPJ lost the 2010 Upper House election, plunging Japanese politics back into a situation in which one party controlled one House and another party controlled the other (Thies and Yanai 2013; Kushida and Lipscy 2013). Like it had done before, the LDP attempted to exploit the disagreements within the DPJ with a motion of no confidence. This failed, but the DPJ prime minister chose not to expel the party members who had voted for the motion. Substantive questions such as whether to restart the nuclear reactors that had been placed offline after the March 2011 earthquake, tsunami, and nuclear meltdown and whether Japan should say yes to the Trans-Pacific Partnership (TPP) also divided the party, with those opposed to their leader's decisions publicly voicing their opposition (Pekkanen and Reed 2013).

In early 2012, a second major transformation of the party system began, which would prove fatal for the DPJ. The engine of this was the efforts of local politicians – mostly governors – to create new parties. As with the events of the early 1990s, these individuals were likely calculating that they could take advantage of conflict within the ruling DPJ, or they were actively encouraged by the protagonists of that conflict themselves. In January 2012, the mayor of Osaka and leader of a party formed the previous year to contest elections to the Osaka City Assembly, Hashimoto Toru, announced the launch of a new party that would run candidates in the next Lower House election. He called this the Japan Restoration Party (JRP). At the same time, Tokyo governor Ishihara Shintaro declared his intention to resign his position and form a new party. In events reminiscent of 1993, a few months later a group of forty-odd DPJ lawmakers voted against their leader's consumption tax bill and left the party (Nyblade 2013). This group formed Peoples' Life First (PLP). Soon after its formation, the PLP tabled a motion of no confidence against Prime Minister Noda, in conjunction with other opposition parties. In exchange for not supporting the motion, which would have brought down the Noda government, the LDP extracted a promise from Prime Minister Noda to hold an election "soon." It also decided to support the DPJ government's consumption tax legislation (Endo, Pekkanen and Reed 2013).

Later that same year, PLP lawmakers secured a new leader, Shiga governor Yukiko Kada, and reconstituted themselves as the Tomorrow Party of Japan (TPJ). Ishihara resigned from his position as governor of Tokyo and formed a small party, only to merge with the JRP almost immediately. Together with Your Party, which had been formed by an LDP defector prior to the 2009 election, these three parties (PLP, JRP, and YP) collectively became known as the Third Force (Pekkanen and Reed 2013; Nyblade 2013). While they were also three parties, this moniker refers to the fact that their goal was to give voters unhappy with both the LDP and the DPJ a third choice in the upcoming election.

By the time the election was held in December 2012, the DPJ had suffered seventy-five defections. It had captured 308 Lower House seats in the 2009 election; by December 2012, it had only 230 lawmakers. Nyblade (2013)'s analysis shows that relatively junior, electorally insecure DPJ lawmakers were more likely to defect than their more-senior, electorally secure counterparts. Such members, he reasons, were likely engaged in a near-continuous calculation that boiled down to asking: Are my political ambitions (most immediately, being reelected) better served by staying *in* the party or casting my lot with *another* party? By mid 2012, when the occasional defection of a DPJ member was giving way to more-frequent defections of groups of DPJ members, polls continued to show that large segments of the population disapproved of Cabinet. In a sign of the reversal in fortunes that the impending election would bring, polls showed that the percentage of respondents supporting the DPJ was now lower than the percentage supporting the LDP. More LDP politicians, Nyblade (2013) argues, would have tried to defect from the LDP prior to the 2009 election if there had been Third Force parties to defect to.

Table 2.3 displays data on the performance of the LDP and other major parties in the four HOR elections held between 2012 and 2021.

Table 2.3 Share of seats (in bold) and votes (in parentheses) captured by parties in Japan's Lower House elections, 2012–2021. Under the total share of seats won, the numbers on the left pertain to seats and votes in the proportional representation tier, while those on the right pertain to seats and votes in the single-seat district tier.

	2012		2014		2017		2021	
LDP	**61.3**		**60.4**		**60.4**		**55.7**	
	31.7	79.0	37.8	74.0	37.5	74.4	40.9	64.7
	(27.6)	(43.0)	(33.1)	(48.1)	(33.3)	(47.8)	(34.7)	(48.0)
Your Party	**3.8**							
	7.8	1.3						
	(8.7)	(4.7)						
SDP	**0.4**		**0.4**		**0.4**		**0.2**	
	0.6	0.3	0.6	0.3	0.6	0.3	0	0.3
	(2.7)	(0.8)	(2.5)	(0.8)	(1.7)	(1.2)	(1.8)	(0.5)
DPJ	**11.9**		**15.2**					
	16.7	9.0	19.4	12.7				
	(16.0)	(22.8)	(18.3)	(22.5)				
TPJ	**1.9**							
	3.9	0.7						
	(5.7)	(5.0)						
CDP					**11.6**		**20.6**	
					21.0	5.9	22.2	19.7
					(19.9)	(8.5)	(20.0)	(30.0)

(continued)

Table 2.3 *(continued)*

	2012	2014	2017	2021
Hope/DPP	6.5	7.3	**10.8**	**2.4**
			18.2 6.2	2.8 2.0
			(17.4) (20.6)	(4.5) (2.2)
Komeito	**1.7**	**4.4**	**6.2**	**6.9**
	12.2 3.0	14.4 3.0	11.9 2.8	13.1 3.1
	(11.8) (1.5)	(13.8) (1.5)	(12.5) (1.5)	(12.4) (1.5)
JCP	**11.3**	**8.5**	**2.4**	**2.2**
	4.4 0.0	11.1 0.3	6.3 0.3	5.1 0.3
	(6.1) (7.9)	(11.4) (13.3)	(7.9) (9.0)	(7.2) (4.6)
JRP/JIP/Ishin				**8.8**
	22.2 4.7	16.7 3.7	4.5 1.0	14.2 5.5
	(20.4) (11.6)	(15.7) (8.2)	(6.1) (3.2)	(14.0) (8.4)
Other	**1.2**	**3.8**	**5.6**	**3.2**
	0.5 2.0	0.0 6.0	0.0 9.1	1.7 4.2
	(1.0) (2.7)	(5.7) (5.6)	(1.2) (8.2)	(1.6) (4.8)
Total	480	475	465	465
	180 300	180 295	176 289	176 289

The total share of seats won by each party appears in bold above each bar. Below this, the party's seat share in the PR (left) and SSD (right) tiers appears in bold. Below that, in parentheses, is the share of votes the party won in the PR (left) and SSD (right) tiers. Parties are CDP (Constitutional Democratic Party); Hope (Party of Hope); Democratic Party for the People (DPP); TPJ (Tomorrow Party of Japan or Nihon Mirai no To); JRP/JIP/Ishin refers to the Japan Restoration Party (2012), the Japan Innovation Party (2014), and Ishin (2017 and 2021). Other includes PNP (2009), PFG and PLP (2014), Party for Japanese Kokoro and Liberals (2017), and Reiwa Shinsengumi (2021), as well as other minor parties and Independents.

2.1 Victorious under Different Electoral Systems

The format is the same as Table 2.2. The first column shows that the 2012 election saw a decisive reversal of fortunes for the LDP: It captured 61.3% of seats, while the DPJ was reduced to just 11.9%. Going into the election, the LDP had 118 seats. Coming out, it had 294, a gain of 176 seats. While the LDP had won only 64 SSDs in 2009, it walked away with 237 in 2012, a gain of 173 SSDs. Furthermore, the LDP–Komeito coalition together captured more than two-thirds of seats in the Lower House, which gave it the ability to override any potential veto from the Upper House. The DPJ, on the other hand, was reduced to only fifty-seven HOR seats, which was only two in excess of the third-largest party, the JRP, which won fifty-five. The TPJ, comprised mostly of recent DPJ defectors, did badly, managing only nine seats.

During the 2012 campaign, the LDP made addressing stagflation (the economic stagnation and deflation that had plagued Japan for more than a decade) the centerpiece of its campaign. Immediately afterward, the new Prime Minister Abe Shinzo took steps to implement two of the three arrows in his economic policy, which would later become known as Abenomics (Hoshi and Lipscy 2021). The first was quantitative easing, which involved instructing the Central Bank to set a 2% inflation target, to be achieved through the purchase of government bonds and other assets. The second was fiscal stimulus, to be financed with the extra money provided by the easy monetary policy (Noble 2016; Tiberghien 2013). A key aspect of this stimulus was construction spending to increase the country's resilience to natural disasters. The stock market rallied temporarily, although other economic indicators in the run-up to the July 2013 Upper House election were less positive. Coming only a short time after the LDP had regained control of government in December, this election promised to determine whether or not the LDP-led coalition would face a "divided Diet" for the remainder of its term, just as the DPJ had done between 2010 and 2012, and the LDP had done between 2007 and 2009, respectively (Thies and Yanai 2013). Helped by the continued unpopularity of the DPJ, fragmentation in the opposition, and low turnout, an indication that voters without partisan attachments were staying at home, the LDP won a comfortable victory, increasing its seat share from 35% of Upper House seats to 48%. The share controlled by the DPJ fell from 36% to 24% (Pekkanen, Reed and Scheiner 2016).

Coming a year and a half after the July 2013 Upper House election, the December 2014 Lower House election took many by surprise. In the wake of the LDP's 2013 election victory, the Abe government had enacted a Special Secrets Law, revised a prohibition on arms exports, and declared that the longstanding interpretation that Article 9 of Japan's constitution prohibited the exercise of collective self-defense, which was Japan's right under the United Nations Charter, would be overturned (Pekkanen and Pekkanen 2015; Repeta 2014). Being unpopular, these policies sparked demonstrations attended by scores of thousands. In April 2014, the scheduled increase in the consumption tax (from 5% to 8%) took place. The product of a decision made two years earlier, under the DPJ government, this led to a contraction in Japan's GDP, prompting the public to exhibit misgivings about Abenomics. Public opinion polls showed that a majority continued to have hope for Abenomics, but an even larger majority reported that they had not personally experienced any tangible benefits from it (Maeda 2016). Despite this, none of the opposition parties were able to present a compelling counterproposal or capitalize on public discontent with other aspects of Abe's agenda (Noble 2016). Suddenly, in November 2014, Abe dissolved the House and called an election. His reasoning was that he was seeking a mandate for his decision to delay the next scheduled increase in consumption tax (from 8% to 10%) from April 2015 to April 2017.

Pekkanen, Reed and Scheiner (2016) argue that two calculations influenced Abe's decision. One was his desire to take advantage of the fact that the opposition was in the process of reconsolidating. The other was his desire to forestall a *within*-party challenge, which could emerge now that the gains from Abenomics appeared smaller than projected. With regard to the opposition, the TPJ had reverted back to the name used upon its formation in 2012 (prior to installing Kada as its head): the PLP. Your Party (YP) had suffered rifts that led to the formation of a splinter party, the Unity Party, and its eventual dissolution in 2014. The JRP had also split, with one faction leaving and calling itself the Party for Future Generations (PFG) and another merging with YP's splinter Unity Party to form the Japan Innovation Party (JIP) (Pekkanen and Reed 2016). In the December 2014 election, Table 2.3 shows that the LDP captured a seat share that was similar to its 2012 share: 60.4%. The next-largest party, the DPJ, managed just 15.2% of seats. Between them, the Third Force parties managed only 9.4% of seats (down from 17% in 2012), nearly all of which were captured by the JIP. The PFG and PLP were decimated, winning only two seats each.[6]

By early 2017, Prime Minister Abe was grappling with declining approval ratings as two instances in which conservative-leaning educational institutions had been given preferential treatment with regard to land sales, allegedly on account of personal connections to the prime minister, came to light. At the same time, scandals involving members of the "friends and ideological allies" Cabinet Abe had put together in

---

[6] These parties are in the Other category in the table.

2.1 Victorious under Different Electoral Systems

the wake of his 2016 Upper House victory were also receiving media coverage (Carlson and Reed 2018b). Against this background, the newly elected governor of Tokyo, former LDP-affiliated Lower House Member Koike Yuriko, announced that she was forming a new party to challenge the LDP's majority party status in the Tokyo Metropolitan Assembly. She called this party Tokyoites First. In a blow to the LDP, Koike convinced the Tokyo branch of the LDP's coalition partner, the Komeito, to abrogate its electoral coordination with the LDP in the upcoming July 2017 Tokyo Assembly election and coordinate with Tokyoites First instead. This strategy was a resounding success: Tokyoites First won a plurality of assembly seats, while the LDP lost more than half the seats it had going into the election. Koike made no secret of the fact that she intended to take her party to the national level and compete in the next Lower House election.

Between 2014 and 2017, the opposition reconstituted itself again. Despite being decimated in the 2014 election, in its wake the PFG had rebranded itself as Party for Japanese Kokoro and the PLP had rebranded itself as the Liberals. The only opposition party that had done well in 2014, the JIP, ended up splitting in 2015 over whether or not to cooperate with the DPJ. The group that opposed cooperation became Initiatives for Osaka and then, in 2016, Nippon Ishin no Kai (JIP). The group in favor of cooperation ended up merging with the DPJ in 2016. Calling itself the DP, this new entity carved out a plan to cooperate with Japan's oldest opposition party, the JCP, in the upcoming election. It had tried out this strategy in the 2016 Upper House election and determined that it had gone well (Pekkanen and Reed 2018).

In September 2017, North Korea launched a missile over Japanese territory. Abe, who had attempted to build a relationship of trust with United States President Donald J. Trump since the latter's election the previous November, decided to dissolve the House and call for an election. Much like in 2014, he told voters that he needed a mandate to deal with the security concerns posed by North Korea and decide how to allocate revenue generated from the consumption tax hike (Scheiner, Smith and Thies 2018; Smith 2018c). Soon after this announcement, Koike (Tokyoites First leader) announced that she was forming a new party called the Party of Hope. The DP leader, Maehara Seiji, announced that the DP would not endorse candidates in the election and instead, DP members would be encouraged to seek endorsement from Hope. Immediately after this announcement, Koike, who declined to resign from the governorship while leading the new party, announced that any DP lawmaker seeking Hope's endorsement had to publicly pledge to support the party's policies, which included constitutional revision. These preferences reflected greater partisan alignment with the LDP, which is a conservative party, than with the more liberal opposition parties. These demands led to the creation of *another* new party at the eleventh hour, the Constitutional Democratic Party (CDP), which was comprised of those DP members who opposed constitutional revision (Pekkanen and Reed 2018).

For the LDP, the results of the 2017 election were nearly a carbon copy of the 2014 election (Scheiner, Smith and Thies 2018, 46). Despite a loss of ten seats between the two elections due to redistricting (four in PR and six SSDs), the LDP won a seat share of 60.4% seats, eerily similar to its seat share in 2014. The share of votes it won in the SSD and PR tier, respectively, were within 1 percentage point of the party's 2014 shares. Hope, which had tried to coordinate with JIP in the SSD tier, managed only 10.8% of seats. The CDP, which pursued what ended up being a relatively successful coordination effort with the JCP (and to a lesser extent, with the SDP), won 11.6% of seats, eclipsing Hope to become the second-largest party (Scheiner, Smith and Thies 2018). Another twenty-six SSDs were won by independents, many of whom were former DP lawmakers who had elected not to join either Hope or the CDP.

As with the 2012 and 2014 elections, the aftermath of the 2017 election saw yet another reconstitution of the party system. The DP had not formally disbanded in 2017, when it said it would not run any official candidates in the Lower House election. This is because it had Upper House lawmakers. In April 2018, DP-affiliated Upper House Diet Members decided to merge with Hope's lawmakers in the Lower House and call the new party the Democratic Party for the People (DPP). A year later, the Liberal Party (formerly the PLP) dissolved, with its members joining the DPP. Then, in August 2020, the leaders of the DPP and CDP agreed to merge, with the reconstituted entity to be named the CDP (Sugiyama 2020). As with prior attempts at merging, select DPP members declined to join the new party, preferring to remain as a separate party under the DPP moniker. After this merger, the CDP became the second-largest party in the Lower House, controlling 110 seats.

The beginning of 2020 saw the onset of the COVID-19 pandemic. The government closed schools and asked people to stay home and businesses not to open. Economic growth, which under Abe had been on a slightly upward trajectory, contracted significantly as businesses recorded fewer profits, so cut work hours and wages, households cut consumption, inbound tourism collapsed with new restrictions on the entry of non-Japanese nationals, and demand for Japanese products abroad declined. Even though his government enacted two supplementary budgets, designed to help blunt the need for layoffs and keep businesses and individuals afloat, Prime Minister Abe's support rate steadily declined. In August 2020, he suddenly declared that he was stepping down from

2.1 Victorious under Different Electoral Systems

his position as the prime minister (and by default, LDP president). The party held an election to decide who would serve out the remaining year of Abe's three-year term, and in it, LDP-affiliated Diet members elected Suga Yoshihide (Liff 2021).

Despite his close association with former Prime Minister Abe, who became the longest-serving prime minister in Japan's history a few weeks before his resignation, and pledge to continue the policies of his predecessor, Suga's support rate fell steadily, as public consternation with pandemic-imposed restrictions, the slow vaccine roll-out, and rising case counts grew. Support for Suga's administration reached a low ebb during a "fifth wave" of infections in summer 2021, during which time the government persisted in holding the Tokyo Olympics, which had been postponed from 2020 (Liff 2022). This prompted Suga to declare that he would not run in the next LDP leadership election, slated to choose a leader for a new three-year term. In September 2021, LDP-affiliated Diet members elected Kishida Fumio in his place. Kishida immediately dissolved the Lower House and called for an election.

Unlike the 2014 and 2017 elections, the 2021 election occurred at the very end of Members' constitutionally mandated four-year term. Having set expectations that the party's seat share would be on the low side, given the pandemic, the LDP still managed to walk away with 55.7% of seats (Maeda 2023). This represented a loss of fifteen seats, but it was still a comfortable majority. Going into the election, the reconstituted opposition comprised the CDP, JCP, JIP, and DPP, respectively. The CDP captured 110 seats, the JCP captured 12 seats, the JIP captured 11 seats, and the DPP captured 8 seats, respectively (Pekkanen and Reed 2023). The CDP and JCP had coordinated their SSD candidacies to avoid running against each other. This strategy ended up being less successful than either party had hoped and both parties lost seats. The JIP, on the other hand, saw its seat tally triple to forty-one seats, which put it in the position of second-largest opposition party. The JIP's support has always been heavily concentrated in the Osaka region, where it emerged, and of the fifteen Osaka-based SSDs in which it fielded candidates, it won all of them.

2.1.3 Untouched by Post-2012 Party System Transformation

Figure 2.1 chronicles the transformations in Japan's party system that have occurred since 1955. The tree begins on the left with the LDP, JSP, and JCP, each of which existed in 1955. The year of each party's formation or dissolution appears in smaller text outside the boxes. The Komeito was formed in 1964 and divisions in the JSP's ranks produced the DSP

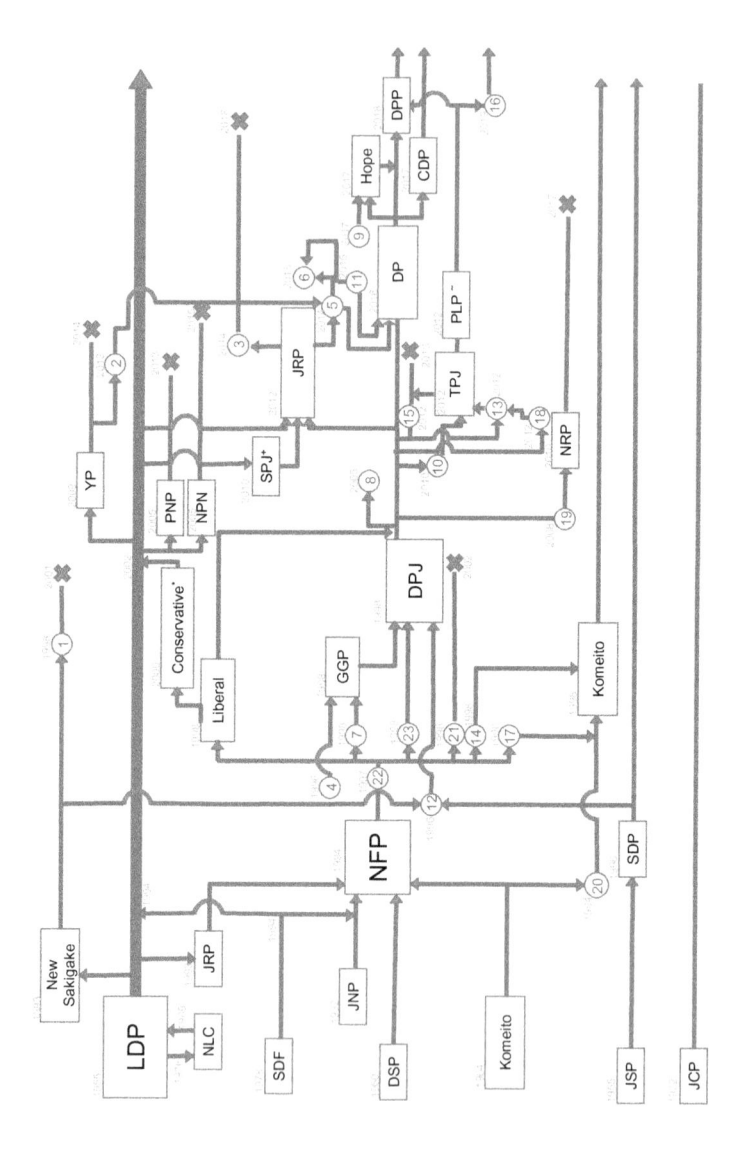

Figure 2.1 Tree depicting the transformation of Japan's party system, 1955–2018. The year of each party's formation or dissolution appears in smaller text outside the boxes.
See Figure A.2 for a key to the parties represented by numbers in the circles. See Figure A.1 for the party tree in Japanese.

in 1960 and the Socialist Democratic Federation (SDF) in 1978, respectively. Moving slightly to the right, the Japan Renewal Party, JNP, and Sakigake were formed in the early 1990s. After the electoral reform in 1994, the JSP changed its name to the SDP and the NFP was formed. The DPJ was formed in advance of the 1996 election, but refounded itself in 1998 under the same label after the NFP collapsed. The NFP's collapse in 1997 begat the formation of the Liberals, and later, the Conservatives. It also led to the reemergence of Komeito (technically under the name New Komeito). In the 2000s, smaller parties were formed when LDP politicians disapproved of Prime Minister's Koizumi's postal privatization plan and defected from the LDP. Then, the formation of several new parties in 2012, and the subsequent splintering of the DPJ, are depicted on the right-hand side of the figure. The tree makes it clear that the LDP, depicted by the large square at the top, has remained completely aloof from the transformation in the party system that has occurred since 2012.[7]

2.2 ECLIPSING OTHER PARTIES IN SUPPORT

Election results are the product of an electoral system that converts votes cast for parties into seats for those parties. Because electoral systems have biases, and voters have a sense of those biases when casting their votes, I supplement the above discussion with data on voter *attitudes* toward the different parties. This table is based on Jiji Press data provided by Kenneth McElwain.[8] Every month, Japan's Jiji Press conducts a survey on a nationally representative sample of 3,000 Japanese citizens of voting age. Examining the share of voters selecting the LDP relative to other parties provides more information as to the sheer dominance of the LDP, and how that dominance has been consolidated in the post-2012 period.

The question we are interested in is "Which party do you support?" In Figure 2.2, the black line captures the percentage of respondents who selected "the LDP" between the forty years from August 1980 until March 2020. It is immediately apparent that, for all its strength in elections, the LDP is not a particularly *popular* political party. The average percentage of respondents who say they support the LDP in this period was 25.8%. This number reached its zenith at 40.2% in December 1991 and its lowest ebb at 11.7% in March 2012. The former occurred immediately after the inauguration of the government of Miyazawa Kiichi, while the latter occurred while the LDP government was negotiating with the DPJ government over a planned increase in the consumption tax. Of

---

[7] Figure A.1 presents the same figure in Japanese, and Figure A.2 presents a key to the English and Japanese names of parties represented by numbers in the circles.
[8] For more information on this data, see Matsumoto et al. 2024.

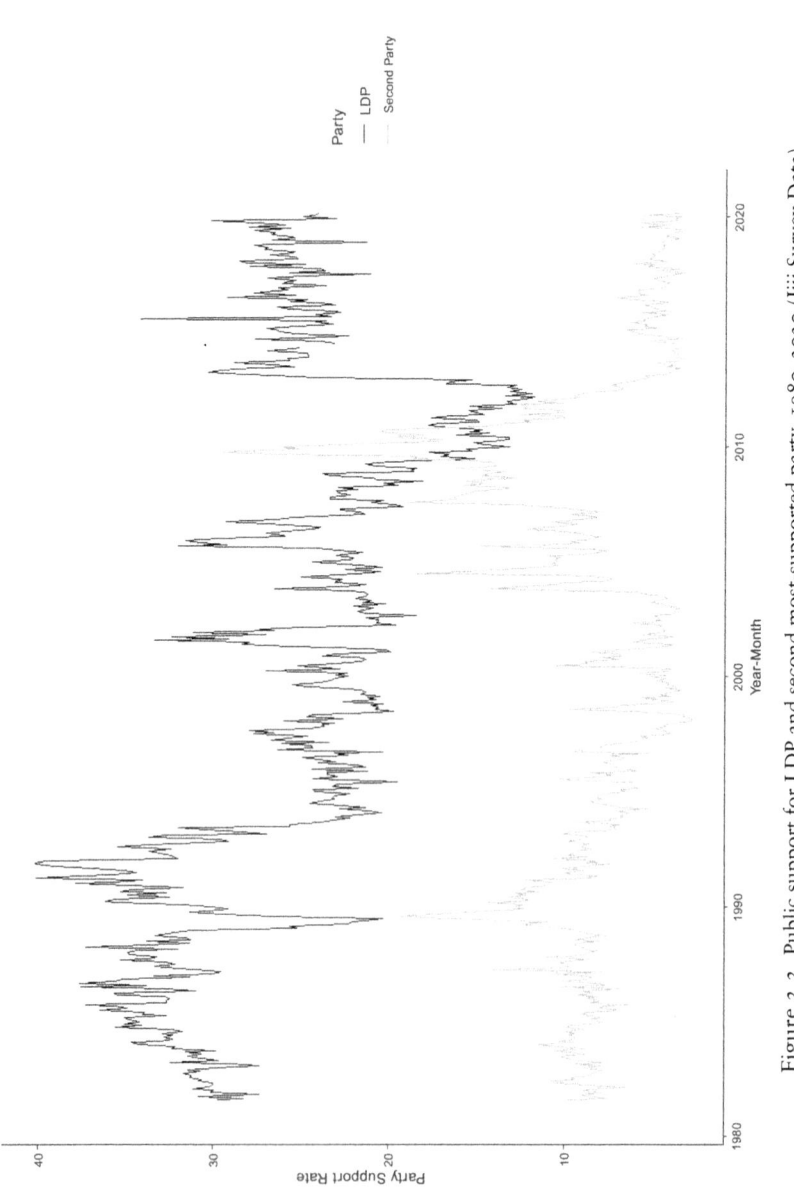

Figure 2.2 Public support for LDP and second most-supported party, 1980–2020 (Jiji Survey Data)

2.2 Eclipsing Other Parties in Support

course, the strength of attachment voters feel to political parties is a function of many context-specific factors that make it difficult to generalize from. Thus, our interest here is less in the *absolute* level of support the LDP commands in these surveys and more in the *relative* level of support it commands.

The gray line depicts the percentage of respondents who selected the second-most-selected party in each month. To construct this, I took the percentages of respondents who supported each of the n non-LDP parties that existed in any given month, and I plotted the maximum of those percentages. Thus, the gray line depicts how much support the second-most-supported party commanded each month.[9] If the LDP commands a surprisingly small share of popular support, given its electoral prowess, the opposition party best poised to take over from the LDP commands an *abysmally small* share of popular support. Across the whole period, the second-most popular party commanded the support of, on average, just 8% of survey respondents. Support for the second-most popular party reached its lowest ebb in February and March of 1998, when just 2.8% of respondents said they supported the second-most-supported party (the JSP) and its highest ebb in October 2009, just after the inauguration of the DPJ government, when 29.4% of respondents supported the second-most-supported party (the DPJ).

It will be immediately apparent that the *gap* between the black and gray lines depicts how much *more* support the LDP has commanded, relative to the next-most-supported party. On average, this gap has been large: 17%. However low the LDP's absolute level of support is, then, it is clear that its support vastly exceeds that commanded by any other party. Three distinct periods are discernible. In the first period, which pertains to the twenty-seven years between 1980 and 2007, the gap was, on average, 19.5%. There was a single month, July 1989, when the gap was only 3.7%, which occurred when a decidedly *unpopular* LDP leader was serving as the prime minister just as a very *popular* leader was at the helm of the JSP. Notice that this twenty-seven–year period includes

---

[9] For those interested, between 1980 and 1993, the second-most-supported party was the JSP. In August 1993, it became the newly established JNP. By November 1993, it was back to the JSP. The JSP continued to command the second-highest rate of support until the NFP was established in December 1994. For the near duration of the NFP's existence until its dissolution in December 1997, it was the second-most-supported party. Between January and June 1998, the second-most supported party oscillated between the JSP, the DPJ, and even the JCP. Then, for the next eighteen years, the second-most-supported party was almost always the DPJ, with the exception of several months in which it was the LDP's coalition partner, the Komeito. Between 2016 and 2017, it was the new party that formed after the DPJ dissolved, the DP. In 2017, the CDP was formed, after which this party has consistently captured the second-highest rate of support.

the inauguration of the first non-LDP government in thirty-eight years (in August 1993). This occurred *without* noticeable changes in the support rates of either the LDP or second-most-supported party. This makes sense when we consider that this alternation in power did not occur through an election in which another party won more seats than the LDP.

In the second period, which extends from 2007 until 2013, the DPJ grew in popularity and eventually superseded the LDP in public support for just over a year between 2009 and 2010. In the 2007–2013 period, the gap was, on average, a much smaller 3.2%. In the third period, however, which extends from 2013 until 2020, the gap has shot back up to 21.2%. In this period, the average level of support commanded by the second-most supported party has been a measly 4.6%, while the average level of support commanded by the LDP has been 25.8%. Looking at these figures and considering the trajectories of the numerous new parties that have been formed since 2012, it is hard to imagine the LDP being unseated by a single opposition party in the immediate future.

2.3 ELECTORAL INSTITUTIONS ADVANTAGE THE LDP?

While numerous factors have contributed to the LDP's electoral dominance, we can distil many of these factors into three main categories. The first draws attention to the ways in which the two electoral systems used to select Lower House Members have advantaged the LDP at the expense of other parties. How?

First, let us take the electoral system used for the Lower House until 1993: single nontransferable vote in multimember districts (SNTV-MMD). Under SNTV-MMD, recall that Japan was divided into between 118 and 131 multimember electoral districts, from which three, four, or five candidates were elected. Generally speaking, political scientists have shown that the number of serious competitors in any given electoral district tends to be one *more* than the number of candidates elected, meaning that an electoral district electing five people will likely see six serious competitors, and so on (Cox 1997; Reed 1990; Duverger 1963). When competition is between four, five, or six serious candidates in a given district, it follows that each candidate will end up needing a relatively *small* share of the vote to be elected. The share can be even smaller when the district attracts nonserious competitors. In an electoral district with five winners (and six serious competitors), for example, candidates can win seats with just 10–15% of votes cast (Bouissou 1999).

In this setting, parties essentially face a choice: They can remain small, which means avoiding intraparty competition but forgoing the chance to

2.3 Electoral Institutions Advantage the LDP?

govern, or they can try to be large, which means grappling with intraparty competition but potentially gaining control of government. When a party is content with being small, it can run a single candidate in each electoral district and tailor its platforms to attract approximately 15% of voters in each district. By not running more candidates, it ensures it will never be majority-seeking, thus forgoing the opportunity to capture a majority and control government, at least by itself. However, it can avoid having its candidates campaign against each other, which can give rise to serious internal disagreement. As a result, the party can remain unified.

As soon as a party has ambitions of controlling government, however, then under SNTV-MMD it has to run more than one candidate in many (if not all) electoral districts. This means it has to find a way for its candidates to compete against each other in a relatively "safe" manner, meaning in a manner that does not create divisions between party members that could threaten its hold on power, were it to reach this point. Whereas in some political systems, disagreements between members of the ruling party might be less consequential, in a parliamentary system like Japan's, the prime minister governs with the confidence of the majority party. Hence, disagreements within the ruling party can prove fatal, in the sense of bringing down government or leading to a new election in which one's career as a lawmaker could come to an end. Under SNTV-MMD, then, majority-seeking parties are buffeted by two conflicting pressures. One, emanating from the bottom (electoral system) up, encourages parties to stay small and the party system to *fragment*. Another pressure, emanating from the top (constitutional structure) down, encourages parties to enlarge themselves and *unify* (McCubbins and Rosenbluth 1995; Ramseyer and Rosenbluth 1993).

A key explanation for LDP dominance under this electoral system holds that the LDP was better able to manage these countervailing pressures than parties in the opposition. Why? Because of its control of central government resources. Specifically, this explanation holds that in the years after its inception, the party decided to allow its members access to central government resources, which they could use to carve out personal bailiwicks in their electoral districts that could then be relied on to get out the vote on election day (Krauss and Pekkanen 2010; Hirano 2006; Tatebayashi 2004; Fukui and Fukai 1999; Bouissou 1999; McCubbins and Rosenbluth 1995; Ramseyer and Rosenbluth 1993). As long as a lid was kept on the *total* amount of particularistic spending inserted into the budget each year, the idea was that the party allowed this spending on the grounds that having members from the same district competing against each other with particularism posed less of a threat to party unity and government stability than competition over programmatic policies

(Catalinac 2015). Having candidates in the same electoral district dueling over national security or judicial reform was deemed risky, as it could too easily spiral into a situation where efforts by one LDP lawmaker to realize her election promises clashed with the efforts of another to realize theirs (Catalinac 2016; Estevez-Abe 2008). Policy clashes of this kind were what could stymie decision-making and create legislative stalemates that could end in the dissolution of parliament. Granting party members the ability to discern which types of infrastructure and other projects were of greatest interest to groups of constituents and deliver those projects was deemed the safer choice.

Critically, this was a choice available to the LDP because of its control over central government resources. Because none of the opposition parties had such access, they did not have this option. In the event that all four of them decided to come together and contest the election as one big opposition party, or in the event that one of the parties decided to field enough candidates to qualify as majority-seeking, this new party would not have had such a convenient means of coping with the divisions within the party that would inevitably crop up. It is not hard to see how, for the *non*-LDP parties, competing *separately*, for 15% of voters in each electoral district, was an attractive choice. Maeda (2012) shows that this choice was in keeping with the preferences of individual members of the largest non-LDP party, the JSP, who did not want the inconvenience of another JSP candidate in their electoral district. The fact that the LDP had a ready means of *solving* the challenges emanating from the conflicting pressures emanating from the combination of SNTV-MMD and Japan's constitutional structure, while opposition parties did not, and instead stayed divided and competed on the ideological fringes, led scholars, pundits, and even Diet Members to fear that under SNTV-MMD, a second majority-seeking party might never emerge.

Toward the end of the 1980s and in the early 1990s, the impediments to the emergence of a second majority-seeking party mixed with other arguments about the pathologies of SNTV-MMD to build public support for reforming the electoral system (Reed and Thies 2001; Curtis 1999). One was the fact that each candidate needed such a small share of votes in each district that they designed their platforms to target relatively *narrow* segments of the electorate (Catalinac 2018). Another was the fact that basing one's election campaign around what could be done for one's constituents, as LDP candidates did, ended up requiring considerable financial outlays, which made corruption more attractive than it might otherwise be (Carlson and Reed 2018*a*; Nyblade and Reed 2008; Otake 1996). It also inclined LDP candidates toward policies that benefited

2.3 Electoral Institutions Advantage the LDP?

narrow segments of the electorate, over policies that helped broad swaths of the electorate (Catalinac 2015). In the series of events chronicled above, the opposition parties, helped by LDP defectors, eventually took power and reformed the electoral system. However, it took *fifteen* years for a party other than the LDP to win a plurality in a Lower House election. Why? What took so long?

It turns out that, far from obliterating the advantages enjoyed by large parties, the new MMM electoral system introduced new ones. Three in particular stand out. First, recall that MMM combines an SSD tier with a PR tier and makes a party's seat tally the sum of those it wins in both tiers. Under this system, it turns out that parties are buffeted by countervailing pressures reminiscent of those bequeathed by the combination of SNTV-MMD with Japan's constitutional structure prior to 1994. What are these?

To begin with, to win seats in the SSD tier, parties have incentives to transform themselves into two blocs, each of which runs a single candidate in each SSD (Duverger 1963). Because there can only be one winner, these two blocs have incentives to choose candidates with the highest chance of winning and concentrate all available resources on this candidate's campaign. These two candidates, in turn, have incentives to position themselves at the *center* of the ideological spectrum, with one slightly to the right and the other slightly to the left. In doing so, both candidates can guarantee themselves the votes of all voters on their respective "side" of the spectrum (Downs 1957). Importantly, in this setting, candidates can be harmed by the emergence of additional candidates on their respective "side": New candidates emerging on the left, for example, might siphon votes away from the candidate positioned at center-left. This would hand an easy victory to the candidate positioned at center-right.

Thus, the existence of an SSD tier, combined with the fact that a large party (the LDP) already existed when MMM was introduced, gives non-LDP parties strong incentives to join forces and *unify*. Without joining forces and getting behind a single candidate in each SSD, the opposition parties stand little chance of defeating the LDP's SSD candidate. However, the addition of a PR tier, and the mechanics of how votes are converted into seats in that tier, generate a countervailing pressure on non-LDP parties to *fragment*. Why? PR tiers allow parties to compete as separate entities, secure in the knowledge that as long as they win some votes, they will win some seats. While competing separately might be counter-productive from the perspective of winning SSDs – and hence, capturing a governing majority – the fact that it is possible for parties to win seats by competing separately, whereas it would be considerably less possible if the electoral system was comprised solely of SSDs, creates a countervailing force encouraging these parties to fragment (Scheiner 2006, 187).

To make matters worse, once a party in the opposition has weighed up these trade-offs and decided against teaming up with other opposition parties to compete under the banner of a single, unified opposition party, then it is likely to realize that fielding SSD candidates can be beneficial, even when they have no chance of winning. This is because parties typically win more PR votes in SSDs where they field SSD candidates. This is thought to be because even when those candidates have no chance of winning their SSD, their campaign activities therein contribute to publicity for the party that pays off in PR votes (Cox and Schoppa 2002; Sugawara 2002).

What this means is that once an opposition party has decided to compete separately, thereby forgoing the opportunity to create a unified opposition party capable of winning SSDs, then it has incentives to engage in behavior that boosts its own PR votes but makes it more likely that the large party's candidate positioned on the *opposite* side of the ideological center emerges victorious. In Japan, this dynamic plays out to the advantage of the LDP because the LDP positions itself at center-right, while most of the opposition parties position themselves on the left (Catalinac 2018). Paradoxically, then, whenever an opposition party eschews coordination with other opposition parties and fields its own candidate, the presence of that candidate ends up creating a playing field that is highly advantageous for the LDP. Intuitively, this is because the opposition candidates usually position themselves on the left, which limits them to voters on the left. This hands the LDP candidate, usually located at center-right, an easier victory than a situation in which her rival had been a single opposition-supported candidate located right next to her, at center-left.

Generally speaking, elections after 1994 have featured SSDs where LDP candidates face multiple opposition candidates and win with relatively small shares of the vote. In the 1996 election, Table 2.2 shows that SSD candidates from the LDP captured an average of 38.6% of votes cast. Yet, helped by the fact that non-LDP votes were split across multiple candidates, this translated into victory in 56.3% of SSDs. The largest discrepancy between votes and seats occurred in the 2012 election, in which LDP candidates won an average of 43% of votes in each SSD, yet walked away with 79% of SSDs. This election occurred after defections from the ruling DPJ resulted in the creation of new parties, which together with one older party (YP), were referred to as the Third Force. In the vast majority of SSDs, competition between two serious

2.3 Electoral Institutions Advantage the LDP?

contenders in the 2009 election became competition between three, four, or five contenders. Reed et al. (2013) show that increases in number of SSD candidates between 2009 and 2012 were associated with lower vote shares for both the LDP and DPJ candidates, but the effect for DPJ candidates was nearly twice that for LDP candidates. According to Scheiner, Smith and Thies (2016), in the 211 SSDs that saw a DPJ and a Third Force candidate, had all the votes cast for these candidates been cast for a *single* opposition candidate, then absent other changes in voter preferences or proclivity to vote, the LDP would have won 112 fewer SSDs. Considering that the LDP's seat tally was 294, a loss of 112 would have left it with a seat share of only 37.9%, considerably less than the majority it won (Scheiner, Smith and Thies 2016, 34).

It is clear that the fragmentation effect of the PR tier in an MMM electoral system advantages the LDP. However, that is not all. The LDP has found at least two other ways to use the PR tier to its advantage. One, recall that in the PR tier, parties present voters with "closed" lists of candidates and voters vote for one list. What "closed" means is that parties decide ahead of time which candidates will be on the list and what rank candidates will be placed at. Seats accrue to parties in proportion to the share of PR votes obtained in each bloc, meaning that a party capturing 30% of PR votes in a given bloc is entitled to roughly 30% of available seats in that bloc. Critically, parties assign the number of seats they are owed to candidates in the order they appear on the list, meaning that a party whose vote share entitles it to four seats in a given bloc will assign those to the candidates ranked at the first, second, third, and fourth positions on the list, respectively. Because candidates at higher ranks have a higher chance of winning seats, candidates prefer to be listed as highly as possible.

After the introduction of MMM, LDP leaders devised a way of using their control over list placements to motivate their SSD nominees to campaign as hard as possible. How? Under Japan's version of MMM, candidates are allowed to be dual-listed in both tiers. When a candidate is dual-listed, this means that she is the party's designated nominee in a given SSD *and* appears on the party list in the PR bloc housing that SSD. The LDP decided that as a general rule, its SSD nominees would be dual-listed in the PR tier and placed at the *same* rank on the list (McKean and Scheiner 2000). After the election, candidates who won their SSD would be struck from the list and the remaining candidates, who lost their SSD, would be reranked in accordance with how closely they lost. This rule has the effect of increasing campaign effort from the party's SSD nominees, even when those nominees have little chance of victory (Christensen and Selway 2017; Reed and Shimizu 2009; Reed 2007; Bawn and Thies

2003). It also means that when an opposition candidate wins an SSD, she can enter parliament only to find her same-district LDP rival also there, presumably availing herself of all the advantages of incumbency and increasing her chances of ensuring the SSD swings back to her next time.

Two, Catalinac and Motolinia (2021a) highlight another way in which the presence of *separate* opposition parties, made possible by the PR tier, redounds to the benefit of the LDP. Essentially, the presence of these parties create an opportunity for the LDP's SSD candidates to craft mutually beneficial electoral coordination agreements, which can help them clinch victory. How? Above, I mentioned that the LDP formed a coalition government with a small party, the Komeito, in 1999. Since then, select LDP candidates have used this party's supporters as a crutch to win their SSD. Specifically, they ask the Komeito not to field a candidate in their SSD and instruct its supporters to cast their SSD votes for them (Liff and Maeda 2019). The presence of the PR tier makes this *possible*, on the one hand, by creating a playing field in which small parties like the Komeito are more likely to exist. They would be less likely to exist if the system was comprised only of SSDs. However, the PR tier also gives LDP candidates a *tool* they can use to make this deal more attractive to the Komeito: They can ask some of their supporters to cast their PR votes for the Komeito in return for receiving the SSD votes of Komeito supporters. For the LDP candidate, giving up PR votes in exchange for SSD votes, a relatively small number of which can be sufficient to put them over the finish line, is a highly beneficial trade (Catalinac and Motolinia 2021a).[10]

2.4 LDP'S POLICIES ARE MORE POPULAR?

We have seen how the electoral systems used to select Lower House Members have given the LDP an edge over other parties. In election after election, these electoral institutions have helped transform modest numbers of *votes* for the LDP into sizeable numbers of *seats*, sufficient to give it virtually uninterrupted control of Japan's government for the past sixty-nine years. The second and third category of explanations look beyond

---

[10] While not the focus of this discussion, the formula used to apportion seats in Japan's PR tier is a divisor-based one, d'Hondt. Gallagher (1991) illustrates that, among all formulae used to apportion seats in a PR system, d'Hondt advantages larger parties. Tables 2.2 and 2.3 reveal that larger parties tend to receive seat shares that exceed their vote shares in the PR tier too, while the reverse is true for smaller parties. In 2021, for example, the LDP won 34.7% of PR votes, but this translated into 40.9% of PR seats. In contrast, the JCP captured 7.2% of PR votes, which translated into just 5.1% of PR seats.

2.4 LDP's Policies Are More Popular?

institutionally derived advantages and focus on answering the question: Why do the millions of people who vote LDP do so?

One category of answers holds that voters choose the LDP because they prefer its policy positions, ideological orientation, image, or reputation to those of other parties.[11] Scholars have pointed out that the LDP has reaped electoral dividends from its effective stewardship of the economy, particularly during the high-growth years (Pempel 1998), its management of the US–Japan alliance during the Cold War (Curtis 1999), and the image of Prime Minister Koizumi Junichiro (2002–2006) as a reform-oriented leader committed to meeting the needs of urban voters (Uchiyama 2010; Kabashima and Steel 2007), respectively. Recently, Maeda (2016) shows that the post-2012 disarray in the opposition camp has meant a "there is no alternative (to the LDP)" logic has permeated public consciousness, contributing to LDP victories. Also on the programmatic dimension, Amano and Katada (N.D.) argue that the LDP's co-opting of innovative policy proposals advanced by opposition parties is an overlooked component of its electoral prowess.

While programmatic explanations for the party's dominance have been around for a long time, many scholars saw them as less decisive determinants of LDP election victories under the old electoral system, on the grounds that the intraparty competition faced by LDP candidates necessarily relegated policy-related factors to the sidelines. Why? While individual LDP candidates may have invoked the party's policies or reputation in their quest for reelection, these are factors *shared* between all LDP candidates in a district. By definition, factors shared between all LDP candidates in a district are not useful for convincing LDP-aligned supporters to choose one LDP candidate over the others (Catalinac 2016; Carey and Shugart 1995). It is on these grounds that distributive politics explanations for LDP election victories reigned supreme under SNTV-MMD, as channeling particularistic spending toward carefully demarcated groups of constituents was seen as offering a relatively safe way in which same-district LDP candidates could compete against each other (Krauss and Pekkanen 2010; McCubbins and Rosenbluth 1995; Cox and Niou 1994; Bouissou 1999; Ramseyer and Rosenbluth 1993). Because the introduction of MMM in 1994 resulted in the elimination of intraparty competition, it was seen as creating incentives for

---

[11] Political science research often separates a party's policy positions from any valence advantages it enjoys (e.g., Eshima et al. N.D.). Here, I lump policy positions and valence advantages together under the category of programmatic politics because my main purpose is to distinguish answers in this category from those in the distributive politics category, discussed below. There is also debate about the extent to which a valence advantage can be separated from policy positions.

the main axis of competition to shift from revolving around distributive politics to revolving around programmatic politics.

The first few elections under MMM saw many signs of a shift to programmatic politics. In spite of the countervailing pressures placed on opposition parties by the combination of SSDs and PR, by 1998 a large opposition party had nevertheless emerged (the DPJ). Moreover, in the first few Lower House elections after its emergence, the percentage of SSDs seeing competition between two serious candidates progressively increased, as did the percentage of SSDs in which voters had a choice between "the government" (the LDP) and "the opposition" (the DPJ) (and critically, not between multiple candidates on either side) (Reed 2007). Correspondingly, elections started to turn on the popularity of a candidate's party and leader, rather than on candidate-specific characteristics such as seniority or local ties, which tended to determine victory under the old electoral system (McElwain 2012). Elections also started featuring manifestos produced by parties, which the media used to compare the priorities parties placed on different policy areas and their stances on those areas (Krauss and Pekkanen 2010). In my analysis of 7,497 election manifestos produced by the universe of LDP candidates competing in consecutive Lower House elections on either side of the 1994 reform, I found that the reform was associated with a decisive shift in discussion: In the three elections prior to reform (1986, 1990, and 1993), the average LDP candidate devoted approximately two-thirds of discussion to particularism (what I call "pork-barrel politics") and one-third to programmatic politics (what I call "policy"). In the five elections after reform, these proportions were reversed: The average LDP candidate devoted approximately two-thirds of discussion to programmatic politics and only one-third to particularism (Catalinac 2015).

The 2005 Lower House election offered a vivid example of what competition on programmatic politics looks like. To understand the circumstances surrounding this election, we must begin with the observation that the LDP has always been stronger in rural areas (Saito 2010; Scheiner 2005). One reason was because LDP governments were slow to address the fact that population changes had created marked disparities in the number of votes needed to elect a Diet Member across electoral districts. The failure to adjust the number of seats available in each district (either by increasing the number of seats in urban areas and decreasing them in rural ones) or redraw district boundaries created a situation where the number of votes required to elect a single Diet Member in a rural district could be as few as *half* those required to elect a single Diet Member in an urban district (Horiuchi and Saito 2003). The fact that it was considerably *easier* to win a seat in a rural area, combined with the fact

2.4 LDP's Policies Are More Popular?

that rural areas were needier, and tended to have greater *demand* for the pork-barrel projects LDP members could provide, meant that over time, the LDP developed relatively steadfast support in rural areas and less support in cities.

By redrawing the boundaries of Japan's electoral districts, the 1994 reform went a long way toward rectifying these vote-seat disparities (McElwain 2012). Conscious of the fact that there were now many more seats in urban areas, LDP Prime Minister Koizumi Junichiro (2001–2006) crafted policies designed to increase the party's appeal to urban voters. One of these was postal privatization, which promised to eviscerate the array of special benefits enjoyed by the so-called commissioned post-masters, individuals who played a key role mobilizing votes for LDP candidates in rural areas (Maclachlan 2006, 2004). Under the banner of liberalization, Koizumi also promised cuts to public works spending and agricultural subsidies and policies to encourage the amalgamation of smaller towns and villages, respectively (Reed, Scheiner and Thies 2012; Noble 2010). In 2005, however, Koizumi met with resistance from fellow LDP members over his postal privatization plan. He responded by dissolving the Lower House and calling for an election in the middle of Lower House Members' four-year terms. In the election, Koizumi declared that he was waging a war against what he called the forces of resistance (LDP members who had tried to block his privatization plan) (Reed and Shimizu 2009). He refused the party's nomination to these candidates and tried to reduce their chances of winning as independent candidates by hand-picking party-anointed "assassins" to run in their place (Nemoto, Krauss and Pekkanen 2008).

In doing so, Koizumi succeeded in making the 2005 election about a single idea (reform), and convincing people that a vote for an LDP candidate was "a vote for reform" (Reed, Scheiner and Thies 2012, 365). This strategy proved enormously successful: The LDP's seat share shot up to 61.7%, whereas the DPJ's decreased to 23.5%. Importantly, relative to the prior election in 2003, the gains made in 2005 were not very large in terms of votes, but because of the winner-take-all nature of SSDs, modest gains in votes translated into large gains in seats. The 2005 election saw the LDP increase its PR vote share from 35% to 38.2%, and its SSD vote share from 43.9% to 47.8%, respectively. Whereas the 3.2% increase in PR votes translated into a 4.5% increase in PR seats, the 3.9% increase in SSD votes translated into a 17% increase in SSDs won. In this way, the 2005 election was a reminder that when competition is between two serious competitors in an SSD, anything that can give one of those candidates an edge over the other is enough to swing the SSD their way. With his compelling programmatic message and broad public appeal, Koizumi provided this edge to all the LDP's candidates, thereby significantly increasing their chances of victory and the party's majority (Christensen 2006).

While the LDP's 2005 victory revealed the dividends of such a strategy, it did not stick to it. A year later, Koizumi stepped down and the party elected a new leader, Abe Shinzo (2006–2007). A decision Abe faced was what to do about the so-called "postal rebels": LDP politicians who had opposed postal privatization and been booted from the party, yet had run in the 2005 election as independents and won against the LDP candidate Koizumi had nominated. Abe allowed these individuals to rejoin the party, a decision that generated negative publicity. As we explained above, his support rate declined and within a year he had resigned. The trajectory of the LDP's two next leaders was similar, with both meeting similar fates. By summer 2009, support for the LDP had dipped below that of the DPJ for the first time. In the ensuing election, DPJ leader Hatoyama Yukio did for his party's candidates what Koizumi had done for LDP candidates in 2009: He made the election about a single idea (change of government) and convinced people that a vote for a DPJ candidate was a vote for this idea. The power of this message ended up increasing the DPJ's PR vote share by 11.2% and its SSD vote share by 11%. Whereas the party had won only 17.3% of SSDs in 2005, it won 73.7% in 2009.

In a world in which electoral competition is taking place on a programmatic dimension, if we still observe LDP victories, then it is reasonable to attribute those victories to its superior performance on this dimension. In other words, the LDP must be winning because its programmatic policies are more attractive than those offered by the other parties. Yet this assumption has been dealt a major blow in recent years by work that uses experiments conducted on nationally representative samples of voters to probe the relative attractiveness of the policies offered by the major parties contesting Japan's 2014, 2017, and 2021 Lower House elections. In one experiment, respondents were presented with pairwise comparisons of different hypothetical bundles of policy positions and asked to select the bundle they most preferred. Presenting respondents with multiple pairwise comparisons of different policy bundles allows the researcher to derive estimates of the degree to which a given policy position increases or decreases overall support for a given policy bundle. Using this design, Horiuchi, Smith and Yamamoto (2018) found that of the eleven policy positions that were distinct from the LDP's in the 2014 election, nine were more popular than the LDP's, and Eshima et al. (N.D.) found that the LDP's policy bundle in the 2017 and 2021 Lower House elections had a lower average evaluation than any other party, with the exception of its coalition partner, the Komeito. In a similar experiment that replaced policy bundles with hypothetical bundles of candidate attributes, Horiuchi, Smith and Yamamoto (2020) found that the addition of "the LDP" onto a given candidate lowered support for that candidate relative to when respondents were told she was an independent.

These experiments made use of the actual policy promises offered by parties in these elections and the actual attributes of candidates running. They also demonstrated consistent results, about the relative unpopularity of the LDP's policy positions, across multiple elections. As a result, these studies deal a major blow to claims that LDP victories in recent years can be attributed to superior performance on the programmatic dimension. Indeed, the main takeaway is not just that the LDP's policies are *unpopular*, it is that they are among the *least popular* of any party competing. Importantly, we cannot go back in time and run these experiments on Japanese voters in the 2000s. It is possible that when LDP candidates were squaring off against a candidate from a single, unified opposition party in their SSD, as many were the 2000s, the pressure to court the median voter would have been so great that it led to a more concerted effort to craft policy proposals catering to this voter. It is possible that the proliferation of opposition parties and SSD candidates in recent years has alleviated this pressure, allowing LDP candidates to move toward their preferred policies and away from those popular with the median voter (Sakaiya 2009). Regardless, these studies suggest that, at least in the post-2014 world, competition on the programmatic dimension is playing less of a role in LDP's election victories than we thought. Put bluntly, these studies offer strong evidence that *something else*, other than competition on policy grounds, is likely driving LDP election victories.

2.5 DISTRIBUTIVE POLITICS?

A second category of explanations holds that people vote for the LDP because there are distributive advantages in doing so. Specifically, LDP politicians are said to be adept at using their access to government resources to craft benefits and allocate spending in ways that create loyal groups of supporters, who can be relied on to turn out and vote for them, election after election (Reed 2021; Christensen and Selway 2017; McMichael 2018; Reed, Scheiner and Thies 2012; Pempel 2010; Krauss and Pekkanen 2010; Saito 2010; Scheiner 2006; Bouissou 1999; Tani 1998; Ramseyer and Rosenbluth 1993; Sone and Kanazashi 1989; Curtis 1971; Thayer 1969). Regardless of whether goods are particularistic spending for one's community or preferential tax treatment, regulatory favors, and protection from international competition for nationally organized groups of voters, distributive politics explanations hold that voters on the receiving end of such goods cannot be certain they would receive them under an alternative government, so continue voting LDP. In this account, an "I'll scratch your back, if you scratch mine" relationship between the LDP and select groups of constituents explains why the party is able to vanquish its opponents, election after election.

What kind of goods do LDP politicians provide? One is government funds for voters in a politician's electoral district, which take the form of what Naoi (2015, 56) calls "geographically targetable public investment projects." Scheiner (2005) makes the case that LDP politicians in rural areas devote an inordinate amount of time trying to secure such projects on account of the fact that municipalities in Japan are fiscally dependent on the central government and this dependence is greatest for rural municipalities. Fiscal dependence, combined with voter expectations that the role of the politician is to provide what he calls "clientelistic goods," creates a situation in which local mayors and assembly members cannot avoid being pulled into relationships with LDP-affiliated Lower House Members, in which the local politician mobilizes votes on behalf of the LDP Diet Member in exchange for the latter's delivery of goods. In her account of how LDP leaders built support for lowering tariffs and signing trade and investment agreements with other countries by distributing "side payments" to LDP members, Naoi (2015) shows that the appeal of such projects was not limited to LDP politicians in rural areas. A second good LDP politicians provide is policy favors for special interest groups whose members reside in more than one electoral district. Groups organized at the national level, whom LDP politicians have courted with all manner of favorable regulatory, protectionist, and tax policies, include farmers, physicians, special postmasters, proprietors of small and medium-sized businesses, the families of deceased soldiers, religious organizations, and declining industries and sectors (Maclachlan and Shimizu 2022; Reed 2021; Gentry 2021; Maclachlan 2006; Naoi 2015; Estevez-Abe 2008; Davis and Oh 2007; Davis 2003).

While particularistic spending geared at narrow segments of the electorate and pandering to special interests are features of politics in many countries, scholars have attributed the outsized role they played in the election campaigns of LDP politicians to the SNTV-MMD electoral system (Catalinac 2016; Krauss and Pekkanen 2010; Estevez-Abe 2008; Ramseyer and Rosenbluth 1993). As I explained above, when candidates from the same party are competing against each other for a limited number of seats, candidates cannot rely exclusively on their party label. Instead, personal popularity and name recognition become key to winning (Carey and Shugart 1995). A body of work contends that the main

2.5 Distributive Politics?

reason LDP politicians devoted such a lot of time to the first good, particularistic spending, is because of the premium placed on cultivating strong, personal ties to constituents (e.g., Catalinac 2015; Hirano 2006; Ramseyer and Rosenbluth 1993). In this account, a causal line can be drawn from the need to cultivate personal ties with constituents to the need to provide particularism. A causal line can further be drawn from the need to provide particularism to other facets of Japanese politics, such as why the LDP is a factionalized party. The LDP politicians struggling to build their reputations as people who could deliver the goods were only too happy to exchange their vote in the party's leadership election – which determines who becomes the prime minister – for the bureaucratic connections, campaign funds, and other resources provided by senior members of their faction.

The party's courting of special interests was also thought to be connected to the electoral system. How? Since its formation in 1955, the LDP has been dedicated to reestablishing Japan's economic prowess and boosting economic productivity. To this end, it pursued "bureaucratically-led industrial policies, tightly balanced budgets, rapid technological improvement of large-scale firms, domestic oligopolization, and the aggressive pursuit of export markets" (Pempel 2010). This medley of policies proved successful, sustaining the double-digit growth rates that had begun during the Korean War through until 1969 and keeping growth roughly double that of OECD countries for many years thereafter. The dramatic expansion of Japan's economy increased the size of the government's budget, on the one hand, but it also created vast disparities in wealth across sector and region, on the other. These disparities gave voters who felt they were *not* enjoying as many of the fruits of the economic miracle reason to seek government protection (Pempel 2010; Estevez-Abe 2008; Scheiner 2006). Voters in rural areas experiencing depopulation and inadequate fiscal resources were in this category, as were voters employed in small businesses and declining industries, who faced stiff competition from firms in urban areas and later, from global firms, as governments made concessions to facilitate the entry of Japanese products into foreign markets (Naoi 2015; Davis 2003).

Under a different electoral system, the emergence of a set of economic losers might have sowed the seeds for a protectionist, redistribution-oriented party to emerge and contest elections *against* the productivity-oriented LDP. In Japan, however, a coalition championing the interests of these voters emerged *within* the LDP, in the form of members hailing from depopulating areas and with sizeable chunks of constituents in declining sectors. These politicians wasted little time in pushing for government resources to be channeled toward propping these sectors up and minimizing any disadvantages they faced (Naoi 2015; Estevez-Abe 2008; Scheiner 2006). As a result, the LDP became a party that mixed "high growth (productivity) with localized protection (pork)" (Pempel 2010, 236).

Given that the electoral system was thought to have underpinned both components of the LDP's distributive politics strategy, it is perhaps unsurprising that the focus of scholarship on the party's electoral strategies shifted away from distributive politics in the wake of Japan's 1994 electoral reform. Above, we explained how MMM provides incentives for competition to take place on a programmatic dimension. However, a second factor may have also played a role in the supplanting of distributive politics accounts of the party's electoral dominance with programmatic ones: the absence of systematic evidence that geographically targeted spending flows to the party's core supporters, however defined. Notwithstanding the trove of studies attesting to the centrality of pork-barreling to the electoral strategies of LDP politicians, which scholars of Japanese politics engaged in fieldwork saw with their own eyes, and the compelling case made that the point of all this pork-barreling was to create and nurture groups of loyal supporters, a survey of the literature reveals that whenever scholars made the effort to collect and analyze data on central government outlays to lower tier entities, whether prefectures, electoral districts, or municipalities, they found little-to-no evidence that the party's *core supporters*, places that deliver higher-than-average vote shares for the party, have been favored when it came to spending (McMichael 2018; Saito 2010; Hirano 2011; Horiuchi and Saito 2003).

Four studies in particular cast doubt on the claim that LDP politicians contest elections by channeling government resources toward core supporters. One, Horiuchi and Saito (2003) analyzed government outlays to Japanese municipalities in the 1991–1998 period. While their research question was whether malapportionment (defined as having more Diet Members per voter) impacted the amount of money municipalities received from the government, their research also found that, controlling for other potential confounders, municipalities in electoral districts with *greater* support for the LDP received *less* money than their counterparts in electoral districts with less support for the party. Two, Hirano (2011), too, studied government outlays to Japanese municipalities. Leveraging the sudden deaths of sixty-seven Lower House Members in the 1977–1992 period (forty-seven of whom were LDP), he found that allocations received by municipalities in the bailiwicks of a recently deceased politician did not decline in the wake of their deaths. He also compared allocations received by municipalities in the bailiwicks of LDP politicians who narrowly won and lost reelection, respectively. While he

2.5 *Distributive Politics?*

found some evidence that municipalities in the bailiwicks of LDP politicians who narrowly won received larger allocations, overall he concluded that LDP politicians were not "pipelines" between the national treasury and their constituents and instead had "limited personal influence over the amount of government transfers directed to their constituents" (Hirano 2011, 1082). Three, McMichael (2018) studied government outlays to Japanese prefectures between 1958 and 1993. His research question was whether prefectures exhibiting greater loyalty to the LDP, defined as electing more LDP-affiliated Diet Members, received more transfers. Controlling for confounders, he found no evidence that prefectures with more LDP politicians among their Diet representatives received more money, and in some regression specifications, he found evidence of the *reverse*: they received less.

Four, in a book-length treatment of this topic, Saito (2010) studied government outlays to municipalities and Lower House electoral districts between 1977 and 1990. His first research question was whether electoral districts with more municipalities and more Diet representatives per voter received more transfers. In a regression with electoral districts as the units of observation, he found no relationship between support for the LDP, measured in share of Diet representatives who are LDP-affiliated, and the amount of transfers received. His second research question was whether municipalities returning greater support for the LDP received more transfers. Operationalizing support for the LDP as the degree to which a given municipality's LDP vote share deviated from that of the *average* LDP vote share in its electoral district, he found evidence for his hypothesis when he operationalized transfers as the degree to which a municipality's transfer allocation deviated from that of its district's average, but not when he used the absolute value of (per capita) transfers it received. In regressions with the absolute value of transfer received, he found a statistically significant *negative* relationship between support and transfers in one specification (municipalities returning more support for the LDP received fewer transfers) and no relationship between support and transfers in another.

Ultimately, the findings in these studies end up reinforcing a key takeaway of Reed (2001), who synthesized all prior work on the political determinants of inter-governmental transfers in Japan and concluded that many of the most plausible anecdotes of political influence over grant allocation "evaporate on closer investigation" (Reed 2001, 181). He contends that anecdotes alleging undue political influence capture scholarly and media attention because they are "interesting stories that play on our sense of cynicism" but are "simply false" (Reed 2001, 125). He points out that these anecdotes can also redound to the benefit of the politician involved, who can use the revelation of undue influence to claim credit for allocations that actually had little to do with her. When it comes to publicly funded construction projects, for example, he writes that all evidence suggests they are allocated according to "impersonal political and bureaucratic criteria," and not political influence (Reed 2001, 124).

2.6 HOW THIS BOOK CONTRIBUTES

As we have seen, literature on the LDP's longevity has furnished a number of compelling explanations, ranging from electoral system–derived advantages to claims that the party captures more votes than other parties because voters prefer its policies or are exchanging their votes for distributive benefits. However, these arguments have shortcomings. Electoral system–based explanations can explain how relatively *small* shares of the vote translate into relatively *large* shares of seats but have little to say about how the party gathers those votes in the first place. Programmatic explanations provide a plausible account of the party's victories for a portion of the elections under study but have been undermined by evidence that the party's issue positions are unpopular with the broader electorate. Moreover, this evidence comes from the 2014, 2017, and 2021 Lower House elections, which saw the LDP walk away with some of its largest seat majorities to date. Distributive explanations, which center on the idea that LDP politicians leverage demand for central government resources to form relationships with voters, in which votes are exchanged for goods, are theoretically compelling and jibe with many other facets of Japanese politics but fall apart when subject to empirical testing.

In this book, I draw on innovations in theory, data, and empirics to make the case that many LDP politicians contest elections by making the distribution of geographically targetable government resources to municipalities in their electoral districts contingent on the level of support each municipality provided them in the most recent election. By making the amount of money a municipality receives contingent on its position in a rank ordering of municipalities in the same electoral district, constructed on the basis of electoral loyalty, I explain how LDP politicians are able to create a situation where voters in relatively supportive municipalities, which stand to gain a lot with a few more votes for the politician, are heavily dissuaded from casting their votes for anyone else. Drawing on prior work, I explain why allocating resources in this manner, according to a "tournament," has the effect of encouraging voters in supportive municipalities to reason that, given their vote holds very little influence over who wins the election, they may as well use it to make sure their municipality remains a priority in the eyes of the politician after she reaches the Diet (Smith and Bueno de Mesquita 2012, 2019; Smith, Bueno de Mesquita and LaGatta 2017; Catalinac, Bueno de Mesquita and Smith 2020). In these municipalities, plenty of voters may *want* another politician elected but draw the line at using their *own* vote to elect her.

Critically, this electoral strategy is possible only when electoral districts are divisible into multiple geographically defined units, at which electoral support is observable and resources targetable. Chapter 5 explains that under Japan's old electoral system, the relatively *small* number of electoral districts and relatively *large* number of municipalities, in addition to the rule that electoral districts be drawn *around* the borders of municipalities, meant that more than 90% of electoral districts met these conditions. The redrawing of electoral districts that accompanied Japan's 1994 electoral reform, plus the municipal amalgamations of the 2000s and ongoing urbanization, has reduced the share of electoral districts meeting these conditions to around 50% of electoral districts in the last election for which we have data (2014). Thus, the electoral strategy illuminated in these pages is not a complete account of LDP dominance, as we can only speculate about what happens in electoral districts that do not meet these conditions.

For Japanese politics scholars, an important takeaway is that it was premature to presume that the rise of programmatic party competition after Japan's 1994 electoral reform, documented by numerous scholars, meant that we could dispense with explanations of LDP victories rooted in distributive politics. In this sense, my findings corroborate Scheiner (2006)'s expectation that the 1994 reform would be unlikely to shift competition to programmatic grounds entirely. My study suggests, however, that the reform may have shifted competition to programmatic grounds almost entirely in places where the new electoral district rules out the possibility of a tournament. In Scheiner (2006)'s account, it is municipalities' dependence on central government resources that drives whether or not LDP politicians rely on a distributive politics–based strategy. Given that the 1994 electoral reform did little to alter this dependence, the implication is that we should observe a similar reliance on distributive politics before and after reform. I contend, in contrast, that whether or not LDP politicians choose distributive politics has less to do with *demand*, as central government resources can be massaged to appeal to wealthier municipalities, and more to do with *institutions*: namely, the way the boundaries of electoral districts are configured, relative to municipalities.

In this way, my study lends empirical support to the observation that the LDP is a *bifurcated* party, with some members investing heavily in old-fashioned vote-mobilization techniques and filling their manifestos with promises of particularism, while other members stake out positions on programmatic politics to win (Koellner 2009; Scheiner 2006). Comparative politics scholars would describe the LDP as "diversified linkage party," meaning that, when viewed in the aggregate, the linkages the LDP cultivates with voters encompass both distributive and programmatic dimensions (Kitschelt and Singer 2018; Magaloni, Diaz-Cayeros and Estévez 2007). My study provides a theory that can account for why these diversified linkages exist and which LDP politicians cultivate each type of linkage. Future scholarship should investigate how the party manages tensions that likely arise from the use of two different electoral strategies and how the tournaments pursued by half its members impact the positions on programmatic policies staked out by the other half, and vice versa. For now, however, let us turn to elucidating the book's theory.

3

A Theory of Group-Based Clientelism

All around the world, politicians harness the material goods they have access to by virtue of being in office in ways that are designed to help them win elections. In some cases, politicians distribute goods in the hope they prove attractive enough to their would-be beneficiaries that they will vote for them on election day. A governing party might enact a programmatic policy that bestows benefits on large classes of voters, such as single parents or the elderly. It might steer infrastructure toward communities containing certain types of voters, such as party supporters, co-ethnics, or people living below the poverty line. It might channel favorable regulatory policies or protection from international competition toward nationally organized groups of voters, such as farmers or local business owners. While the goods in these examples are quite different, the rationale underpinning their distribution in these cases is similar: It is being distributed *in the hope* it moves the needle in favor of the party conferring it in the next election, whether by inducing feelings of loyalty among recipients, creating a perception that the party is competent and cares about the welfare of people like the recipients, or another such mechanism.

In other cases, politicians are not content with the one-sidedness of a relationship in which they deliver goods in the hope they turn into votes. A qualitatively different mode of distribution occurs when a politician is able to *tie* the distribution of a valued good to a person's voting behavior. By "ties," I mean the good is conferred on the understanding that the politician will receive a vote in return, and if it should become apparent that she is not, will not, or did not, the good is withdrawn. Unlike in the former case, in which politicians use the distribution of goods to try to make themselves attractive to voters, the latter case embodies contingency: The distribution of the good is made *contingent* on how a person votes, such that if a vote is not forthcoming or did not materialize, the good is withdrawn.

A Theory of Group-Based Clientelism

The contingent mode of distribution is what comparative politics scholars call clientelism. As with the former mode of distribution, nonclientelism, the good changing hands in a clientelistic exchange can be virtually anything, so long as the politician has access to it and the recipient values it. What differentiates the nonclientelistic mode of distribution from the clientelistic mode of distribution is that in the former, voters retain the freedom to pocket the good, whether it be a programmatic policy, infrastructure spending, or favorable regulation, and *vote for someone else* on election day. This freedom is taken away in a clientelistic exchange. In a clientelistic exchange, at least as clientelistic exchanges have traditionally been conceptualized, if a voter wants the good on offer, she has to vote for the politician proffering it. Because her access to the good is tied to her voting behavior and will be cut off if she is found to have voted for anyone other than her politician benefactor, clientelistic exchanges are troubling from the perspective of democratic integrity. They prevent voters from exercising free choice in their decision of who to vote for, and they can keep voters wedded to incumbents who will have few incentives to represent their other, programmatic, interests.

In this book, I make two theoretical claims. The first stems from the observation that the literature on clientelism in political science has been preoccupied with the idea that politicians form clientelistic relationships with *individual voters*. This preoccupation has led scholars to be overly concerned with a particular set of questions, which center on how a politician seeking to buy the vote of an individual voter can consummate the deal to her satisfaction, given that the secret ballot prevents her from being able to observe how this person votes. The secret ballot means that there are hardly any scenarios under which a person's vote choice will be observable to the politician. If a politician receives every vote cast in a given locale, then she will know that everyone there voted for her. If she receives no votes, then she will know that no one did. But outside of those two scenarios, as soon as we are in a world in which the politician receives a *modicum* of votes in a given locale, then anyone who received goods from the politician in exchange for her vote will be able to credibly claim that they supplied one of those votes, and the politician will not know difference. The assumption that politicians' inability to observe how people vote means that they must be using every tool at their disposal to try to ascertain how the people they gave resources to voted on election day has shaped answers to questions ranging from which types of voters are embedded in clientelistic exchanges to what role the politician's intermediaries play in implementing it.

I make the case that under a certain configuration of political institutions, it makes more sense for politicians to form clientelistic relationships

A Theory of Group-Based Clientelism

with *groups of voters*. To form this relationship, a politician's electoral district must be divisible into groups of voters, at which levels of electoral support are observable and to which resources are targetable. While clientelistic relationships are possible with any group meeting these conditions, the practice of counting votes at the level of a small, geographically defined group within electoral districts, very common across democracies today, means that *geographically defined* groups are particularly susceptible to being pulled into clientelistic exchanges with politicians. However, to consummate such an exchange, it is not enough for the politician to be able to *observe* disaggregated vote totals at distinct geographic areas within her electoral district; she must also be able to *deliver resources* to those units. The key insight of my theory, group-based clientelism (GBC), is that both conditions must be met: The group has to be able to make its level of electoral support for the politician observable *and* it must be an entity to which resources can be delivered. When both conditions are met, I argue that the ease of relying on publicly available election returns to glean levels of support makes forming clientelistic relationships with groups of voters more attractive to reelection-seeking politicians than forming them with individual voters.

In this chapter, I flesh out this claim. I point out that the possibility that politicians form clientelistic relationships with groups was present in foundational work on clientelism but has been overlooked in recent years, eclipsed by the presumption that politicians prefer to form clientelistic relationships with individuals. Today, almost every study of goods-for-votes exchanges – what the literature calls clientelism – conceives of them as being between politicians and individuals. However, if resource allocations to groups are found to be tied to their voting behavior, meaning that they increase when the group performs "well" for the politician, however defined, and decrease when it performs "badly," then this is observationally equivalent to an exchange in which an individual's access to resources is tied to his or her voting behavior. As such, this behavior should not be considered *outside* the purview of clientelism. I offer reasons why a politician worried about winning the next election might prefer to form clientelistic relationships with groups over individuals, and I elucidate the conditions under which they will be able to do so. I conclude by taking four longstanding questions of interest in the clientelism literature and explaining how the possibility that politicians are forming clientelistic relationships with groups has the potential to open up new lines of inquiry, which promise to significantly advance our understanding of how politicians use resource allocations to further their electoral interests.

Chapter 4 is devoted to my second theoretical claim, which concerns *how*, exactly, politicians tie group-level allocations to electoral support.

Politicians can do this in several ways. They could set a target vote share for each group and promise to reward any group that meets the target. They could promise to reward any group whose support exceeds that which it delivered to the politician in the previous election. Alternatively, the politician could promise to divvy up any material goods she has access to after the election in proportion to the number of votes she receives from each group, such that a group contributing 20% of the politician's votes would receive 20% of resources, and so on. Drawing on prior work, I explain that when politicians are members of a party that everyone knows is going to win the next election – in other words, a "dominant party" – they will be able to get the most votes, conditional on resources delivered, by converting voting into a competition over which group is the most electorally supportive (Smith and Bueno de Mesquita 2012, 2019; Smith, Bueno de Mesquita and LaGatta 2017; Catalinac, Bueno de Mesquita and Smith 2020).

In such a competition, what this work calls a "tournament," the incumbent creates the perception that groups will be ranked on the basis of their loyalty in the most recent election, and prizes (in the form of resource allocations) will be awarded on the basis of rank. By offering a very large prize to the highest-ranked group, the incumbent can encourage supportive groups to compete for this position. Among supportive groups, the promise of a very large prize for placing first drives up the incumbent's support, such that rankings can hinge on handfuls of votes. When a handful of votes is enough to change a group's ranking, and a significant increase or decrease in resources awaits any change in rank, voters in these groups have incentives to set aside whatever personal feelings they harbor toward the incumbent or her policies, and think primarily about the influence their vote wields over their group's prize. When resources are structured this way, plenty of voters may dislike the incumbent and her policies but have few incentives to translate that dissatisfaction into their voting behavior. They may *want* another politician elected, but with other people's votes. For the incumbent, structuring resources in this manner increases her support. Moreover, because she uses the *same prize* to motivate support in more than one group, she can deliver less than if she had pursued an alternative scheme through which goods are tied to support.

3.1 WHAT IS CLIENTELISM?

Clientelism has been the subject of sustained attention by comparative politics scholars since as early as the 1970s (Piattoni et al. 2001; Chubb 1982; Shefter 1994, 1977; Scott 1972). Yet it was seminal studies in the

3.1 What Is Clientelism?

2000s that catapulted it to the forefront of scholarly inquiry. Kitschelt and Wilkinson (2007) observed that party competition looked very different in countries that democratized later, in the Third Wave, versus countries that democratized earlier, despite the use of similar electoral systems and other political institutions in both. In the late democratizers, parties lacking coherent ideologies, programmatic policies, or records of competence were nevertheless regularly able to attract solid levels of electoral support. In the early democratizers, however, parties of this nature tended not to even exist. The authors attributed this to variation in "citizen–politician linkages," a concept examined in Kitschelt (2000). Citizen–politician linkages were qualitatively different, the authors argued, in different countries and tended to be remarkably durable over time.

In countries where citizen–politician linkages were what they called programmatic, the authors observed that parties fought elections by coming up with policies targeted at broad swaths of voters in the hope that those policies would prove attractive enough to entice at least some of their intended beneficiaries to vote for them on election day. In contrast, in countries where citizen–politician linkages were deemed "clientelistic," parties contested elections by using what the authors called direct material inducements – direct payments to voters, or continuing access to employment, goods, or services – to target individuals and small groups of citizens whom the politician felt would be "responsive to such side-payments and willing to surrender their vote for the right price" (Kitschelt and Wilkinson 2007, 2). These inducements were offered on the condition that the voter or small group of citizens vote for the party or politician. Whereas the authors pointed out that programmatic linkages were "indirect" (not targeted at any specific individual voter or small group) and "noncontingent" (there might be a hope that the beneficiary votes for the politician but she does not have to do so), clientelistic linkages were the opposite: "direct" and "contingent."

Other scholars writing around the same time made similar observations. Stokes (2007) observed that all politicians offered material goods to voters in the expectation that those goods would influence whether or not the intended recipient voted for them. Further, she observed that all types of material goods entailed the redistribution of resources away from larger classes of voters toward smaller classes of voters. A good distributed to a large class of voters on the basis of an ascriptive characteristic such as employment or single parent status was defined as programmatic. A good distributed to a narrower class of voters on the basis of, for example, the type of electoral district in which they resided was defined as pork-barrel politics. Stokes (2007) was primarily concerned with differentiating these two categories from a third category, which she labeled clientelistic. In a clientelistic mode of redistribution, she pointed out that the sole criterion a politician uses to determine whether to deliver a good to a voter, or whether to end a voter's access to a good she was already enjoying, is "did you (will you) support me?" Whereas in the programmatic and pork-barrel modes of redistribution just described, the criteria was whether or not a voter qualified as a member of said group, in the clientelistic mode of distribution, it was how they voted. A central insight of her study, which has been adopted in virtually every subsequent study of clientelism, is that it is not the *nature* of a good that determines whether or not a politician is distributing it clientelistically, but the *criteria* (the rules) governing its distribution.

Synthesizing some of this work, Hicken (2011) defined clientelism, at least for the purpose of mobilizing votes, as a transaction between politicians (the patrons in the exchange) and clients (voters), in which politicians offer particularistic benefits in exchange for votes. The nature of these benefits were "limited only by politicians' and voters' imaginations, and could range from cash to cookware to corrugated metal" (Hicken 2011, 291). To qualify as clientelistic, he suggested that a transaction had to exhibit two characteristics: "contingency" and "iteration." With regard to the former, he explained that both the politician and voter have to know that the exchange is conditional upon holding up their end of the bargain. The voter has to know that she will only receive the good if she votes for the politician, while the politician has to know that she will only receive the vote if she delivers the good. This "quid pro quo" feature of the clientelistic exchange is what distinguishes it from other forms of particularistic targeting (Hicken 2011, 291).

The second characteristic, iteration, was deemed necessary because exchanges of goods for votes were not, generally speaking, simultaneous. This means that there tends to be a lag between when the voter delivers the vote and when the politician delivers the good (Hicken 2011). This presents opportunities for both sides to defect from the exchange. For the voter, defection means pocketing the good and not voting for the politician on election day, while for the politician, it means receiving the vote but not delivering the good. The promise of an *iterated* exchange is seen to help both sides credibly commit to following through on their promises to the other. More specifically, iteration helps the voter see that, if she receives a good but fails to vote for the politician, the politician will be around long enough to punish her by withholding the good next time. It also helps the politician see that, if she receives a vote from the voter but does not deliver the good, the voter will be around long enough to withhold her vote next time. If the exchange was a single-shot transaction, in contrast, both sides would have powerful incentives to defect and the exchange would be difficult to consummate (Stokes 2005).

What implications does clientelism have for democracy? Stokes et al. (2013) consider this question in depth. They point out that in democracies, almost all individuals over a certain age are given the right to participate in the selection of leaders who will go on to formulate policies that apply to them. The right to the exercise of free choice in this decision of who to vote for is treated as sacrosanct. Elections are critical moments in which the preferences of citizens are translated upwards: Citizens have the right to evaluate, to the best of their knowledge, what their leaders have been doing while in office. If they approve, they can give those leaders a green light to continue; if they disapprove, they have the right to throw their support behind a different set of individuals. The expectation that citizens will be able to use elections to reward or punish their elected representatives for their performance while in office is known as democratic accountability (see also the chapters in Brun and Diamond 2014).

In earlier work, Stokes (2005) made the case that clientelistic exchanges made a "mockery" of democratic accountability. This is because in a clientelistic exchange, it is no longer the politician who is being held accountable by the voter at election time, but the *voter* who is being held accountable by the *politician*. Accountability is thus reversed. Any politician with the ability to punish or reward voters on the basis of their performance at the ballot box will likely be able to subvert (at least partially, if not completely) the ability of voters to use elections in the manner they were intended: as a means of sanctioning politicians for poor behavior while they were in office. In this way, clientelism is thought to undermine voter autonomy. Whenever voters know that they will suffer retaliation for voting for anyone other than their politician benefactor, they will be less likely to do so. This means they are no longer exercising free choice when casting their votes (Stokes et al. 2013).

Extending this logic further, politicians rarely try to buy the votes of *everyone*. The division of the electorate into voters whose votes are being bought and voters whose votes are not is likely to give rise to a fundamental inequality in representation and policymaking, whose consequences for the broader political system are likely to be profound: Namely, the politician benefactor knows that as long as she continues the flow of clientelistic goods to the voters whose votes she is buying (her "clients"), she can afford to ignore their preferences on virtually any other matter (Stokes et al. 2013). Essentially, she is able to bribe her clients to forget their other concerns. Because of the implied threat of retaliation, voters whose votes are being bought cannot credibly threaten to exit the relationship, which means that they may struggle to convince the politician to pay attention to their other concerns. This creates a situation in which differences in the *type* of voter who is pulled into clientelistic exchanges could be carrying over to quite pronounced biases in public policy. If politicians make a calculated decision to buy votes from the poor, for example, on account of the fact that their votes can be bought with fewer resources, then the risk is that policy will come to reflect the prefectures of other, *less* needy groups, which is not socially desirable (see also Diaz-Cayeros, Estévez and Magaloni 2016).

The fact that clientelistic practices are observed in so many countries and pose a threat to democratic integrity helped propel clientelism to the forefront of scholarly inquiry in comparative politics. Central questions of interest have been the types of voters politicians form clientelistic exchanges with and what form those exchanges take (Higashijima and Washida 2024; Yıldırım and Kitschelt 2020; Cruz 2019; Bussell 2019; Nichter 2014; Cammett and Issar 2010; Magaloni 2006; Calvo and Murillo 2004; Chandra 2007), whether clientelistic exchanges are always aimed at changing how a person votes ("persuasion") or whether they are also used to encourage people to turn out to vote ("mobilization") (Nichter 2018; Rosas, Johnston and Hawkins 2014; Gans-Morse, Mazzuca and Nichter 2014), and what role brokers play in helping politicians consummate their exchanges (Ravanilla, Haim and Hicken 2022; Holland and Palmer-Rubin 2015; Stokes et al. 2013; Larreguy, Marshall and Querubín 2016).

Other studies have tried to identify the conditions under which politicians turn to clientelism to build coalitions of loyal supporters, as opposed to relying on nonconditional modes of distribution (Diaz-Cayeros, Estévez and Magaloni 2016; Weitz-Shapiro 2012; Calvo and Murillo 2004; Wantchekon 2003; Magaloni, Diaz-Cayeros and Estévez 2007), with the aim of shedding light on what brings about the demise of clientelism (Rizzo N.D.; Golden and Nazrullaeva 2023; Kuo 2018; Weitz-Shapiro 2014; Camp, Dixit and Stokes 2014). How clientelism impacts the interests that get represented in politics, and whether clientelism is bad for democracy and economic development and if so, why, have also been the subject of research (Diaz-Cayeros, Estévez and Magaloni 2016; Szwarcberg 2015; Stokes et al. 2013).

3.2 PROBLEM OF CONTINGENCY

Virtually all clientelism research, at least as it pertains to the exchange of goods for votes, whether iterative or single-shot, has following feature. On the one hand, clientelism is deemed worthy of study because of the threat it poses to the form and functioning of democracy. As we mentioned, clientelistic exchanges are thought to undermine voter autonomy, limit voter choice, pervert the functioning of elections as a means of holding elected officials accountable, and create unequal representation and a bifurcated electorate (Stokes et al. 2013; Brun and Diamond 2014). Yet on the other hand, clientelism is a practice that, by all accounts, should not be observed in democracies. Why not? In a democracy, the secret ballot affords voters the right to vote in secret (Mares 2015). This means that only in exceptional circumstances – such as when a politician receives every vote or no votes in a locale – is it ever revealed how a given individual voted. The secret ballot gives the people whose votes a politician tries to buy the freedom to pocket the good from the politician, in exchange for a promise to vote for her, but then on election day, renege on this promise and vote for someone else. As long as the politician receives a *modicum* of votes in the voter's locale, then the voter will always be able to credibly claim that *she* was responsible for one of those votes (and is therefore worthy of continued targeting in the next election), and the politician will not have the means of discerning whether or not she is telling the truth.

The fact that politicians cannot verify how people vote means that they have no way of monitoring whether a person with whom they are attempting to cultivate a clientelistic exchange held up their end of the bargain and voted for the politician like they said they would. This creates a fundamental imbalance in the clientelistic exchange: Whereas the *voter* can discern whether or not they receive the good from the politician, the *politician* will not be able to discern whether or not they received the vote from the voter. Without this information, the politician cannot even *identify* clients who reneged on their promises, let alone *punish* the clients who did renege by stopping the flow of resources.[1] And yet, as we explained above, it is the politicians' ability to *retaliate* against clients who renege on their promise, and defect from the goods-for-votes exchange, that is thought to be the glue that binds those clients tightly to them, in ways that undermine voter autonomy, restrict vote choice, and pervert democratic accountability.

The problem of contingency places clientelism scholars in the peculiar position of studying a practice on account of the fact that it poses a threat to democracy, but having to begin by acknowledging that democracies are precisely the kinds of places where clientelistic practices are unlikely to take root. It is not my contention that *no* politician will attempt a clientelistic exchange in a democracy, it is that, by depriving politicians

---

[1] The exception to this is when a politician receives zero votes in a locale; then she will know that everyone she attempted to buy votes from reneged.

of the means of enforcing such an exchange, the secret ballot should, all else equal, *decrease* the attractiveness of clientelistic practices, relative to alternative ways of soliciting votes. To return to the dichotomy introduced above (between programmatic and clientelistic citizen–politician linkages), we might expect that being unable to enforce the terms of a clientelistic exchange would make electoral strategies on the *programmatic* end of the spectrum more attractive to the politician. By definition, a politician or party pursuing nonclientelistic electoral strategies offer voters policies that they would enact if elected, on the understanding that everyone qualifying for the policy will benefit from it, regardless of whether they voted for the politician.

Given the vast size of the clientelism literature, it is reasonable to surmise that politicians may have found a way around the "contingency problem," such that they *can* observe individual votes. Have they? The answer appears to be "no." In a review of all research on clientelism published in comparative politics journals and university press books between 2008 and 2018, which amounts to eighty-two studies, Hicken and Nathan (2020, 280) found that "very few recent studies, if any, document full contingency, with the commitment problem perfectly resolved and no chance for defection by voters." Of the studies they examined, 41% explicitly rejected the assumption that politicians had to be able to monitor how people voted in order to cultivate an exchange that otherwise met the criteria as clientelistic. Of the remainder, 16% made no claims about monitoring. 38% assumed that the ability to monitor individual votes *was* necessary, but of these, two-thirds presented no evidence of monitoring, while one-third presented evidence that was either from historical cases where the secret ballot was not yet in place or cases in autocratic or semi-autocratic regimes (with one exception, Hungary, but the evidence in that study did not point to widespread monitoring) (Hicken and Nathan 2020, 280–281). Importantly, their survey of the literature did not reveal a single case of the widespread monitoring of vote choices in a modern-day democracy.

The authors argue that the exchanges actually documented by clientelism scholars are better described as "not-quite-clientelism" or "clientelism-adjacent" (Hicken and Nathan 2020, 279). By this, they mean that the exchanges studied hardly ever satisfy the contingency requirement (meaning there were always opportunities for defection), and in some cases, do not even satisfy the iteration requirement (meaning there was little expectation the relationship would continue into the future). Clientelism, the authors report, appears to have become a catch-all phrase applicable to essentially any situation in which politicians are distributing particularistic, excludable benefits to voters around the time of elections. As a result, they conclude that "real clientelism – with a clearly contingent, iterated quid pro quo – appears substantially rarer across the world than the size of the literature on clientelism implies" (Hicken and Nathan 2020, 280). Indeed, of the five cases of real clientelism in these eighty-two works, four were in autocratic or semi-autocratic regimes.

One response to this observation might be to double down on the centrality of contingency to the definition of a clientelistic exchange and demand that any exchange in which this condition is not met is given some other label. The authors take a different path. They recommend a reassessment of the centrality of this characteristic to an exchange qualifying as clientelistic. They reason that if a politician without the ability to monitor votes (and thus, enforce the terms of a clientelistic exchange) nevertheless dedicates herself to cultivating one, then the appropriate conclusion to draw is that the politician may not *need* to be able to monitor votes to make clientelism a viable electoral strategy. One reason a politician might choose clientelism even when she cannot verify individual votes is because distributing resources in this fashion buys her credibility in the eyes of voters. If every candidate distributes handouts prior to elections, and evidence suggests that voters like handouts (Wantchekon 2003), then any candidate choosing not to partake in this goody-mongering risks being seen as unconcerned for voters' welfare. In such a setting, politicians might choose clientelism to avoid the negative signal that they worry opting out of it incurs (Aspinall et al. 2022, 13). They may also choose clientelism, even if they lack the ability to monitor votes, because they see it as insurance against encroachments on their supporters by rival candidates, or because it increases their name recognition in the electorate and builds their brand (Aspinall et al. 2022, 13).

Hicken and Nathan (2020) point out that all electoral strategies involving the tactical allocation of resources with an eye to influencing how people vote can be scaled according to their "yield rate," meaning the number of votes the politician receives, per dollar spent. At one end of the spectrum is a programmatic electoral strategy. Because politicians promising programmatic policies cannot deny them to voters who qualify for those policies but voted for the opposition, this electoral strategy is expected to have a low yield rate (many people who receive the good will vote for the opposition). At the other end is "real clientelism," which is expected to have a high yield rate. Because real clientelism is expected to have such a high yield rate, the authors argue that it makes sense for politicians to invest considerable energy and resources into trying to make this strategy work, which amounts to trying to circumvent the secret ballot. To this end, it pays to cultivate intermediaries known as brokers, whose job is to penetrate social networks in an attempt to identify which types of voters, if bribed, are most likely to follow through on their promise to vote for the politician (Finan and Schechter 2012; Stokes et al. 2013). Recognizing that investing in such surveillance of individuals is costly and decreases the amount of resources available for vote buying, the authors conclude that many politicians are likely to just muddle through, giving particularistic benefits to select voters and making it clear that they expect a vote in return, but anticipating that their yield will be far less than if they had the means of monitoring their votes. By their calculation, however, a "weakly enforced clientelistic exchange" is still likely to yield vastly more votes than the decidedly inferior (from the perspective of yield) programmatic strategy (see also Aspinall et al. 2022).

Golden and Nazrullaeva (2023) also make the point that exchanges need not satisfy the contingency requirement in order to qualify as clientelistic. They define clientelism as "the discretionary use by politicians of resources for electoral purposes" (Golden and Nazrullaeva 2023, 1). Central to this definition is the potential for voters to be excluded from outlays and the explicitly electoral goals of the politician. Critically, however, their definition "omits any notion of exchange, conditionality, or contingency" (Golden and Nazrullaeva 2023, 5). Thus, clientelistic exchanges should be distinguished from other exchanges not by their contingent nature but by their discretionary nature and electoral goals. Thus, clientelism consists of all the ways in which politicians use discretionary resource allocations to win office, whether used defensively (to recoup waning support), proactively (to win over new voters), or as a general signal of their competence, clout, and willingness to work on behalf of certain types of voters. Other studies that adopt definitions that do not embody contingency include Kramon (2017), who defines clientelism as the allocation of material benefits to voters during elections, and Diaz-Cayeros, Estévez and Magaloni (2016, 7), who define it as "discretionary programs targeted to individuals," which are "unambiguously administered through clientelistic networks."

3.3 SHIFTING THE TARGET OF THE EXCHANGE FROM INDIVIDUAL TO GROUP

As we have seen, the clientelism literature runs up against the problem that clientelistic exchanges, at least as they have traditionally been conceived, are unenforceable in democracies. Given this, one might think it would make little sense for politicians to make them the core of their electoral strategies. But clientelistic exchanges appear rampant, at least in certain democracies. Faced with this disconnect between what we observe empirically and the theories that have been developed to account for those empirical observations, recent work posits that we should reconsider the centrality of contingency to our definitions of clientelism. Essentially, this work suggests that we should treat any attempt to strategically confer resources on select sets of voters, with the goal of influencing how those people vote, as "clientelism." As a result, the field of clientelism scholarship appears poised to move in this direction.

However, there is an alternative path scholars could take, which does not require us to jettison this requirement. Instead, it reinstates contingency as the hallmark of a clientelistic exchange. The reason we may want to treat contingency as special, and demarcate goods-for-votes exchanges in which this condition is met from goods-for-votes exchanges in which it is not met, is because it is the characteristic of a goods-for-votes exchange that poses the gravest threat to democracy. As I explained above, in *non*contingent exchanges, voters retain the freedom to pocket goods from the politician but vote for someone else on election day. In contingent exchanges, when politicians have the means of monitoring whether the people they gave goods to voted for them on election day, voters lose this freedom and become locked into voting for their politician benefactor. While both types of exchanges confer advantages on politicians with access to resources, and those advantages may also be troubling from the perspective of democratic integrity, a voter's freedom to cast her vote however she sees fit is more seriously undermined in the latter.

I posit that the reason contingency has loomed so large in the clientelism literature, to the extent that it is labeled a problem, is because scholars tend to view clientelism as a relationship politicians form with *individual voters*. Emblematic of this approach is Weitz-Shapiro (2014, 5–7), who defines clientelism as the "individualized, contingent exchange of goods or services for political support or votes." She writes that "in a clientelist exchange, benefits are targeted at the individual and linked to individual political behavior" (Weitz-Shapiro 2012, 569). Diaz-Cayeros, Estévez and Magaloni (2016, 8), also, differentiate discretionary programs targeted at individuals, which they call clientelism, from "discretionary social transfers spent on infrastructure, electrification, street pavement, road construction, and so on," which they call pork-barrel politics. Lindberg and Morrison (2008, 102), too, write: "It is only when there is a promise or implicit agreement about personal favors or goods to be exchanged in return for political loyalty that a clientelistic relationship is established." More generally, returning to the aforementioned review piece, Hicken and Nathan (2020) found that of the seventy-three articles and nine books on clientelism they surveyed, seventy-eight (95%)

concerned exchanges between politicians and individuals, leaving only four that looked at exchanges between politicians and groups.

It is not hard to see how a focus on individuals leads straight to the realization that, because individual votes are unobservable, clientelism in its purest form is unenforceable. In the literature, this has led to a presumption that politicians must be on a never-ending quest to try to solve this problem and figure out how people vote, and it to this end that much of their energy is devoted. This presumption underpins most of the work done in the strand of clientelism research that focuses on the intermediaries who help politicians implement their clientelistic exchanges (Ravanilla, Haim and Hicken 2022; Bussell 2019; Brierley and Nathan 2021; Mares and Young 2019, 2016; Larreguy, Marshall and Querubín 2016; Finan and Schechter 2012; Holland and Palmer-Rubin 2015; Stokes et al. 2013; Larreguy, Montiel Olea and Querubin 2017; Wang and Kurzman 2007). Known as brokers or vote mobilizers, these intermediaries are presumed to help politicians with two tasks, both designed to help with the contingency problem. One is identifying which voters a politician should forge clientelistic exchanges with. This is thought to require intimate knowledge of the partisan preferences, short-term situational changes (such as a job loss or sick family member), and attitudes toward helping others of the voters in a politician's jurisdiction. The second task is helping the politician discern whether someone who received a good in exchange for a vote followed through and voted for the politician on election day. This, too, is thought to require intimate knowledge about voters. The fact that clientelism saddles politicians with this "problem" (of being unable to observe individual votes) leads to the presumption that intermediaries are employed to help them solve it. Correspondingly, a trove of studies examine how politicians manage these individuals.

However, the foundational literature referenced above adopted a more expansive definition of clientelism. Kitschelt and Wilkinson (2007, 2), for example, theorized that politicians could cultivate clientelistic exchanges with individuals or "small groups of citizens." In the case of the latter, the authors reasoned that the politician could deliver local club goods to groups "who have already delivered or who promise to deliver their electoral support" (Kitschelt and Wilkinson 2007, 10). They argued that group members would be motivated to vote for their politician benefactor in exchange for the local club goods their group would become eligible for. Beyond pointing out that it was decidedly less costly to monitor votes at the level of a group, especially when election results are reported at a fine-grained level such as a polling station, the authors did not theorize as

3.3 Shifting the Target from Individual to Group

to the conditions under which politicians might want to form clientelistic relationships with groups over individuals, or vice versa.

Writing in the same volume, Medina and Stokes (2007) argued that when votes are counted at a disaggregated level such as a precinct, politicians could use the promise of large rewards or punishments to induce voters to vote for them. When the reward or punishment was very large, they argued that politicians who cannot observe how individuals vote will nevertheless be able to create the perception that a voter's livelihood will be significantly affected by how they vote. To illustrate this, the authors describe a situation where voters are threatened with paramilitary attacks on their communities if their politician benefactor does not emerge as the top vote-getter in the community. In this scenario, they argue that even though voters will know that the probability that the politician places first will hardly be affected by whether or not they *personally* make the effort to vote, many voters will nevertheless decide that turning out and voting for the politician is worth it to avoid an attack on the community that could kill those close to them.

From the politician's perspective, key to the effectiveness of such a strategy is being able to count votes at a disaggregated level (Medina and Stokes 2007). The authors contrast this with a situation in which returns are counted at a much higher level of aggregation, like a city with a million people. Under these conditions, they explain that such a threat will not be as effective at inducing people to turn out and vote for the politician because each voter will realize that the impact their vote holds over whether or not their politician places first in the city as a whole is negligible. In this setting, the politician will find it harder to create the perception that the welfare and safety of any one voter is meaningfully influenced by how they cast their vote.

Building on these insights, I posit that when vote counts are discernible at the level of groups within a politician's electoral district, and resources are targetable at those same groups, politicians will find it advantageous to kick the clientelistic exchange up a notch, from the level of the individual voter to the level of the group of voters. The advantage in doing so is that the level at which vote tallies are *discernible* is the level at which the terms of any goods-for-votes exchange they cultivate are *enforceable*. Moreover, they are enforceable at virtually no cost to the politician.

To elaborate, consider a politician whose electoral district is divided into a number of geographically defined groups, such as precincts or municipalities, at which votes are counted and tallies reported. After the election, all the politician has to do is consult the public record to glean the number of votes she received from each group. Using these tallies, she will be able to map out the geographic distribution of her support within the electoral district, with the level of granularity determined by the number of groups into which the electorate is divided and vote tallies are reported. Then, providing she has access to resources that are targetable at the same group, she will have the tools to implement a clientelistic exchange with these groups. By this, I mean that if a group's level of support for her was found to have declined in a given election, she will be able to observe this and retaliate by withholding resources. Importantly, the politician will be able to discern changes in her support from one election to the other without having to divert *any* resources to creating and maintaining a surveillance operation capable of telling her which of the many individuals she attempted to buy votes from voted for her on election day. By setting up the clientelistic exchange with *groups of voters*, how any given *individual voter* casts their ballot is no longer her concern.

In what I am proposing, *group-based clientelism*, the politician's partner in the exchange is no longer the individual but the *group*, and the goal is not to buy the votes of individuals but to buy *support* from groups. This claim differs from existing research on groups in the clientelism literature in subtle yet important ways. One set of studies assume that politicians are trying to buy the votes of individuals, but reason that, because individual votes are unobservable, politicians will come up with ways of using group-level election returns to discern how many individuals they tried to buy votes from followed through and voted for them on election day. Rueda (2017), for example, argues that when a relatively small number of voters are assigned to vote at a given polling station, brokers will set a target number of votes they want for the politician at that station and imply that the flow of goods to the bribed voters assigned to vote therein will be cut off if the target is not met. Because the number of voters assigned to that station is small, bribed voters will be more likely to vote for the politician on account of the fact that their vote wields influence over whether or not their polling station meets its target. Caselli and Falco (2019) make a similar point, arguing that voters behave differently when assigned to small polling stations as opposed to larger ones, due to the greater risk that their vote choice is revealed to politicians. In both of these studies, politicians are thought to be targeting *individuals* (not groups), and mete out rewards and punishments to *individuals* (not groups).

A second set of studies share the assumption that politicians are trying to buy the votes of individuals. To this end, they are presumed to devise ways of using group-level election returns to discern how hard the intermediaries they hire to deliver individual votes are working for them. Larreguy, Marshall and Querubín (2016), for example, argue that local party operatives lack on-the-ground insight into voter preferences and willingness to vote on election day. As a result, they hire brokers capable

3.3 Shifting the Target from Individual to Group

of supplying this information. Preventing shirking by their brokers thus emerges as a central concern for the politician. The authors argue that when an electorate is divided into more groups at which vote tallies are reported, politicians will be better able to distinguish between changes in voter turnout that are a function of broker shirking, and changes in voter turnout that are a function of shocks outside of broker control. Leveraging the fact that Mexican electoral precincts gain an additional polling station for every 750 voters, they compare otherwise-similar precincts with and without an extra polling station and find that turnout is higher in precincts with the extra polling station. This is evidence, they argue, that brokers shirk less at smaller polling stations. In this study, the partner in the clientelistic exchange remains the *individual* (not the group), and group-level returns are seen as useful only insofar as they give politicians the tools to monitor how hard others are working to deliver the votes of *individuals* (not groups).

A third set of studies look at the allocation of group-level benefits. It is widely acknowledged that politicians all over the world have access to material goods targetable at groups of voters, whether those groups are geographic-based (such as villages), association-based (such as religious organizations), or sector-based (such as occupational organizations) (Aspinall et al. 2022; Harris and Posner 2019; Hutchcroft et al. 2014; Scheiner 2006; Maclachlan 2006). Politicians in the ruling party are especially blessed when it comes to resources they control. They routinely have access to funds they can use to deliver infrastructure and other projects to geographic areas of their choosing. Because benefits funneled to groups are enjoyed by all group members, they fit the definition of club goods and are variously referred to as "local public goods," "pork-barrel politics," or "partisan bias" in the literature (Stokes et al. 2013; Diaz-Cayeros, Estévez and Magaloni 2016).

In contrast to my claim, which is that club goods can be exchanged for electoral support in a clientelistic fashion, a consensus has emerged in the clientelism literature that club goods are analytically distinct from clientelism. Why? Scholars emphasize that while the decision to bestow benefits on certain groups and withhold them from others might be *political*, meaning that it is undertaken with explicitly political (and usually electoral) goals, it is not *contingent*, on the grounds that these benefits cannot be tied to votes in the way that clientelistic goods aimed at individuals are (Diaz-Cayeros, Estévez and Magaloni 2016; Stokes et al. 2013; Weitz-Shapiro 2014; Lindberg and Morrison 2008; Aspinall et al. 2022; Hutchcroft et al. 2014; Hicken 2011).

In what will by now be a familiar refrain, underpinning the claim that group-level allocations lie outside the purview of clientelism is the assumption that politicians are focused on buying the votes of *individuals*. Because club goods are bestowed on everyone in a group and cannot be withheld from group members who fail to vote for the politician, members receive the (club) good regardless of whether they personally contributed to the quality that made the group eligible for the good. On these grounds, scholars stress that club goods cannot be used to enforce a clientelistic exchange. Lindberg and Morrison (2008, 102), for example, write that club goods such as schools, roads, and electricity for the community are enjoyed by everyone, so cannot be used to enforce patron–client relationships between politicians and individuals. Diaz-Cayeros, Estévez and Magaloni (2016, 8) write that "a key difference between clientelism and the pork barrel is that within a given district politicians cannot screen users with the latter instrument." Weitz-Shapiro (2014, 7) writes that pork-barreling, defined as the redistribution of funds away from citizens toward residents of select geographic areas, is not tied to how any given individual in the groups votes, and therefore does not fit the definition of "clientelistic" (see also Weitz-Shapiro 2012, 569). In support of this, Aspinall et al. (2022) find that politicians regularly seek to influence allocations of club goods for political ends (this is "meso-particularism" in their language) but rarely make references to any quid pro quo in which the group receiving the good is expected to reciprocate with votes (Hutchcroft et al. 2014). On this basis, the authors conclude that club goods are not being used to buy electoral support; therefore, they are not being used clientelistically. Instead, they argue that the purpose of meso-particularism is to buy the politician credibility, build her brand, and protect her turf from encroachment by rivals.

If we relax the requirement that clientelistic relationships are necessarily between politicians and individuals and devote serious consideration to the possibility that under a certain configuration of political institutions, politicians might be able to form them with *groups*, we can see that the fact that club goods are not targetable at individuals within groups does not negate the possibility they are being used clientelistically. Recently, scholars have begun to investigate the possibility that group-level benefits are used to purchase support from groups, without the presumption that they are used to buy the votes of individuals (Cooperman 2024; Gottlieb and Larreguy 2020; Gottlieb et al. 2019). These studies do not explicitly tout the relationships between group-level support and benefits they observe as "clientelistic." However, the definition of clientelism offered in the seminal studies discussed above hold that it is not the *nature* of a good that determines whether it is used clientelistically, but the *criteria* governing its distribution. These studies emphasized that if the sole criteria under which a good is delivered is "did you vote for me?," then the good is being distributed clientelistically (Hicken 2011; Stokes 2007; Kitschelt and Wilkinson 2007). I argue that if the sole criteria under which a club good is delivered to a group is "how many votes did you return for me?," then there are few compelling reasons why we cannot also say that the (club) good is being distributed clientelistically.

My claim is not that club goods are always being used clientelistically. Rather, it is that when institutions are configured a certain way, politicians will be able to form clientelistic relationships with groups, in which club goods are exchanged for support from the group as a whole. While *how* the club good is used to buy support from the group will vary according to contextual factors such as the presence of a dominant party, the basic idea is that the politician will make it known that the amount of money to be delivered to each group will be a function of its level of electoral support. It will be made *contingent* on its level of electoral support. If a group's level of support for a politician drops relative to a previous election or if it is found to be lower than that of other groups (again, we can expect the precise allocation rule to vary according to contextual factors), the politician will penalize it with less money (fewer goods). Conversely, if a group's level of support for the politician increases relative to a previous election or is found to be higher than that of other groups, the politician can reward it with more goods.[2]

3.4 POLITICAL INSTITUTIONS ARE KEY

My claim is that politicians can pursue GBC under a certain configuration of political institutions. What is that configuration? GBC is possible when politicians can observe their electoral support at the level of a group within their electoral district and have the ability to target resources at that same level. It is the degree to which the units at which vote shares are observable and resources targetable *overlap*, and are *nested* within broader electoral districts, that determines the viability of this electoral strategy.

Let us unpack this further. When setting up their democratic institutions (or having them set up by someone else), countries have many decisions to make. One of those decisions is where the votes cast in elections will be *counted*. While all countries have voters cast votes at

---

[2] While Weitz-Shapiro (2014, 7) argues that politicians' inability to tie the provision of pork to how an individual within the group votes means that pork is "analytically distinct" from clientelism, she acknowledges in a footnote that "if that degree of contingency is possible, then clientelism, rather than pork is a more accurate description."

polling stations, countries vary with regard to whether the votes cast in polling stations are counted at the polling station itself or transported somewhere else and counted there. That "somewhere else" could be a central location in the electoral district as a whole, or it could be an entity such as a precinct or municipality located within the electoral district but sitting atop the polling station. When the votes cast at polling stations are transported to a central location at the level of the electoral district and counted there, politicians are usually prevented from being able to observe their vote shares at the level of a group within their district. In this setting, then, GBC will not be a viable electoral strategy. In contrast, when the votes cast at polling stations are counted either at the polling station itself, or are transported to a jurisdiction such as a precinct or municipality located within the electoral district and counted there, the condition that politicians can observe their vote shares at the level of a group within their electoral district is met, and GBC becomes viable.

How many countries enable politicians to observe their vote shares at a disaggregated unit within the broader electoral district? Data on the unit at which votes are counted in 218 countries, both democracies and nondemocracies, was collected by ACE: The Electoral Knowledge Network (2013). Of these, four held no elections, while eight did not make this information available. Of the remaining 206 countries, 178 countries (86% of the total) are coded as counting votes at the polling station or polling center.[3] The remaining twenty-eight countries (14%) transport the votes cast in several polling stations to a "special counting center" and count them there.[4] While a special counting center means that votes cast at polling stations are transported somewhere else to be counted, further investigation was necessary to determine whether the special counting centers used in each country were coterminous with the borders of the electoral district as a whole (ruling out GBC), or were jurisdictions located *within* the electoral district (making GBC viable). Of the twenty-eight countries using special counting centers, the special counting center appears to be coterminous with the borders of an electoral district in four countries: the United Kingdom, Ireland, Namibia, and Botswana.

---

[3] This number includes the 177 countries coded this way in the data, as well as Canada, which counts ordinary votes cast on election day in polling stations (mail-in ballots are counted differently).

[4] This number includes the twenty-six countries coded as counting votes in special counting centers, as well as the United States and Anguilla, which were coded as "Other" in the data. In the United States, votes are counted in electoral precincts, while in Anguilla, votes are transported to "a place" designated ahead of time for the purpose of counting. Both these cases fit the definition of "special counting center," even if they are not coded as such in this data (this may have been because this terminology is not used in their electoral legislation).

In the remaining twenty-four, special counting centers are units within the broader electoral district. Putting together the 177 countries counting votes at polling stations or centers, and the 24 countries counting votes at special counting centers located within broader electoral districts, we find that 202 out of 206 countries (98%) enable politicians to observe their vote shares at a disaggregated unit within the broader electoral district.

In this discussion, I am equating the *counting* of votes at the level of a unit within the broader electoral district with the *reporting* of vote tallies at the same unit. In other words, I am assuming that if votes are counted at the level of a given subdistrict unit, the results of those counts, in terms of votes cast for the politicians and parties competing, will also be available at the same unit. Unfortunately, data on the unit at which vote tallies are reported or made available does not appear to have yet been collected. To gauge the plausibility of this assumption, I narrowed down the 218 countries in the ACE: The Electoral Knowledge Network (2013) data to the 88 democracies and semi-democracies included in the Democratic Accountability and Linkages Project (DALP) (Kitschelt et al. 2013).[5] Of these eighty-eight countries, eighty-four count votes at a disaggregated level.[6] A search of the national electoral commission websites in these eighty-eight countries revealed that thirty-five reported disaggregated vote tallies matching the unit at which votes were said to be counted. Of the remaining forty-nine countries, I was unable to ascertain whether the absence of these tallies on commission websites meant that they were not reported, or that they *are* reported, but are simply not published on these websites.[7]

On balance, the assumption that votes counted at a disaggregated level are observable (by politicians at least) at that level is reasonable on two grounds. First, one reason votes are counted at a disaggregated level is to enhance transparency. This suggests that publication of vote tallies is likely to accompany vote counting. Second, politicians are often allowed to send observers to places where votes are counted, also in the name of enhancing transparency and count legitimacy. The fact that the count

---

[5] This project collected data from eighty-eight countries in the 2008–2009 period. The criteria for inclusion was that a country had more than 2 million inhabitants and had conducted at least two rounds of national elections under "democratic or semi-democratic conditions." Five countries not meeting these conditions (Egypt, Indonesia, Malaysia, Pakistan, and Russia) were also included.

[6] The United Kingdom, Ireland, Namibia, and Botswana were the four that did not.

[7] In Japan's case, for example, votes are counted at special vote-counting centers (we explain what those are in Chapter 5) and published by local electoral commissions after elections are held. But with the national electoral commission does not make these counting-center-level vote tallies available on its website.

takes place with witnesses suggests it is not intended to be kept shielded from the eyes of political actors.

Thus, it appears that, in 98% of countries (and 95% of democracies), politicians are able observe their vote shares at a disaggregated unit within their electoral district. In how many of these countries do politicians have access to resources targetable at or around the same level? The vast literature in political science on pork-barreling and the allocation of club goods suggests that controlling government is synonymous with having access to goods targetable at select groups, whether geographically defined or otherwise, at least for countries above a certain threshold of development.[8] In some countries, being a member of parliament, not necessarily a member of the governing coalition, is a sufficient condition to be able to influence the allocation of such goods. Critically, however, the degree to which the jurisdictions to which such benefits are deliverable *overlap* with the units at which vote shares are observable is a much subtler question, about which we know relatively little.

To elaborate, *perfect overlap* occurs when vote shares are observable at the exact same unit to which central government resources are deliverable and units are perfectly contained within the boundaries of a single electoral district. In Chapter 5, I explain that many politicians seeking election to Japan's all-important Lower House compete in electoral districts with perfect overlap. Votes are counted and reported at the level of the municipality, which is also a jurisdiction to which central government resources are delivered. With some exceptions, municipalities are perfectly contained within a single electoral district. The fact that many municipalities belong exclusively to a *single* electoral district, and politicians can observe their vote tallies in each municipality and influence resource allocations to municipalities, creates a situation where each and every municipality can be pulled into a clientelistic relationship with the politician representing the district. These are *perfect storm conditions* for GBC: Any politician with influence over government resources will be able to tie the amount of resources municipalities receive to the level of support it provided the politician in the most recent election.

In other settings, votes might be counted and reported at the level of a polling station. While central government resources are not normally deliverable to polling stations, polling stations are often perfectly

---

[8] For work on pork-barreling, consult Jensenius and Chhibber (2023); Malik (2023); Motolinia (2021); de Kadt and Lieberman (2020); Rickard (2018); Harris and Posner (2019); McMichael (2018); Kramon (2017); Catalinac (2015); Funk and Gathmann (2013); Huber and Ting (2013); Tavits (2009); Golden and Picci (2008); Magaloni (2006); Diaz-Cayeros, Estévez and Magaloni (2016); Hirano (2006); Lee (2004); Horiuchi and Saito (2003); Dahlberg and Johansson (2002); Ward and John (1999) and Dixit and Londregan (1996).

3.4 Political Institutions Are Key

contained within the boundaries of a jurisdiction to which central government resources *are* deliverable, such as a town. If those jurisdictions are then perfectly contained within the boundaries of a single electoral district, then we have something akin to perfect overlap, although it requires the politician to take the extra step of *aggregating* their polling station-level vote tallies to a town-level tally. Politicians contesting Lower House elections in Italy and Mexico operate in electoral districts that meet these conditions.

In contrast, *imperfect overlap* occurs when vote shares are either not observable at the same unit to which central government resources are deliverable or they *are* observable at this level, but this unit is not perfectly contained within the boundaries of a single electoral district. When the jurisdictions to which central government resources are deliverable are relatively *large*, for example, they can be coterminous with the boundaries of a single electoral district or encompass several electoral districts. In the former, a politician might be able to observe her vote shares at a disaggregated level within the electoral district, if votes are counted in polling stations, but will not be able to deliver resources to those units (resources are deliverable only to the jurisdiction as a whole, which is coterminous with electoral district). In the latter case, the fact that the jurisdictions to which resources are deliverable contain several electoral districts nestled within them mean that politicians do not even have the means of delivering resources to their *own* electoral district, as any resources delivered to the broader jurisdiction containing their electoral district could hypothetically end up in the hands of voters in other electoral districts.

In South Korea, for example, the jurisdiction to which central government resources can be delivered is the municipality. In elections to the National Assembly, three types of electoral districts exist: districts whose borders are coterminous with a single municipality, districts that are part of a larger municipality, and districts containing multiple municipalities. The conditions for GBC are not met in the first two types but are met in the third.[9] In the case of elections to the House of Commons in the United Kingdom, the central counting system precludes politicians from even viewing their vote shares at a disaggregated unit within their electoral district. Even if they were able to observe disaggregated vote counts, however, the jurisdictions to which central government resources are deliverable (local authorities) are relatively large, with many encompassing more than one electoral district (Fouirnaies and Mutlu-Eren 2015; Ward and John 1999). Thus, the conditions for GBC are not met in elections to the House of Commons.

---

[9] Calculated with data collected by myself and Lucia Motolinia.

Other cases of imperfect overlap occur when the units to which central government resources are deliverable might not be particularly large but are nevertheless not contained within the boundaries of a single electoral district and straddle more than one. In Japan, Italy, Mexico, and Ukraine, for example, many politicians operate in settings characterized by perfect overlap (electoral districts are perfectly divisible into units at which vote shares are observable and resources targetable). But some of the politicians in these countries operate in electoral districts in which one or more of the jurisdictions making up the electoral district, at which vote shares are observable and to which resources are targetable, straddle the boundaries of a neighboring electoral district.[10] In these electoral districts, politicians will be able to pull all the perfectly nested jurisdictions into clientelistic relationships with them but would have trouble incorporating the jurisdiction straddling the boundaries of the neighboring electoral district. While the politician would be able to observe her vote shares in the area of that jurisdiction located in her electoral district, she would find it difficult to target resources at that area only. Because resources are targeted at the jurisdiction as a whole, then she would likely find it difficult to ensure that any resources she delivers to the jurisdiction are spent in the section of the jurisdiction located in her electoral district.

A different case of imperfect overlap occurs when the unit to which central government resources are deliverable bears absolutely no resemblance to the unit at which vote shares are observable. Because national governments tend not to administer national elections themselves but *delegate* this task to the lower-tier administrative entities that make up the state, such as municipalities, my research has not unearthed a case like this. Thus, I mention it as a hypothetical. When the lower-tier entities that make up the state are tasked with establishing polling stations, supervising voting, and counting and reporting the votes, then the result is a situation in which vote tallies tend to be observable at the level of this lower-tier administrative entity. A municipality charged with administering national-level elections within its borders would have no reason to establish polling stations or count votes in another municipality. Nor would it have any reason to *mix* the votes cast within its borders with those cast within the borders of other municipalities.[11] However, if a national government decided to administered elections directly, without delegating this task to lower-tier units, then theoretically, we might observe a situation in which votes are counted and reported at

---

[10] Calculated with data collected by myself and Lucia Motolinia.
[11] Note that mixing votes is a feature of vote counting in certain countries, such as Japan and Belgium, but this appears to entail the mixing together of votes cast in different polling stations (before they are counted) within the same jurisdiction.

units it established, which might not correspond with the borders of the lower-tier units already in existence.

While I was able to establish that politicians can observe their vote shares at a disaggregated level within their electoral district in 95% of democracies, establishing the degree of overlap between those units and the units to which central government resources are deliverable is more difficult, and requires the collection of new data. In gathering it, researchers must be mindful of the possibility that the degree of overlap between the unit at which vote shares are observable and resources deliverable not only varies across country but might also vary within country and over time. As we saw with South Korea, for example, it can be the case that among politicians running for election to the same legislature, some may be running in electoral districts where GBC is possible and others may be running in electoral districts where it is not possible. In Chapter 5, I explain that in the case of Japan, the drawing up of new electoral districts for Lower House elections, combined with municipal amalgamations and urbanization has created variation in the degree to which electoral districts meet these conditions over time. Whereas it used to be the case that virtually every politician competed in electoral districts in which GBC was possible, a growing number of politicians compete in districts where it is not.

Beyond matching up units at which vote shares are observable and resources deliverable, researchers interested in gauging whether GBC is happening in their countries of interest should also consider the following three questions. First, what types of *resources* are available to politicians? The vast literature on pork-barreling suggests that three categories of geographically targetable spending are amenable to serving as fodder for politicians seeking clientelistic exchanges with groups, at least those that are geographically defined.[12] The first category, *project-based funds*, is when the central government takes revenue generated from taxes levied on all citizens and makes a pot of money available for the purpose of funding specific projects in lower-tier administrative units. The units often have to come up with proposals for funding (and sometimes, commit to shouldering part of the cost themselves) and central government bureaucrats weigh up the merits of each project and decide which

---

[12] In this chapter, I have focused discussion on how politicians could go about cultivating clientelistic relationships with geographically defined groups. It is also possible that politicians could cultivate these relationships with *non*geographically defined groups, such as sectoral associations. They could do this on the condition that the level of support they receive from each group is observable. Politicians might use goods such as preferential tax rates or regulatory favors to buy the votes of nongeographically defined groups, provided those benefits could be adjusted, upwards or downwards, with an eye to the group's electoral performance.

to fund. Project-based funds are distinct from funds allocated to lower-tier units on the basis of a formula that takes into account need, broadly defined. Several studies tackle the question of whether politicians can influence formula-decided allocations, and while their results are suggestive of influence, their analyses underscore the difficulty of controlling for the myriad factors that go into the formula (McMichael 2017; Ward and John 1999; Banful 2011).[13]

The second category, *supranational funds*, are funds granted to central governments from supranational bodies such as the European Union and the World Bank, on the condition that they are used to create programs designed to alleviate poverty, enhance economic development, improve health outcomes, and so on. It is not implausible that these funds could also serve as fodder for GBC. The European Union Cohesion and Structural Funds, for example, was created to foster convergence in all areas of the EU. Recipient governments receive funds each year, which they are required to use to fund projects at the local level (Dellmuth and Stoffel 2012). While recipient governments must comply with rules in deciding which projects to fund, Muraközy and Telegdy (2016, 324) argue that there is scope for political manipulation, not least because the EU exercises "limited supervision" over this process. Concessionary loans from the World Bank, for example, funded the Ugandan government's Youth Opportunities Program, which grants funding to help groups of young people in underdeveloped regions start a small business (Blattman, Emeriau, and Fiala 2018).[14]

The third category, the *constituency development fund* (CDF), is when a government sets aside a percentage of its annual budget to be allocated directly to members of parliament, for the purpose of funding projects aimed at fostering development in their electoral districts (Malik 2023; Jensenius and Chhibber 2023; Keefer and Khemani 2009; Harris and Posner 2019; Malik 2019). In some of the countries with CDFs, the same

---

[13] Project-based funds can include temporary grant programs, such as the local investment grants provided by the Swedish government for investments in ecological sustainable development (Dahlberg and Johansson 2002), and the Australian government's sports grants (Denemark 2000).

[14] A type of supranational funding that has received sustained attention by political scientists is the conditional cash transfer (CCT). This encompasses cash payments and other in-kind transfers to low-income individuals and families in exchange for ensuring their children attend school, health clinics, and so on (e.g., Conover et al. 2020; Imai, King and Rivera 2019; Correa and Cheibub 2016; Layton and Smith 2015; De La O 2015; Tobias, Sumarto and Moody 2014; Linos 2013; Zucco 2013; Labonne 2012). Because most (although, not all) CCTs consist of money for individuals or families (not groups), these funds may be less likely to serve as fodder for GBC.

amount of money is given to all electoral districts, while in others, a formula is used to determine how much each electoral district receives. In still others, electoral districts receive allocations that are in part determined by a need-based formula and in part made up of the same amount all districts receive. The fact that the sitting member of parliament representing the district tends to have complete discretion over how the funds are used within her electoral district, combined with the fact that funds are replenished every year and politicians do not have exert effort to secure them, makes CDFs a near-ideal resource with which politicians could tie the dollar value of projects awarded to groups within the district to their voting behavior.

A second question researchers should consider is: How do politicians exert *influence* over the allocation of these resources? As our discussion of the types of resources that are amenable to GBC has implied, the way influence is exercised will depend on the nature of resources available. In the case of CDFs, politicians gain access by virtue of winning the election. In other settings, tying the amount of resources groups receive to their performance in the most recent election will be less straightforward. While the decision to establish a pot of money that can be used for local development projects and other infrastructure might have been made by politicians, and usually by politicians in the ruling party, decisions about which areas will actually receive the funding are usually delegated to bureaucrats. Rickard (2018, 188) explains why delegating these decisions to bureaucrats helps shield the politician from criticism that she is using these funds for electoral ends and gives her the power to scapegoat bureaucrats for decisions that might later come under criticism. In these settings, we can expect that politicians will seek to influence bureaucratic decision-making via lobbying. In Chapter 5, I explain how in Japan, politicians make calls to bureaucrats on behalf of municipalities and occasionally accompany local politicians to the offices of the relevant government ministry, such that they can make the case for a particular project in person. When the only means of influencing resource allocations is via lobbying, we can expect that politicians will devote more time to lobbying for groups they intend to reward, very little time lobbying for groups they are indifferent to, and the cumulative output of all this lobbying could be allocations that track electoral support.

A third question researchers should consider is: How *dependent* is the lower-tier entity on the funds politicians have to offer? Ultimately, given that the lower-tier jurisdictions to which central government resources are deliverable are local governments, answering this question boils down to unpacking the fiscal relationship between tiers of government in a given country. Scheiner (2006) made the case that the value lower-tier units will place on the resources controlled by politicians at the national level will be a function of the degree of fiscal autonomy enjoyed by the lower-tier unit. In countries characterized by "fiscal centralization," the vast majority of lower-tier units could be in a situation where most of their revenue comes from central government transfers, in part because they lack autonomous revenue streams. In countries not characterized by fiscal centralization, lower-tier units can also exhibit high dependence on central government transfers when they lack robust revenue streams, whether due to poor economic conditions, economic shocks, or mismanagement. On balance, higher dependence will mean that a higher value is placed on the government resources proffered by politicians. As a result, the attractiveness of GBC as an electoral strategy, as well as the nature of the groups that are likely to emerge as core supporters of politicians, will likely also be influenced by dependence.[15]

3.5 CONTRIBUTIONS

I have argued that under the right configuration of political institutions, politicians will have incentives to pursue GBC, which means they will tie the amount of resources groups in their electoral districts receive to how much support those groups gave them in the most recent election. In Chapter 4, I consider the nuts and bolts of how this can be done. I offer a series of hypotheses centered on how politicians in a dominant party can design allocations to groups such that they lead to the most votes, conditional on resources delivered. The rest of the book turns to the case of Japan to test these hypotheses. In that sense, it returns to the puzzle posed in Chapter 2, about the extraordinary staying power of Japan's Liberal Democratic Party (LDP), through electoral reforms, transformations to the party system, bumpy economic performance, corruption scandals, and policy mistakes. My results show that GBC has been a central component of the electoral strategies of many LDP politicians since at least 1980, which is when my data begins.

Before doing so, however, let me spell out four ways in which the theory of GBC opens up new avenues of inquiry. These new avenues of

---

[15] Here, I have discussed the nature of resources available to politicians (the second question) and the degree to which lower-tier units depend on those resources (the third question) as if they are exogenous to the theory. However, in a setting where the institutional conditions for GBC are met, it is possible that politicians find this electoral strategy so attractive that they *create* resources that can be used for this purpose and take actions to prevent municipalities becoming more independent. Under these circumstances, both the nature of resources available and the degree to which lower-tier units depend on them might be partly endogenous.

3.5 Contributions

inquiry have the potential to further our understanding of how politicians use the selective targeting of resources under their control to further their electoral ends, in ways that are likely to have broad consequences for democracy.

3.5.1 Bringing Institutions Back

A key finding in the early work on clientelism, which still carries considerable weight in research in the area today, was that formal political institutions mattered relatively little and could not account for why politicians sought to cultivate programmatic versus clientelistic linkage strategies with voters (Kitschelt and Wilkinson 2007). When "other imperatives" made it attractive for politicians to cultivate clientelistic linkage strategies with voters, Kitschelt and Wilkinson (2007, 43) argued that politicians would essentially "work around" formal political institutions such as the electoral system or constitutional structure, such that they would be able to do so. The authors argued that at most, political institutions structured how the exchange was conducted (for example, whether the party was the key actor orchestrating it, or the politician), but not the *demand* for the exchange.

In a systematic treatment of the role of political institutions, Mueller (2007, 259) reached the same conclusion, finding that neither federal, electoral, legislative, nor executive structures appeared to decisively impact the likelihood that a politician would "go clientelistic." Of the institutions examined, this study found that no specific institution was necessary, nor specific configuration of institutions sufficient, for clientelism to emerge as the dominant linkage strategy in a given country. While institutions might bequeath politicians with incentives to pursue clientelism, he observed that those incentives did not appear "not overwhelmingly strong" (Mueller 2007, 275). Thus, he agreed with the above scholars that the balance of evidence appeared to be that institutions did not influence the demand for clientelism but might influence the form it took. Writing in the same volume, Scheiner (2007, 276) considered the role that Japan's personalistic electoral system, described in the last chapter, played in pushing Japanese politicians to adopt clientelistic electoral strategies. He concluded that this electoral system was "neither necessary nor sufficient for clientelism in Japan." Hicken (2007) echoed this claim, arguing that personal vote-oriented electoral systems might increase the probability that politicians would try to buy votes, but did not determine whether or not they did so.

To the extent that the finding that institutions matter less than we think reflects a consensus in the literature, the theory offered in this book breaks with this consensus. As I explained above, GBC is possible only when institutions are configured a certain way. It is not possible when they are not. This conclusion is important because it suggests that reconfiguring a country's political institutions could eradicate, or at the very least minimize, a politician's ability to pursue GBC. Specifically, taking ballot boxes from all the polling stations within a given electoral district to a central location in the district, and mixing them together first, before votes are counted, would significantly diminish a politician's ability to divide her electoral district up into sections and discern how much support she received from each. To the extent that disaggregated vote counts are preferable on transparency grounds, politicians interested in reform could instead choose to tackle rules governing the drawing up of the boundaries of electoral districts and the relationship between those boundaries and those of lower-tier administrative units. Specifically, doing away with rules that electoral districts must respect the boundaries of existing administrative units, which is another way of saying they must to be drawn *around* administrative units, or pursuing amalgamations of those administrative units such that they are larger than a single electoral district or straddle more than one, would also go a long way toward undoing the conditions that make GBC possible.

Early work on clientelism called for scholars to "move beyond the current focus on structures and institutions" (Kitschelt and Wilkinson 2007, 6). Indeed, this call is understandable because the institutions that were the focus of their analyses bore little correlation to the clientelistic practices they were observing. Nevertheless, the seeds of a research agenda focused on the aspect of a country's political institutions identified in my theory, *overlap*, are found throughout the literature on clientelism, in any study that makes use of disaggregated vote counts or documents the prevalence of club goods or transfers targetable at groups (e.g., Cooperman 2024; Gottlieb and Larreguy 2020; Gottlieb et al. 2019; Rueda 2017; Medina and Stokes 2007; Scheiner 2006). The findings of this book lead me to urge anyone interested in the question of how politicians engage in the selective distribution of benefits around the time of elections to consider whether the institutions in their country of interest are conducive to GBC, and if so, to collect evidence that would enable them to evaluate whether or not it is a component of politicians' electoral strategies. Once this research has been carried out on numerous countries, we will have the tools to examine whether, conditional on meeting the conditions for GBC (overlap), it is always pursued by politicians, or whether the degree to which it plays a role in politicians' electoral strategies is contingent on the presence of other institutions, such as a particular electoral system.

3.5 Contributions

3.5.2 New Ideas about the Role of Brokers

The main conclusion emanating from the vast sub-genre of clientelism research that looks at brokers is that in countries where clientelistic practices are observed, politicians are nowhere without their brokers (e.g., Ravanilla, Haim and Hicken 2022; Brierley and Nathan 2021; Larreguy, Marshall and Querubín 2016; Holland and Palmer-Rubin 2015; Stokes et al. 2013; Baldwin 2013). Brokers are thought to play a critical role helping politicians sustain their clientelistic electoral strategies, first by helping them identify who to buy votes from and second by helping them discern which voters they bought votes from actually held up their end of bargain and voted for the politician on election day.

When politicians are pursuing GBC, however, how a given individual within their electoral district voted will no longer be their primary concern. Because politicians are buying support from groups, not votes from individuals, I expect they will have less of a need for the intimate knowledge and surveillance of individual voters that brokers in many settings are presumed to carry out. When politicians are pursuing GBC, their main concerns will likely boil down to how to create an equilibrium in which voters understand that the amount of resources their group receives will be contingent on its level of support for the politician, on the one hand, and how to harness the resources available to them to generate bite-sized goodies that can be channeled at the groups in their electoral district, on the other. In a democracy, creating the perception that one's access to resources is contingent on how one votes has to be done in subtle ways that avoid raising red flags that the integrity of voting is being undermined. In settings where GBC is occurring, then we expect that the main function of brokers will be to help politicians with these two tasks. It is perhaps the settings in which politicians are *unable* to pursue GBC – again, this is likely be to be a function of the configuration of political institutions – that the main function of brokers is to anticipate and monitor individual votes.

In support of this, recent research has unearthed findings that are difficult to square with the claim that brokers are employed mainly for their ability to anticipate and monitor individual votes. Brierley and Nathan (2021) conducted a large-scale voter survey in Ghana. Some of their respondents were employed as brokers, while some were not. Comparing brokers with non-brokers, they found that brokers only had slightly more information about the voting intentions of their fellow voters than non-brokers. Moreover, brokers did not have noticeably deeper ties with their fellow voters than non-brokers and were not more politically active during or after election campaigns than non-brokers. On balance, they found that if anything, brokers appeared to have stronger ties *upward* (to local elites, defined as local party leaders, bureaucrats, and politicians), rather than *downward* (to voters). They acknowledge that their findings are hard to reconcile with the idea that brokers are agents of *politicians*, helping them anticipate and monitor votes. Instead, they suggest that, at least in the Ghanaian context, brokers might be agents of *voters*, helping them identify and secure resources from their politician benefactor.[16]

Baldwin (2013)'s research in Zambia lends further credence to the possibility that brokers might be helping with the task of *delivering goods*, not with the task of inferring individual votes. She argues that in settings characterized by low state capacity, voters attach great value to politicians who can bring home central government resources in the form of infrastructure projects and the like. In these settings, she posits that the main function of brokers ("patrons," in her terminology) is to help politicians bring to fruition the projects for which they secure funding.[17] The help brokers provide likely ranges from identifying problems in the local community that need to be addressed, organizing local resources, and ensuring buy in from the community for projects. In short, brokers "serve as the technology by which local goods and services are demanded and delivered" (Baldwin 2013, 795). She reasons, in turn, that voters are more likely to believe that their elected representatives will be able to bring funds to the community if those representatives have good ties with brokers. She finds that elections tend to turn on which candidates have managed to secure the backing of the broker, and winning candidates with that backing end up providing more local public goods.

The theory offered in this book helps us see that the role of brokers may be systematically different in settings where GBC is possible, relative to settings where it is not possible. Once we have established that politicians are engaging in GBC, future scholarship should subject this hypothesis to rigorous empirical scrutiny. The fact that all three types of the club goods politicians generally have access to require the identification of projects in a community, for which funds can be granted, and two require communities to put together proposals for projects ahead of time (project-based funds and supra-national funds, respectively), imply that elected representatives will need *someone* to help them with this task. That someone may be the broker.

---

[16] However, Ravanilla, Haim and Hicken (2022) conducted a similar survey in the Philippines and found evidence that was more in line with the possibility that brokers are agents of politicians.

[17] Essentially, patrons play the role that bureaucrats might play in a setting with higher state capacity.

3.5 Contributions

3.5.3 Clientelism Occurring at High Levels of Development

The assumption that politicians are buying votes from individuals, combined with the observation that politicians do not try to buy votes from all individuals, led scholars to ponder the question of which types of voters politicians try to pull into clientelistic exchanges. This produced an early consensus that poverty was a critical factor (Brusco, Nazareno, and Stokes 2004; Chubb 1982). From a politician's perspective, the weight of a poor person's vote is equivalent to the weight of a wealthy person's vote, but cheaper to buy. The politician knows that the poor voter is likely to surrender her vote for less (in terms of resources) than the wealthy voter, making it far more expedient to target the former (Hicken 2011).

It follows that as economic development proceeds and incomes rise, voters will require more and more resources in exchange for their vote and may even develop an antipathy toward clientelism on account of its perceived damage to the integrity of their country's democracy (Weitz-Shapiro 2014). Businesses, too, can be expected to start resenting the corrupt practices associated with clientelism and begin to lend their support to politicians championing reforms to clean up the state apparatuses facilitating it (Kuo 2018). At a certain point, the literature suggests that politicians will decide to walk away from clientelism in favor of alternative electoral strategies that do not encompass such explicit quid pro quos. In support of this, research shows that within countries, it is the poorer voters who are more likely to end up in clientelistic exchanges with their politicians, and across countries, it is the poorer countries that supply the bulk of evidence of clientelism (e.g., Golden and Nazrullaeva 2023; Kitschelt and Wilkinson 2007; Calvo and Murillo 2004; Scott 1972).

As I have explained, GBC is an electoral strategy, which means it is designed to help politicians win elections and reduce uncertainty surrounding reelection. It is safe to assume that these goals are shared by politicians everywhere. In my theory, the main factor determining whether a given politician will alight on GBC as a means of mobilizing votes is whether the political institutions under which she is competing afford her the ability to observe her vote share at a disaggregated level within her electoral district and deliver resources to that same level. In principle, then, providing that these institutional conditions are met, GBC is possible at varying levels of economic development, provided that the pool of resources controlled by the central government and disbursed by politicians in exchange for electoral support is sizeable enough to be of interest to the jurisdictions at which votes are counted and resources targetable.

At low levels of economic development, resources commanded by the central government will likely be of interest to almost all of the lower-tier administrative entities. As countries become wealthier, the degree of attractiveness of those resources will become a function of their value, relative to the value of the administrative entity's autonomous revenue. Looking around the world, we can see plenty of examples of countries at the highest echelons of economic development that nevertheless have a relatively large number of lower-tier administrative entities that lack robust revenue streams, whether due to a weak local economy, rules surrounding taxation, or economic shocks such as natural disasters or mismanagement. While the question of how politicians will go about tying the amount of resources groups receive to their voting behavior is the subject of Chapter 4, we expect that when politicians are cultivating clientelistic relationships with groups, groups with the *least* robust autonomous revenue sources will be disproportionately represented among the groups at the *highest* echelons of electoral support for the politician.

Viewed in this light, then, the theory of GBC expects that shifts in a country's wealth, international standing, or technological prowess will not be sufficient to shift politicians away from this electoral strategy, unless they are accompanied either by reforms that end politicians' ability to observe their vote shares at a disaggregated unit within the electoral district and target resources to those units, or a situation where the lower-tier units become so wealthy that the resources commanded by the central government are no longer of interest. This, too, represents a proposition that should be subject to rigorous empirical scrutiny in future work.

3.5.4 Democracy Is Undermined, But by Club Goods

Studies widely credited for laying the foundation for the modern-day study of clientelism did not conceive of it as a relationship limited to politicians and individual voters (e.g., Kitschelt and Wilkinson 2007; Medina and Stokes 2007; Hicken 2011). Nevertheless, somewhere along the way, scholars began to restrict their focus, theoretically and empirically, to individual-based clientelism. In doing so, they ran up against the reality that virtually all democracies today safeguard the right of voters to cast their ballots in secret. This means that politicians cannot enforce the terms of any clientelistic bargain struck with individuals. Because individuals can always renege on such a deal, politicians can shower material goods on individuals during election campaigns, and they can do so with an eye to influencing how those individuals vote, but they will not be able to even *discern* whether a given individual has held up her end of the bargain and voted for the politician, let alone *retaliate* against anyone

3.5 Contributions

who reneges. Thus, the practice of showering material goods on individuals during election campaigns, documented all over the world in a variety of capacities, does not, strictly speaking, satisfy the requirements of clientelism.

One might think there is little to be gained from quibbling over definitions. Why does it matter if a practice that does not fit the definition of clientelism continues to be given this moniker? It matters because the exchange of material goods for electoral support poses a graver threat to the integrity of a country's democracy than the practice of treating voters with material largess in the *hope* this influences how they vote. The latter practice might unfairly advantage politicians with more largess to deliver and could end up amounting to a colossal waste of government resources, but fundamentally, the recipients of that largess retain the right to rebuff the politician's attempts to influence them and will suffer few consequence for doing so. This is not the case with the former practice. With real clientelism, voters know that they will only receive certain resources or avoid having their resources taken away if they cast their vote correctly. This means that its consequences for democracy and democratic accountability are more troubling. For this reason, it is important to delineate a politician's attempt to *tie* the provision of material goods to how people vote (the original definition of clientelism, which embodies contingency) from a politician's attempt to use material goods to *try to influence* how people vote (the more catch-all definition of clientelism in recent work).

Once we reinstate contingency as *the* component that differentiates electoral strategies based on the selective targeting of material goods, we can see that attempts to *buy* levels of electoral support from groups in a politician's district (GBC) poses a graver threat to democracy than attempts to *treat* individuals with material goods in the hope that this wins the politician more votes (the "clientelism-adjacent" strategies characteristic of the clientelism literature today). By extension, this means that a whole category of material goods that scholars have assumed posed *less* of a threat to democracy – club goods – may be posing a much bigger threat than we realized. The flip side of this is that the mode of distribution scholars have been most troubled by, essentially any good given to an individual by a politician who seeks a vote, may be posing less of a threat than we realized. To this end, we urge future scholars to devote more attention to the possibility that, conditional on their country of interest meeting the conditions for GBC, politicians are pursuing it. This will entail investigating whether club goods are being used clientelistically. We also urge future scholars to engage in a more considered comparison of the downsides of all electoral strategies involving the use of material goods to influence votes, those embodying contingency and those not.

4

Second Prize Is a Set of Steak Knives

We're adding a little something to this week's sales contest ... first prize is a Cadillac El Dorado ... second prize is a set of steak knives. Third prize is: you're fired (line from the film "Glengarry Glen Ross").

In Chapter 3, I argued that whenever politicians can observe their vote shares at a disaggregated unit within their electoral district and deliver resources to the same unit, they will have incentives to pursue group-based clientelism (GBC). This is an electoral strategy in which politicians make the amount of resources received by groups in their electoral district contingent on how each group votes. From the perspective of a politician seeking reelection, I explained why this electoral strategy has clear advantages over one that seeks to use the targeted distribution of material benefits to influence the vote choices of individual voters. Because GBC undermines voter autonomy, restricts voter choice, and reverses the accountability relationship at the heart of democracy, such that *voters* become accountable to *politicians* and not the other way around, I exhorted researchers around the globe to devote concerted effort to classifying countries in accordance with whether or not they meet the institutional conditions for GBC, and in those that do, examining whether allocations of group-level benefits in those countries bear the hallmarks of GBC.

In this chapter, I turn to the question of *how* politicians do this. What exactly do I mean when I say that under certain conditions, politicians can cultivate clientelistic relationships with groups of voters? There are many different ways this could be done. Consider an incumbent politician who contests elections in an electoral district in which all voters reside in one (and only one) of ten groups (let us call these "municipalities"), all of which are perfectly contained within the electoral district. After elections, local electoral commissions in each municipality publish the number of registered voters residing in their municipality, as well as the number of votes cast for each of the electoral district's candidates in the municipality. Because municipalities are also lower-tier administrative entities to which central government resources can be delivered, and some of those resources are distributed at the discretion of bureaucrats (and thus, can be influenced by politicians), the conditions for GBC in this scenario are met: Namely, the politician can observe the amount of electoral support she received from each group, and she can use her influence over the allocation of those resources to steer money toward groups she wants to reward and deny them to groups she wants to penalize.

In this setting, a politician interested in cultivating a clientelistic relationship with these ten groups could do so in a variety of ways. One possibility is that she decides ahead of time on a target vote share she wants to receive from each group and communicates, presumably through her brokers, that all groups meeting their target will be rewarded with a set amount of government resources after the election, while any group not meeting the target will receive nothing. The target vote shares could be the same for each group, or tailored to a group's past performance, where "performance" refers to level of support the group delivered the politician in a prior election. Alternatively, the politician could communicate that any group that manages to return a higher level of support for her than it did in the previous election will be rewarded with more resources, while any group whose support was found not to have exceeded its prior level misses out. Yet another possibility is if the politician decides that the amount of resources each group receives after the election will be a function of the share of her votes that came from that municipality, such that a group contributing 20% of the politician's total votes would end up receiving 20% of the resources the politician had to deliver, and so on.

In this chapter, I do not consider every possible way in which resources can be tied to support, as there are many. Instead, I focus on elucidating one way, which I argue that members of a party widely expected to win the next election – a "dominant party" – are likely to choose. This aspect of my argument is drawn from the formal models offered in a series of studies that should be widely credited as introducing the "tournament theory" to political science (Smith, Bueno de Mesquita and LaGatta 2017; Smith and Bueno de Mesquita 2019, 2012). These works offer rationalist microfoundations that clearly explain why this electoral strategy is so attractive from the perspective of the reelection-seeking politician. One of the purposes of this book is to flesh out the main implications of these models in the most intuitive way possible, so that the advantages tournaments offer politicians and the mechanics of how they can be pulled off in different settings can be better understood by political scientists.[1] An earlier study considered the applicability of these models in the real-world setting of Japan between 1980 and 2000 (Catalinac, Bueno de Mesquita and Smith 2020). This book picks up where that study left off, expanding the range of implications tested, the types of evidence gathered, and the time period examined. In tandem with that earlier work, the aim is to help lay a theoretical and empirical groundwork upon which researchers can devote serious attention to the possibility that tournaments are occurring in their countries of interest.

The central insight of these studies is that when there is low uncertainty surrounding who is going to win the next election, the politicians projected to win will be able to win the most votes, conditional on resources delivered, by pitting the groups in their electoral district against each other in a competition for resources. As Chapter 3 made clear, a necessary condition for politicians to be able to do this is that electoral districts are divisible into groups of voters, from whom electoral support is observable and to whom resources are targetable (that is, the conditions for GBC are met). In such a competition, a "tournament," the politician creates the perception that groups will be ranked according to their loyalty in the most recent election and prizes, in the form of resource allocations, will be awarded on the basis of rank. By making it clear that the highest-ranked group will receive a very large prize, the politician can encourage groups with a chance of achieving this position to compete for it. This drives up the politician's support in groups that are supportive of the politician, creating neck-and-neck competition for first place. Neck-and-neck competition, in turn, creates a situation in which a group's ranking can hinge on a handful of votes. When a handful of votes is enough to change a group's ranking, and a significant increase or decrease in resources awaits any change in rank, voters in these groups will have reason to set aside whatever *personal* feelings they may harbor toward the politician or her policies, and think primarily about the amount of influence their vote wields over their group's prize.

When resource allocations are structured in this manner, sizeable numbers of voters in supportive groups may actually prefer the opposition and its policies but will draw the line at using *their votes* to elect them. Instead, they will reason that, given that the incumbent politician's reelection is so likely, they are better off using their votes to make sure their group attains as many resources as possible after the election. For some voters, this will mean using their vote to *defend* the high rank their group attained last time, while for others, it will mean using their vote to try to *improve* the rank attained last time. In this way, the incumbent is able to make

---

[1] As such, I do not reproduce the formal models in these studies, but rather, flesh out the intuition behind several of their implications.

the costs of voting for anyone other than herself unpalatable for sizeable share of the electorate. Many voters may want the opposition elected but with other people's votes. This is likely to have profound consequences for the political system. When incumbents are using tournaments to win, it will be very hard for the opposition to make inroads. No matter how popular their policy platforms are with ordinary voters, or how unpopular the incumbent's policy platform is, opposition parties will find it nearly impossible to defray the costs of voting for them, which have been imposed on voters by the incumbent. As such, opposition parties are likely to find it extraordinarily difficult to unseat the incumbent.

In Chapter 3, I argued that under the right conditions, it makes more sense for politicians to cultivate clientelistic relationships with groups of voters, not individual voters. One reason why prior work has not paid enough attention to the possibility that politicians were doing this is likely because buying support from groups imposes a *collective action* problem on each group (Morton 1991). Namely, if a politician wants a target number of votes from each group, somebody within the group has to be responsible for gathering those votes. Absent a powerful incentive or sanction, group members have incentives *not* to vote, on the grounds that their vote adds a single vote to their group's tally and thus has a minuscule effect on whether it meets the target. Thus, while GBC might solve one problem (politician's inability to observe individual votes), it would seem to introduce another (how group leaders can overcome the collective action problem). When politicians are conducting tournaments, however, this problem is solved. How? By structuring resources so that the highest-ranked group gets significantly more than the second-highest-ranked group, even when it is within striking distance of that first group, and maintaining this structure of resources all the way down, as groups drop in rank, politicians can essentially *reach inside groups* and give *individual group members* a reason to vote for her. Under a tournament, the prize structure *itself* presents a solution to the collective action problem.

In what follows, I explain what tournaments are, when they are likely to be adopted and how they can be structured to maximize support for a politician seeking reelection. I then derive six testable hypotheses pertaining to resource allocations and turnout rates in Lower House elections in Japan, 1980–2014. These hypotheses, examined in subsequent chapters, help us ascertain whether or not LDP politicians use tournaments to win elections. Just as I did with the theory of GBC in Chapter 3, I then identify longstanding areas of interest in the distributive politics literature, such as why politicians tend to direct resources at "core supporters" when it makes more sense to direct them at "swing voters" and elucidate the tournament's implications for each.

4.1 THE TOURNAMENT THEORY

The genesis of the tournament theory lies in labor economics. Lazear and Rosen (1981) showed that employers could elicit high levels of worker productivity by proposing a contest for a prize for the most productive worker. Under the simplest contest-based compensation scheme, workers are ranked in accordance with their productivity and the worker at the top of the ranking, judged to be most productive, wins the prize while the others miss out. An alternative compensation scheme, output-calibrated compensation, is one in which workers' compensation is calibrated to be proportional to their output. The main difference between the two is that under contest-based compensation, what matters is a worker's *rank*, not how *close* workers came to one another. A worker ranked second could be within striking distance of the worker who ranked first, but under contest-based compensation, would receive nothing. Her compensation would thus not be significantly different from a worker whose performance placed her at the very bottom of the ranking. Under output-calibrated compensation, in contrast, it is not rank that matters, but *output*. The worker judged to be most productive still receives the most compensation, but those closing in on her productivity levels would receive only slightly less. Workers whose productivity places them at the bottom of the ranking would receive significantly less than a worker in second place.

Lazear and Rosen (1981) used a formal model to show that contest-based compensation schemes boost worker productivity. Their study also drew attention to the fact that the salary differentials of executives at many large corporations already reflected these incentives. Why else, the authors asked, would a vice president promoted to company president find her salary tripling overnight? It is not the case that the value she adds to the company as president has increased threefold in a single day. It *is* consistent, however, with the notion that the promotion is a *prize* she has won in a *contest* among vice presidents, presumably over who has contributed the most to the company's profits. By constructing such a promotion and dangling the possibility of winning it over the heads of a pool of employees, companies can extract high levels of effort from those employees. As this example suggests, such differentials in salary structure are not calibrated to reward *output* but to elicit high levels of effort from workers over the entirety of their working lives.

Galanter and Palay (1991) used these insights to explain the rise of the "big American law firm." The authors point out that the standard practice in many law firms is to admit a group of associates each year and tell them that, in addition to their annual wages, their performance

4.1 The Tournament Theory

over a fixed number of years will be evaluated for a "super-bonus" of promotion to partner. This prize, associates are told, will be bestowed on a small number of associates on the basis of their productivity, defined as the quality of their legal work and accumulated human capital. In this "promotion-to-partner" tournament, associates are ranked. Those at the very top of the ranking are awarded the prize, while the others are all let go, although the authors point out that as long as the compensation differential between winners and losers is kept large, those missing out do not need to be fired. A key insight of their study is that as long as promotion-to-partner tournaments are the preferred means of boosting worker productivity, firms grow exponentially. They grow first and foremost because the pool of associates has to be replenished every year to replace those promoted to partner; but they also grow because the pool of associates itself has to grow each year to match growth in the partner pool, so as to make sure there are always enough associates competing for every promotion (Galanter and Palay 1991, chapter 5).

In political science, Bruce Bueno de Mesquita and Alastair Smith were the first to harness these insights to consider whether contest-based compensation schemes could be useful for incumbents seeking reelection (Smith and Bueno de Mesquita 2012, 2019; Smith, Bueno de Mesquita and LaGatta 2017). The formal models in this work, as well as expectations of those models that were fleshed out and subject to empirical testing in Catalinac, Bueno de Mesquita and Smith (2020), collectively make up what I refer to as "tournament theory" in this book. The starting point of their work was the observation that the situation facing *employers* is not entirely unlike the situation facing *incumbents*. Employers are concerned with maximizing firm productivity and want a compensation scheme that will elicit the highest level of effort from their employees. Incumbents, on the other hand, are concerned with maximizing their chances of reelection. One of their biggest fears, the authors conjecture, is that the people who supported them in the last election will decide to sit out the next election. Incumbents have this concern partly because of what is known as the paradox of voting (Fedderson 2004; Geys 2006). This is the notion that voting is costly, in that it takes time and requires effort, and the probability that a single voter will cast a decisive vote, meaning one that determines who wins the election, is negligible. It follows that incumbents, like employers, need a compensation scheme that minimizes shirking, where for them, shirking means not turning out to support them.

Schwartz (1987) had a similar insight. He explained that even though a single voter is rarely pivotal when it comes to who wins the election, a single voter *can* be pivotal (or at least, more pivotal) on other dimensions.

The dimension he examined was which candidate garnered the most votes in the voter's precinct or other subelectoral district jurisdiction. Because of the decentralized way in which votes tend to be counted in the democratic world, voters are more likely to be pivotal on this dimension – which candidate *carries* his or her subdistrict jurisdiction – than on the dimension of which candidate *wins* the election. Describing a voter in a mayoral election, Schwartz (1987) writes "if votes are pooled and counted citywide ... her vote would count for nought. But votes are not pooled and counted citywide; they are counted separately for each of the many small voting precincts" (Schwartz 1987, 104). This gives the individual voter a "nonnegligible" chance of determining which candidate *carries* her subdistrict jurisdiction. This might matter, the author conjectures, when distributive benefits such as "road repairs, snow removal, police patrols and the like" can be targeted at these same subdistrict jurisdictions. It is possible that incumbents could use the selective distribution and removal of these benefits to subdistrict jurisdictions within the broader electoral district to motivate voters who know their vote is unlikely to influence the outcome of the election to turn out and support them.

Expanding on this, the tournament theory holds that one way in which reelection-seeking incumbents can motivate their supporters to turn out and vote for them is by making the allocation of resources to the group in which the supporter resides (her "subelectorate") contingent on the level of electoral support the group provides. Moreover, rather than setting a target vote share for each group and awarding resources to all groups that meet that target, or doling out resources in proportion to the size of each group's contribution to one's total vote share, incumbents can elicit the highest levels of support by making groups compete for those resources, in exactly the same manner employers have their workers compete for promotions. To administer such a tournament, a necessary condition is that the incumbent's electoral district is divided into subelectorates from which levels of support – namely, vote totals – are discernible. A second necessary condition is that the incumbent has sufficient clout to influence resource allocations in ways that disproportionately benefit certain subelectorates over others.

How, exactly, can subelectorates be made to compete? Consider an incumbent member of the ruling party whose district is divided into two subelectorates, each of which contains a similar number of voters. In this setting, the incumbent can elicit the highest levels of support from both groups by proposing a contest for a prize for the subelectorate that provides the most votes. The "prize" could be money for a project such as a new hospital, community center, train station or park, which will benefit everyone in the group. Or it could be some amount of a central government transfer that the subelectorate is free to spend however it likes. After the election, the incumbent would simply observe her vote totals in each of the subelectorates, rank them on the basis of number of votes delivered, and award the prize to the subelectorate ranked first.

In developed democracies, allocations of central government resources are usually the purview of central government bureaucrats. It is rare that incumbent politicians have pots of money they can dole out at their discretion. How, then, could an incumbent go about "awarding" the subelectorate placing first with a "prize"? The balance of evidence suggests that the preferred way in which incumbents, particularly those in the ruling party, influence government resources is by leaning on bureaucrats to fund certain projects over others (e.g., Rickard 2018; Saito 2010; Horiuchi and Saito 2003; Ramseyer and Rosenbluth 1993). It follows that an incumbent who wants to reward a particular subelectorate for its performance in a given election would simply lobby the bureaucracy on behalf of that subelectorate and not lobby the bureaucracy on the behalf of other subelectorates. If the incumbent is a member of the ruling party, then we can expect that the cumulative output of this lobbying will be more money for that subelectorate at the expense of the others. Rickard (2018) explains why delegating decisions over the allocation of targetable government resources to the bureaucracy, thereby keeping any influence wielded by incumbents over the process out of the public's view, is an effective means of insulating politicians from excessive rent-seeking behavior. She writes "they can exert control over the allocations of subsidies for electoral gain and at the same time they can 'scapegoat' bureaucrats for unpopular decisions" (Rickard 2018, 188).

Making the amount of resources a subelectorate receives contingent on its rank, and denying resources to the subelectorate that did not attain that rank, has the effect of galvanizing voters in both subelectorates to actively compete for first place. This drives up the incumbent's vote share in both subelectorates, which helps her gather the votes she needs to win. This is akin to the way a promotion-to-partner tournament drives up the law firm's profits, as pools of associates strive to be among the precious few chosen for promotion. Importantly, positioning a subelectorate's access to resources on its performance in elections has the effect of raising the stakes of voting considerably. While a single vote continues to hold virtually no sway over who wins the election, it has been made to hold considerably more sway over the amount of resources a voter's subelectorate receives. This is because structuring resources like this induces neck-and-neck competition for first place. This neck-and-neck competition, in turn, reduces the number of votes that are needed to *change* a subelectorate's ranking. When a subelectorate's position in the ranking can be changed with a handful of votes, and a very large resource allocation awaits the subelectorate placing first, individual votes are suddenly much more pivotal than they would be in the absence of a tournament.

To use Schwartz (1987)'s terminology, the tournament works by creating an "alternative dimension" upon which votes are pivotal. Incumbents can raise (or lower) the stakes of voting even further by adjusting the value of the prize. This will have the effect of further increasing (or decreasing) the level of electoral support she receives from the two subelectorates. If an incumbent desires a very high level of electoral support, she can offer a very large prize. Voters will be even less likely to shirk (stay home on election day) because none of them will want to be the reason their subelectorate misses out on winning this large prize. If the incumbent is content with merely *beating* her opponent, on the other hand, and seeks a more modest level of electoral support, she can offer a smaller prize, but one she knows will be sufficient to generate the competition necessary to put her level of electoral support over the threshold for winning. Because government resources are usually scarce, and more money for prizes means less money for other things, we can assume that on balance, incumbents will prefer prizes that are just large enough to guarantee their reelection, and nothing more.

The formal models in the body of work making up the theory make it clear that alternative compensation schemes that incumbents in this setting could adopt are inferior to a tournament. This is because they do not *magnify* the influence of a single vote in the same way. For example, an incumbent could offer to tailor the amount of resources a subelectorate receives to its contribution to her reelection. Returning to labor economics, this would be akin to tailoring a worker's compensation to their output. The incumbent could take the number of votes provided by each subelectorate and calculate the proportion of her vote total that came from each. Then, she could divvy up any government resources she has access to, including her attempts to influence those allocations through lobbying, to match those proportions. Under this scheme, a subelectorate contributing 35% of her votes could expect to receive 35% of resources allocated.

While this might appear to be a more straightforward way of using geographically targetable resources to motivate individuals to turn out and vote for you, it can be shown that this produces a smaller vote yield, conditional upon resources allocated, than could be realized with a tournament. This is because under output-calibrated compensation, voters know that the amount of resources their subelectorate will receive after the election will hardly be affected by whether *they*, personally,

4.1 The Tournament Theory

make the effort to vote. If a voter's subelectorate contributed 20% of the incumbent's votes in a previous election, which entitled it to 20% of any resources the incumbent had to deliver, then a single voter is likely to reason that if she stays home on election day, her subelectorate's contribution to the incumbent's vote total will be virtually unchanged. By extension, her subelectorate's resource allocation will also be virtually unchanged. Her subelectorate's access to resources is not positioned on a knife edge the way it is with a tournament, in which tiny numbers of votes can translate into very large differences in rewards.

From this example, we can see that the problem is not that one voter will make this calculation, it is that *many* voters probably will. A non-negligible number of voters are likely to reason that, if they stay home on election day, the amount of resources their subelectorate stands to receive after the election will only be slightly less than if they had voted. These sorts of calculations risk imperiling an incumbent's reelection prospects. Even if the incumbent is so far ahead of her competitors that she does not need to worry about losing, doling out resources on the basis of each subelectorate's contribution to her reelection will lead to a lower level of support, conditional upon resources allocated, than that which could be achieved by making subelectorates compete. Incumbents using output-calibrated compensation thus need to offer much larger prizes to try to overcome the fact that many voters will stay at home. Or they need to outsource the problem of motivating voters to turn out and vote for them to the leaders of each subelectorate.

In practice, incumbents are not usually seeking reelection in electoral districts that are perfectly divided into two subelectorates with similar numbers of voters. What happens when incumbents are in electoral districts comprised of numerous subelectorates, each of which has a different number of voters? In this setting, the tournament theory expects that contest-based compensation can still be used to elicit high levels of support, but incumbents will structure it slightly differently. Rather than pitting two subelectorates against each other in a single competition for a single prize, it behooves incumbents to create multiple competitions between pairs of subelectorates. Concretely, incumbents in these districts will be able to elicit high levels of support by promising to award a prize to the subelectorate placing first, a much smaller prize to the subelectorate placing second, an even smaller prize to the subelectorate placing third, and so on. The contest structure of the compensation can be maintained by calibrating the *size* of the prize so that the subelectorates vying for first place are fighting over a much larger prize than the subelectorates vying for second place, which are in turn fighting over a larger prize than the subelectorates vying for third place, and so on.

Second Prize Is a Set of Steak Knives

A scene from the 1992 movie Glengarry Glen Ross, starring Alec Baldwin, nicely captures the intuition behind this prize structure. Four real estate salesmen are paid a visit by a representative from the corporate office (Baldwin), who declares "we're adding a little something to this month's sales contest." He then announces that he plans to observe them all for a week, after which two will be fired. In one of the film's most famous scenes, he announces that first prize in the contest is "a Cadillac El Dorado," second prize is "a set of steak knives," and third prize is "you're fired." In this contest, the prize for first place is exponentially larger than the prize for second place, and those placing third or fourth do not get prizes. This prize structure has the effect of galvanizing all four salesmen to go to extreme lengths to be one of the two winners left standing at the end of the week. This is the kind of prize structure the tournament theory envisions for incumbents operating in districts with numerous differently sized subelectorates.

Above, I explained how a tournament consisting of a single competition between two same-sized subelectorates raises the stakes of voting considerably. Because no voter wants to be the reason their subelectorate is ranked second and misses out on the prize, voters will be more motivated to turn out and vote for the incumbent than they would be in the absence of such a competition. Conducting multiple competitions between pairs of differently sized subelectorates, in which the size of the prize being fought over becomes smaller at lower ranks, raises the stakes of voting in a *heterogeneous* fashion across subelectorates. The use of a tournament in which a subelectorate's resource allocation is contingent on its rank already raises the stakes of voting in all subelectorates, relative to no tournament. But in this setting, voters in subelectorates with a shot of placing *first* are competing for a much larger – indeed, an *exponentially* larger – prize than their peers in subelectorates that anticipate placing lower in the ranking. Thus, the stakes of voting are exponentially larger for voters in subelectorates that anticipate placing at the top of the ranking. This means that their incentives to turn out and support the incumbent are also exponentially larger.

In sum, an incumbent who ranks the subelectorates in her electoral district on the basis of their relative levels of support, awards prizes based on rank, and calibrates the size of those prizes such that the amounts being fought over at higher ranks are larger than the amounts being fought over at lower ranks, creates a setting in which relatively small differences in support between groups – handfuls of votes, in some cases – can translate into relatively large differences in rewards. This magnifies the influence of a single vote. Whereas a single vote is rarely pivotal when

4.1 *The Tournament Theory*

it comes to deciding who wins the election, a single vote *can* be pivotal when it comes to deciding how many resources a voter's subelectorate receives. The influence of a single vote is magnified to the greatest degree in subelectorates projected to perform well in the tournament.

For incumbents, a tournament offers a means of using contest-based compensation to motivate one's supporters to turn out to vote for them, election after election, irrespective of the degree to which a given election is forecast to be competitive. The theory expects that incumbents will choose contest-based compensation whenever they can, on the grounds that positioning a subelectorate's access to resources on a knife edge – thereby giving voters reason to turn out and vote for them – enables incumbents desiring a given level of support to expend fewer resources than under alternative schemes. As I explained above, if the incumbent relied on output-calibrated compensation, she would need to promise a very large resource allocation initially, which would later be used to compute each subelectorate's share of resources, based on their contribution of votes. A very large resource allocation would be needed to compensate for the fact that no subelectorate's allocation is poised on a knife edge in the same way, which means that unless a very large reward is promised, many voters would sit the election out.

Alternatively, if the incumbent sets a target level of support that she wants from each subelectorate and promises to reward all the subelectorates that meet it, she would need to offer a reward large enough to encourage people to turn out, but if it was too large, she would run the risk of many subelectorates meeting it, which would require an exorbitantly large amount of resources. Contest-based compensation schemes are cheaper because the *same* prize is used to motivate more than one subelectorate. Under target-based compensation schemes, *all* subelectorates that meet the target would expect to be paid, requiring the use of more resources.

Critically, while tournaments offer an attractive means of mobilizing votes for all incumbents, they are less likely to be an effective electoral strategy for incumbents whose reelection prospects are uncertain. When an incumbent's reelection prospects are uncertain, she will find it harder to create the perception that resource allocations to a voter's subelectorate are poised on a knife edge and convince voters to act on that perception. This is not only because people will not know if she will be around to dole out spoils after the election but also because the fact that her reelection prospects are uncertain gives voters a modicum of influence over who wins the election that they lack in a situation in which the incumbent's reelection is a foregone conclusion. It is the perception that one's vote *cannot* influence the outcome of the election, because the incumbent is likely to win, that makes voters susceptible to being primed to think only about their subelectorate's resource allocation.

4.2 TOURNAMENTS IN MANY ELECTORAL DISTRICTS

We have seen that in electoral districts that satisfy the conditions for GBC and have relatively uncompetitive races, incumbents have incentives to pit groups against each other in the tournament. Let us now turn to a different question: How do the tournaments conducted in different electoral districts compare to each other? The theory expects that while the nature of the tournaments conducted in different electoral districts will be similar, more money will be delivered to some districts over others, creating a distinct pattern of resource allocations across districts.

To elaborate, the tournament theory holds that the amount of resources needed to garner a given level of support in an electoral district will vary systematically with the ease with which a tournament can be administered. What do I mean by "ease?" A feature of an electoral district that makes a tournament difficult to administer is heterogeneity in the size of subelectorates (the "contestants" in the tournament). Pitting differently sized subelectorates against each other in the same competition for resources is like pitting workers doing completely different jobs against each other in the same competition for promotion. Intuitively, holding a contest between a pool of law firm associates is easier than holding a contest between those associates, IT support staff, personal assistants, and janitors. I have already pointed out that whenever subelectorates are not the same size, incumbents will gain from splitting a single competition for a prize into numerous competitions between pairs of subelectorates, in which the size of the prize increases with rank in a convex manner. It turns out that heterogeneity in subelectorate size not only influences how a tournament is administered but also the *size* of the prizes offered. Incumbents in electoral districts in which subelectorates vary greatly in size have to expend more money for a given level of support than their counterparts in districts where subelectorates vary less in size.

To see why, it helps to recall that, unlike employers who might have few qualms advocating a compensation scheme that promises to boost their firm's profits, incumbents are unlikely to make their use of a tournament explicit. This is because using government resources to buy votes, which is what tournaments boil down to, is not in keeping with the tenets of democracy, for the reasons discussed in Chapter 3 (Stokes et al.

4.2 Tournaments in Many Electoral Districts

2013). In a democracy, *voters* are supposed to be able to hold *incumbents* accountable for their behavior, not the other way around (Stokes 2005). Dangling the promise of central government resources over the heads of voters, to be granted on the condition that they demonstrate fealty to the incumbent in an election, overturns the principle that voters should not be held accountable for their votes. It risks trapping voters in a situation where casting an "expressive vote," meaning a vote for a party whose policies the voter may support, becomes much riskier. If a voter votes for the opposition but the incumbent is reelected, then the voter has not only jeopardized her subelectorate's access to needed resources, but she has also opened her group up to reprisal by an incumbent intent on dissuading her and others from voting this way again. It is unsurprising that many voters in this situation will think twice before casting expressive votes, which leads to an unfair advantage for incumbents.

All of which is to say: Incumbents are unlikely to make their use of a tournament explicit. Any understanding between incumbent and voter that resources will be allocated in this manner is likely to be *implicit*. The tournament theory expects that this implicitness will create ambiguities in how the performance of subelectorates will be compared to each other and how the ranking of subelectorates will be determined. Critically, while this ambiguity exists in all electoral districts, it is expected to have more pernicious consequences, in terms of dampening voter incentives to turn out and support the incumbent, in electoral districts where subelectorates are asymmetrically sized. As a result, the theory expects that incumbents in "asymmetric districts" will be forced to offer larger prizes for a given level of support than their counterparts in districts with less asymmetrically sized subelectorates, where the same ambiguity exists, but has less serious consequences.

It is worth unpacking this expectation with a concrete example. Let us consider two straightforward methods of ranking subelectorates. One, the *Number of Votes* metric, ranks subelectorates in terms of the raw number of votes they supplied to the incumbent. Another, the *Vote Share* metric, ranks subelectorates in terms of the share of subelectorate's voting population who voted for the incumbent. When a district's subelectorates are exactly the same size, the same set of vote totals produces the same ordering under both metrics. To see this, consider District A, which consists of two subelectorates, each consisting of 50,000 voters. One supplies 31,000 votes for the incumbent, while the other supplies 30,900. On the Number of Votes metric, the first subelectorate wins the tournament (31,000 votes to 30,900). On the Vote Share metric, the first subelectorate also wins (62% of its voters voted for the incumbent, compared to 61.8%

in the other subelectorate). Regardless of metric, for a given set of vote totals, the ordering is the same: the first subelectorate wins.

When subelectorates are asymmetrically sized, in contrast, the two metrics no longer produce the same ordering for a given set of vote totals. Consider District B, which consists of two subelectorates, one with 80,000 voters and the other with 40,000. The former supplies 35,000 votes for the incumbent, while the latter supplies 31,000. On the Number of Votes metric, the first subelectorate wins the tournament (35,000 votes to 31,000). On the Vote Share metric, in contrast, the second subelectorate wins (77.5% of its voters voted for the incumbent, compared to 44% in the first subelectorate). The fact that incumbents cannot easily clarify which metric they will use to construct the ranking, and the fact that different metrics produce different orderings for the same vote totals, complicates voters' ability to calculate how many votes are needed to change the ranking. Because voters find it more difficult to calibrate how many more votes would increase their subelectorate's rank (or how many *fewer* votes would *decrease* it), the amount of influence their vote holds over the size of their subelectorate's prize is unclear. Hence, their incentives to turn out are diminished.

Returning to this example, in District A, where both subelectorates have 50,000 voters, the ranking of subelectorates can be changed with just 101 votes, regardless of metric. If the second subelectorate cast an additional 101 votes for the incumbent, it would have 31,001 votes overall, which exceeds the first subelectorate on *both* the Number of Votes Metric (31,001 to 31,000 votes) *and* on the Vote Share metric (62.002% to 62%). In District B, on the other hand, the number of votes required to change the ranking differs significantly depending on metric. Under the Number of Votes metric, the first subelectorate is ranked first (35,000 to 31,000). To change the ranking, the second subelectorate needs an additional 4,001 votes. Under the Vote Share metric, in contrast, the second subelectorate is ranked first (77.5% to 44%). To change the ranking, the first subelectorate needs to increase its share of voters who voted for the incumbent from 44% (35,000) to in excess of 77.5% (more than 62,000 votes). At minimum, then, the first subelectorate needs an extra 27,001 votes (77.501% of voters) to change the ranking and put itself in the lead.

In District A, then, the same subelectorate wins regardless of metric, and the same number of votes is needed to change the ranking regardless of metric. In District B, the first subelectorate wins under one metric, while the second subelectorate wins under the other. The number of votes needed to change the ranking *differs* based on metric. Because incumbents

4.2 Tournaments in Many Electoral Districts

cannot make their use of a tournament explicit, voters will not know which metric the incumbent plans to use to rank subelectorates. This ambiguity does not matter in District A, but it does matter in District B. In District B, voters cannot calculate the amount of influence their vote holds over the size of their subelectorate's resource allocation. This matters because it is this influence – the fact that one's vote could *significantly* alter the amount of resources their subelectorate receives – that generates the high level of support for the incumbent that makes a tournament attractive. When subelectorates are asymmetrically sized, the theory expects that incumbents can still conduct a tournament but will need to offer larger prizes to offset the heightened incentives voters have to stay at home. Depending on the ease with which they can access resources, incumbents in electoral districts with asymmetrically sized municipalities are likely to settle for lower levels of electoral support. But to win those, they will likely still need to deliver larger prizes.

It is prudent to pause and consider the question: In electoral districts where subelectorates vary greatly in size, would it not make sense for incumbents to jettison the use of a tournament altogether, in favor of buying votes from the *larger* subelectorate only? In the above example, the first subelectorate in District B contains twice as many voters as the second. Why would a savvy incumbent not decide to concentrate her vote-gathering on the *larger* subelectorate, on account of the fact that it contains more voters?

As soon as an incumbent restricts her vote-gathering to a narrower set of subelectorates, she diminishes the incentives of voters in *all* subelectorates to turn out and vote for her, relative to a situation where she conducts a tournament between all subelectorates. This is because, in narrowing the set of subelectorates from whom she seeks votes, she is creating a situation in which many voters lose the incentive to vote for her. Voters in the smaller subelectorates are unlikely to vote for her because they will see that her vote-seeking (and thus, any resources that flow from that vote-seeking) are being concentrated on the larger subelectorates. Yet in the larger subelectorates, too, the incentive to vote is diminished because voters know that their group will receive a large prize, irrespective of whether they make the effort to vote. As we saw in my discussion of output-calibrated compensation above, many voters are likely to make these calculations and stay home. The incumbent would *again* be placed in a position where she is forced to offset the likelihood of abstentions in the larger subelectorate with larger prizes. But she could get away with smaller prizes if she conducted the tournament between *all* subelectorates, large *and* small.

4.3 HYPOTHESES

In Chapter 5, I explain that many electoral districts used in Japan's Lower House elections meet the conditions for a tournament. These conditions are: One, incumbents can discern relative levels of support from different subelectorates; two, incumbents can influence the allocation of central government resources to those subelectorates; and three, there is a dominant party, meaning low uncertainty over who will win the next election. Thus, tournaments have likely been an overlooked component of the electoral strategies of politicians from Japan's dominant party, the Liberal Democratic Party (LDP). To examine this possibility, I use the theory to derive six hypotheses for what we would observe about the world if LDP politicians were conducting tournaments.[2]

The first two hypotheses concern the distribution of resources to subelectorates within electoral districts. These are examined in Chapter 6. In Japan's case, the relevant subelectorates are municipalities. If LDP politicians are administering tournaments between municipalities, then the amount of money that municipalities receive after Lower House elections will be a function of their position in a rank ordering of municipalities in the same electoral district, constructed on the basis of the share of eligible voters in the municipality who voted for the politician. We will also find that the largest sums of money will have accrued to the municipalities whose level of support put them in first place, after which the amounts awarded to each municipality in the same electoral district will decline with rank not in a linear fashion, but in a *convex* fashion. This would indicate that LDP politicians made the amounts of money being fought over larger at higher ranks. This is a critical piece of evidence that distinguishes a tournament from output-calibrated compensation, which I explained above. In sum, the hypotheses tested in Chapter 6 are as follows:

- **Hypothesis 1**: Within electoral districts, resource allocations are a function of a municipality's position in a rank ordering of municipalities, constructed on the basis of support for the LDP winner in the most recent election.
- **Hypothesis 2**: Within electoral districts, the impact of increases in rank on a municipality's postelection resource allocation increase as municipalities climb the ranks.

---

[2] Chapter 5 describes the data collected to test these hypotheses. Several of these hypotheses were evaluated with data spanning a shorter time frame in Catalinac, Bueno de Mesquita and Smith (2020).

4.3 Hypotheses

My third and fourth hypotheses concern the distribution of resources and support across electoral districts. These are examined in Chapter 7. If LDP politicians are administering tournaments between the municipalities in their electoral districts, then if we take the *sum* of the postelection resource allocations received by all municipalities within each electoral district, we will find that the total amount of money received by electoral districts is a function of the degree of heterogeneity in size of their municipalities. All else equal, we will observe that districts characterized by a greater degree of asymmetry in municipality size receive larger allocations than districts characterized by less asymmetry in municipality size. This, too, is a critical piece of evidence that helps distinguish the use of a tournament from alternative allocation schemes. Under an alternative allocation scheme such as output-calibrated compensation, we might still observe allocations to municipalities within districts being a function of electoral support (Hypothesis 1), but we would have little reason to expect that the degree of asymmetry in municipality size would exert a decisive impact on the total amount of money received by the municipalities in each electoral district.

Further, the tournament theory holds that the reason "asymmetric" electoral districts receive more money is because voters will not know how their municipality is going to be compared to other municipalities in the same district (politicians will have difficulty clarifying this), so will not be able to *calibrate* the degree of influence their vote wields over the size of their municipality's prize in the same way as they can in other districts. Anticipating that their support is likely to be *lower* in asymmetric districts for this reason, politicians have incentives to offer a larger prize (as we just explained). In spite of this larger prize, however, we can still expect that politicians will recoup a *lower* level of support in those districts, relative to their counterparts in less asymmetric districts. Why? In asymmetric districts, politicians are working with voters who have drastically reduced incentives to turn out and support them. In other words, they are starting from a much lower baseline level of support, relative to their counterparts in less asymmetric districts. A larger resource allocation will bring support up, but that allocation, usually secured via lobbying bureaucrats, is also costly and requires effort by the politician. Thus, we are likely to observe an equilibrium in which these electoral districts are receiving more money *and* exhibiting less support for the politician. Evidence of this equilibrium, in turn, is further evidence that politicians are conducting tournaments within electoral districts. In sum, the hypotheses tested in Chapter 7 are as follows:

- **Hypothesis 3**: Across electoral districts with LDP winners, resource allocations are a function of the degree of asymmetry in municipality size. All else equal, districts characterized by greater asymmetry in municipality size receive larger resource allocations.
- **Hypothesis 4**: Across electoral districts, support for the LDP is a function of the degree of asymmetry in size of municipalities therein. All else equal, electoral districts characterized by greater asymmetry in municipality size exhibit less support for the LDP.

It is worth mentioning that, if the above four hypotheses are borne out in our data, then this equates to a pattern of spending within electoral districts that is the *reverse* of what happens across electoral districts. Within electoral districts, the expectation is that places (municipalities) exhibiting more support for the LDP politician receive more resources (Hypotheses 1 and 2). But across electoral districts, the expectation is that places (electoral districts) exhibiting more support for the LDP politician receive fewer resources (Hypotheses 3 and 4). Other scholars, too, have noticed that answers to the question of who receives targetable government spending can depend on the level at which data on spending and votes is aggregated (e.g., Albertus 2019). The tournament theory offers rationalist microfoundations for why such different patterns can occur. It is not that politicians are targeting one type of voter at one level and a different type of voter at another level. Politicians are essentially doing the same thing everywhere, but a *third variable*, the degree of asymmetry in municipality size, is exercising an *independent impact* on the baseline level of support politicians are likely to enjoy in their electoral districts, and through that impact on support, changing the amount of *resources* they have to deliver to guarantee victory.

My fifth and sixth hypotheses pertain to voter decisions to turn out. These are examined in Chapter 8. If LDP incumbents are administering tournaments between the municipalities in their electoral districts, then we will find that the share of eligible voters who make the decision to turn out and vote will be function of the municipality's position in a rank ordering of municipalities in the same electoral district, constructed on the basis of support for the politician. More specifically, we will observe higher turnout in municipalities projected to do well in the tournament. This is similar to Hypothesis 1 but examines turnout not resource allocations. Moreover, we will also find that the impact of increases in rank on voter decisions to turn out and vote will increase as municipalities' projected position in the ranking increases. This is similar to Hypothesis 2 but examines turnout not resource allocations. In sum, the hypotheses tested in Chapter 8 are as follows:

- **Hypothesis 5**: Within electoral districts, turnout rates are a function of a municipality's position in a rank ordering of municipalities, constructed on the basis of support for the LDP winner in the most recent election.
- **Hypothesis 6**: Within electoral districts, the impact of increases in rank on turnout in a municipality increases as municipalities climb the ranks.

4.4 IMPLICATIONS

In Chapter 3, I explained how the GBC theory contributes new insights to four areas of interest to clientelism scholars. These insights were that political institutions matter more than we realized, brokers' roles might be qualitatively different in settings where politicians conduct GBC, high levels of economic development may not dampen politicians' enthusiasm for GBC, and allocations of club goods may be posing more of a threat to democracy than we realized. In the rest of this chapter, I explain how the form GBC is likely to take when there is a dominant party, a tournament, also has implications for longstanding areas of interest in comparative politics.

4.4.1 Raising the Costs of Voting for the Opposition

A vast literature ponders the question of why people vote, given the probability that a single vote will influence the outcome is virtually nil. For the average voter, the costs of voting (having to travel to a polling station, familiarize oneself with the candidates or parties on the ballot, and wait in line) vastly outweigh any benefits they can expect. In spite of these costs, many people vote. This is known as the paradox of voting (Fedderson 2004; Geys 2006). The tournament theory and GBC more generally join a subgenre of research on voting, which holds that people vote because politicians in control of central government resources have found ways to offset the costs of voting with targeted material benefits, one of which is "pork," defined as club goods that are bestowed on everyone in a given group of voters.[3] Pork usually takes the form of geographically focused

---

[3] For an introduction to the literature on pork-barreling, see Jensenius and Chhibber (2023); Malik (2023); Motolinia (2021); de Kadt and Lieberman (2020); Rickard (2018); Harris and Posner (2019); McMichael (2018); Kramon (2017); Catalinac (2015); Funk and Gathmann (2013); Saito (2010); Tavits (2009); Golden and Picci (2008); Magaloni (2006); Diaz-Cayeros, Estévez and Magaloni (2016); Golden and Picci (2008); Nichter (2008); Huber and Ting (2013); Dixit and Londregan (1996); Hirano (2006); Lee (2004); Horiuchi and Saito (2003); Dahlberg and Johansson (2002); McCubbins and Rosenbluth (1995); and Ward and John (1999).

benefits, such as new libraries, community centers, roads, or parks, the beautification of beaches or train stations, or the extension of train lines.

The tournament theory offers an original take on the question of *how* targeted material benefits can be deployed to maximize the incentives of voters to turn out and support politicians who are widely expected to win the next election. As I explained, politicians whose reelection chances are high can deploy material benefits most effectively by promising to allocate them according to a group's position in a rank ordering of groups in the same electoral district, constructed on the basis of support for the incumbent. By making it known that the largest prize will accrue to the group ranking first, the second-largest prize to the group ranking second, and so on, and making the difference in size of the prize largest between the first- and second-placed groups, after which it decreases in a convex fashion as groups decline in rank, politicians can create fierce competition for the highest ranks. This fierce competition increases her support in the district, and it also creates a situation in which rankings, at least at the top, tend to hinge on small numbers of votes. When a small number of votes stands between a high rank and a not-so-high rank, and a large resource allocation awaits the group that attains the higher rank, ordinary voters become much more pivotal than they would be in the absence of a tournament. Critically, because the politician's victory is likely, voters are not going to be pivotal when it comes to who wins the election. But because of the step-wise function under which resources are allocated under a tournament, and the particularly steep steps at the top of the stairs, voters become more pivotal when it comes to the rank their municipality attains and as a consequence, the money it receives.

By structuring resources this way, politicians in a dominant party actively dissuade people from voting for anyone other than them. They have created a situation in which people have to put their group's access to resources on the line in order to do so. Because the differences in amounts of money received at different ranks are largest at the highest ranks, meaning that the difference in amounts received by the first- and second-placed groups will be much larger than the difference in amounts received by the fifth- and sixth-placed groups, for example, people in groups with a chance of attaining a high rank are particularly dissuaded from voting for anyone other than the politician slated to win. Voters in these groups have to turn their backs on a very large sum of money in order to vote for anyone other than her. In this way, the *pressure* on voters to support the politician slated to win the election is not evenly distributed across groups and is more severe in groups that are ordinarily quite supportive of the politician. People in those groups have the least incentive to translate whatever policy preferences they have into their

4.4 Implications

actual voting behavior. They may want someone else elected, but with *other people's votes*, not theirs.

In this way, tournaments have profound consequences for the political system. When politicians in a dominant party are using tournaments, opposition parties will struggle. No matter how popular their policy platforms are, or how *unpopular* the dominant party's policy platform is, they will not be able to win unless they can find a way to defray the costs the dominant party has imposed on voters for voting for them. Opposition parties will thus find it extraordinarily difficult to win enough votes to unseat the incumbent. Their best shot of gaining power might be appealing to politicians in the dominant party who are unhappy with the widespread use of such an electoral strategy and all it entails, and using relationships with those individuals to try to chip away at the dominant party's seat majority.

4.4.2 Policy Positions Matter Little to Incumbent Reelection

Correspondingly, when politicians in a dominant party are using tournaments, they know that factors such as the popularity of their policy positions or conduct in office matter far less than their ability to convert government resources into bite-sized pieces of different sizes that can be channeled to groups in their electoral districts as a function of support. So long as they can keep this up, they know that they will be able to stave off most threats to their reelection, whether they originate in dissatisfaction with their policies or the rise of new, reform-minded opposition parties. This means that when it comes to formulating policy, tournament-reliant politicians will be less constrained than politicians whose policy positions played a bigger role in getting them elected. After elections, the tournament-reliant politician will be able to point to the election results as evidence of her numerous supporters in the electoral district, who, she can plausibly argue, have given her a mandate to formulate policies as their agent. Importantly, however, this masks the fact that the bulk of her support is not coming from voters who liked her *policies*, but from voters who reasoned that, given the incumbent will be elected anyway, they may as well make their group a priority when it comes to *resources*.

4.4.3 Money Flows to Core Supporters

Above, I mentioned that a subgenre of research on voting holds that people vote because politicians use targeted material benefits to offset the cost of voting. In this literature, there is debate over *who* politicians will deliver these targeted material benefits to. Stokes (2005) and Dixit and

Londregan (1996) are the studies most closely associated with the idea that incumbent politicians will focus resources on "swing voters," defined as voters with less rigid preferences for one party over another. Stokes (2005) considers a setting in which incumbent politicians (in her parlance, "machines") have ways to circumvent the secret ballot and deduce how individuals cast their votes. She points out that an incumbent's core supporters, defined as voters with fairly rigid preferences for the incumbent, cannot credibly commit to voting for someone else. Thus, it makes little sense for an incumbent to waste precious resources on them. It also makes little sense for the incumbent to focus resources on "strong opponents," defined as voters whose preferences for the opposition are similarly rigid, on the grounds that it is possible that no amount of money would persuade them to switch their vote to the incumbent. Instead, in the setting she examines, she argues that it makes sense for incumbents to target resources at voters "in the middle of the distribution of partisan predispositions: ones who are indifferent about whether to vote for or against the machine" (Stokes 2005, 323).

Dixit and Londregan (1996) consider a different setting, one in which an incumbent politician cannot infer how individuals vote and is seeking reelection in a single-seat district (SSD) consisting of multiple groups of voters. In their model, voters have preferences over one of two parties but can be induced to switch their votes to the party they do not currently support in exchange for geographically targeted resources. The amount of resources an incumbent needs to deliver to induce someone to vote for her is assumed to be a function of how tightly wedded the voter is to the other party. The model also assumes that incumbents vary in the amount of information they possess about what it would take for a given individual in each group to vote for them. When the amount of information incumbents possess about individuals is the *same* across groups, meaning they have no "special relationship" with the voters in any given group, the model shows that focusing geographically targeted resources on groups with higher concentrations of "swing voters" is the most effective electoral strategy. Targeting groups with swing voters minimizes the possibility that resources are wasted, either on voters who would have voted for the incumbent anyway, or on voters for whom no amount of resources would induce them to change their minds and vote for the incumbent (Dahlberg and Johansson 2002; Lindbeck and Weibull 1987).

Conversely, an incumbent who does possess a strong relationship with voters in some of these groups will have relatively good information about what type of benefits are likely to sway them. Under this second scenario, Dixit and Londregan (1996), as well as an earlier model by Cox

4.4 *Implications*

and McCubbins (1986), show that an incumbent politician has incentives to focus geographically targeted resources on groups with higher concentrations of "core supporters" (see also Zarazaga 2016). The extra information incumbents have about what those voters in those groups wants enables them to avoid the possibility that, in trying to buy votes from swing voters by targeting resources at groups with more swing voters (the first scenario), their efforts will miss the mark and fail to woo those swing voters. In their models, an incumbent with core supporters will get the most electoral bang for her buck by focusing resources on core supporters. This differs from the prediction in Stokes (2005)'s model, which is that incumbents with core supporters will avoid focusing resources on them, on account of the fact that they would receive their votes anyway. Empirical evidence that incumbents focus geographically targeted resources on core supporters, defined as places where the incumbent garnered a disproportionately high vote share in the previous election, include Tavits (2009) and Rickard (2018, chapter 7).

These foundational studies on the question of who receives targeted material benefits sparked a rich literature on the "core supporters-versus-swing voters" debate. Much of this work boils down to trying to explain why incumbents would ever choose to focus resources on core supporters when those voters would have voted for them anyway. At least three distinct answers can be discerned. Nichter (2008) argued that because parties cannot observe how individuals vote, they will never be able to verify whether someone they gave money to in exchange for their vote actually voted for them on election day. Thus, it makes little sense for a party to use money to buy votes, which he defines as persuading people to switch their vote to the incumbent. Instead, they will use money to "buy turnout," meaning entice its core supporters to turn out, with the expectation that once they are at the polling station, they will vote for the party. This is because whether someone shows up at the polls is verifiable. His empirical tests line up with the claim that parties concentrate resources on core supporters, but he acknowledges the difficulties of substantiating his assertion that this is to make sure they turn out.

Magaloni (2006) offers a second answer. She argues that one of the central ingredients in the longevity of Mexico's Institutional Revolutionary Party (PRI) – a "hegemonic party" in her parlance – was its funneling of resources toward core supporters whom it judged were most "vulnerable" to defection to an opposition party in an upcoming election. Her analysis revealed that allocations under the poverty-relief program Programa Nacional de Solidaridad (PRONASOL) were governed by a political logic under which allocations were denied to places that were already governed by the opposition and concentrated in places that were former bastions of support for the PRI, but whose support had waned in a recent election (Magaloni 2006, chapter 4). By spending more on municipalities in which support for the PRI was "wavering" and less on municipalities that continued to support the PRI in large numbers, the PRI was using PRONASOL to halt further deteriorations in support.

A third answer is that politicians concentrate resources on core supporters to deter them from withdrawing their support for her and coordinating around a new candidate, either from their party or another party. Cox (2009) argues that observed instances of "splintering" might be rare, but they pose an ever-present threat to incumbents, particularly "if the group threatening to split has some chance of forcing a re-coordination of the party system and emerging as the dominant party in its ideological niche" (Cox 2009, 350). Making sure the lion's share of government resources is kept in the hands of one's core supporters minimizes the incentives of those voters to coordinate around a new candidate or party. This rationale for why incumbents target core supporters features prominently in work on geographically targeted spending under proportional representation (PR) electoral systems. McGillivray (2004) argues that under closed-list PR, incumbent parties carve out policies designed to bind their core supporters more tightly to them, rather than policies designed to expand their appeal to new voters. Because new parties can be created relatively easily under PR, parties remain fearful of appearing to alienate their core supporters with appeals to new sets of voters, whose interests may appear to conflict with those of their core supporters. Golden and Picci (2008) offer a similar rationale for why legislators prioritize core supporters under open-list PR.

The tournament theory offers a distinctive answer to this debate. As we explained, politicians administering tournaments will end up delivering the most money to the groups in their electoral districts that exhibited the most electoral support. This is observationally equivalent to targeting one's core supporters. Critically, however, politicians are not *targeting* any particular *type* of voter on the basis of an ascriptive characteristic such as strength of attachment to the incumbent. Rather, the incumbent is *rewarding* groups that won a competition over which group is the most supportive. She is steering these rewards to groups without regard to who lives in each group. The largest reward could just as easily have gone to a group full of people who had never voted for her before and disliked her intensely, *if* voters in that group had swallowed their dislike for her and voted for her in large numbers. Conversely, a group filled with an incumbent's most die-hard supporters would have to

4.4 Implications

settle for last place in resource allocations if many of them had decided to sit out the last election.

4.4.4 All Groups Are Subject to the Same Competition

The idea that under a tournament, no *specific* group is targeted, and politicians essentially treat all groups in their electoral district in the *same* manner, subjecting them to the *same* competition, differs from claims made in a strand of clientelism literature that has begun to consider how allocations of group-level benefits can buy levels of support from groups. Gottlieb and Larreguy (2020), for example, argue that when politicians have access to transfers targetable at groups (e.g., villages) and the party system is not institutionalized, they have incentives to direct transfers toward groups with a "high coordination capacity," which vote as a bloc. These transfers are intended to persuade the group to continue voting (en masse) for the politician from whom they receive transfers or to switch to voting (en masse) for this politician from a different one. In related work, the authors argue that when incumbents face increased competition and need support from many groups, they will offer different things to different groups (Gottlieb et al. 2019). To groups they have a track record of providing transfers to (because, for example, the group votes as a bloc), promises to deliver local public goods are credible and will suffice as a means of winning votes. To groups the politician does not have a track record of providing transfers to, incumbents must make a credible commitment to their welfare. To do this, they embrace a different strategy: They create a new administrative unit for the group.

What these studies have in common is the idea that politicians use ascriptive characteristics of a group to decide whether to try to buy support from it, and conditional upon deciding to do so, deploy those same ascriptive characteristics to determine what to offer each group in return for support. Essentially, this mirrors a central claim in work on individual-based clientelism, discussed in Chapter 3. This claim is that politicians use ascriptive characteristics of individuals, such as income or partisanship, to decide whether to try to buy their votes, and conditional upon deciding to do so, deploy those same ascriptive characteristics to decide what to offer in return and how much. In contrast, politicians administering tournaments do not look around their electoral district and weigh up which groups to pull into the tournament on account of their ascriptive characteristics. This is because tournaments work best when *all* groups are subject to the *same* competition, and the sole determinant of the size of the prize groups receive is their position in the ranking.

As such, tournaments work best by making ascriptive characteristics of groups *immaterial* to whether or not they will be subject to a competition, what they will be offered in return for support, and how much they will be offered. The fact that group-level characteristics do not determine whether a group is included in the tournament and how much it receives is not to say that a group's ascriptive characteristics will have no bearing on how it *fares* in the tournament. Because groups will likely vary in their *need* for the resources the politician has to offer, in the same manner as individuals vary in their need for the goods proffered by politicians, then we may observe groups that place a higher value on the resources politicians have to offer, perhaps because of ascriptive characteristics such as strength of the local economy, being overrepresented among the groups returning the highest levels of support for the incumbent. However, this is not because politicians have decided to buy support from the needier groups only, eschewing the wealthier groups, but because that need made voters in the needy groups even less willing to put their group's access to resources on the line by voting for the opposition. In other words, these groups are likely to score highly in the tournament because the voters within them are less willing to resist the pressure placed on them by the incumbent.

4.4.5 Resource Allocations Take Place after Elections

Tournaments accord with accounts of the inner workings of political machines in the United States (Allen 1993), which depict how machine bosses used the targeted distribution of benefits such as snow plowing to reward neighborhoods that supplied them with lots of votes and penalize neighborhoods that had not. In line with how political machines worked, the tournament theory is unambiguous that allocations happen after elections, once a group's relative rank can be discerned from its voting behavior. This claim puts it at odds with a lot of work on distributive politics. According to Golden and Min (2013, 86), many studies assume that pork is best allocated prior to elections, "so that voters will have the provision of goods and services fresh in their minds when they head to the polls." Evidence that governing parties flood selected areas with construction and other geographically targeted projects in advance of elections, with a view to influencing the number of votes they receive in the election, has been documented in different contexts (Fukumoto, Horiuchi and Tanaka 2020; Denmark 2000; Tavits 2009; Kohno and Nishizawa 1990; Magaloni 2006, chapter 3).

The tournament theory, in contrast, depends on the idea that incumbent politicians can change resource allocations on a whim, for example,

4.4 Implications

after observing the results of a particular election. If it looks like an election had little impact on the allocation of resources to groups within a politician's electoral district, then the theory would expect that this was because the rank order of groups had not been changed by the election. If the group placing first last time had successfully defended the title from its most viable contender (the group that had placed second last time), and there was little change in other groups' positions in the ranking, this would give the impression that resources allocations were unaffected by election results. However, this would not be the correct inference to draw. Resource allocations *are* being impacted by elections, but we only observe decisive shifts in resource allocations when rankings change. An implication of this is that, to the extent that voting behavior is sticky, and groups that rank highly in support of a politician are likely to continue ranking highly, it will be difficult to detect the tournament empirically.

4.4.6 Asymmetry in Group Size Matters

Above, I explained that when tournaments are being carried out in many electoral districts, the degree to which the groups in each electoral district vary in size has profound consequences for both the amount of money politicians have to deliver and the support they receive. When groups are vastly different sizes, I explained that voters will not know how the incumbent plans to construct the ranking. Because the same set of vote totals can produce different rankings, voters will find it difficult to calibrate the degree of influence their vote holds over the size of the prize their group is poised to win. All else equal, this can be expected to *dampen* incentives to turn out and support the incumbent in "asymmetric districts." The theory expects that to increase the incentives of voters to turn out and support them in asymmetric districts, the politician will offer more resources. But because politicians usually have to incur costs to obtain resources, and in most cases, do not automatically receive them, we can expect that politicians may struggle to totally offset the drastically reduced incentives to support them in these districts. As a result, when electoral districts are characterized by variation in group size, and resources are not easily obtainable, we will observe asymmetric districts receiving more money, but exhibiting less support for the incumbent.

Observationally, then, this leads to a pattern of spending across electoral districts that is the *reverse* of what happens within electoral districts. Within districts, the theory expects that money flows to relatively *supportive* groups. Across districts, however, the theory expects that money flows to relatively *unsupportive* electoral districts, where the incumbent's performance was worse. Because the theory also expects that allocations happen after the election, this pattern of spending makes it look like the incumbent is rewarding districts for supplying fewer votes and penalizing districts for supplying more votes. Or, it will look like the incumbent is prioritizing swing districts and ignoring core districts. Importantly, under the theory, she is doing no such thing. Instead, district-level asymmetry is exercising an *independent* effect on the price of votes in each district. Increases in asymmetry drive up the price of votes. Because votes are more expensive in those districts, incumbents buy fewer of them. But because votes are still more expensive there, even if incumbents buy fewer of them, this will still lead to more spending in asymmetric districts than an incumbent can get away with in less asymmetric districts.

We would be less likely to observe this pattern of resources and support across electoral districts if resources were easy to come by. If resources were easy to come by, incumbents in asymmetric districts, who presumably want to get elected just as much as their peers in less-asymmetric districts, would simply deliver the resources needed to increase their support. They may be especially inclined to do this if their overall level of support in the electoral district mattered for other things of value, such as promotion to Cabinet. We would also be less likely to observe this pattern of resources and support if party leaders wielded control over the process through which individual politicians conduct their tournaments, perhaps by serving as a gatekeeper to the bureaucracy. To the extent that party leaders seek a *majority*, and are less concerned with winning every district, and asymmetric districts require larger resource allocations than less asymmetric districts, it would be reasonable, depending on how many asymmetric districts there are and how asymmetrically sized the groups are in those districts, for those leaders to decide to *forgo* trying to win in those districts and concentrate resources on the less asymmetric districts, where votes are cheaper. Viewed in this light, evidence that politicians deliver more resources but receive less support in exchange for those resources in asymmetric districts could also be evidence of the *decentralized* nature of parties and the *weakness* of party leaders.

Now that we have fleshed out implications of the tournament theory for longstanding areas of interest in distributive politics, let us return to the real-world setting in which we plan to test the six hypotheses derived above: Japan, 1980–2014. Is there evidence that politicians in Japan's ruling party are using tournaments to get elected? Can this shed light on the party's extraordinary electoral performance?

5

Perfect Storm Conditions for Tournaments in Japan

In Chapter 3, I argued that when incumbents can discern their vote shares at a disaggregated unit within their electoral districts and influence allocations of central government resources to those units, they will have the tools to pursue an electoral strategy of "group-based clientelism" (GBC). Under GBC, the amount of resources groups receive is tied to the level of support they provide the politician in elections. Whereas scholars have tended to treat the allocation of central government resources to geographically defined groups of voters as a mode of distribution distinct from clientelism, I argue that whenever incumbents are tying the amount of resources groups receive to the level of electoral support provided, such that resources ebb and flow as a function of support, it makes more sense to conceptualize this as a *clientelistic* electoral strategy.

By carving out a clientelistic exchange with groups of voters, whose levels of support can be observed, I explained that incumbents are able to sidestep the myriad problems that arise when clientelistic exchanges are attempted with individual voters, whose votes are never (or hardly ever) observed. The problems GBC solves for the reelection-seeking politician, coupled with the fact that geographically targetable spending is a staple of government budgets in many countries, opens up the possibility that goods ordinarily believed to be *outside* the purview of clientelism – namely, discretionary spending on geographically defined groups of voters, otherwise known as pork-barrel politics – are actually being allocated clientelistically, in ways that tether voters to their incumbents and take away their freedom to vote for whomever they choose. On this basis, I argued that comparative politics scholars interested in elections, pork-barreling, and clientelism should devote serious attention to the possibility that GBC is occurring in their countries of interest. This could either be on a large scale, if all electoral districts meet these conditions, or on a smaller scale, if only a handful of electoral districts do. Either way, it should be studied.

In Chapter 4, I explained that when electoral districts meet the conditions for GBC *and* there is a dominant party, incumbents in this party will be able to get the most bang for their buck – meaning the most *votes*, conditional on *resources* delivered – by converting voting into a *competition* over which groups are the most electorally loyal. This aspect of the book draws on earlier work, both theoretical (Smith and Bueno de Mesquita 2012, 2019) and applied (Catalinac, Bueno de Mesquita and Smith 2020). In such a competition, the incumbent makes it known that she plans to rank groups according to their loyalty in the most recent election and allocate "prizes" (central government resources) on the basis of rank. More specifically, when electoral districts consist of multiple groups, the incumbent can promise the largest prize (the most resources) to the unit that ranks first in electoral loyalty, the second-largest prize to the unit that ranks second, and so on. Moreover, if she makes the difference in size of the prize received by the first and second place-getter larger than the difference in size of the prize received by the second and third place-getter, and so on, she can create a situation in which voters in groups with a chance of placing first will vie for first place. Vying for first place drives up her support in these groups such that neck-and-neck competition ensues. Neck-and-neck competition, in turn, means that group rankings can turn on handfuls of votes. By committing to dispense resources in this manner, the incumbent creates an environment in which voters in supportive groups have reason to set aside whatever personal feelings they may harbor toward her or her policies and reason that, because the incumbent's reelection is very likely, they are better off using their vote to influence the size of their group's prize.

In this book, I provide a blueprint for how researchers should go about testing the theory in their countries of interest. First, a deep dive into the country's political institutions is required, to ascertain whether electoral districts meeting these conditions exist and if so, how many and which ones. As will be clear below, this is not as straightforward as it first appears. It involves the aggregation of subtle information about electoral districts, subnational governance, and the interaction of the two. After this information has been gathered and districts meeting the conditions identified, the researcher should gather data on voting behavior, resource allocations, and other confounding variables for all groups within these (tournament-possible) districts and devise stringent empirical tests capable of pitting the theory's propositions against those of rival theories. This chapter is concerned with the first stage of the empirical strategy, while the tests in Chapters 6–8 implement the second stage.

Perfect Storm Conditions for Tournaments in Japan

The conditions that must be satisfied for politicians to implement GBC (and a tournament) are that electoral districts are divisible into groups of voters, at which electoral support is discernible and resources deliverable. Are these conditions met in Japan? In Section 5.1, I focus on the "observing support" side of the equation. I explain that the laws governing the administration of elections, the drawing up of electoral districts, and subnational governance in Japan create many electoral districts in which candidates in Lower House elections can observe their support at a disaggregated level. This level is the *municipality*. Switching to the "delivering goods" side of the equation, Section 5.2 explains how the fiscal relationship between tiers of government in Japan creates a situation in which municipalities are tasked with many responsibilities yet have insufficient revenue. As a result, the vast majority of Japanese municipalities are highly dependent on transfers from the central government, some of which are allocated at the discretion of central government bureaucrats (Scheiner 2006). I spell out what is publicly known about how one particular fund, national treasury disbursements (NTD), is allocated, and I present evidence that year-to-year allocations are vulnerable to political influence.

In Section 5.3, I explain that the confluence of these laws mean that the conditions for tournaments were satisfied for the vast majority of politicians in Japan's Lower House elections until the 1994 electoral reform. I explain how the redrawing of electoral district boundaries that accompanied the reform, as well as an increase in the raw number of districts (necessitated by the switch from larger, multiseat districts to smaller, single-seat districts [SSDs]), reduced the share of districts in which tournaments are possible from approximately 91% of all districts to approximately 73%. This share was further reduced by municipal mergers, which took place from 2002 until 2006, and ongoing urbanization, such that as of 2014, the last year for which I have data, tournaments were possible in approximately *half* of all Lower House electoral districts.

Finally, I explain that the theory would expect that the creation of more tournament-impossible electoral districts over time has created a *bifurcation* in LDP electoral strategies: LDP candidates in tournament-possible districts conduct tournaments, in which they use the promise of central government resources to buy votes, while their counterparts in tournament-impossible districts do not. While the theory is agnostic about what happens in tournament-*impossible* districts, the balance of theory and evidence suggests that politicians who cannot use tournaments will revert to policy competition and use positions on policy to win. Regardless of what politicians in tournament-impossible districts do, it is reasonable to expect that this bifurcation would manifest itself in qualitatively different election outcomes across the two types of districts. I present simple analyses showing that, controlling for other differences between electoral districts and election years, tournament-possible electoral districts exhibit higher support for LDP candidates, have higher turnout, are more likely to produce LDP winners, and are less likely to see no LDP candidate fielded.[1] At the aggregate level, then, tournaments appear to contribute to LDP election victories. The next three empirical chapters, which focus on municipalities within tournament-possible districts, decipher *how*, exactly, they do this.

5.1 OBSERVING SUPPORT

During the Allied Occupation of Japan (1945–1952), four laws were passed, the combination of which enable candidates to discern relative levels of electoral support from groups in their electoral district. One was the Constitution (1947), which has remained unamended to this day.[2] The Constitution awards sovereignty to the Japanese people, recognizes universal adult suffrage, designates the Diet as the nation's sole lawmaking body, states that the Diet is comprised of two Houses, explains how the House of Representatives (the Lower House) can override the opinion of the House of Councilors (the Upper House) on certain matters and under certain conditions, and includes a host of other stipulations. Importantly, the Constitution stipulates that the electoral system used to select Members of both Houses and the electoral districts in which those Members would compete are to be "fixed by law" (Article 47). The Constitution also provides for a system of local self-government through "local public entities," the details of which would also be "fixed by law."

Also in 1947, Law No. 43 was enacted, which stipulated that the system to be used to elect Members of the Lower House would be what is known in Japan as the "medium-sized district system" (Chusenkyoku Seido). Comparative politics scholars call this "single-non-transferable-vote in multi-member districts" (SNTV-MMD). The law established 117

---

[1] Chapter 6 presents further evidence of this bifurcation with analyses showing that LDP candidates in tournament-possible districts promise more money for their communities in their election manifestos than their counterparts in tournament-impossible districts, and survey evidence showing greater congruence between policy preference and vote choice in tournament-impossible districts than in tournament-possible districts, respectively.

[2] An English translation of the Constitution can be found here: https://japan.kantei.go.jp/constitution_and_government_of_japan/constitution_e.html.

5.1 Observing Support

multimember districts, each of which would elect three, four, or five representatives.[3] Initially, the total number of Members to be elected was set at 466. Law No. 43 also stipulated that voters would have a single vote to cast and the top second, third, fourth, or fifth vote-winners in the district would win a seat, depending on the total number to be elected in that district (district magnitude).[4] Critically, the law upheld another principle that had been a feature of Japanese elections ever since the Meiji Government enacted the very first Lower House Law in 1889.[5] This was the principle that electoral districts would, to the extent possible, respect the boundaries of existing administrative entities (chihou kokyou dantai) (Hayashida 1967, 27).

What are those administrative entities? The Local Autonomy Law, also passed in 1947, stipulates that the units of elected local government are prefectures and municipalities. Prefectures, which cover a much larger area than municipalities, have existed as formal administrative entities since 1878. In 1947, Japan had forty-six prefectures. Since Okinawa was reverted to Japanese control in 1972, Japan has had forty-seven. In 1947, when the Local Autonomy Law was passed, there were more than 10,000 municipalities, which consisted of cities, towns, and villages, respectively.[6] The Act conferred new responsibilities on municipalities, which included providing social welfare and operating junior high schools. Following this, the Law to Promote the Merger of Towns and Villages (1953) and the New Municipality Creation Promotion Law (1956) encouraged smaller villages and towns to merge and new cities to be created, with the goal of enhancing the fiscal and administrative capabilities of municipalities. By 1961, the number of municipalities had fallen to approximately 3,400 (Yokomichi 2007). With minor changes, the number of municipalities stayed at around 3,300 until the 2001–2006 period, when another law encouraging mergers led to further consolidations (Horiuchi and

---

[3] Amami Oshima was added as an electoral district in 1953. It was the only district that elected a single representative (Ward 1966, 552). In 1992, it ceased to exist, with its area being incorporated into Kagoshima 1st District.

[4] The same system, down to the total number of elected representatives, the three-, four-, and five-member districts, and even the boundaries of most electoral districts had been in place from 1925 to 1934 (Ward 1966).

[5] Prior to the promulgation of the 1947 Constitution, sovereignty had been vested in the Emperor. However, the Meiji Government, which ruled after the Meiji Restoration (1868) and was the architect of the extraordinary modernization program that took place in this period, declared that it intended to decide matters on the basis of public opinion, and to this end, had established elected bodies.

[6] As part of Japan's modernization, a 1889 law had established cities, towns, and villages as local administrative units, appointing them responsibilities that included levying taxes and operating elementary schools.

Saito 2003). By 2006, the number of municipalities had been whittled down to approximately 1,800, and this number remains only slightly less today. For the duration of our study (1980–2014), there have been four types of municipalities: cities, special wards (administrative units within the Tokyo metropolitan area), towns, and villages.[7] The Local Autonomy Law stipulates that regardless of type, all municipalities are to be headed by a mayor (or chief) and assembly. Separately elected, mayors and assembly members are both appointed to four-year terms (conditional on not losing their positions due to dissolution or no-confidence motion).

The fourth law of interest to us, also passed during the Occupation, was the Public Office Election Law (POEL), enacted in 1950. This is a lengthy law that details almost every rule imaginable pertaining to elections to Japan's Lower House, Upper House, prefectural governor and prefectural assemblies, and municipal mayor and municipal assemblies (McElwain 2008).[8] The law assigns two important functions to municipalities. One is the responsibility of *administering elections*, which involves managing the voter roll (senkyonin meibo), establishing polling stations (touhyoujo), advertising the location of polling stations ahead of time, and facilitating voting on election day (Chapter 3, Article 17). The other is the responsibility of counting the votes cast and reporting the vote tallies to the Election Chief (Senkyo Cho), an individual charged with receiving the results and reporting them (Chapter 3, Article 18).[9] To carry out these tasks, municipalities establish Election Management Commissions (Senkyo Kanri Iinkai), which appoint individuals to serve in the roles of Presiding Officer for Voting (Tohyou Kanrisha), Witnesses to Voting (Touhyou Tachiainin), Presiding Officer for Counting (Kaihyou Kanrisha), and Witnesses to Counting (Kaihyou Tachiainin), respectively.

---

[7] Cities with populations greater than 500,000 can be a "designated city" (seirei shitei toshi). This is discussed further below. Since 1996, cities with populations greater than 200,000 can be designed a "core city." Until 2015, a further designation, that of "special city" (tokureishi) was also used.

[8] The law (Koshoku Senkyo Hou) can be found at https://elaws.e-gov.go.jp/document?lawid=325AC1000000100.

[9] Strictly speaking, the law assigns the responsibility of administering the election to a "Vote Casting Unit" (Touhyouku) and the responsibility of counting the votes to a "Vote Counting Unit" (Kaihyouku). But it says that those units are coterminous with a municipality, unless there are extenuating circumstances. A circumstance mentioned is when different sections of a municipality are located in different electoral districts. I discuss this further below.

5.1 Observing Support

5.1.1 How Votes Are Counted

According to the POEL, voting takes place in the following manner. On election day, voters go to one of the polling stations administered by their municipality's Election Management Commission to cast their vote.[10] Each polling station is overseen by a Presiding Officer for Voting and between two and five Witnesses to Voting. Voters go into a private booth (tohyoukisaidai) by themselves. On a government-issued ballot, they are instructed to write the name of the candidate or party, depending on the election in which they are voting (Chapter 6, Article 46).[11] At 8 p.m., the time polling stations are scheduled to close, the Presiding Officer fastens the door to the polling station and closes the ballot box (touhyoubako), after which no additional votes may be added (Chapter 6, Article 53). The Presiding Officer for Voting, together with at least one Witness to Voting, are responsible for transporting the closed ballot boxes to the physical location at which they will be counted, which the municipality has designated ahead of time.[12] The Law suggests that votes be counted at the municipal office (Shiyakusho or Choson Yakuba) but also says that municipalities can designate another place, if necessary (Chapter 7, Article 63).

After every ballot box has arrived, the Presiding Officer for Counting and Witnesses to Counting oversee the process by which votes are counted. First, these individuals open the ballot boxes and decide whether or not to "accept" the votes brought to them by the Presiding Officer and Witnesses to Voting (Chapter 7, Article 66). Second, they take the votes from polling stations in the municipality, as well as votes from polling stations that had been established for the purpose of early voting in the municipality, and *mix them together* (kondo suru), making sure to keep votes cast for different elections – for example, the SSD tier and the proportional representation (PR) tier, which are held simultaneously –

---

[10] Many municipalities mail registered voters pamphlets explaining where the polling stations will be located on election day and an entrance ticket with the voter's name on it (nyuujoken). Designed to speed up the process of verifying voters' identity on election day, these entrance tickets are not required of voters. In the event a voter shows up without one, voters are encouraged to use their driver's license or other identification to verify their identity.

[11] Japan introduced the secret ballot for the first time in 1900. The right to vote in secret is enshrined in the Constitution and mentioned in the POEL (Hayashida 1967). In Lower House elections, Japan uses "voting in your own handwriting" (jishoshiki touhyou).

[12] Strictly speaking, votes are transported to the place the Vote Counting Unit (see the above footnote) has designated as the physical location at which votes will be counted. But the Vote Counting Unit *is* the municipality, unless the municipality has established more than one Vote Counting Unit.

separate.[13] After this mixing, counting ensues. After the count is over, the Presiding Officer for Counting, after having consulted with the Witnesses and secured their consent, reports the tally of votes won by candidate or party to the Chief Election Officer (Chapter 8, Article 75).[14]

Christensen and Colvin (2009) studied the occurrence of "election-night corruption" in Japan, Canada, and the United States. They argue that this type of corruption happens when communities can delay the reporting of results. This enables corrupt election administrators to observe other communities' returns, calculate how many extra votes their preferred candidate needs to win, and manufacture those votes. The authors find no evidence of this in Japan, and they attribute this to five factors: the fact that laws governing election administration are codified in national law (and are not under the control of elected leaders at the local level); the fact that members of local Election Management Commissions are selected in municipal assemblies by public vote; the fact that candidates can nominate Witnesses to Counting; the fact that counting does not begin until all ballot boxes designated to be counted at that polling station have arrived; and the fact that votes from different polling stations are mixed together before counting, respectively (Christensen and Colvin 2009, 213).

In sum, these four laws create a situation where, in elections to Japan's most-powerful legislative body, voters cast their votes in the municipality in which they live and the vast majority of municipalities are perfectly nested within a single electoral district. For incumbents competing in these districts, the fact that votes are counted and reported at the level of the municipality means that they can easily discern the number of votes they received in each municipality in their district. The flip side of these rules is that incumbents *cannot* discern their vote totals at a more disaggregated level within each municipality, such as the neighborhood, precinct, or polling station.[15] Indeed, in a frequently asked question (FAQ) section of its website, Atsugi City's Election Management Commission explains that the mixing of votes from different polling stations is a

---

[13] Municipalities may be comprised of more than one Vote Counting Unit. As I described above, this tends to happens when sections of a municipality span more than one electoral district. Municipalities with more than one Vote Counting Unit can count votes for these different Units in the same physical location. Under these circumstances, the Presiding Officer and Witnesses for Counting have to be careful not to mix votes from polling stations in one Vote Counting Unit with votes from polling stations in a different Vote Counting Unit.

[14] More information about the Chief Election Officer's role can be found here: www.soumu.go.jp/senkyo/senkyo_s/naruhodo/naruhodo06.html#chapter4.

[15] The inability of politicians to discern their vote totals at a more disaggregated level within each municipality is discussed in Curtis (1971).

5.1 Observing Support

tactic designed to safeguard the secrecy of the ballot. As such, the Commission emphasizes that it cannot provide breakdowns of candidate or party votes at a more granular level because these are not available.[16]

5.1.2 How the Level at Which Support Is Discernible Varies

How has the level at which politicians can discern their support in Lower House elections varied across electoral districts and election? We can answer this question by looking at the number of municipalities in each electoral district. This book focuses on the 1980–2014 period. From 1980 until 1994, the relatively *large* number of municipalities (approximately 3,300) and relatively *small* number of (multimember) electoral districts (initially 117, but rising to as many as 131 as new districts were created to cope with the growth of the electorate in large cities) meant that the average electoral district consisted of twenty-six whole municipalities. The fewest municipalities in an electoral district was 2 and the greatest was 64. During this period, only four municipalities in total (out of approximately 3,300) spanned more than one district.[17]

In 1994, Japan reformed its electoral system, introducing a mixed-member majoritarian (MMM) system comprised of two tiers. One tier consisted of 300 SSDs, from which a single candidate was elected via first-past-the-post and the other tier consisted of 11 regional blocs, from which 200 members were elected according to closed-list proportional-representation. My focus is on districts in the first (SSD) tier.[18] Since then, the number of electoral districts in this tier was decreased to 295 and is now 289, while the number of seats in the second tier was also decreased, first to 180. Today, it is 176. Critically for our purpose, the principle that electoral districts should respect the borders of existing administrative entities was maintained.

To draw up the 300 new electoral districts in 1994, the government created a Deliberative Council, which consisted of seven members, who were appointed by the Prime Minister and assented to by the Houses.[19] The law establishing the Council charged it with drawing up the new electoral districts in a "rational" fashion, taking into account the need to respect the borders of existing "administrative entities" (gyosei kukaku) and the need to keep the vote-seat disparity across electoral districts to

[16] See www.city.atsugi.kanagawa.jp/soshiki/senkyokanriiinkai/2/2021.html.
[17] These were Koriyama City in Fukushima prefecture, Chiba City's Midori Ward, Okayama City, and in the 1990 election, Osaka's Chuo Ward.
[18] For research on districts in the PR tier, see Catalinac and Motolinia (2021*b*).
[19] The Deliberative Council was established with the Law for the Establishment of a Deliberative Council for the Demarcation of House of Representatives Election Districts. This can be found here: https://elaws.e-gov.go.jp/document?lawid=406AC0000000003_20160527_428AC0000000049.

two or under, respectively (Article 3).[20] To this end, the Council was given an explicit mandate to consult with local government bodies (Article 8). After drawing up the boundaries, the Council was required to submit them to the Prime Minister, who would present them to both Houses. If agreed upon, they would appear as Appendix One of the revised POEL.[21] Between 1994, when the electoral system was reformed, until the 2003 election, the average electoral district contained twelve whole municipalities. The fewest number of municipalities in a district was 1 and the greatest was 42. Of the approximately 3,300 municipalities in existence at this time, the number that spanned more than one district was fifteen in 1996 and 2000 and seventeen in 2003.

In 1999, as part of a decentralization drive that began in the mid 1990s, the government embarked on a plan to encourage municipalities to undertake mergers by the end of the 2005 fiscal year (Yokomichi 2007; Yamada 2016; Yamada and Arai 2021). The officially stated objectives of the plan were couched in rationalization terms: The central government wanted municipalities to become more self-reliant, so that the money it was having to distribute in the form of intergovernmental transfers each year could be reduced (Horiuchi, Saito and Yamada 2015, 113). By 2005, many municipalities had taken the government up on its offer, which reduced the total number of municipalities to approximately 1,800. Of the 3,252 municipalities that existed as of January 2000, 1,992 (61%) of them underwent mergers, while the remaining 1,260 municipalities stayed, borders intact (Horiuchi, Saito and Yamada 2015, 100). Since 2005, the average electoral district has contained seven municipalities. The fewest number of municipalities in a district was 1 and the greatest, 34. In addition, the number of municipalities spanning more than one electoral district increased. It was fifty-one in 2005, eighty-five in 2009, eighty-eight in 2012, and eighty-five in 2014, respectively.

The distribution in Number of Municipalities Per Electoral District across these three periods is displayed in Figure 5.1. Two patterns are evident. One is that as time goes on, the average electoral district has consisted of fewer municipalities. Another is that as time goes on, variation in the number of municipalities per district has declined.

---

[20] According to Reed (1995, 1077), requiring that the wishes of local government bodies be respected in the drawing up of the new electoral districts made it nearly impossible to make the populations of those electoral districts equal; hence, the need for the statement about vote-seat disparity.

[21] The POEL also included provisions for how changes in district boundaries would be determined in the event population changes necessitated it and in the event municipalities merged with other municipalities (Chapter 3, Articles 12 and 13).

5.2 Delivering Goods

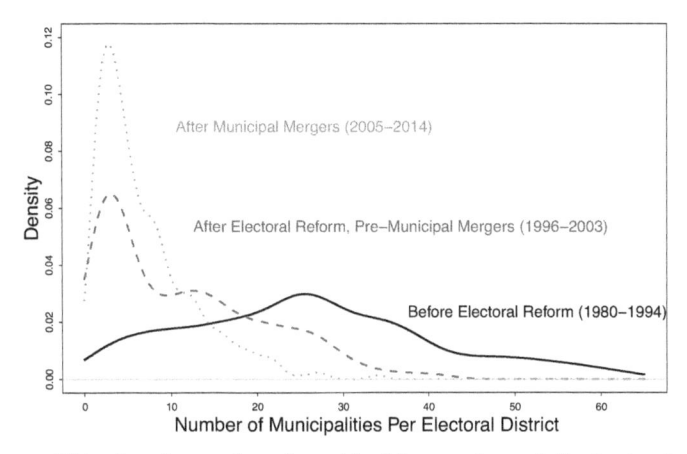

Figure 5.1 This plots the number of municipalities per electoral district for the twelve elections to Japan's Lower House, 1980–2014.
The data is divided into three periods to show how the number of municipalities per district changed, first with electoral reform (1994), which increased the number of electoral districts, and then with municipal mergers (2001–2005), which decreased the number of municipalities.

5.2 DELIVERING GOODS

The above discussion established that many candidates in Lower House elections compete in electoral districts divisible into groups of voters, from which electoral support is discernible. Let us now turn to the second condition: money. Do Lower House Members have access to resources that they can target at the municipalities in their districts? An abundance of evidence implies that the answer to this question is "yes." Importantly, Japan is characterized by "centralized tax administration, decentralized provision of public services, and dependence of local government on intergovernmental transfers" (Mochida 2001, 85). What this means is that the bulk of *taxes* in Japan are collected by the central government, but the bulk of *spending* is carried out by local government entities, both prefectures and municipalities. The relationship between Japan's central and local governments is thus characterized by a "vertical fiscal imbalance," meaning that revenues typically exceed spending at the central level and fall short at the local level (Mihaljek 1997; Yonehara 1986). Each year, this imbalance is redressed by vast sums of money being transferred from the central government to local governments via a series of intergovernmental transfers.

In this section, I describe the features of intergovernmental relations in Japan that give rise to a situation where the vast majority of local governments are highly dependent on central government transfers (Scheiner 2006). I then present qualitative evidence that annual allocations of one transfer, NTD (kokko shishutsukin), are vulnerable to manipulation by politicians.

5.2.1 Vertical Fiscal Imbalance in Japan

First, Figure 5.2 plots the share of tax revenue in Japan collected by the central government (dark gray bars) and local government(s) (both prefectures and municipalities) (light gray bars) for each year, 1980–2015. Figure 5.3 plots the share of government expenditure by the central government and local governments, respectively, for the same period. On average, local governments collect only 39.4% of tax revenue but are responsible for 61.4% of government spending. Viewed as shares of gross domestic expenditure (GDE), of which the bulk is household spending, spending by local governments accounted for an average of 18.5% of GDE during this period, whereas spending by the central government accounted for just 11.6% of GDE. Municipalities, of special interest to us, make up approximately half of all local government spending, with the remaining half the preserve of prefectures. In 2000, municipalities spent 51.1610 trillion yen, which equates to approximately $381 billion USD (in today's exchange rate).[22]

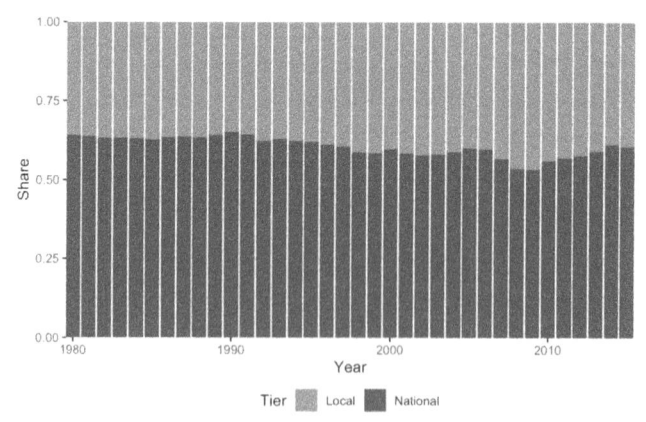

Figure 5.2 This plots the share of tax revenue collected by the central government (dark gray) and local governments (light gray) annually for the period 1980–2015.

[22] This data was assembled from the annually published White Paper(s) on Local Public Finance (Japanese versions). Tax revenue data comes from a table called Kokuzei Oyobi Chihouzei no Ruinen Hikaku. Spending data, including as a share of GDE, comes from a table called Chihou Zaisei to Kuni no Zaisei to no Ruinen Hikaku. As is customary, central government spending is calculated after subtracting transfers to local governments (described below), and local government spending is calculated after subtracting transfers to the central government (these are very small and are the local government's share of public works projects undertaken by the central government in the locale). Spending by prefectures and municipalities is reported in a table called Dantai Shurui Betsu Kessan Kibo no Jyoukyou.

5.2 Delivering Goods

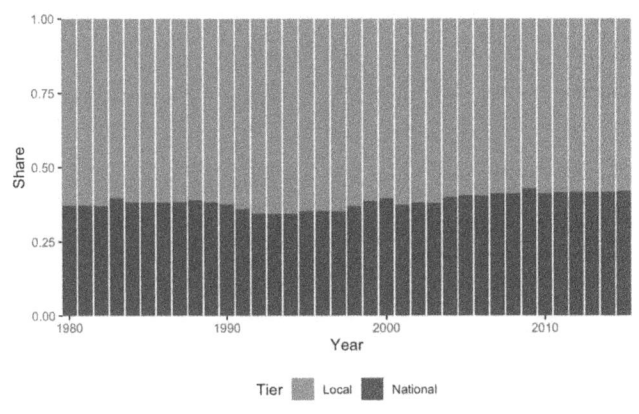

Figure 5.3 This plots the share of government expenditure by the central government (dark gray) and local governments (light gray) annually for the period 1980–2015.

The vertical fiscal imbalance apparent in these figures arises for two reasons: one, because the central government assigns more functions to local governments than they are capable of performing with their own revenue; and two, because the central government demands a certain degree of uniformity in the performance of these functions by all local governments, regardless of fiscal capacity (Bessho 2016; Mihaljek 1997). This latter point is important: A "defining feature" of intergovernmental relations in Japan is a "strong collective preference for equal access to public goods" (Mihaljek 1997, 289). Since the immediate aftermath of the Second World War, there has been widespread support in Japan for the idea that people should experience the same level of taxation and be supplied with the same quality of government services, regardless of where they live. Correspondingly, there is widespread support for the idea that any local government projected to experience difficulty providing services that meet this standard should be able to count on money from the central government to bring up the level of service provided. Scholars have pointed out that the commitment to local autonomy enshrined in Japan's Constitution sits somewhat uneasily alongside this deeply ingrained preference for equal access to public goods. Why? Because the desire for equality provides a justification for the central government to exercise "detailed and stringent controls over the revenues of local governments and a wide range of local expenditures" (Mihaljek 1997, 285). While local governments enjoy autonomy in theory, in practice "almost all activities of local governments" are subject to "guidelines, standards, and regulations" set by the central government (Yonehara 1986, 159). On this basis, one analyst concluded that "the degree of effective revenue and expenditure centralization in Japan is among the highest in industrial countries" (Mihaljek 1997).

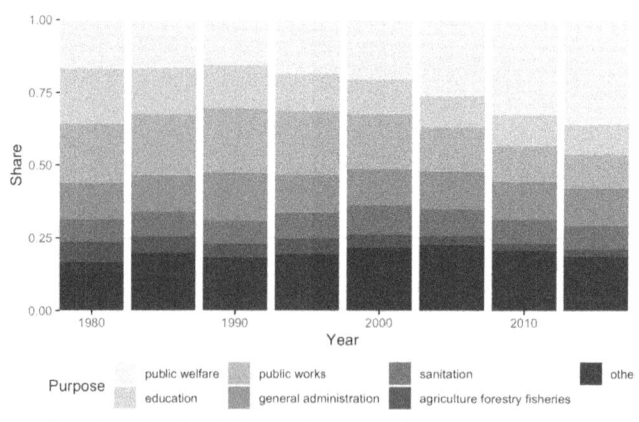

Perfect Storm Conditions for Tournaments in Japan

Figure 5.4 This plots the breakdown of municipal spending by purpose at five-year intervals between 1980 and 2015.

Under Japanese law, the functions performed by the central government are limited to defense, diplomacy, judicial affairs, social security (specifically, pensions), national universities and research facilities, national hospitals and medical facilities, national highways, and first class rivers (Mochida 2008, 48). All other functions are the preserve of local governments. Prefectures are charged with police, high schools, salaries of teachers in the compulsory education sector, social assistance, certain roads, and second-class rivers. Municipalities are responsible for urban planning and infrastructure, public housing, sewerage and waste disposal, clean drinking water, municipal roads, firefighting, residential records and the family registry, social insurance (specifically, the national health insurance and long-term care insurance), the maintenance of kindergartens, elementary and secondary schools, and the administering of elections (Yamada 2018; Weese 2015; Mochida 2008). As these lists show, it is not that one level of government is entrusted with *all* tasks falling in the categories of education or social welfare; broad policy sectors have *many* responsibilities associated with them, which are assigned to different government entities (Mochida 2008, Chapter 3).

Figure 5.4 plots the breakdown of municipal spending by "purpose" at five-year intervals between 1980 and 2015.[23] Until 2000, expenses related to public works (dobokuhi) comprised the largest share, after which came expenses related to public welfare and education. Public works expenses include the cost of constructing and maintaining public facilities, such

---
[23] The Japanese government prepares annual breakdowns of local government spending according to both "purpose" (mokutekibetsu) and "type" (seishitsubetsu). Data in this section come from annually published White Paper(s) on Local Public Finance (Japanese versions). See tables and figures entitled "Dantai Shurui Betsu Mokuteki Betsu Saishutsu no Jyoukyo."

5.2 Delivering Goods

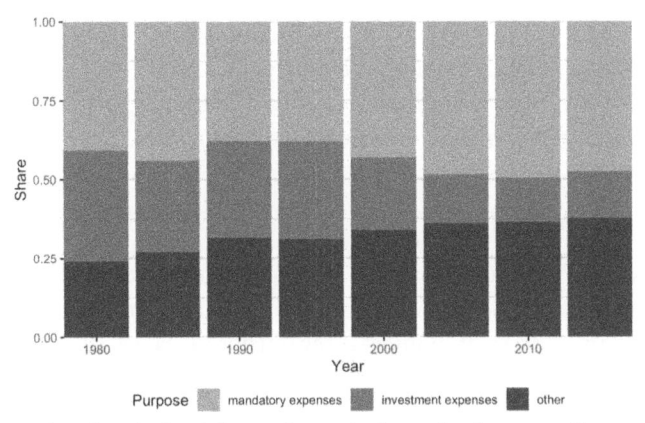

Figure 5.5 This plots the breakdown of municipal spending by type at five-year intervals between 1980 and 2015.

as roads, bridges, housing, parks, harbors, and rivers that fall under the purview of the municipality. Expenses for public welfare include the cost of constructing and operating welfare facilities for children, the elderly, and the disabled, as well as dispensing the public assistance municipalities are responsible for. Education expenses include the cost of constructing and maintaining school buildings and gymnasiums. Since the late 1990s, welfare expenses have doubled, relegating public works to second and then third place, respectively. Education expenses have also fallen, reflecting the declining birthrate, as have expenses related to agriculture, forestry, and fisheries. Expenses in the Other category, which include debt servicing, firefighting, labor, and commerce and industry, have increased since the 2000s.

The second breakdown of municipal spending available is by "type." Here, the two overarching categories are Mandatory Expenses, which are those municipalities have little discretion over (and thus, would have difficulty reducing), such as personnel expenses and social assistance expenses, and Investment Expenses, more than 95% of which consist of ordinary construction projects. Expenses that do not fit neatly into either Mandatory or Investment expenses are characterized as Other and include reserves and transfers to other accounts. Figure 5.5 plots the breakdown of municipal spending by type at five-year intervals between 1980 and 2015.[24] While Investment expenses comprised almost one-third of municipal spending in the years prior to 2000, they have dropped to less than 15% in recent years. Still, the massive scale of municipal spending in Japan means that in 2015, for example, the 14.7% of spending

[24] See the White Papers' tables and figures entitled "Seishitsu Betsu Saishutsu Kessan Gaku no Kouseihi."

on Investment translated into 8,310.6 billion yen (approx. $61 billion USD in today's exchange rate). Similarly, the 11.8% of spending in the public works category (in Figure 5.4) translated into 6,671.1 billion yen (approx. $48.7 billion USD in today's exchange rate).

5.2.2 Municipalities Depend on Central Government Transfers

Why, exactly, are municipalities so dependent on central government transfers? We can answer this question by looking at revenue data. There are four main sources of municipal revenue: local taxes, the Local Allocation Tax (LAT), NTD, and local bonds. Figure 5.6 plots the breakdown of local government revenue sources at five-year intervals between 1980 and 2015.[25] The largest revenue source is local government taxes. On average, 37% of local government revenue comes from taxes levied locally. It is on this basis that Japan's local governments are often described as being only "30% autonomous" (sanwari jichi). Of the two entities, municipalities derive most of their tax revenue from a municipal inhabitants tax (akin to a personal income tax) and a fixed asset tax (a property tax levied on land, buildings, and tangible depreciable assets). Prefectures derive most of their tax revenue from a prefectural inhabitants' tax (personal income tax) and an enterprise tax (corporate income tax) (Ishihara 1986).[26]

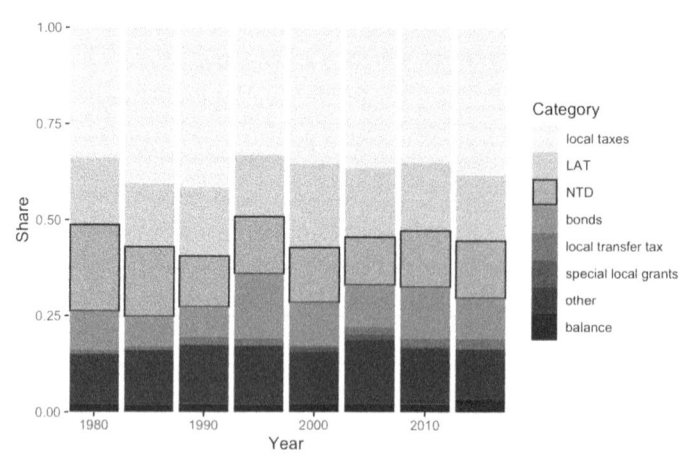

Figure 5.6 This plots the revenue structure of local governments at five-year intervals between 1980 and 2015.
The share captured by national treasury disbursements is highlighted with a black border.

[25] Data for this figure comes from a Table called Chihou Sainyuuchuu ni Shimeru Chihouzei Shyuunyuu no Wariai no Suii.
[26] Because corporate activities are more prone to business cycles, municipalities' tax revenue tends to be more stable than that of prefectures.

5.2 Delivering Goods

Under Japanese law, local governments lack sufficient authority to introduce new taxes and adjust tax rates to suit local conditions (Shirai 2005). The taxes they are permitted to levy, the standard rates of those taxes, and where applicable, upper and lower limits to those standard rates, are codified in national legislation: the Local Tax Law (Chihouzei). Local governments are permitted to levy discretionary taxes or non-standard rates but have to receive special permission from the central government to do so.[27] Their ability to issue special local bonds to fund longer-term projects, a revenue source described below, is also tied to the rates at which they levy taxes. As a result, local governments "almost always" levy the standard taxes at the standard rates and "do not consider local tax rates a plausible choice variable." In 2013, only 1.5% of local government tax revenue came from excess taxation or discretionary taxes (Bessho 2016, 8).

After local taxes, the next largest revenue sources are two categories of intergovernmental transfers: the LAT, at 17.8% of local government revenue, and NTD, at 15.7%, respectively. Together, the data in Figure 5.6 reveal that they made up an average of 33.4% of local government revenue in our period.[28] Despite its name, LAT is not a tax but a mechanism for revenue-sharing between the central government and local governments, in which tax collected at the national level is redistributed to local governments (DeWit 2002). Established in 1954, LAT is the main vehicle through which the central government ensures that all local governments are able to provide their residents with a minimum level of public services and infrastructure, regardless of population, demographics, geographic location, weather conditions, economic vitality, and so on (Akizuki 1995). To this end, its purpose is to "adjust imbalances in tax revenue among local governments" and "guarantee revenue sources so that local governments in whatever region can provide a certain level of administrative services" (Bessho 2016, 12). Importantly, LAT allocations are a *general* revenue source, meaning that local governments are allowed to spend their LAT on whatever services they like.

How are LAT allocations determined? Every year, a fixed percentage of revenue from five major national taxes (personal income, corporation, liquor, consumption, and tobacco) are earmarked for the Local

---

[27] Examples of discretionary taxes include a merchandise certificate tax, an advertisement tax, and a nuclear fuel tax (Ishihara 1986, 142).
[28] In 1982, LAT and NTD made up close to 98% of the revenue local governments received from intergovernmental transfers. Three other categories of transfers made up the remaining 2%: special traffic safety grants; local transfer taxes; and transfer as a substitution of fixed property tax (Yonehara 1986, 158).

Allocation Tax Special Account (Chihou Koufuzei Tokubetsu Kaikei).[29] This forms the pot of money available for LAT. To determine each local government's allocation, the central government calculates the local government's cost of providing services (called its standard financial requirement, or demand), and its expected revenue from taxation (the "standard financial revenue," or supply) (Shirai 2005, 217).[30] Dividing the former by the latter generates an index capturing the degree to which each local government is capable of funding services within its jurisdiction. Of the pot of money in the Special Account, 94% is designated as "Ordinary LAT" and divvied up among all local governments whose demand exceeds supply (local governments whose tax revenue outstrips supply are ineligible for LAT). In 2000, 97% of local governments received LAT (DeWit 2002, 358). The remaining 6% in the Special Account is designated as "Special LAT," and divvied up among local governments experiencing circumstances not anticipated when their demand was calculated (Akizuki 1995; Reed 1986; Ishihara 1986).[31]

Can LDP politicians influence LAT? Akizuki (1995, 359) argues that there is "no room for political negotiation or special consideration" as far as LAT allocations are concerned. He credits this to mechanisms adopted by the ministry in charge of LAT (and relations with local governments more generally): the then-Ministry of Home Affairs (MOHA, or Jichisho).[32] These mechanisms include the use of fixed percentages of earmarked national taxes to determine the total pool of money available for LAT; the use of a standard, publicly known formula to calculate each local government's supply and demand; and the cap of 6% for Special LAT. Together, these rules ensured that allocations were decided upon "without political considerations (pressure from interest groups and

[29] These percentages have fluctuated a little over time. Until 1989, 32% of the first three taxes was reserved for the Special Account (Reed 1986). In 1989, 25% of the consumption tax and 24% of the tobacco tax were added to the first three (Fukui and Fukai 1996, 274). Incremental adjustments have been made since then (DeWit 2002, 370).

[30] For the former, it calculates the number of service functions (e.g., police officers, city planning, parks, or garbage collection) deemed necessary for each local government. It then multiplies that number by the unit cost of each item, adjusted by a modification coefficient that takes into account factors specific to the local government in question, such as snowfall and other geographical features (Yonehara 1986, 163). An English translation of the Local Allocation Tax Law, which includes the formula for calculating demand and supply, is here: www.chihousai.or.jp/english/07/pdf/Local_Allocation_Tax_Law.pdf.

[31] Special LAT is used for expenses related to local elections, protection of historical properties, and disaster relief, among others (Yonehara 1986, 164).

[32] In 2001, a process of government reorganization took place, which saw MOHA merge with sections of the Ministry of Posts and Telecommunications and sections of the Management and Coordination Agency to form the Ministry of Internal Affairs and Communications (MIC, or Soumusho).

5.2 Delivering Goods

political parties)." As indirect evidence of the absence of political meddling, he points out that LDP politicians' interest in MOHA is low, the Minister of Home Affairs is one of the least popular Cabinet positions, and posts in the corresponding Diet and party committees are unpopular (Akizuki 1995, 359). Others have agreed with his assessment that the formula under which LAT allocations are determined, and over-time adjustments to the formula to incorporate context-specific factors, have been key factors *limiting* the ability of ruling party politicians to influence LAT allocations (DeWit 2002, 361).[33]

Saying that politics plays little role in the *distribution* of LAT is not the same as saying that politics plays no role in the LAT regime itself. Instead of trying to influence LAT allocations, local governments appear to have directed their efforts toward maintaining, enlarging, and protecting the pool of money in the LAT Special Account. For example, they lobbied for larger percentages of the earmarked national taxes to be placed in the Special Account, and whenever recessions caused shortfalls between the amount in the Special Account and the amount required for LAT, they persuaded the central government to cover the shortfall by borrowing from other accounts. In doing so, they have avoided having to reduce expenditure or engage in any serious rationalization or restructuring (Shirai 2005; DeWit 2002).[34] A key reason they were successful is that in these instances, their interests dovetailed with those of MOHA bureaucrats, who are charged with ensuring the fiscal health of local governments and overseeing the pot of money in the LAT Special Account. Local governments have also been successful at weathering critiques of LAT that have emerged since the early 2000s. These center on the observation that decades of LAT funding has created local governments that are relatively *well*-endowed, infrastructure-wise, even in rural areas experiencing depopulation. Critics allege that the quality of services provided by many local governments go "far beyond" that of any national minimum and question whether continued levels of LAT funding are warranted, especially when funded by borrowing (Shirai 2005, 119).

5.2.3 National Treasury Disbursements

The third-largest source of local government revenue, and our focus in this book, is NTD. National treasury disbursement is money the central

---

[33] Technically, the central government can make local governments repay their LAT allocations if it deems they have been used in ways "not in accordance with local autonomy" (Akizuki 1995, 346).
[34] Mihaljek (1997, 295) notes that occasionally, political pressure influences what is included in the calculation of "standard financial requirement."

government transfers to local governments for the purpose of funding specific programs or projects undertaken by the local government. It is not a *general* revenue source (like LAT), but a *specific purpose* revenue source, meaning that it is awarded for specific programs or projects and must be spent on those. While NTD is treated as another vehicle through which the central government can realize its commitment to the equalization of services across Japan, to the best of our knowledge, there is no formula determining how much NTD each local government deserves (unlike LAT) (Mihaljek 1997; Yonehara 1986). Nor does it appear that there any predefined rules governing the size of the total pool of money available for NTD each year.[35] The total amount of NTD received by each local government in a given year is the culmination of separate, project-specific disbursements issued at the discretion of the central government ministry with jurisdiction over that area. A local government might receive money for one project from the Ministry of Construction (later Ministry of Land, Infrastructure, Transportation and Tourism) and money for another from the Ministry of Agriculture, Forestry and Fisheries. The *sum* of monies it receives for these disbursements constitutes the total amount of NTD it receives in a given year. In 2015, 15,282.2 billion yen was disbursed to local governments as NTD (this equates to approximately $113 billion USD in today's exchange rate).

Unlike LAT, there is no law establishing NTD. The Local Public Finance Law (Chihou Zaisei Hou) specifies two categories of transfers that collectively make up transfers under the umbrella label of NTD (Mihaljek 1997; Yonehara 1986).[36] One category is central government disbursements to local governments for the purpose of "central government functions." These are functions that are inherently the central government's responsibility, but whose execution is entrusted to local governments. Specified in Article 10-4 of the law, until 2000, these were known as agency-delegated tasks (kikan inin jimu); since 2000, they have been called statutory entrusted tasks (hotei jyuutaku jimu). Examples of these functions include the administration of national elections and the provision of a national pension. The second category is central government disbursements for the purpose of "local government functions" (jichi jimu). Within this category, there are two subcategories: one, disbursements to cover the central government's obligatory share in the cost of certain prespecified local government functions (Article 10-1, 10-2,

---

[35] Like LAT, NTD comes under (the central government's) budgetary income. This is separate from income derived from the Fiscal Investment and Loan Program (FILP) and earmarked national taxes, both of which also consist of money that can be used to fund investment at the local level (Mochida 2008).

[36] The law can be found here: https://elaws.e-gov.go.jp/document?lawid=323AC0000000109.

5.2 Delivering Goods

and 10-3); and two, disbursements for "specific projects" undertaken by the local government that the central government deems "important" (Article 16). The law specifies thirty-four functions in the first subcategory (partially funded by the central government). These include public schoolteacher salaries, expenses for poor relief, national health insurance benefits, medical treatment for the elderly, firefighting, and certain public works projects. Regarding the second subcategory, neither the type of projects deemed important, nor the criteria under which they would be considered important, are specified.

In its Local Finance White Papers, MIC's Local Public Finance Bureau describes NTD as a "collective term for the national obligatory share (futankin), commissioning expenses (itakuhi), and incentives or fiscal support for specific measures (tokutei no shisaku no shourei mata ha zaisei enjo), disbursed from the central government to local governments."[37] While the White Papers provide a breakdown of the sum of NTD disbursed by the central government to all local governments in different categories, these categories do not clearly map onto the three categories in the Local Public Finance Law (money for central government functions; money covering the central government's obligatory share of local government functions; and money for important projects undertaken by local governments). For the first twenty-five years of our study (1980–2005), NTD allocations to municipalities consisted of, in order of largest to smallest, expenses related to ordinary construction (on average, 33.6%), cash benefits for the poor (25%), Other (21.5%), welfare allowance for children (8%), and welfare allowance for the aged (3.4%).[38] The government has used slightly different categories since then.[39] In 2010 and 2015, NTD allocations to municipalities consisted of, in order of largest to smallest, expenses related to cash benefits for the poor (29.3%), child

---

[37] See, for example, page 421 of www.soumu.go.jp/main_content/000785192.pdf.
[38] See the table entitled Kuni, Ken Shishutsukin no Jyoukyou. Categories comprising smaller shares of the total include postdisaster restoration (3.1%), tuberculosis patients' medical expenses (2%), unemployment benefits (0.7%), commission money (2.7%), and fiscal support (0.2%). Note that these averages were computed from data collected at five-year intervals across my sample. In 1980, two additional categories reported were compulsory education at 0.5% and medical expenses for the elderly at 8%, respectively.
[39] The categories added were support for the independence of individuals with disabilities, child allowance, support for the noncollection of tuition fees at public high schools, support for hosting national facilities (Self Defense Force and US bases), traffic safety, support for power source areas, support for areas surrounding defense facilities, support for social infrastructure development, support for regional revitalization, and support for reconstruction in the wake of the earthquake and nuclear disaster on March 11, 2011. Old categories no longer in the breakdown are welfare allowance for the elderly and tuberculosis patients' medical expenses, respectively.

allowance (17.9%), ordinary construction (10.6%), support for the independence of disabled people (9.9%), support for social infrastructure development (6.8%), and Other (12.9%).[40]

In contrast to LAT, there is a scholarly consensus that NTD allocations *are* vulnerable to political influence, especially by LDP politicians. How, exactly, is political influence exercised? The process through which money for a specific program or project is awarded begins with a ministry specifying categories of projects for which local governments can seek funds (Akizuki 1995, 342). To our knowledge, ministries do not publicize lists of these categories; nor is there a central repository of categories under which NTD is awarded. However, in 2016, the central government decided that local governments would be obliged to share information regarding the degree to which a certain program or project for which they received funding had met the goals of the umbrella category under which it was awarded. To facilitate this, the central government published "performance indicators" for certain categories of NTD. While gauging the representativeness or exhaustiveness of the publicized categories is difficult, the list provides us with a sense of the *type* of NTD categories that exist. Categories include the Regional Revitalization Promotion Grant (administered by the Cabinet Office), the Certified Center for Early Childhood and Care Maintenance Grant (Ministry of Education, Culture, Sports, Science, and Technology) the Employment Development and Support Subsidy and Water Maintenance Subsidy (Ministry of Health, Labour and Welfare), Measures for Projects that Nurture and Secure Local Leaders Subsidy (Ministry of Agriculture, Forestry and Fisheries), Comprehensive Subsidy for Social Infrastructure Development and Comprehensive Subsidy for the Maintenance and Promotion of Housing in Urban Areas (MIC), Promotion of a Recycling-Oriented Society Subsidy and Carbon Dioxide Emission Control Measures Subsidy (Ministry of the Environment), respectively.[41]

Local governments put together applications for specific programs or projects for which they seek to receive funds under different categories. These applications, known as Requests (Yobousho) or Petitions (Teian),

---

[40] Categories comprising smaller shares of the total include postdisaster restoration (0.7%), unemployment benefits (0.7%), commission money (1.2%), and fiscal support (0.06%), support for hosting national facilities (0.4%), traffic safety (0.3%), support for power source areas (0.4%), support for areas surrounding defense facilities (1.9%), regional revitalization (2.2%, only reported in 2015), support for reconstruction after earthquake and nuclear disaster on March 11, 2011 (3.0%, only reported in 2015).

[41] The policy under which this change occurred was the Basic Policy on Economic and Fiscal Management and Reform. See: www5.cao.go.jp/keizai-shimon/kaigi/special/reform/mieruka/db_top/link/performance.html.

5.2 Delivering Goods

describe the project and use diagrams, maps, photographs, and other data to explain its importance to the local economy and/or livelihoods of residents. While local governments can always *send* their application to the relevant ministry to be evaluated alongside applications in the same category from other local governments, in practice, many local governments seek the opportunity to present bureaucrats in the ministries with their applications *in person* (Yonehara 1986, 166–168). To do this, local governments dispatch groups to Tokyo. In the case of municipalities, these groups are usually headed by the mayor and/or municipal assembly members and can include representatives from local construction firms and interest groups. Reed (1986, 39) calls the "floods" of municipal representatives who arrive in Tokyo to petition the central government each year "one of the most visible aspects of Japan's intergovernmental relations." In his assessment:

Local governments act as interest groups, trying to get benefits from the central government. Although they are actually competing against each other for a piece of a limited pie, they act as if each request is independent of all the others. (Reed 1986, 153)

After arriving in Tokyo, it is customary for these groups try to meet with bureaucrats in the line ministry (with jurisdiction over the project), as well as with bureaucrats in the Ministry of Finance, which is in charge of the disbursal of monies, to make the case for their project (Saito 2010, 115). For assistance setting up these meetings, they turn to their local Diet Member(s). Meeting with a Diet Member right before making their way to the relevant ministry gives them the opportunity to hand over their application and personally request the Diet Member's "backing" (atooshi) in delivering it. The Diet member might send her secretary to the meetings with bureaucrats on her behalf. She might also place a phone call to the relevant ministries during the meeting with the local group. In Saito (2010)'s assessment, the "petition politics" (chinjyo seiji) Japanese municipalities engage in each year has become institutionalized to the extent that it resembles an art. Alongside meetings with Diet Members and bureaucrats, other events on the group's agenda while in Tokyo, particularly for large-scale projects such as the extension of a highway or bullet train line, can include social gatherings. Euphemistically called Demand-Realization Gatherings (Yokyuu Jitsugen Shuukai), the point of these parties is to invite the Diet Member and bureaucrats and showcase, via speeches by local residents, the consensus and enthusiasm in the community in support of the project (Saito 2010, 115).

While the process suggests there is ample room for the involvement of politicians, what grounds do we have that bureaucrats listen to them, such that year-to-year NTD allocations reflect politicians' electoral concerns? This question taps into one of the oldest debates in the Japanese politics literature, which concerns who retains the ultimate "say": bureaucrats or politicians. Ramseyer and Rosenbluth (1993) make the case that it is politicians (and specifically, politicians in the ruling LDP). By retaining vetoes over work done by bureaucrats, controlling promotions within the bureaucracy and access to postretirement jobs, and cultivating private sources of information about bureaucratic performance, the authors argue that while it can look like bureaucrats act autonomously, they actually "administer in the shadow of the LDP." By this, the authors mean that bureaucrats "write the bills that will best promote LDP electoral odds, and administer them in ways that will best lead to the same end" (Ramseyer and Rosenbluth 1993, 120–121). By using the bureaucracy as their own private think tank, the authors point out that LDP politicians gain a major advantage over non-LDP politicians. They can use government resources to bring "highways, schools, airports, and cash" into their electoral districts (Ramseyer and Rosenbluth 1993, 122). In support of this, the authors cite a bureaucrat interviewee:

When an LDP politician asks for information, we give him a hundred pages. When an opposition politician asks, we give him two pages. Basically, we're here to be the LDP's Secretariat. (Ramseyer and Rosenbluth 1993, 106)

Later studies lend further support to the idea that power is vested in ruling party politicians, not bureaucrats. Estevez-Abe (2008), for example, presents examples of senior LDP politicians riding roughshod over plans that had been carefully drawn up by bureaucrats to deliver social protection to unorganized voters such as working families or unemployed people. She explains how universalistic welfare policies were all quashed on the grounds that they were not in keeping with the interests of the organized groups that senior LDP politicians courted for electoral support and financial contributions. In their place, senior LDP politicians pushed through a hodgepodge of policies that put into place a system under which social protection was delivered to targeted groups of beneficiaries, such as select industries, certain geographic areas, occupational groups, and business organizations, all of whom LDP politicians depended on for votes. Bureaucratic initiatives, she finds, only see the light of day when they accord with the "distributive priorities" of LDP lawmakers (Estevez-Abe 2008, 119). Saito (2010, 13), who studied the allocation of NTD, goes even further, arguing that the bureaucracy is so completely under the thumb of LDP lawmakers that the two entities should be considered one and the same (ittaika).

5.2 Delivering Goods

Anecdotal evidence of the influence ruling party politicians supposedly wield regularly surfaces in the news media. In the wake of the 2021 Lower House election, for example, a newspaper article noted that the election had deprived both electoral districts located in Kitakyushu City (Fukuoka 9 and 10, respectively) of their LDP incumbents. Both Mihara Asahiko, the longtime representative of Fukuoka 9th, and Yamamoto Kozo, the longtime incumbent in Fukuoka 10th, had lost their races, with their advanced age disqualifying them from winning PR seats and entering the Diet that way.[42] The article quoted officials in the city administration, who expressed concern that the city's demands of the central government would no longer be heard (Asahi Shimbun 2021).

5.2.4 Impact of Decentralization

Beginning in the mid 1990s, the Japanese government embarked on a decentralization drive (Machidori 2023). Limits on the right of local governments to introduce new taxes, adjust tax rates, and issue government bonds for longer-term projects, combined with the burdens placed on local governments in terms of service provision, had come to be seen as factors preventing the development of more flexible and autonomous fiscal policies. Critics alleged that the current system of local government financing might have been necessary to recover from the economic devastation of the Second World War but was now doing more harm than good. Specifically, the system was said to be contributing to an overdependence on central government transfers and insufficient attention paid to fiscal discipline, particularly among overly dependent local governments (Shirai 2005).

The first phase of decentralization tackled the aforementioned "agency-delegated functions," under which local governments were statutorily deemed to be carrying out tasks on behalf of the central government (Machidori 2023). The second phase, dubbed the Trinity Reforms, was pushed by LDP Prime Minister Koizumi Junichiro (2001–2006). As its name suggests, there were three components. One was cuts to NTD funding: The government announced that in the 2004–2006 period, the amount of money spent on NTD would be cut by 4.7 trillion yen. The second component was cuts to LAT: Here, the announced reduction was 5.1 trillion yen. The third component was a transfer in tax resources from the central to local government: The central government announced a plan to cut national personal income tax and increase individual inhabitant tax, which was a key revenue source for local governments. Together,

---

[42] Dual candidacy is permitted under Japan's mixed-member electoral system. This is discussed further in Chapter 6.

the government claimed that these changes amounted to a transfer in tax resources of approximately 3 trillion yen (Mochida 2008).

Could the cuts in spending and transfer of tax resources have made it more difficult for LDP politicians to use NTD to reward electoral support? While this is certainly possible, scholars have described the impact of the reforms as limited. Naoi (2015, 31), for example, calls the impact of decentralization "moderate" and stresses the fact that municipalities still relied on the central government for approximately 60% of their revenue after the Trinity Reforms. Moreover, because the reform aimed to relax the regulations imposed on local governments, with the idea that they would then be freer to develop programs suited to the needs of their residents (Mochida 2008), the cuts to NTD may have been concentrated in the categories through which the central government enforced its regulations. This is not NTD distributed under Article 16 (for projects deemed necessary), but NTD distributed under Article 10 (for the local government's fulfillment of certain central government functions and for the central government's obligatory share in the cost of certain local government functions). While this is merely a conjecture and further research is needed, it is supported by the fact that, when the National Governor's Association was asked to come up with a proposal for where the NTD cuts would come from, only 16% of those proposed, which were eventually accepted by the Cabinet, came from Article 16-style NTD allocations (Suzuki and Takahashi 2015, 47). Reflecting this, one analyst concluded that "the effect of the cut in earmarked grants in practice was less than it appeared in principle" (Mochida 2008, 155).

In sum, the majority of municipalities in Japan depend on central government transfers for large shares of their operating revenue. One of those transfers, NTD, is allocated at the discretion of central government bureaucrats. Because NTD are funds for specific projects, with amounts designed to cover either the full or partial cost of a project, the total amount of NTD municipalities receive in a given year is not determined by formula. Instead, it is the product of *municipalities'* efforts (to put together proposals and persuade bureaucrats to fund them), *politicians'* efforts (to connect municipalities and bureaucrats and persuade bureaucrats), and *bureaucratic priorities*. In this setting, it is possible that LDP incumbents apportion their lobbying in ways that could translate into NTD allocations that track levels of electoral support. If an LDP politician devotes the most effort to persuading bureaucrats to fund projects in the municipality that ranked first in electoral loyalty, slightly less effort to persuading bureaucrats to fund projects in the municipality that placed second, and so on, then we can expect that the cumulative output of all this lobbying will be NTD allocations that reflect their incentives under a tournament.

5.3 FEWER TOURNAMENT-POSSIBLE DISTRICTS OVER TIME

The above section made it clear that many candidates in Japan's Lower House elections compete in electoral districts divisible into groups of voters, from which support is discernible and to which resources are targetable. This section offers precise figures on the number and share of electoral districts meeting these conditions in every Lower House election held in our period of study (1980–2014). Doing so first requires us to be explicit about the type of districts in which these conditions are *not* met. Broadly speaking, in the Japanese case, there are three categories of district in which tournaments are not possible.

One, owing to the way votes are counted in Japan, electoral districts consisting of a single municipality do not give politicians a means of discerning their support at a disaggregated level therein. Nor do they offer a means of targeting money at this disaggregated level. Thus, the conditions for tournaments are not met in districts comprising a single municipality, even if that municipality is perfectly contained within the district. Table 5.1 presents tallies of the number of electoral districts in all three categories in the Lower House elections in my sample and their percentage of the total number of electoral districts used. To classify electoral districts into each category, I relied on the comprehensive, municipality-level data I gathered for this project, which is described in Chapter 6. The numbers in the first row capture the number of electoral districts in this first category.

Two, electoral districts in which a sizeable share of voters reside in a municipality whose area spills out into another electoral district also do not meet these conditions. Japan's vote counting rules mean that municipalities whose area straddles more than one electoral district can set up distinct Vote Counting Units to correspond with each of the electoral districts they are located in. Thus, politicians in electoral districts that contain a section of a municipality whose other sections lie in other electoral districts will be able to observe how many *votes* they received in their section of the municipality (these vote tallies are needed to calculate district-level vote tallies). However, because NTD is targeted at the municipality as a whole, they lack the means of *targeting* their section of the municipality with resources. Any resources they deliver will go to the municipality as a whole, which means that they could be spent in the sections of the municipality located in a different electoral district.

Table 5.1 *Tally of electoral districts not meeting the conditions for a tournament in Japan's Lower House elections, 1980–2014.*

Election year	1980	1983	1986	1990	1993	1996	2000	2003	2005	2009	2012	2014
Solo-municipality districts	0	0	0	0	0	18	18	16	13	12	13	12
Split-municipality districts	3	3	3	3	2	27	27	32	65	89	102	93
(only split, not only split)	(0, 3)	(0, 3)	(0, 3)	(0, 3)	(0, 2)	(11, 16)	(11, 16)	(13, 19)	(19, 46)	(17, 72)	(16, 86)	(16, 77)
Ordinance-designated city districts	9	9	9	9	9	35	35	36	37	41	40	38
Total tournament-impossible districts	12	12	12	12	11	80	80	84	115	142	155	143
Percentage of total districts	9	9	9	9	9	27	27	28	38	47	52	48
Total districts	130	130	130	130	129	300	300	300	300	300	300	295

Each row identifies a different reason why a district does not meet these conditions.

5.3 Fewer Tournament-Possible Districts over Time

Within this second category of tournament-impossible electoral district, my data revealed that there are two subcategories: districts consisting *solely* of split municipalities and districts consisting of some municipalities whose borders are perfectly contained in the district, *plus* one or more split municipalities, whose borders are not. Districts in the first subcategory do not meet the conditions for tournaments. When it comes to districts in the second subcategory, it is reasonable to expect that if the vast majority of a district's voters resided in municipalities whose borders were perfectly contained in the district, then a politician could still implement a tournament, even if a small sliver of the district's voters resided in a municipality whose area spilled out into another district. On the other hand, if a sizeable share of a district's voters resided in the split municipality, then it is reasonable to assume that a tournament would be difficult. For each Lower House election, for all districts falling in this second subcategory, I counted the number of districts in which a sizable share of voters resided in a split municipality.[43] In Table 5.1, the second row reports the number of districts in this second category. Underneath this value, the numbers in parentheses capture the number in the first and second subcategories, respectively.

Three, when cities in Japan reach a population threshold of 500,000, they can apply for a status as an ordinance-designated city (seirei shitei toshi).[44] Ordinance-designed cities have fiscal relationships with the central government that are different from other municipalities (Horiuchi and Saito 2003). They are comprised of wards, at which Vote Counting Units are established and thus, vote tallies reported, but these wards do not appear to be entities to which the central government delivers NTD.[45] The central government delivers NTD to the city, but how the

---

[43] I used 10% as a rule of thumb. If more than 10% of a district's voters resided in a split municipality, I coded the district as not meeting the conditions for a tournament. To do this, I calculated the number of voters in the average electoral district in each election and took 10% of this. If a given electoral district had a split municipality within it whose population exceeded this value, the district was placed in this subcategory and coded as tournament-impossible.

[44] Cities with this designation across the full period are Kyoto, Osaka, Yokohama, Kobe, Nagoya, Sapporo, Kawasaki, Fukuoka, Hiroshima, and Kitakyushu cities. To these, Sendai City was added in 1989, Chiba City in 1992, Saitama City in 2003, Shizuoka City in 2005, Sakai City in 2006, Niigata City and Hamamatsu City in 2007, Okayama City in 2009, Sagamihara City in 2010, and Kumamoto City in 2012, respectively. Tokyo has a special designation as a "to" (metropolis), which puts it on equal footing (at least with regard to the conditions for GBC) to the other forty-six prefectures (which are "ken," "fu," and "do", respectively).

[45] For ordinance-designated cities, the central government reports financial statistics at the level of the city as a whole, including amounts of NTD delivered (to the city), but not at the level of the wards within the city (see "Shichoson no Sugata" at

Perfect Storm Conditions for Tournaments in Japan

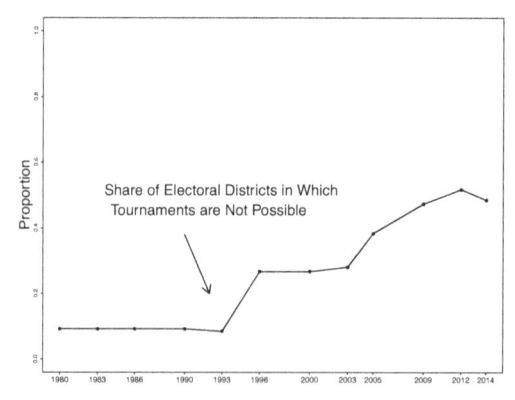

Figure 5.7 Share of electoral districts in Japan's Lower House elections (1980–2014) in which tournaments are not possible.

city decides to divvy this up to the wards is not well understood.[46] Thus, while candidates competing in electoral districts located in these cities can observe their vote tallies at a disaggregated level within their district (at least, if their district is made up of more than one ward), they cannot deliver funds to these units in the same manner as they do to other units. Thus, electoral districts located within ordinance-designated cities do not meet the conditions for a tournament, at least according to my criteria. In Table 5.1, the third row reports the number of districts in this third category.[47]

In the bottom rows of Table 5.1, the number of tournament-impossible districts in each Lower House election is reported, as well as their percentage of the total number of districts. Figure 5.7 presents this percentage as a share, plotting the share of all electoral districts used in Lower House elections from 1980 to 2014 that are tournament-impossible. We can discern several changes over this period. In the five elections prior to electoral reform in 1994, this coding reveals that tournaments were possible in more than 90% of electoral districts. Table 5.1 tells us that there were no districts in the first category, only two or three in the second, and only nine in the third. The 1994 electoral reform created new districts, just over a quarter of which were tournament-impossible. This was the result of an increase in number of districts in all three categories. This makes sense when we recall that the reform introduced single-member districts,

---

www.stat.go.jp/data/s-sugata/naiyou.html). I could not find any evidence that NTD is deliverable by the central government to these wards.

[46] I consulted the budgets of several ordinance-designated cities, and they did not record how NTD was divvied up across wards.

[47] In 2009, 2012, and 2014, there were a total of forty-three electoral districts in this category, but several of those were Split-Municipality Districts, so are accounted for by the figures in the second row.

5.3 Fewer Tournament-Possible Districts over Time

so necessitated the division of the same geographic area (the country of Japan) into a much larger number of districts. As a result, the number of Solo-Municipality, Split-Municipality, and Ordinance-Designated City Districts all increased.

The share of tournament-impossible districts remained relatively stable from the 1996 election through the 2003 election (at 27–28%), before increasing again, to almost 40% of districts in 2005. As I mentioned above, the 2001–2005 period saw thousands of municipal amalgamations. As municipalities became bigger, it was no longer possible to have as many electoral districts drawn *around* the borders of municipalities. Table 5.1 tells us that the increase in share of tournament-impossible districts between 2003 and 2005 is primarily due to an increase in number of Split-Municipality Districts, in which a sizeable share of voters reside in a municipality whose borders spill out into another district. The decrease in number of Solo-Municipality Districts across the postreform period, from 1996 until 2014, is another by-product of already-populous municipalities becoming even more populous and spilling out into neighboring districts.

The share of tournament-possible districts jumped again between 2005 and 2009 and between 2009 and 2012, respectively, to constitute just under and over 50% of all districts, respectively. This was again due to increases in the number of Split-Municipality Districts. Between 2012 and 2014, there was a redistricting, which saw the total number of districts cut from 300 to 295. This means that the average electoral district contained slightly more voters in 2014 than in 2012. The fact that districts got slightly "bigger" between 2012 and 2014 is reflected in a slight reduction in number of Split-Municipality Districts and Ordinance-Designated Districts, respectively, and a decrease in share of tournament-possible districts (from 52% of the total in 2012 to 48% in 2014).

In Figure 5.8, I plot the share of all voters in Japan who reside in tournament-possible electoral districts. To construct this, I took my classifications of electoral districts as tournament-possible and -impossible, respectively, and I merged them with elections data in Reed and Smith (2015). Using their variable capturing the number of eligible voters in each electoral district, I calculated the share of all voters in Japan who reside in districts in which the theory posits that tournaments are being conducted. The data show that the voting population in Japan has ranged from just over 80 million (in 1980) to a high of just over 104 million (in 2012; by 2014, it had declined slightly to 103.9 million). In elections prior to 1994, my calculations show that about 90% of all Japanese voters resided in these districts (this is between 71 and 85 million people). In 1996, 2000, and 2003, it was about 70% of voters (around 70 million

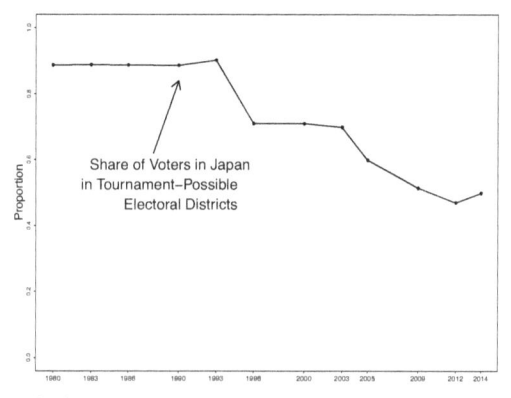

Figure 5.8 Share of all voters subject to a tournament in Japan's Lower House elections, 1980–2014.

people). In 2005, it was about 60% (around 61 million people). Then, in 2009, 2012, and 2014, respectively, it was about 50% of all voters (or around 50 million people).

5.4 ELECTION OUTCOMES DIFFER IN TOURNAMENT-POSSIBLE DISTRICTS

We have established that the share of electoral districts meeting the conditions for a tournament in Japan's Lower House elections has decreased over our period of study, first in the wake of electoral reform (in 1994) and second in the wake of municipal amalgamations (2001–2006). Ongoing urbanization, a process separate from electoral reform or municipal mergers, has also contributed to the decrease in share of electoral districts in which tournaments are possible. In Chapters 6–8, I leverage a comprehensive new dataset on geographically targeted spending and voting behavior at the level of the municipality in Japan to conduct rigorous empirical tests designed to gauge whether tournaments are being conducted inside tournament-possible districts. My evidence shows that LDP politicians in tournament-possible districts contest Lower House elections by pitting the municipalities in their districts against each other in a competition over which is the most electorally supportive. After observing each municipality's performance for them in an election, LDP politicians use the transfer system, ostensibly under the control of central government bureaucrats, to generate prizes that disproportionately reward the more supportive municipalities in their district over less supportive ones.

Before embarking on this analysis, however, the increase in share of tournament-impossible districts over our period of study affords us the opportunity to conduct a simple comparison of election outcomes across the two types of electoral districts. If the theory offered in this

5.4 Outcomes Differ in Tournament-Possible Districts

Table 5.2 *Tournament-possible districts have higher support for LDP candidates, are more likely to see an LDP winner, are less likely to see no LDP candidate fielded, and have higher turnout in Lower House elections, 1980–2014.*

	Dependent variable			
	LDP VS$_{d,t}$ (1)	LDP Winner$_{d,t}$ (2)	No LDP Candidate$_{d,t}$ (3)	Turnout$_{d,t}$ (4)
Tournament-possible district	0.057*** (0.004)	0.113*** (0.017)	−0.035*** (0.008)	0.038*** (0.002)
District magnitude	−0.029*** (0.004)	0.019 (0.017)	−0.003 (0.008)	−0.009*** (0.002)
Constant	0.445*** (0.017)	0.823*** (0.076)	0.043 (0.037)	0.742*** (0.010)
Observations	2,636	2,636	2,744	2,744
Year FE	Y	Y	Y	Y
R^2	0.257	0.257	0.029	0.640

***$p < 0.001$.

book is correct, and LDP politicians are conducting tournaments in tournament-possible districts and a different electoral strategy entirely in tournament-impossible districts, then leaving aside the question of what that latter strategy is, we should observe election outcomes diverging systematically as a function of the type of electoral district LDP candidates are in. Evidence of qualitative differences in election outcomes strengthens my claim that there is a *distinct* electoral strategy being undertaken by LDP candidates in tournament-possible districts.

In Table 5.2, I present the results of four ordinary least squares regressions. These regressions are based on a dataset I created by merging my classifications of electoral districts described above with data from Reed and Smith (2015). The unit of observation in the dataset is the electoral district, and the sample is the universe of electoral districts in Lower House elections, 1980–2014. My first question of interest is whether, controlling for other differences across electoral districts, tournament-possible districts exhibit a statistically discernible difference in electoral support for LDP candidates. In Model 1, I limit the sample to districts with at least one LDP candidate running. The dependent variable is LDP VS$_{d,t}$, the share of eligible voters in the district who voted for any one of the LDP candidates who ran (this ranges from 0.06 to 0.68).[48]

[48] In Japanese, this is zettai tokuhyouritsu. Another means of calculating electoral support is to use sotai tokuhyouritsu, which is votes cast for LDP candidates divided by valid votes cast.

The coefficient on Tournament-Possible District is positive and statistically significant, controlling for election year and number of seats in the district (district magnitude).[49] On average, districts in which tournaments are possible return a vote share for the LDP that is 5.7% higher than districts where tournaments are not possible.

My next question of interest is whether, controlling for other differences across electoral districts, tournament-possible and tournament-impossible districts differ in the probability of seeing an LDP candidate *win* the election. In Model 2, I use the same sample as in Model 1: districts with at least one LDP candidate in all Lower House elections in the sample. My dependent variable of interest is LDP Winner$_{d,t}$, a dummy variable indicating that the district had at least one LDP winner (it ranges from 0 to 1).[50] The coefficient on Tournament-Possible District is positive and statistically significant, controlling for year and district magnitude. It tells us that on average, districts where tournaments are possible are 11% more likely to see at least one LDP winner emerge.

My third question of interest is whether, controlling for other differences between districts, tournament-possible and tournament-impossible districts differ in the probability of seeing no LDP candidate fielded. In Model 3, the sample is all electoral districts in all elections in the sample. My dependent variable of interest is No LDP Candidate$_{d,t}$, a dummy variable indicating districts without any LDP candidate (it ranges from 0 to 1).[51] The coefficient on Tournament-Possible District is negative and statistically significant, controlling for year and district magnitude. On average, districts in which tournaments are possible are 3.5% less likely to see no LDP candidate fielded.

My final question of interest is whether, controlling for other differences between districts, tournament-possible districts exhibit statistically discernible differences in turnout. In Model 4, the sample is all districts in all elections in the sample. My dependent variable is interest is Turnout$_{d,t}$, which is the share of a district's voting population who cast valid votes in the relevant Lower House election (it ranges from 0.39 to 0.93). The coefficient on Tournament-Possible District is positive and statistically significant, controlling for year and district magnitude. On average, districts in which tournaments are possible exhibit a turnout level that is 3.8% higher.

In sum, Table 5.2 offers evidence that election outcomes vary systematically by the type of electoral district candidates are competing in. While my primary goal with these tests was to evaluate whether

---

[49] I limit the controls out of concern for posttreatment bias.
[50] This is a linear probability model.
[51] This is a linear probability model.

5.4 Outcomes Differ in Tournament-Possible Districts

tournament-possible districts produce election outcomes that differ systematically from those in tournament-impossible districts, the results also suggest that tournaments also produce stronger electoral performance by LDP candidates (Models 1, 2, and 3) and higher political participation (Model 4), respectively. This accords with the main claim of this book, which is that tournaments help LDP politicians win elections, and the mechanism through which they do this is by increasing the incentive to turn out and vote for LDP candidates among voters in supportive municipalities in tournament-possible districts, whose votes have been made to matter enormously for the amount of money their municipality receives. As such, the direction of the differences in outcomes across the two types of electoral districts, with *stronger* performance by LDP candidates and *higher* political participation in tournament-possible districts relative to tournament-impossible ones, is also in keeping with the theory's predictions.

While the theory holds that LDP politicians will conduct tournaments in tournament-possible districts, it is agnostic about the type of electoral strategy LDP politicians will adopt *outside* these districts. However, almost every study of vote buying described in Chapters 2 and 3, both theoretical and applied, models it as a choice between vote buying *or* competition on policy grounds, where policy refers to broad programmatic policies. On these grounds, it is reasonable to expect that in tournament-impossible districts, LDP politicians will be using positions on policy issues to try to win. If that is the case, then it follows that the growth of tournament-impossible districts after electoral reform and municipal mergers, respectively, should have injected a large amount of policy competition into an otherwise particularism-oriented electoral landscape.

This is exactly what has occurred: A host of studies have documented the rise of programmatic policy competition in the wake of Japan's 1994 electoral reform and have attributed it to changes in the behavior of LDP politicians (Catalinac 2016, 2015; Reed, Scheiner and Thies 2012; Krauss and Pekkanen 2010; Rosenbluth and Thies 2010; Krauss and Pekkanen 2004). Other studies have pointed out that this "new" policy competition has sat, somewhat uneasily, alongside more traditional campaign tactics adopted by LDP politicians, which emphasize particularistic favors and personalized help for community members (Christensen and Selway 2017; Krauss and Pekkanen 2010; Koellner 2009; Scheiner 2006; Tani 1998). Moreover, policy competition received a noticeable "boost" in the 2005 and 2009 elections, respectively. Chapter 2 documented how the 2005 election was successfully framed by the LDP leader (Prime Minister Koizumi Junichiro) as one in which voters had to decide whether they were for or against reform, which in this case was postal privatization (Nemoto, Krauss and Pekkanen 2008; Maclachlan 2006). In 2009, the Democratic Party of Japan (DPJ), which had been the LDP's main rival since the 1990s, framed the election similarly, calling on voters to decide whether they wanted a change of government or more of the same. The LDP lost this election.

In Table 5.1, we saw that the biggest increases in share of tournament-impossible districts occurred in the 1996 election, the 2005 election, and the 2009 election, respectively. These increases correlate perfectly with the three elections in which policy competition suddenly appeared to play a much more prominent role in Japanese elections. In Chapter 6, I present stronger evidence that the rise of policy competition since 1994 is indeed connected to the increase in share of tournament-impossible districts after 1994. First, however, we turn our attention to the core question this book seeks to answer: Are LDP politicians using tournaments in tournament-possible districts? This is the subject of Chapters 6–8.

6

How Politicians Tie Money to Electoral Support

This book offers a theory for how incumbents operating under a certain configuration of political institutions can use government resources to stay in power. The theory holds that when incumbents can discern their electoral support at a disaggregated unit within their electoral district and influence allocations of central government resources to those units, they will be able to tie the amount of resources units receive to their voting behavior. I call this electoral strategy *group-based clientelism* (GBC). I further hold that when incumbents are able to create the impression that they are so dominant no one stands a chance of unseating them, they will be able to go even further, and make those units compete for resources. In such a competition, a *tournament*, the amount of resources units receive will be a function of the relative level of support they provided the incumbent in the most recent election. Testing the theory first requires a deep dive into a country's political institutions to ascertain whether these conditions are met and in how many electoral districts. After this has been verified, the researcher must gather data on voting behavior, resource allocations, and other confounding variables, and devise stringent empirical tests capable of pitting the theory's propositions against those of rival theories.

In this book, I provide a blueprint of how this is done by turning the spotlight onto an understudied case in political science: Japan. In Chapter 5, I explained how the laws governing election administration, government structure, and fiscal relations between the central government and lower-tier administrative entities in contemporary Japan combine to create many electoral districts in which tournaments are possible. In this chapter, I describe a comprehensive panel dataset I have put together, with data on voting behavior, central government transfers, and numerous other fiscal and demographic variables, all measured at the level of the relevant lower-tier entity, which in Japan's case is the municipality. Altogether, my dataset spans the twelve Lower House elections held between 1980 and 2014 and contains more than one hundred thousand observations pertaining to the universe of municipalities in existence in this period. Using these data, I explain how I constructed variables to capture my quantities of interest and use those variables to conduct rigorous tests of Hypotheses 1 and 2, which pertain to the theory's expectations about resource allocations to municipalities within this subset of (tournament-possible) districts. These tests are rigorous because they take confounders seriously, pit the predictions of the tournament theory against those of rival theories, and are tailor-made to the specifics of the electoral system under which incumbents were competing. The results of these quantitative tests provide compelling evidence that LDP politicians in tournament-possible districts use tournaments to win elections.

In the second part of the chapter, I break down the theory's assumptions about LDP politicians, central government bureaucrats, and voters. I present evidence for these assumptions from the Japanese politics literature, anecdotes in the news media, interviews, data on the backgrounds of LDP politicians, and even popular fiction. This qualitative evidence further decreases the chance that the relationships between variables uncovered in the statistical analyses could be the product of a set of dynamics orthogonal to my theory.

In the third part of the chapter, I point out that my book is by no means the first to tackle the relationship between votes and money in Japan. Numerous studies have looked at this question; some with statistical analyses of the exact same data I use herein. Critically, these studies are notable for their *lack* of findings: They either found no clear relationship between votes and money in Japan, or a relationship that ran in the *opposite* direction than what we have been led us to expect (places delivering *fewer* votes for the LDP got *more* money). The absence of systematic evidence that LDP politicians tie money to votes has been hard to reconcile with qualitative evidence that paints a clear picture of LDP politicians spending a lot of time trying to secure funds for their constituents and using election campaigns to advertise their ability to do so. It suggests that while there might be a few bad apples, meaning LDP politicians who threaten to withhold resources from groups who fail to exhibit sufficient electoral loyalty, this is not a *systematic* component of the electoral strategies of LDP politicians. If this is the case, then we should be looking at *non*distributive explanations for the puzzle articulated in Chapter 2: the LDP's electoral success.

I explain that the tournament theory can account for why prior studies reached strikingly different conclusions about the relationship between money and votes in Japan. In a nutshell, tournaments are conducted by relatively autonomous LDP politicians, who face variation in the number and size of municipalities in their respective electoral districts. This creates variation across electoral districts in the total amount of money LDP politicians must offer to entice their municipalities to compete against each other. The LDP politicians facing a set of municipalities that are relatively evenly sized can realize competition with less (money) than their counterparts facing a set of municipalities that are unevenly sized. To uncover the relationship between money and votes, then, it is critical to compare the amount of support delivered and money received by municipalities in the same electoral district after the same election. This is a point not appreciated in prior work, which did not have the tournament theory upon which to draw.

I show that the robust relationship between money and votes documented in this chapter emerges only in regression specifications with district-year fixed effects, which limit the comparison to municipalities in the same district in the same election. When these fixed effects are not used, the relationship appears to run in the *opposite* direction. This result likely obtains because most Japanese municipalities are in electoral districts characterized by relatively evenly sized municipalities. These municipalities receive significantly *less* money than their counterparts in districts characterized by relatively *unevenly* sized municipalities for the same level of support. Thus, without district-year fixed effects, money and support can appear negatively correlated across municipalities. Critically, though, this is the outcome of numerous LDP politicians adjusting the contours of their tournaments to features of their districts, and *not* the outcome of a concerted party strategy of directing spending toward districts where the LDP does worse.

6.1 EMPIRICAL STRATEGY

Chapter 4 fleshed out the theoretical underpinnings of the hypotheses this book tests. To recap, Hypothesis 1 holds that if LDP politicians are administering tournaments between the municipalities in their electoral districts, then the amount of money municipalities receive after Lower House elections will be a function of their position in a rank ordering of municipalities in their electoral districts, constructed on the basis of the level of support the municipality provided the LDP incumbent in the most recent election. Hypothesis 2 holds that if LDP politicians are using tournaments, then the most money is expected to accrue to the municipality whose level of electoral support puts it in first place, after which the amounts awarded are expected to decline with rank, not in a linear fashion but in a convex fashion. This would be evidence that LDP politicians deliberately make the amounts of money being fought over larger at higher ranks. As I explained in Chapter 4, this is done to increase the influence of a single vote over the amount of money one's group receives and is a critical piece of evidence that distinguishes a tournament from alternative logics under which incumbents could be using money to buy support. For ease of access, here are these hypotheses again:

- **Hypothesis 1**: Within electoral districts, resource allocations are a function of a municipality's position in a rank ordering of municipalities, constructed on the basis of support for the LDP winner in the most recent election.
- **Hypothesis 2**: Within electoral districts, the impact of increases in rank on a municipality's postelection resource allocation increases as municipalities climb the ranks.

6.1.1 Data

To examine these, I put together a comprehensive new dataset on the universe of Japanese municipalities that existed in any form between 1980 and 2015.[1] The data is a panel and consists of yearly observations (where t indicates year) of municipalities (m). Because fiscal and other demographic variables pertain to the fiscal year, which runs from April 1 to March 31 in Japan, the unit of analysis in the dataset is municipality-fiscal year (with one exception, which is explained below). There were twelve Lower House elections held during this thirty-five-year period. In the fiscal years in which elections were held, distinct variables capture the electoral districts (d) municipalities are located in and record the numbers of votes cast for the candidates and parties competing therein.[2]

The process through which the data was assembled is described in the Appendix. Let me highlight four pertinent features of it here. One, as I explained in Chapter 5, Japanese municipalities can be cities, special wards, towns, or villages. There were around 3,300 municipalities in existence until the 2002–2005 period, after which a series of amalgamations whittled this number down to around 1,800. My data uses unique municipality codes to account for every single instance of a boundary change. Because a boundary change between two elections means that the pool of voters in municipality m in the second election is different from that in the first, we can reason that politicians will not treat these municipalities as identical and neither should we. Carefully recording each and every

---

[1] This is an expanded, cleaned up version of the data compiled for Catalinac, Bueno de Mesquita and Smith (2020).
[2] The 1990 Lower House election was held on February 18, so is recorded as happening during the 1989 fiscal year.

6.1 Empirical Strategy

boundary change allows us to study what happens to resource allocations when the exact same municipality increases or decreases its support for the LDP incumbent.

Two, in the five Lower House elections held under the old electoral system (in 1980, 1983, 1986, 1990, and 1993, respectively), between 129 and 130 multimember electoral districts (MMDs) were used. As Chapter 2 explains, these districts collectively elected between 511 and 512 Lower House members, with districts selecting between one and six members. In 1994, a mixed-member electoral system was introduced, under which a share of members are elected via first-past-the-post in single-member districts (SMDs) and another share via votes cast for their parties in eleven regional blocs according to closed-list proportional representation. In the first six Lower House elections held under the new system (in 1996, 2000, 2003, 2005, 2009, and 2012, respectively), 300 Members were elected from 300 SMDs. In the seventh election (in 2014), the number of SMDs was reduced to 295. The number of Members elected via proportional representation was 200 in the 1996 election, after which it reduced to 180 prior to the 2000 election. It was reduced further, to 176, prior to the 2017 election.

Three, as Chapter 5 explains, the vast majority of Japan's municipalities are perfectly nested within a single electoral district. Concretely, in the five elections held under the old electoral system (1980–1993), a maximum of four municipalities (out of more than 3,300) straddled more than one district.[3] After electoral reform, the number of split municipalities increased but remains low as a share of the total number of municipalities.[4] Municipalities perfectly contained within a single district appear once in the dataset for every year they exist. Because municipalities straddling more than one district have sections of themselves in different districts, they appear n times in the dataset in election years, with n capturing the number of distinct electoral districts they are located in.

Critically, as Chapter 5 explains, for municipalities straddling more than one district, we can observe voting behavior for the section of the municipality in each district, but we cannot observe fiscal or demographic data at this level. Nonvoting variables are measured at the level of the municipality as a whole. This means that an LDP politician with a split municipality in her district can observe how much *support* this section

---

[3] These were Koriyama City in Fukushima prefecture, Chiba City's Midori Ward, and Okayama City. In the 1990 election, Osaka's Chuo Ward was a fourth.
[4] The number of split municipalities increased to fifteen in the 1996 and 2000 elections, seventeen in the 2003 election, fifty-one in the 2005 election, eighty-five in the 2009 election, eighty-eight in the 2012 election, and eighty-five in 2014.

of the municipality gave her but do not possess the same degree of influence over the amount of *money* voters in this section receive. This LDP politician could lobby for money for the municipality as a whole but cannot guarantee that it will be spent in *her* section of the municipality. For this reason, we assume that LDP politicians focus their attention on the *nonsplit* municipalities within their districts. To this end, we drop split municipalities from the data prior to the creation of the variables used in the below empirical analyses. These variables are thus constructed with municipalities that are perfectly contained within a single district.

Four, as Chapter 5 explains, the fiscal transfers I am interested in are national treasury disbursements (NTD). For annual allocations of NTD, I rely on data made available after the conclusion of the fiscal year, which records the total amount of funds municipality m received in this category during fiscal year t. As such, my data is not the amount of NTD *promised* to municipality m, nor the amount of NTD the government *planned* to send to municipality m, but the amount of NTD municipality m received from the central government during fiscal year t.

6.1.2 Variables

With this data, I constructed four electoral support variables.[5] These capture, in slightly different ways, the level of electoral support municipality m supplied to its LDP incumbent(s) in a Lower House election held at t. Let $n_{d,t}$ capture the number of municipalities in electoral district d in year t.[6] Let $v_{c,m,t}$ represent the number of votes obtained by candidate c in municipality m at time t. This is available for $t \in E = \{e_1, e_2, ...\} = \{1980, 1983, ...\}$, the years in which Lower House elections were held. Let $p_{m,t}$ represent the voting population in municipality m at time t (the number of eligible voters). Thus, $VS_{c,m,t} = \frac{v_{c,m,t}}{p_{m,t}}$ is the number of votes captured by candidate c in municipality m at time t, divided by the number of eligible voters in municipality m at time t. Several indicator functions can also be defined: $w_{c,t}$ indicates whether candidate c won a seat in district d at time t, and $LDP_{c,t}$ indicates whether candidate c was a member of the LDP at time t.

First, I calculate:

$$\text{Best LDP } VS_{m,t} = max_{c \in m}\{LDP_{c,t} w_{c,t} VS_{c,m,t}\} \quad (6.1)$$

---

[5] Where possible, I use the variable operationalizations in Catalinac, Bueno de Mesquita and Smith (2020).
[6] The average electoral district prior to 1994 contained twenty-six municipalities. Between 1994 and the 2001–2005 period, the average district contained twelve municipalities. Since 2005, it has contained seven municipalities.

6.1 Empirical Strategy

This takes the $VS_{c,m,t}$ scores of the universe of LDP winners in district d at time t, and for each municipality, records the maximum. Intuitively, this variable captures the level of electoral support the municipality gave to the LDP winner it supported the most. As an illustration, if there were three LDP winners in district d at time t and they captured 0.6, 0.1, and 0.05 of the available votes in municipality m, respectively, then municipality m's Best LDP $VS_{m,t}$ score would be the maximum of these, or 0.6. Second, I calculate:

$$\text{Sum LDP } VS_{m,t} = \sum_{c \in m} \{LDP_{c,t} w_{c,t} VS_{c,m,t}\} \quad (6.2)$$

This takes the $VS_{c,m,t}$ scores of the universe of LDP winners in district d at time t, and for each municipality, takes the sum of these scores. Intuitively, this variable captures how supportive the municipality was for *all* the LDP winners in its electoral district. Continuing with the above example, if there were three LDP winners in district d at time t and they captured 0.6, 0.1, and 0.05 of the available votes in municipality m, then municipality m's Sum LDP $VS_{m,t}$ score would be the sum of these, or 0.75. When a district has a single LDP winner, Best LDP $VS_{m,t}$ and Sum LDP $VS_{m,t}$ are identical. Thus, my analyses of the Lower House elections *after* Japan's 1994 electoral reform use Sum LDP $VS_{m,t}$ only.

While Best LDP $VS_{m,t}$ and Sum LDP $VS_{m,t}$ are indicators of the absolute level of support for the LDP in municipality m, the tournament theory emphasizes the importance of a municipality's relative *rank* in its electoral district. Thus, I also construct ranked versions of these electoral support variables. To do this, I first identify district-years with LDP winners, in which at least one of the LDP candidates competing in the district emerged victorious. For each of these district-years, I took the Best LDP $VS_{m,t}$ scores of all the municipalities therein and ranked them, so that the lowest-ranked municipality received 0 and the highest-ranked municipality received one less than the total number of municipalities in the district (in other words, $n_{d,t} - 1$). If there were sixteen municipalities in a given district-year, the lowest-ranked (least supportive) municipality receives 0, while the highest-ranked (most supportive) municipality receives 15.

Then, dividing each municipality's number on this ranking by the total number of municipalities in its district-year minus 1 ($n_{d,t} - 1$) has the effect of standardizing the index across district-years. The result is that in every district-year, the municipality supplying the *lowest* level of electoral support for the district's LDP winner(s) (with the lowest Best LDP $VS_{m,t}$ score) received 0 and the municipality supplying the *highest* level of electoral support (with the highest Best LDP $VS_{m,t}$ score) received 1.

I then did the same for Sum LDP VS$_{m,t}$. These calculations leave me with ranked versions of the two electoral support variables, which I refer to as Rank (Best LDP VS$_{m,t}$) and Rank (Sum LDP VS$_{m,t}$), respectively.

Next, I constructed my dependent variable: Postelection Per Capita Transfers (log). This is the total amount of NTD received by municipality m in the fiscal year following each Lower House election, divided by population in municipality m, and logged. I also construct Log(Transfers$_{m,t}$), which is the lagged dependent variable. This is the total amount of NTD received by municipality m in fiscal years in which Lower House elections were held, divided by the population in municipality m, and logged. Specifications with the lagged dependent variable help isolate the impact of a municipality's behavior in the election held at t, by guarding against the possibility that postelection resource allocations are explained by features of the municipality present before the election.

6.2 WITHIN DISTRICTS, MONEY FOLLOWS SUPPORT

Is the amount of money municipalities receive after Lower House elections a function of their position in a rank ordering of municipalities in their district, constructed on the basis of the share of eligible voters in the municipality who voted for the LDP politician? This is Hypothesis 1. To answer this question, I conduct a series of fixed effect regressions on observations from Lower House elections held in the 1980–2014 period, excluding the 2009 election.[7]

Before doing so, let me make three points about the sample. One, my analyses begin in 1980 and end in 2014 because of data availability: putting together historical data on Japanese municipalities from scratch is an arduous task, which made it difficult to go back further than 1980. Furthermore, when I began the project, fiscal data for the years following the 2017 and 2021 Lower House elections was not available, which is why my analyses end in 2014. I exclude 2009 because the LDP lost the 2009 election, which meant it did not control government during the fiscal year following this election (2010). While the LDP was also deprived of its majority in the 1993 election, it managed to put itself back in the saddle the following June, a mere three months into fiscal year 1994. Thus, LDP politicians spent most of fiscal year 1994 *in* government, whereas they spent the entirety of the 2010 fiscal year *out* of government.[8]

---

[7] The empirical tests in this chapter were inspired by those in Catalinac, Bueno de Mesquita and Smith (2020).

[8] As a reminder, my data on NTD allocations capture the amounts *delivered* to municipalities during a given fiscal year, not the amounts *promised* to municipalities

6.2 Within Districts, Money Follows Support

Two, my electoral support variables were constructed after having dropped the small share of municipalities whose area straddles more than one electoral district. Thus, these (split) municipalities are not the subject of the following analyses. Three, in Chapter 5, I explained that in Japan's Lower House elections, tournament-possible electoral districts co-exist with tournament-impossible districts. Tournament-impossible districts are districts comprised of a single municipality, districts with large chunks of voters residing in municipalities whose area is not perfectly contained within the district, and districts located in ordinance-designated cities. The following analyses focus on discerning whether tournaments are occurring in tournament-possible districts. Correspondingly, the sample is limited to nonsplit municipalities in tournament-possible districts.

Table 6.1 presents fixed effect regression models for the logarithm of per capita transfers received by municipalities in the years following the eleven Lower House elections held between 1980 and 2014 as a function of my four independent variables of interest, prior transfers, and other controls.[9] The dependent variable is Postelection Per Capita Transfers (log). My independent variables are Best LDP VS$_{m,t}$ (Model 1), Rank (Best LDP VS$_{m,t}$) (Model 2), Sum LDP VS$_{m,t}$ (Model 3), and Rank (Sum LDP VS$_{m,t}$) (Model 4), respectively. All specifications control for prior transfers, captured with the logarithm of per capita transfers received by the municipality the year of the Lower House election. All specifications also control for six time-varying features of municipalities that could influence the relationship between voting and transfers. These are the municipality's population, per capita income, population density, fiscal strength, the proportion of residents employed in primary industries, and the proportion of residents aged fifteen and under and sixty-five and over, respectively.[10]

All specifications use district-year fixed effects. This controls for features of district d at time t that could be influencing the transfers received

(which could have been decided upon the year prior). An assumption I make is that LDP politicians can influence NTD allocations to municipalities within a given fiscal year. This assumption is also made by others (e.g., Hirano 2011, 1086). In Japan, the government's budget must be approved prior to the start of a fiscal year, but governments can (and regularly do) enact supplementary budgets, which authorize new spending. In an interview with a former House of Councilors member from the Komeito, I was told that spending for a given locale can be inserted into supplementary budgets (Interview, Tokyo, Japan, December 13, 2023.)

[9] Descriptive statistics pertaining to the variables used in these regressions appears in Table A.1.
[10] I use the log of population and per capita income. Population density is created by dividing the municipality's population by its size (kilometers squared). Following Catalinac, Bueno de Mesquita and Smith (2020), I scaled it so that the variable captures the number of *thousands* of people per square kilometer.

How Politicians Tie Money to Electoral Support

Table 6.1 *Within electoral districts, municipalities exhibiting higher levels of support for their district's LDP winner(s) in Lower House elections received more per capita transfers after the election, 1980–2014.*

	Dependent variable: Postelection Transfers (log)			
	(Model 1)	(Model 2)	(Model 3)	(Model 4)
Best LDP VS$_{m,t}$	0.160***			
	(0.034)			
Rank (Best LDP VS$_{m,t}$)		0.029**		
		(0.010)		
Sum LDP VS$_{m,t}$			0.152***	
			(0.034)	
Rank (Sum LDP VS$_{m,t}$)				0.031**
				(0.011)
Log(Transfers$_{m,t}$)	0.720***	0.722***	0.720***	0.722***
	(0.008)	(0.008)	(0.008)	(0.008)
Fiscal Strength$_{m,t}$	0.090***	0.087**	0.091***	0.088**
	(0.025)	(0.028)	(0.024)	(0.028)
Dependent Population$_{m,t}$	0.822***	0.761***	0.840***	0.768***
	(0.138)	(0.145)	(0.138)	(0.145)
Farming Population$_{m,t}$	−0.102	−0.087	−0.109	−0.093
	(0.082)	(0.094)	(0.082)	(0.095)
Log(Population$_{m,t}$)	−0.009	−0.011*	−0.008	−0.010
	(0.005)	(0.005)	(0.005)	(0.005)
Log(Per Capita Income$_{m,t}$)	−0.071*	−0.076*	−0.069*	−0.075*
	(0.032)	(0.035)	(0.032)	(0.035)
Population Density$_{m,t}$	0.007*	0.008*	0.007*	0.008*
	(0.004)	(0.004)	(0.004)	(0.004)
Observations	27,225	23,909	27,225	23,909
District-year FE	Y	Y	Y	Y
R^2	0.538	0.537	0.538	0.537

Robust standard errors clustered on municipality in parentheses.
*$p < 0.05$, **$p < 0.01$, ***$p < 0.001$.
Regression models estimated with R's plm() package.

by all municipalities in that district. For example, a district-year might see the victory of an exceptionally well-connected or competent LDP politician. As I explained above, the tournament theory expects that the total amount of money needed to realize competition among municipalities differs by electoral district, making this a critical part of our empirical strategy. A district-year fixed effect effectively enables us to look *within* district-years, to see whether the hypothesis that municipalities returning higher levels of electoral support for the LDP relative to their same-district counterparts receive more per capita transfers after

6.2 Within Districts, Money Follows Support

the election is supported. For each specification, I report robust standard errors clustered on municipality.

As a reminder, municipalities in districts without any LDP winner receive zero on Best LDP VS$_{m,t}$ and Sum LDP VS$_{m,t}$. Our use of district-year fixed effects means that these observations drop out of the regressions because municipalities in district-years without LDP winners have identical scores on these support variables. This means that our estimates of the impact of electoral support are derived solely from municipalities in districts with at least one LDP winner. In contrast, municipalities receiving zero on Rank (Best LDP VS$_{m,t}$) and Rank (Sum LDP VS$_{m,t}$) are not municipalities in districts without LDP winners, but municipalities who ranked *last in electoral loyalty* for their LDP winner. As such, the number of observations differs across the models in Table 6.1. Models 2 and 4 have fewer observations than Models 1 and 3 because municipalities in districts without a single LDP winner receive NA on Rank (Best LDP VS$_{m,t}$) and Rank (Sum LDP VS$_{m,t}$), respectively.

The positive, significant coefficients on all the support variables indicate that within district-years, controlling for other time-varying features of municipalities, higher levels of support for winning LDP candidates translated into significantly more transfers in the year after the election. The coefficients on the variables measuring prior transfers are also positive and highly statistically significant. This makes sense if we consider first that the amount of transfers a municipality received in previous years would have been influenced by previous levels of electoral support, and second, that voting behavior can be relatively sticky. In addition, within district-years, municipalities with larger proportions of their population who are dependent tend to receive more transfers, as do municipalities whose fiscal situations are sound and which have higher population density. In contrast, municipalities with higher-than-average per capita income and a larger population tend to receive fewer transfers.

What does this mean in substantive terms? Importantly, the coefficients in these models capture the *average* effect of a given increase in support, no matter *where* in the distribution of support it takes place. As Chapter 4 explains, the tournament theory expects that increases in support at the top of the ranking will translate into much larger (indeed, exponentially larger) increases in transfers than the same increase at the middle or bottom of the ranking. Put simply, a municipality ranking second in support will be rewarded with a much larger payoff for a one-rank increase (putting it in first place), than a municipality ranking seventh would receive for the same one-rank increase (putting it in sixth place). This convexity is examined in more detail below. For readers interested in the average effect of increases in support, even though this is less informative,

Model 1 in Table 6.1 tells us that a one-standard-deviation increase in Best LDP VS$_{m,t}$ is expected to net a municipality a 2.61% increase in per capita postelection transfers. Given that the mean postelection per capita transfer in this sample was 29,705 yen, this amounts to a per person increase of 776 yen. The average municipality in this sample has 13,663 people, which translates into an increase of 10,601,462 yen (approx. $68,064 USD at today's exchange rate).[11]

6.2.1 Before Electoral Reform, 1980–1993

Next, to increase confidence in these findings, I divide the data into elections held under the old electoral system (pre-1993) and elections held under the new (post-1994). This allows me to craft nuanced tests of Hypothesis 1, which are tailor-made to the specifics of each period. In the Lower House elections held between 1980 and 1994, I have a set of approximately 3,300 municipalities whose borders were stable *and* which were located in a relatively small number of electoral districts, whose borders were also stable. I can take advantage of these features of this period in two ways: first, by conducting what I call a "snapshot regression." This looks within district-years and ascertains whether, after controlling for the possibility that underlying differences between municipalities are driving any observed relationship between electoral support and transfers, municipalities exhibiting higher levels of support receive more postelection transfers.

Table 6.2 presents the results of the same four regression specifications in Table 6.1, but with the addition of municipality fixed effects and with the sample limited to observations in the 1980–1993 period. The purpose of a municipality fixed effect is to control for time-*invariant* features of municipality *m* that might be influencing both its voting behavior and the amount of transfers it receives. It is conceivable that certain municipalities

---

[11] Could the relationship between money and votes depicted in Table 6.1 be due to the inclusion of districts with dominant municipalities, defined as those with 80% or more residents in a single one? Of the 1,724 tournament-possible districts in this sample, only 113 (6.6%) have a dominant municipality. Rerunning the models in Table 6.1 after removing observations in dominant-municipality districts yields results that are similar in both substance and statistical significance. In Chapter 4, I offered reasons why politicians in dominant-municipality districts would not concentrate their vote-gathering on these dominant municipalities, even though they have more voters. This is because in doing so, the politician runs the risk of reducing the incentives of *all* voters, in both dominant and nondominant municipalities, to vote for them. While further work is needed, preliminary analyses shows that the largest municipality in dominant-municipality districts delivers a level of support that is similar to that provided by the largest municipality in *non*dominant-municipality districts but receives more money for this support. Thus, resource allocations do appear to be different in dominant-municipality districts.

6.2 Within Districts, Money Follows Support

Table 6.2 *Within electoral districts, municipalities exhibiting higher levels of support for their district's LDP winner(s) in Lower House elections received more per capita transfers after the election, 1980–1993.*

	Dependent variable: Postelection Transfers (log)			
	(Model 1)	(Model 2)	(Model 3)	(Model 4)
Best LDP VS$_{m,t}$	0.162** (0.051)			
Rank (Best LDP VS$_{m,t}$)		0.041* (0.016)		
Sum LDP VS$_{m,t}$			0.163*** (0.047)	
Rank (Sum LDP VS$_{m,t}$)				0.055** (0.017)
Log(Transfers$_{m,t}$)	0.435*** (0.012)	0.436*** (0.012)	0.435*** (0.012)	0.436*** (0.012)
Fiscal Strength$_{m,t}$	−0.011 (0.075)	−0.020 (0.076)	−0.012 (0.075)	−0.020 (0.076)
Dependent Population$_{m,t}$	0.689* (0.334)	0.593 (0.331)	0.698* (0.334)	0.593 (0.330)
Farming Population$_{m,t}$	−0.567 (0.328)	−0.619 (0.329)	−0.556 (0.326)	−0.615 (0.328)
Log(Population$_{m,t}$)	−0.515*** (0.116)	−0.520*** (0.116)	−0.511*** (0.116)	−0.517*** (0.116)
Log(Per Capita Income$_{m,t}$)	0.027 (0.071)	0.024 (0.072)	0.030 (0.071)	0.027 (0.072)
Population Density$_{m,t}$	0.026 (0.075)	0.032 (0.077)	0.025 (0.074)	0.032 (0.077)
Observations	15,526	15,416	15,526	15,416
District-year FE	Y	Y	Y	Y
Municipality FE	Y	Y	Y	Y
R^2	0.205	0.205	0.205	0.206

Robust standard errors clustered on municipality in parentheses.
*$p < 0.05$, **$p < 0.01$, ***$p < 0.001$.
Regression models estimated with R's plm() package.

might be better at coming up with projects likely to attract central government funding or building a consensus in their community about the need for those projects. They might have local politicians who are better able to elicit the help of their LDP-affiliated Diet representatives. A municipality fixed effect takes care of the possibility that systematic differences of this nature between the municipalities in a given district-year could be driving any observed effect of electoral support on transfers.[12]

---

[12] Note that municipalities were placed in new electoral districts in 1994 and changed their borders or experienced neighboring municipalities in the same district change

In specifications with municipality fixed effects, the effects of time-varying municipality-level variables such as electoral support can be estimated separately from the municipality fixed effect only when they exhibit sufficient over-time variation. When municipalities have the same or very-similar values on a variable over time, this variable could be influencing postelection transfer allocations, but the lack of over-time variation means that its effect would be subsumed by the municipality fixed effect. Table 6.2 nevertheless reveals that the coefficients on the four electoral support variables are positive and statistically significant, even with municipality fixed effects. This means that, controlling for idiosyncratic features of municipalities that could have consequences for voting and transfers, as well as features of the district-years that municipalities are part of, higher levels of support for winning LDP candidates in elections in the 1980–1993 period translated into larger per capita transfer allocations after these elections. Other time-varying features of municipalities found to influence transfer allocations are prior transfers, the proportion of a municipality's population that is dependent (though not in Models 2 and 4), and population.

A second way I can take advantage of the stability in municipality and district boundaries in this period is by conducting a "first-difference regression." This takes advantage of the fact that municipalities are in the same electoral districts over time, which means they face the same set of competitors in the tournament, election after election. Unlike a snapshot regression, which looks within district-years, leveraging variation in the degree of support between municipalities in the same district-year, a first-difference regression looks within *municipalities*, leveraging variation in the degree to which the same municipality supported the LDP over time. If, controlling for changes in other time-varying municipality-level features, such as population, as well as features of a municipality's district-year that likely influence the amounts of transfers received by all municipalities, municipalities that increase their support for the LDP between two elections are found to receive larger transfer allocations after the second election, this would further bolster confidence in these results.

Table 6.3 examines the effect of changes in support between two consecutive elections on change in the amount of per capita transfers received in the years following those elections for municipalities in the 1980–1993 period. Because my data begins in 1980, the 1983 election is the first election for which I can compute change variables (I call these Δ

---

their borders between 2002 and 2005. The magnitude of these changes mean that municipality fixed effects make less sense in the above analyses, which examined observations from the full period.

6.2 Within Districts, Money Follows Support

Table 6.3 *Increases in support between two consecutive elections in the same municipality translate into increases in the amount of per capita transfers received after the election, 1980–1993.*

	Dependent variable: Δ Postelection Transfers (log)			
	(Model 1)	(Model 2)	(Model 3)	(Model 4)
Δ Best LDP VS$_{m,t}$	0.180** (0.067)			
Δ Rank (Best LDP VS$_{m,t}$)		0.052* (0.022)		
Δ Sum LDP VS$_{m,t}$			0.195** (0.061)	
Δ Rank (Sum LDP VS$_{m,t}$)				0.071** (0.023)
Δ Fiscal Strength$_{m,t}$	−0.045 (0.087)	−0.049 (0.088)	−0.040 (0.087)	−0.046 (0.088)
Δ Dependent Population$_{m,t}$	0.977 (0.752)	0.907 (0.757)	0.995 (0.753)	0.919 (0.756)
Δ Farming Population$_{m,t}$	−0.476 (0.614)	−0.451 (0.614)	−0.460 (0.612)	−0.449 (0.613)
Δ Log(Population$_{m,t}$)	−1.228*** (0.371)	−1.170** (0.371)	−1.217** (0.371)	−1.164** (0.371)
Δ Log(Per Capita Income$_{m,t}$)	−0.071 (0.128)	−0.041 (0.133)	−0.068 (0.128)	−0.039 (0.132)
Δ Population Density$_{m,t}$	0.583* (0.259)	0.540* (0.272)	0.581* (0.260)	0.536* (0.272)
Observations	12,393	12,224	12,393	12,224
Municipality FE	Y	Y	Y	Y
District-year FE	Y	Y	Y	Y
R^2	0.003	0.002	0.003	0.003

Robust standard errors clustered on municipality in parentheses.
*$p < 0.05$, **$p < 0.01$, ***$p < 0.001$.
Regression models estimated with R's plm() package.

variables). Thus, the sample is municipalities in the 1983, 1986, 1990, and 1993 elections. In all four specifications, the dependent variable is ΔLog(Transfer), which is the municipality's per capita transfer allocation in the year following the Lower House election, minus its per capita transfer allocation in the year following the previous Lower House election (in logs). In Model 1, Δ Best LDP VS$_m$ is the municipality's Best LDP VS$_{m,t}$ in the Lower House election, minus its Best LDP VS$_{m,t}$ in the previous Lower House election. Model 2 uses Δ Rank(Best LDP VS)$_m$, Model 3 uses Δ Sum LDP VS$_m$, and Model 4 uses Δ Rank(Sum LDP VS)$_m$, all constructed analogously.

In all four specifications, I control for changes in the six time-varying municipality-level variables, constructing analogous Δ variables for each. I also use municipality fixed effects, which control for time-invariant features of a municipality that could plausibly be correlated with changes in support and transfers, and district-year fixed effects, which control for the possibility that systematic differences between district-years in the second election could influence the degree to which transfers to all municipalities in the district changed relative to the previous election. Because municipalities are located in the same districts in this period, any change in district-level features that have consequences for transfers, such as the victory of a particularly competent LDP politician or an increase in number of LDP winners, will act on all municipalities in that district simultaneously. This means that all district-level changes of this type are accounted for with district-year fixed effects.

In all four models in Table 6.3, the coefficients on the Δ electoral support variables are positive and statistically significant. Models 1 and 3 show that municipalities that managed to increase their absolute level of support between two elections, measured with votes for a single LDP winner (Model 1) or votes for all LDP winners (Model 3), received more transfers after the second election. Models 2 and 4 show that municipalities that managed to increase their position in a rank ordering of municipalities in their district, constructed on the basis of electoral support for a single LDP winner (Model 2) or all LDP winners (Model 4), also received more transfers after the second election. By extension, of course, this means that municipalities that *decreased* their absolute level of support between two elections, or let their ranking *slip* between the two elections, are penalized with smaller transfer allocations after the second election. The results of both the snapshot regressions, which leveraged variation in support across municipalities in the same district-year, and first-difference regressions, which leveraged variation in support within the same municipality over time, lend strong support to my hypothesis.

6.2.2 Competing Explanations and Placebo Tests, 1980–1993

This section reports the results of tests that pit the predictions of the tournament theory against those of rival theories. First, prior to Japan's 1994 electoral reform, districts were multimember, which means they usually sent more than one LDP winner to the Diet. A rival theory might hold that the most *powerful* LDP politician in the district has a stranglehold over transfers. If so, where municipalities placed in a ranking constructed on the basis of electoral support for *this* LDP winner, not *any* LDP winner,

6.2 Within Districts, Money Follows Support

could be a more powerful determinant of how much money it receives after the relevant election.

To evaluate this, I ran the same four specifications in Table 6.2 with a control for the $VS_{c,m,t}$ (vote share) captured by the LDP's highest place-getter in the district, High LDP $VS_{m,t}$.[13] The results appear in Table A.2. The coefficient on High LDP $VS_{m,t}$ is statistically insignificant in all four models, while our four variables of interest, Best LDP $VS_{m,t}$, Rank(Best LDP $VS_{m,t}$), Sum LDP $VS_{m,t}$, and Rank(Sum LDP $VS_{m,t}$), remain positive and statistically significant. Thus, my results cannot be explained by this rival theory.

Second, another rival theory might hold that *senior* LDP politicians are the only members of the ruling party with enough clout to be able to influence transfer allocations to the municipalities in their districts. To evaluate this, I constructed versions of the four support variables using votes cast for *senior* LDP winners only (not all LDP winners), defined as those who have served at least four prior terms.[14] Concretely, let $Sen_{c,t}$ indicate whether candidate c was a senior politician. I constructed the following:

$$\text{Best Senior LDP VS}_{m,t} = max_{c \in m} \{Sen_{c,t} LDP_{c,t} w_{c,t} VS_{c,m,t}\} \quad (6.3)$$

$$\text{Sum Senior LDP VS}_{m,t} = \sum_{c \in m} \{Sen_{c,t} LDP_{c,t} w_{c,t} VS_{c,m,t}\} \quad (6.4)$$

Intuitively, Best Senior LDP $VS_{m,t}$ captures the level of electoral support the municipality gave to the senior LDP winner it gave the highest level of support to, while Sum Senior LDP $VS_{m,t}$ captures how supportive the municipality was for all LDP senior winners in the district.

In Table 6.4, Model 1 pits this rival theory against the tournament theory, by including both Best LDP $VS_{m,t}$ and Best Senior LDP $VS_{m,t}$ as independent variables. The specification is otherwise identical to that presented in Model 1 of Table 6.2 (thus, it includes time-varying municipality-level controls, district-year fixed effects, municipality fixed effects, and limits the sample to elections in the 1980–1993 period). The coefficient on Best Senior LDP $VS_{m,t}$ is positive but not statistically significant, while the coefficient on Best LDP $VS_{m,t}$ remains positive and

---

[13] Concretely, in district-years with LDP winners, I identified the LDP winner who won the most votes. Then, for each municipality in that district-year, I recorded the share of eligible voters who had voted for this LDP winner.

[14] Krauss and Pekkanen (2010, 157) explain that LDP politicians begin receiving leadership posts in their fifth terms.

Table 6.4 *Within electoral districts, transfers to municipalities are not determined by support for senior LDP winners, non-LDP winners, or losing LDP candidates, 1980–1993. But independent winners who join the LDP after elections distribute transfers according to a similar logic as LDP winners.*

	Dependent variable: Postelection Transfers (log)			
	(Model 1)	(Model 2)	(Model 3)	(Model 4)
Best LDP VS$_{m,t}$	0.145**			
	(0.053)			
Best Senior LDP VS$_{m,t}$	0.040			
	(0.050)			
Best LDP+ VS$_{m,t}$		0.196***		
		(0.053)		
Best Non-LDP VS$_{m,t}$			0.035	
			(0.064)	
Best Losing LDP VS$_{m,t}$				−0.255***
				(0.061)
Log(Transfers$_{m,t}$)	0.435***	0.436***	0.436***	0.435***
	(0.012)	(0.012)	(0.012)	(0.012)
Fiscal Strength$_{m,t}$	−0.011	−0.011	−0.014	−0.011
	(0.075)	(0.075)	(0.075)	(0.075)
Dependent Population$_{m,t}$	0.686*	0.682*	0.693*	0.700*
	(0.334)	(0.334)	(0.333)	(0.332)
Farming Population$_{m,t}$	−0.568	−0.561	−0.589	−0.567
	(0.328)	(0.327)	(0.328)	(0.326)
Log(Population$_{m,t}$)	−0.516***	−0.515***	−0.526***	−0.529***
	(0.116)	(0.116)	(0.116)	(0.117)
Log(Per Capita Income$_{m,t}$)	0.027	0.028	0.020	0.026
	(0.071)	(0.071)	(0.071)	(0.071)
Population Density$_{m,t}$	0.026	0.025	0.029	0.027
	(0.075)	(0.075)	(0.075)	(0.074)
Observations	15,526	15,526	15,526	15,526
District-year FE	Y	Y	Y	Y
Municipality FE	Y	Y	Y	Y
R^2	0.205	0.205	0.205	0.206

Robust standard errors clustered on municipality in parentheses.
*$p < 0.05$, **$p < 0.01$, ***$p < 0.001$.
Regression models estimated with R's plm() package.

statistically significant. Thus, there is little evidence to suggest that it is the level of electoral support municipalities supply to senior LDP politicians that determines the amount of transfers they receive.[15]

---

[15] In Model 1 of Table A.3, I conduct the same test with Sum Senior LDP VS$_{m,t}$ instead of Best Senior LDP VS$_{m,t}$ and find that the results are substantively similar.

6.2 Within Districts, Money Follows Support

Third, a different way to build confidence in the theory is to deduce additional observable implications about what we would observe under a tournament and evaluate those. Given what we know about the internal workings of the LDP in this period, we have reason to believe that conservative-aligned independents who were admitted into the LDP after winning an election would have also been able to lobby central government bureaucrats such that NTD allocations could be calibrated to municipalities on the basis of electoral support, just like their counterparts who had obtained the party's endorsement prior to the election. In many cases, these conservative candidates were campaigning with the backing of an LDP faction that was not currently endorsing an LDP candidate in that district (Reed 2009). Given that senior faction members tend to help junior faction members with introductions to bureaucrats, it is reasonable to assume that if LDP-aligned independents were in a faction, they would have been able to elicit the help of senior faction leaders.

To test this, let LDP+$_{c,t}$ indicate whether candidate c was a member of the LDP at the time of the election *or* was a conservative-aligned independent who was permitted to join the LDP after the election. I constructed:

$$\text{Best LDP+ VS}_{m,t} = max_{c \in m}\{LDP +_{c,t} w_{c,t} VS_{c,m,t}\} \qquad (6.5)$$

$$\text{Sum LDP+ VS}_{m,t} = \sum_{c \in m}\{LDP +_{c,t} w_{c,t} VS_{c,m,t}\} \qquad (6.6)$$

Intuitively, Best LDP+ VS$_{m,t}$ captures the level of electoral support the municipality gave to the LDP winner it supported the most, where LDP winner is defined more expansively to include independents who were permitted to join the party after the election. Similarly, Sum LDP+ VS$_{m,t}$ captures how supportive the municipality was for all LDP winners in the district, where LDP winner is defined in this more expansive way.

In Table 6.4, Model 2 examines the effect of Best LDP+ VS$_{m,t}$ on transfers. The specification is identical to that of Model 1 of Table 6.2 but with Best LDP+ VS$_{m,t}$ instead of Best LDP VS$_{m,t}$. The coefficient on Best LDP+ VS$_{m,t}$ is positive and statistically significant. This shows that winning candidates who joined the LDP after the election also had access to transfers such that they were able to dole out prizes to municipalities in accordance with their level of support.[16]

---

[16] In Model 2 of Table A.3, I conduct these same tests with Sum LDP+ VS$_{m,t}$ and find that the results are substantively similar.

Fourth, the tournament theory holds that it is *winning LDP* candidates who will be able to convert voting into a competition over which municipality is the most electorally supportive. By making it clear that resources after the election are contingent on levels of support delivered in the election, LDP candidates who look like they are going to win the election will be able to motivate voters in supportive municipalities to actively compete for first place. In the eyes of voters, being a member of the party controlling the purse strings makes these promises significantly more credible. By extension, it is not winning candidates affiliated with *other parties*. Nor is it LDP candidates who *lost* the election. Thus, if the tournament theory is correct, we would not observe municipalities ranking highly in support of *non*-LDP candidates being rewarded with more money after the election. Nor would we observe municipalities ranking highly in support of *losing* LDP candidates being rewarded with more money. To evaluate this, we constructed:

$$\text{Best Non-LDP VS}_{m,t} = max_{c \in m}\{(1 - LDP_{c,t})w_{c,t}VS_{c,m,t}\} \quad (6.7)$$
$$\text{Sum Non-LDP VS}_{m,t} = \sum_{c \in m}\{(1 - LDP_{c,t})w_{c,t}VS_{c,m,t}\} \quad (6.8)$$

Intuitively, Best Non-LDP VS$_{m,t}$ is the level of electoral support the municipality gave to the non-LDP winner it supported the most, while Sum Non-LDP VS$_{m,t}$ captures how supportive the municipality was for all non-LDP winners in the district. Next, I constructed:

$$\text{Best Losing LDP VS}_{m,t} = max_{c \in m}\{LDP_{c,t}(1 - w_{c,t})VS_{c,m,t}\} \quad (6.9)$$
$$\text{Sum Losing LDP VS}_{m,t} = \sum_{c \in m}\{LDP_{c,t}(1 - w_{c,t})VS_{c,m,t}\} \quad (6.10)$$

Intuitively, Best Losing LDP VS$_{m,t}$ is the level of electoral support the municipality gave to the LDP loser it supported the most, while Sum Losing LDP VS$_{m,t}$ captures how supportive the municipality was for all losing LDP candidates.

In Table 6.4, Model 3 examines the effect of Best Non-LDP VS$_{m,t}$ on transfers after the election. The coefficient is not statistically significant, which means that municipalities scoring highly in support of non-LDP politicians did not receive more money after elections. Model 4 examines the effect of Best Losing LDP VS$_{m,t}$. The coefficient is negative and statistically significant. This means that scoring highly in support of a losing LDP candidate is associated with receiving less money after the election. To the extent that concentrating one's support on a losing LDP candidate means that a municipality has forgone the opportunity to concentrate its support on a winning LDP candidate, it is unsurprising that we observe this negative relationship. Because winning LDP candidates

6.2 Within Districts, Money Follows Support

reward municipalities in their districts on the basis of support, municipalities scoring low in support for winning candidates will, on average, receive less money.[17]

Fifth, the Japanese politics literature provides ample evidence that incumbents have preexisting ties to select municipalities in their electoral districts, on account of the fact that the municipality is their hometown or has a concentration of voters in certain occupations who support the LDP (Hirano 2006; Curtis 1971). In the presence of such ties, these municipalities may consistently return high levels of support for their LDP incumbents *and* receive larger transfer allocations, but it is possible that this is because of their special relationship with the incumbent, not because they are performing well in any tournament. Table 6.3 went some way toward addressing this rival hypothesis by leveraging within-municipality changes in support, showing that increases and decreases in support within the same municipality impact the amount of transfers it receives, but it is still possible that the positive, statistically significant coefficients on the Δ support variables in these models reflect the effect of changes in support among relatively *unsupportive* municipalities. These models do not adequately address the possibility that the highest-performing municipalities may be *exempt* from the tournament.

To evaluate this, I examined whether the results in Table 6.3 hold among municipalities offering the *highest* levels of support for their LDP winners in the previous election. I restricted the sample to the 921 municipalities that placed first or second in the ranking of municipalities in their (tournament-possible) district in the previous election for elections between 1980 and 1993. In other words, I took those that scored the highest and second-highest on Rank (Sum LDP $VS_{m,t}$) in the previous election. Of these 921 municipalities, 173 municipalities (51.3%) remained in the top two in the subsequent election, with 34.9% retaining the same rank in both elections. The average municipality in this sample, however, dropped 4.4 places in the next election.

Table 6.5 examines the effect of Δ Rank(Sum LDP $VS_{m,t}$) between two consecutive elections on change in the per capita transfers received in the years following these two elections for this sample of highly supportive municipalities. In Model 1, I control for prior transfers (measured in the year of the election), while in Model 2, I control for prior transfers *and* time-varying municipality-level characteristics. Because I only have two observations in each district (municipalities that placed first and second in the previous election) and municipalities are not always in the sample for

---

[17] In Models 3 and 4 of Table A.3, I conduct the same test with Sum Non-LDP $VS_{m,t}$ and Sum Losing LDP $VS_{m,t}$ and find that the results are substantively similar.

Table 6.5 *Municipalities ranking first or second in support for their LDP winner in the previous election are penalized with fewer transfers after the next election if they drop in rank, 1983–1993. There is little evidence that highly supportive municipalities are insulated from the tournament.*

	Dependent variable: Δ Postelection Transfers (log)	
	(Model 1)	(Model 2)
Δ Rank (Sum LDP VS$_{m,t}$)	0.158*	0.185*
	(0.080)	(0.091)
Log(Transfers$_{m,t}$)	0.092***	0.111***
	(0.025)	(0.030)
Fiscal Strength$_{m,t}$		0.190
		(0.139)
Dependent Population$_{m,t}$		−1.241
		(0.845)
Farming Population$_{m,t}$		0.355
		(0.376)
Log(Population$_{m,t}$)		−0.002
		(0.028)
Log(Per Capita Income$_{m,t}$)		−0.135
		(0.117)
Population Density$_{m,t}$		0.003
		(0.024)
Constant	0.087	0.395
	(0.101)	(0.424)
Observations	905	843
Year FE	Y	Y
R^2	0.163	0.173

*$p < 0.05$, ***$p < 0.001$.
Regression models using lm() function in R.

two consecutive elections, I cannot incorporate district or municipality fixed effects. Instead, I use year fixed effects.

The positive, statistically significant coefficient on Δ Rank(Sum LDP VS$_{m,t}$) indicates that highly supportive municipalities that drop in rank between two elections are penalized with fewer transfers after the second election. Correspondingly, municipalities that increase their rank between two elections, which in this sample means municipalities that placed second last time and first this time, were rewarded with more transfers after the election. This confirms that even though highly supportive municipalities tend to *remain* highly supportive over time, when those highly supportive municipalities *slip* in support, they are penalized

6.2 Within Districts, Money Follows Support

with fewer transfers after the election. This suggests that our results cannot be explained by the possibility that select municipalities return high levels of support and receive large transfer allocations for other reasons. Highly supportive municipalities are subject to the same conditions as others: They are forced to compete with each other for resources.

6.2.3 After Electoral Reform, 1996–2014

Next, I turn to the postreform period. As I explained in Chapter 5, Japan's 1994 electoral reform increased the share of tournament-impossible electoral districts. Under the old electoral system, only 9% of districts were tournament-impossible. With the electoral reform, the share increased to 27%. The municipal amalgamations that occurred between 2001 and 2005 and urbanization further increased the share to around 40% of districts in 2005 and then to around 50% in 2009, 2012, and 2014. Thus, the analyses in this section pertain to a smaller share of electoral districts.

Table 6.6 presents the results of fixed effect regression models for the logarithm of per capita transfers received by municipalities in tournament-possible districts in the years following the six Lower House elections held between 1996 and 2014 (excluding 2009) as a function of electoral support, prior transfers, the same six time-varying municipality-level controls, and district-year fixed effects. Model 1 examines the effect of Sum LDP $VS_{m,t}$ on postelection transfers, while Model 2 examines the effect of Rank (Sum LDP $VS_{m,t}$).[18] I report robust standard errors clustered on municipality. In the parlance introduced above, these are snapshot regressions. This means that the coefficients on the support variables will tell us whether, within a given district-year, municipalities exhibiting higher levels of support for their LDP winner received more money after elections. In both models, coefficients on the support variables are positive and statistically significant.

In my analyses of the 1980–1993 period (Tables 6.2 and 6.3), I used both the lagged dependent variable and municipality fixed effects to guard against the possibility that time-invariant features of municipalities could be driving the observed relationship between electoral support and transfers. Adding municipality fixed effects to the specifications in Table 6.6 renders the coefficients on the support variables no longer statistically significant. However, as I explained above, a specification with municipality fixed effects is able to estimate the effect of an independent variable of interest only if municipalities exhibit enough variation in that variable

---

[18] We do not need to separately examine the effects of Best LDP $VS_{m,t}$ and Rank (Best LDP $VS_{m,t}$) because values on these variables are identical to their Sum equivalents in this period. This is because districts produce a single winner.

Table 6.6 *Within electoral districts, municipalities exhibiting higher support for their district's LDP winner in Lower House elections received more per capita transfers after the election, 1996–2014 (excluding 2009).*

	Dependent variable: Postelection Transfers (log)	
	(Model 1)	(Model 2)
Sum LDP VS$_{m,t}$	0.232**	
	(0.071)	
Rank (Sum LDP VS$_{m,t}$)		0.034*
		(0.017)
Log(Transfers$_{m,t}$)	0.677***	0.664***
	(0.011)	(0.013)
Fiscal Strength$_{m,t}$	0.164***	0.200***
	(0.032)	(0.040)
Dependent Population$_{m,t}$	1.521***	1.707***
	(0.217)	(0.246)
Farming Population$_{m,t}$	0.008	0.160
	(0.116)	(0.164)
Log(Population$_{m,t}$)	−0.001	−0.002
	(0.006)	(0.007)
Log(Per Capita Income$_{m,t}$)	0.019	0.035
	(0.048)	(0.060)
Population Density$_{m,t}$	0.013**	0.019***
	(0.004)	(0.006)
Observations	11,699	8,493
District-year FE	Y	Y
R^2	0.534	0.531

Robust standard errors clustered on municipality in parentheses.
*$p < 0.05$, **$p < 0.01$, ***$p < 0.001$.
Regression models estimated with R's plm() package.

over time. If they do not, the effect of the variable will be "washed out" (absorbed) by the municipality fixed effect.

As I explained in Chapter 5, the post-1994 period is very different from the pre-1994 period. In the pre-1994 period, changes in municipality and electoral district borders were rare. As a result, we have observations for more than three thousand unique municipalities spanning five elections. Moreover, because a relatively large number of municipalities were squashed into a relatively small number of electoral districts, each district contained an average of twenty-six municipalities. More municipalities in a district means greater potential for shifts in the ranking, which generate the variation in our support variables needed to estimate their effect

6.2 Within Districts, Money Follows Support

independently of a municipality fixed effect. With my data, I calculated the standard deviation in the Sum LDP VS$_{m,t}$ and Rank (Sum LDP VS$_{m,t}$) for all unique municipalities across the five elections prior to 1994. The average municipality experienced a standard deviation of 0.11 in Sum LDP VS$_{m,t}$ and 0.17 in Rank (Sum LDP VS$_{m,t}$), respectively. Translated into absolute rankings, the average municipality in this time period experienced a standard deviation of 5.8 rankings.

In the post-1994 period, we have more electoral districts, which means fewer municipalities per district and less potential for shifts in the ranking. We also have the government's attempts to encourage municipalities to merge. By 2005, only 39% of municipalities that had existed in 2001 remained with their borders intact; 61% had undergone amalgamations of some kind (Horiuchi, Saito and Yamada 2015). This further reduces the number of municipalities per district; thus, further limiting the potential for movement in our independent variable of interest. Chapter 5 explains that a by-product of the increased number of electoral districts and reduced number of municipalities, especially after 2005, was growth in the number of electoral districts in which tournaments cannot be conducted. Municipalities in tournament-impossible districts are not the subject of the above empirical analyses. This confluence of factors means that many municipalities in the postreform period are in the data for only two or three elections before disappearing, either because they were subject to a merger (and ceased to exist), or because population changes meant that their district became tournament-impossible. Many municipalities created by a merger in the mid 2000s are also in the data for only one or two elections before their district qualifies as tournament-impossible and they drop out.

Of the universe of unique municipalities that existed in the post-1994 period ($n = 3,606$), my data show that only 25% ($n = 898$) existed for five or more elections, the length of time municipalities in the pre-1994 period existed. Almost 70% of municipalities ($n = 2,492$) in existence in the post-1994 period existed for one, two, or three elections. Looking at the standard deviation in Sum LDP VS$_{m,t}$ and Rank (Sum LDP VS$_{m,t}$) for all unique municipalities in the postreform period, we find that the average municipality experienced a standard deviation of 0.10 in Sum LDP VS$_{m,t}$ and 0.10 in Rank (Sum LDP VS$_{m,t}$), respectively. Translated into absolute rankings, the average municipality experienced a standard deviation of 2.1 rankings. Thus, while the degree of within-municipality change in Sum LDP VS$_{m,t}$ is similar under both systems, the degree of within-unit change in Rank (Sum LDP VS$_{m,t}$) is less. It is possible that we would observe statistically significant coefficients on our support variables in a specification with both the lagged dependent variable and municipality fixed effects if we had more elections after the mid 2000s mergers were complete.

6.2.4 Competing Explanations and Placebo Tests, 1996–2014

As I explained above, the theory expects that resource allocations after elections will not be a function of support for LDP candidates who *lost* the election. Nor will they be a function of support for winning candidates from *other parties*, with the possible exception of LDP-aligned independent candidates who were allowed to join the LDP after emerging victorious in their districts. This section derives and implements tests of these propositions tailored to the specifics of the post-1994 environment.

First, Table 6.7 presents the results of fixed effect regression models for the logarithm of per capita transfers received by municipalities in the years following the six Lower House elections held between 1996 and 2014 (I continue to exclude 2009). In these models, the sample is limited to municipalities in tournament-possible districts in which the LDP candidate *lost* the election (did not place first). Of the 1,138 tournament-possible districts used in these six elections, 341 (30%) did not produce an LDP winner. In both models, the independent variable of interest is Sum Losing LDP VS$_{m,t}$. Defined above, this is the number of votes cast in the municipality for the district's LDP loser, divided by the number of eligible voters in the municipality. It captures how supportive municipality m was for the losing LDP candidate. Both models include prior transfers, the same six time-varying municipality-level controls, and district-year fixed effects. I report robust standard errors clustered on municipality.

In Model 1, the coefficient on Sum Losing LDP VS$_{m,t}$ is positive but not statistically significant. This means that municipalities in tournament-possible districts in which the LDP candidate lost the election do not appear to have received postelection NTD allocations commensurate with their relative levels of support for this candidate. The lack of a statistically discernible relationship between support for LDP losers and the amount of money municipalities received after the election is evidence that tournaments are conducted by *winning* LDP candidates.

Under Japan's MMM electoral system, electoral districts can have LDP candidates who lose their district (meaning, did not place first) but win a seat in parliament anyway. These candidates are said to have been "resurrected" via the PR tier.[19] This outcome is not a function of the

---

[19] They have also been nicknamed "zombies" due to their ability to "rise from the dead" (that is, an SSD loss) (Krauss, Pekkanen and Nyblade 2006).

6.2 Within Districts, Money Follows Support

Table 6.7 *Within electoral districts, municipalities exhibiting higher levels of support for their district's LDP loser in Lower House elections did not receive more per capita transfers after the election, 1996–2014 (excluding 2009) (Model 1). This holds even in the subset of districts in which the LDP loser was resurrected via PR (Model 2).*

	Dependent variable: Postelection Transfers (log)	
	(Model 1) (LDP candidate loses SSD)	(Model 2) (LDP candidate loses SSD, wins PR seat)
Sum Losing LDP VS$_{m,t}$	0.133	0.115
	(0.157)	(0.258)
Log(Transfers$_{m,t}$)	0.715***	0.779***
	(0.017)	(0.027)
Fiscal Strength$_{m,t}$	0.091*	−0.047
	(0.043)	(0.097)
Dependent Population$_{m,t}$	1.336***	0.331
	(0.391)	(0.703)
Farming Population$_{m,t}$	−0.242	−0.162
	(0.230)	(0.253)
Log(Population$_{m,t}$)	−0.005	0.021
	(0.011)	(0.015)
Log(Per Capita Income$_{m,t}$)	0.001	−0.092
	(0.083)	(0.131)
Population Density$_{m,t}$	0.003	−0.007
	(0.006)	(0.008)
Observations	3,206	1,047
District-year FE	Y	Y
R^2	0.543	0.598

Robust standard errors clustered on municipality in parentheses.
*$p < 0.05$, ***$p < 0.001$.
Regression models estimated with R's plm() package.

electoral system itself, but a function of a feature of the electoral system that allows candidates to be dual-listed in both tiers, *combined* with internal rules parties have adopted to make themselves more competitive in this system. In a nutshell, the LDP (and other parties) encourage their candidates to be dual-listed in both the SSD and PR tier. For a given candidate, this means that she would be the party's nominee for a given SSD, while also appearing on the party's list in the PR bloc that houses that SSD. The LDP adopts the rule that its dual-listed candidates appear at the same rank on the party's list for that bloc. Then, once votes are counted, dual-listed LDP candidates who won their districts are struck from the list, leaving only the dual-listed LDP candidates who lost their districts. These LDP losers are then reranked in accordance with how closely they lost their SSDs, with the LDP candidate who lost by the smallest margin of victory relative to her SSD winner being placed at the top of this list.[20] If the LDP is entitled to n seats in a particular PR bloc, it will then distribute those seats to the n highest-placed candidates on this reranked list (McKean and Scheiner 2000).

For our purpose, this means that voters in some of the 341 district-years without LDP winners (analyzed in Model 1 of Table 6.7) have their losing LDP candidate in parliament anyway. Precisely, voters in 119 (34.9%) of the 341 district-years without LDP winners had their district's LDP loser in the Lower House by virtue of the PR tier. Krauss, Pekkanen and Nyblade (2006) reasoned that the desire these politicians might feel to place first in the SSD the next time around gave them particularly strong incentives to pork-barrel. As evidence, these authors found that LDP politicians who were resurrected in PR were more likely to be appointed to parliamentary standing committees charged with distributive politics (defined as Construction, Transportation, Trade and Industry, Agriculture, Local Affairs, House Budget, and Posts and Telecommunications). In Model 2 in Table 6.7, I conduct the same regression as in Model 1 but limit observations to municipalities in districts in which the LDP candidate lost the district but entered parliament via PR. The results are similar to those in Model 1: The coefficient on Sum Losing LDP VS$_{m,t}$ is positive and not statistically significant. Thus, there is little evidence that PR-resurrected LDP candidates distribute money after elections on the basis of electoral support.

Next, the theory expects that winners from *other parties* will not be able to implement GBC, on account of the fact that they have less influence over central government bureaucrats, upon whose cooperation the distribution of resources depends. One possible exception is LDP-aligned independent winners, who did not obtain the LDP's endorsement prior to the election but make it clear during their campaigns that they will join the LDP after the election, should they win. In an interview with one such LDP politician, who joined the LDP after emerging victorious against an (older) LDP incumbent, I was told "everyone knew that I was planning on joining the LDP if I won" (Interview, LDP Lower House Member, Tokyo, Japan, December 12, 2023). My analyses of the pre-electoral reform period showed that district winners from parties other than the LDP did not make resource allocations a function of support

---

[20] This is called sekihairitsu in Japanese.

6.2 Within Districts, Money Follows Support

(Model 3, Table 6.4), but LDP-aligned independents who won the election did (Model 2, Table 6.4). While the theory expects similar results in the postreform period, a key difference between the old and new systems is that under the old, districts had *several* winners, whereas under the new, they have *one*. It is possible that this has changed the bargaining power between opposition-affiliated district winners and central government bureaucrats. It may have been easier for bureaucrats to ignore the demands of non-LDP Lower House Members when they were one of *several* representatives in a district (which also had an LDP winner) than when they are the *sole* representative in a district.

To examine this, I constructed District Winner $VS_{m,t}$, which is the number of voters in municipality m who voted for the candidate who placed first in the district, divided by the number of eligible voters in municipality m. Table 6.8 presents the results of fixed effect regression models for the logarithm of per capita transfers received by municipalities in the years following the six Lower House elections held between 1996 and 2014 (I continue to exclude 2009). In all models, our independent variable is District Winner $VS_{m,t}$, and I examine how its effect varies based on which party's candidate won the electoral districts in the sample. All models also include prior transfers, the same six time-varying municipality-level controls, and district-year fixed effects. I report robust standard errors clustered on municipality.

In Model 1, the sample is municipalities in electoral districts with LDP-aligned independent winners who joined the LDP after the election (forty-one districts). The coefficient on District Winner $VS_{m,t}$ is positive and statistically significant, indicating that LDP-aligned independent winners were able to make resources a function of support, just like their counterparts in prereform elections. In Model 2, the sample is municipalities in districts with winners from the New Frontier Party (NFP), which ran in 1996 only (sixty districts). The coefficient on District Winner $VS_{m,t}$ is positive and not statistically significant, indicating a lack of evidence that these candidates distributed money on the basis of support.

In Model 3, the sample is municipalities in districts with winners from the Democratic Party of Japan (DPJ). If GBC is in part a numbers game, with any party capable of sustaining a critical mass of Diet Members over a period of time gaining the influence over central government bureaucrats to implement it, then we might observe DPJ district winners tying resource allocations to the municipalities within their districts to their relative levels of support. Altogether, there were 172 of these districts. The coefficient on District Winner $VS_{m,t}$ is negative and not statistically significant, indicating no evidence of this. Of these 172 districts, however, 68 also produced LDP candidates who lost by such small margins that

Table 6.8 *In electoral districts without LDP winners in elections 1996–2014 (excluding 2009), LDP-aligned independents who joined the LDP after the election distributed money in accordance with support (Model 1) but winners from the New Frontier Party and Democratic Party of Japan did not (Models 2 and 3). The lack of a relationship between money and votes in DPJ-won districts is not explained by their rival LDP loser winning a PR seat (Model 4).*

	Dependent variable: Postelection Transfers (log)			
	(Model 1) (LDPI winner)	(Model 2) (NFP winner)	(Model 3) (DPJ winner)	(Model 4) (DPJ winner, no LDP PR candidate)
District Winner VS$_{m,t}$	0.636**	0.267	−0.076	−0.235
	(0.234)	(0.222)	(0.240)	(0.300)
Log(Transfers$_{m,t}$)	0.746***	0.617***	0.761***	0.706***
	(0.041)	(0.035)	(0.026)	(0.038)
Fiscal Strength$_{m,t}$	0.013	0.338**	0.023	0.121
	(0.149)	(0.103)	(0.058)	(0.071)
Dependent Population$_{m,t}$	0.028	3.377***	0.531	1.462
	(0.887)	(0.932)	(0.612)	(0.923)
Farming Population$_{m,t}$	0.700	−0.552	−0.301	−0.139
	(1.171)	(0.360)	(0.299)	(0.417)
Log(Population$_{m,t}$)	0.006	−0.042	0.007	−0.008
	(0.023)	(0.022)	(0.017)	(0.025)
Log(Per Capita Income$_{m,t}$)	−0.144	−0.008	0.059	0.152
	(0.270)	(0.152)	(0.128)	(0.195)
Population Density$_{m,t}$	0.030	0.022	−0.011	−0.009
	(0.035)	(0.013)	(0.008)	(0.012)
Observations	501	614	1,388	812
District-year FE	Y	Y	Y	Y
R^2	0.574	0.593	0.557	0.508

Robust standard errors clustered on municipality in parentheses.
**$p < 0.01$, ***$p < 0.001$.
Regression models estimated with R's plm() package.

they gained a PR seat. In Model 4, I implement the same specification as in Model 3 but limit the sample to municipalities in districts with DPJ winners and *without* LDP PR-resurrected LDP candidates. The coefficient on District Winner VS$_{m,t}$ is similarly negative and not statistically significant. Thus, the lack of relationship between votes for DPJ winners and postelection NTD allocations in Model 3 is not explained by the fact that

6.2 Within Districts, Money Follows Support

some of those districts have LDP candidates in parliament, who may be working at cross-purposes to the DPJ winner.[21]

6.2.5 LDP Winners Double Down after 2009 Election

As I explained in Chapter 2, the years of 2005–2009 were tough ones for the LDP. In 2001, the party chose a leader who succeeded in keeping his approval rate above his disapproval rate for the near-length of his five-year term. The party was not so lucky with its next three leaders, all of whom lasted only a single year. The one-year terms of Abe Shinzo (2006–2007), Fukuda Yasuo (2007–2008), and Aso Taro (2008–2009) exhibited similar pathologies: Disapproval began exceeding approval relatively early on, and it proved difficult to reverse or even stem this trend. In July 2009, with a disapproval rate of 70% to an approval rate of 21%, Aso found himself at the very end of the four-year term of Lower House Members. Indicators of the drubbing the party was about to receive were communicated first by the Tokyo Metropolitan Assembly election in July, in which 40% of ballots went to DPJ candidates and only 25% to LDP candidates, and second, by polling data released by national newspapers (Daily Yomiuri 2009). In one, 41% of respondents reported that they planned to cast PR ballots for the DPJ (compared to 24% for the LDP), while 41% reported that they planned to cast SSD votes for the DPJ candidate (compared to only 23% for the LDP candidate) (Yomiuri Shimbun 2009).[22] Being unable to wait for more fortuitous circumstances, Aso dissolved the House. In the election held at the end of August, the DPJ won a landslide victory. The LDP won only 64 SSDs, while the DPJ won 221.

Because the LDP did not control government during the 2010 fiscal year, the above analyses excluded the 2009 election. However, this election offers the opportunity to examine what happens when a long-standing dominant party fails to capture a majority and loses control of government. In this situation, the party's *majority* is gone, but its *presence in parliament* is not. A number of outcomes are possible: Politicians

---

[21] In the post-2001 era, Catalinac and Motolinia (2021a) find that select LDP politicians seek district votes from Komeito supporters and ask their own supporters to cast PR votes for the Komeito in return. The authors found that resource allocations are also used to reward LDP supporters for switching their PR votes. To the extent that Komeito supporters contribute to their municipality doing well in the tournament, the findings in this book are evidence that rewards flow to Komeito supporters, too.

[22] In the same poll, when asked who they thought would be a suitable Prime Minister, 46% named DPJ leader Hatoyama Yukio (compared to 21% who named the current LDP Prime Minister, Aso Taro) (Yomiuri Shimbun 2009).

in the party slated to win the election (the DPJ) may have used tournaments, such that postelection NTD allocations to municipalities reflect levels of support for those politicians, leaving LDP politicians out in the cold. Alternatively, politicians in the dominant party who manage to retain their seat in spite of the headwind against their party may have lost their status as ruling party members but may still be able to harness their connections to bureaucrats in ways that sway NTD allocations. We might be more likely to observe the latter outcome when the amount of money municipalities receive is not inserted into government budgets, but left up to the discretion of individual ministries, which are vulnerable to lobbying by Diet Members.

Table 6.9 presents three regression models, all of which focus on municipalities in 2009. The outcome of interest in each is the logarithm of per capita transfers received by municipalities in the year after the 2009 election. Each model controls for prior transfers (measured the year of the election) and the same six time-varying municipality-level characteristics included above and includes a fixed effect for electoral district. In Model 1, my question of interest is whether municipalities delivering higher levels of electoral support for winning DPJ politicians were rewarded with more money after the election. The independent variable of interest is Sum DPJ $VS_{m,t}$. Constructed analogously to Sum LDP $VS_{m,t}$, it captures the share of eligible voters in the municipality who voted for a winning DPJ candidate. Its coefficient is positive but not statistically significant. Thus, municipalities exhibiting higher levels of support for their DPJ incumbents do not appear to have been rewarded with more money after the election.[23] Even though the election put DPJ politicians in control of both the Upper and Lower Houses, respectively, there is little evidence that DPJ politicians used a tournament.[24]

In Model 2 of Table 6.9, my question of interest is whether municipalities exhibiting higher levels of support for their LDP winners continued to be rewarded with more money after the election, just as they had been in prior elections. The independent variable of interest is Sum LDP $VS_{m,t}$, the share of eligible voters in the municipality who voted for a winning LDP candidate. Its coefficient is positive and statistically significant. This

---

[23] I checked whether this could be explained by the fact that select DPJ winners had same-district LDP rivals in parliament. To do this, I reran the specification in Model 1 on the sample of municipalities in electoral districts with DPJ winners and without PR-resurrected LDP candidates. I found a similar lack of statistical significance on Sum DPJ $VS_{m,t}$. This means that even when the coast is clear, and efforts to reward supporters are not being overturned by same-district LDP rivals with clashing electoral incentives, there is still little evidence that DPJ SSD winners engaged in GBC.

[24] It had secured a majority in the Upper House in the 2007 election.

6.2 Within Districts, Money Follows Support

Table 6.9 *Within electoral districts in the 2009 election, municipalities exhibiting higher support for DPJ winners did not receive more transfers (Model 1) but municipalities exhibiting higher support for LDP winners did (Model 2). In districts without LDP winners, support for the LDP has no relationship with transfers (Model 3).*

	\multicolumn{3}{c}{Dependent variable: Postelection Transfers (log)}	
	(Model 1)	(Model 2)	(Model 3)
Sum DPJ VS$_{m,t}$	0.264		
	(0.424)		
Sum LDP VS$_{m,t}$		1.303***	
		(0.370)	
Sum Losing LDP VS$_{m,t}$			−0.054
			(0.416)
Log(Transfers$_{m,t}$)	0.569***	0.555***	0.569***
	(0.049)	(0.049)	(0.049)
Fiscal Strength$_{m,t}$	0.190	0.203	0.190
	(0.106)	(0.104)	(0.106)
Dependent Population$_{m,t}$	1.491	1.243	1.522
	(0.794)	(0.773)	(0.794)
Farming Population$_{m,t}$	0.801*	0.746*	0.786*
	(0.383)	(0.379)	(0.381)
Log(Population$_{m,t}$)	−0.038*	−0.032*	−0.040**
	(0.015)	(0.015)	(0.015)
Log(Per Capita Income$_{m,t}$)	−0.249	−0.230	−0.238
	(0.157)	(0.152)	(0.154)
Population Density$_{m,t}$	0.025*	0.025*	0.026*
	(0.010)	(0.010)	(0.010)
Observations	1,072	1,072	1,072
District FE	Y	Y	Y
R^2	0.391	0.401	0.391

Robust standard errors clustered on municipality in parentheses.
*$p < 0.05$, **$p < 0.01$, ***$p < 0.001$.
Regression models estimated with R's plm() package.

means that in the small number of electoral districts with LDP winners, municipalities exhibiting higher levels of support for those LDP winners were found to have been rewarded with more money after the election. Despite having lost control of government, LDP electoral district winners appear to have had no problems influencing NTD allocations in the wake of this loss.

In Model 3, I examine municipalities in districts without LDP winners. Here, I am interested in whether municipalities returning more votes for *losing* LDP candidates received more money after the election. The independent variable of interest is Sum Losing LDP VS$_{m,t}$. Defined above, this is the number of votes cast for the LDP's losing candidate, divided by the number of eligible voters in the municipality. In this regression, the coefficient on Sum Losing LDP VS$_{m,t}$ will tell us whether municipalities exhibiting more support for their district's LDP loser received more NTD after the election than same-district municipalities exhibiting less. Its coefficient is positive and not statistically significant. Thus, like all other elections in our sample, it is only when LDP candidates *win* the election that municipalities receive NTD allocations commensurate with their levels of electoral support.

These findings suggest that being knocked out of government did little to interrupt the ability of LDP Lower House members to use NTD to reward their supporters. Because the 2009 election reduced the number of LDP SSD winners to a mere one-fifth of the total, however, this does mean that a much larger share of Japanese voters were *not* subject to a tournament in this election.

In sum, the above analyses lend support to the theory: Voters in districts won by the LDP, including LDP-aligned independents who were permitted to join the party after winning a seat, are subject to a tournament, in which the amount of resources their municipality receives after the election is tied to the level of support they provided in the election. Voters in districts without LDP winners are not. These findings cannot be explained by certain municipalities having strong ties with their LDP incumbents. Nor can they be explained by the inclusion of electoral districts with dominant municipalities. Nor are they limited to senior LDP politicians. Rather, the balance of evidence suggests that this is an electoral strategy pursued by the rank and file.

6.3 A CONVEX RELATIONSHIP BETWEEN SUPPORT AND TRANSFERS

In Chapter 4, I drew on the formal models in Smith, Bueno de Mesquita and LaGatta (2017) and Smith and Bueno de Mesquita (2019, 2012) to introduce two distinct ways an incumbent could use geographically targetable resources to garner votes from groups of voters in her district. One is "output-calibrated compensation." Under this scheme, incumbents might promise to deliver a prize commensurate with the group's contribution to her reelection. A group contributing 35% of an incumbent's votes could expect to receive 35% of the resources incumbents have access to after the election. A problem with this scheme is that votes are converted into resources in a relatively *proportional* manner. Thus, an individual voter might decide not to vote on the basis that the amount of resources

6.3 Relationship between Support and Transfers

her group would receive would only be slightly less than if she had voted. From the perspective of the incumbent, the danger is that *many* voters will make this calculation. If so, the incumbent would struggle to realize enough votes to actually win the election. The use of output-calibrated compensation would likely result in the incumbent having to deliver a very *large* amount of resources, to try to give voters with incentives to abstain reasons not to.

In Chapter 4, I explained that incumbents who want to protect themselves from this type of abstention can adopt "contest-based compensation." Under contest-based compensation (a tournament), incumbents in districts consisting of two groups can promise a large prize to the group whose support puts it in first place. In the same spirit, incumbents in districts consisting of more than two groups can offer the largest prize to the group that places first, the second-largest prize to the group that places second, and so on. If the incumbent in the multiple group-district designs the prizes such that the difference in amounts received between the first and second place-getter exceeds the difference in amount received between the second and third place-getter, and so on, she will give members incentives to *compete* for first place, second place, and so on, just as groups do in the two group-district scenario. Competition ensues because the amount of money that an already fairly supportive group stands to gain by becoming *even more supportive* is large. This induces voters in the already fairly supportive groups to set aside whatever personal feelings they harbor for the incumbent and turn out and vote for her. Critically, these voters are not turning to influence who wins the election, but to avoid the possibility that *their vote* ends up costing their group a large resource allocation after the election.

Hypothesis 2 concerns this observable implication of a tournament. To subject this to empirical scrutiny, I examined whether the positive relationship between support and transfers within district-years (documented above in Tables 6.1, 6.2, and 6.6) is convex, as implied by the theory.[25] Is there evidence that the amount of money municipalities are competing over are larger at higher ranks? To do this, I use the dependent variable in its raw values (the per capita amount in yen received by municipalities in the years following the Lower House elections held between 1980

---

[25] Because the above specifications used a logged dependent variable, they could also be considered tests of Hypothesis 2, which holds that the relationship between support and per capita transfers among same-district municipalities is *convex*. However, positive significant coefficients on our support variables could still be obtained in the above specifications even if the relationship is *not* convex. The below is a more stringent test.

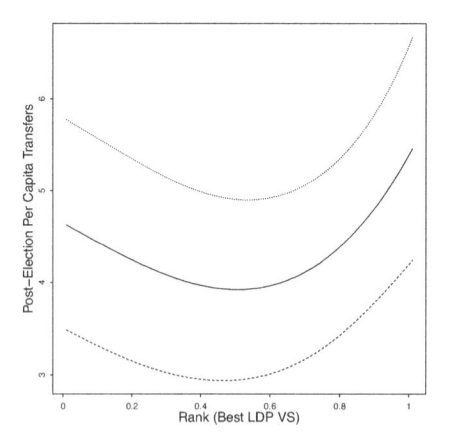

How Politicians Tie Money to Electoral Support

Figure 6.1 The relationship between rank and transfers is convex, 1980–2014. Predicted values (with 95% confidence intervals) from a regression of postelection per capita transfers received by municipalities (1980–2014) on a cubic specification of Rank(Best LDP VS$_{m,t}$), municipality-level controls, and district-year fixed effects.

and 2014, excluding 2009).[26] I conduct fixed effect regressions of this (non-log-transformed) dependent variable as a function of a municipality's position in a rank order of municipalities in its district-year (captured with Rank(Best LDP VS$_{m,t}$) and Rank(Sum LDP VS$_{m,t}$), respectively), as well as quadratic and cubic transformations of these (rank) variables. In this specification, a joint hypothesis test will tell us whether the coefficients on my rank variables and their quadratic and cubic transformations are *jointly significant*.

Table A.4 presents the results of these two specifications, run on municipalities in tournament-possible districts in Lower House elections, 1980–2014 (I exclude 2009). Both specifications include the same six time-varying municipality-level controls and district-year fixed effects. I report robust standard errors clustered on municipality. In both specifications, the joint hypothesis test is statistically significant. This is evidence that the relationship between support and transfers is not linear.

To visually depict the convexity, Figure 6.1 plots predicted values and 95% confidence intervals from the regression in Model 1 of Table A.4. It demonstrates that once a municipality is at the median or above in terms of support (0.5 to 1 on Rank (Best LDP VS$_{m,t}$)), the returns to moving up in rank increase at an increasing rate. For municipalities at the very top

---

[26] The units of this variable are in millions of yen. A municipality with a value of 0.07 receives 70,000 yen per capita. For this regression, I multiplied these values by 100 to make the units of the variable 10,000 yen (ichi man yen in Japanese).

6.3 Relationship between Support and Transfers

of the ranking, the returns to increasing one's rank are very large. Translating these coefficients into real yen amounts reveals that a municipality that increases its Rank(Best LDP VS$_{m,t}$) from 0.95 to 1, which would put it in first place, can expect to net itself an increase of 3,206 yen per capita (approximately $20.60 USD) in per capita transfers after the election. In this sample, the mean per capita transfer received by a municipality in the year after a Lower House election was 40,884 yen (approximately $262 USD). Thus, this amounts to a 7.8% increase in its per capita transfer allocation. In the average municipality of slightly more than 13,000 people, this would translate into an increase of a little more than 43 million yen (or US $275,000 in today's exchange rate).

As expected, the same increase in support translates into smaller increases in transfers for municipalities at lower ranks. A municipality that increases its Rank(Best LDP VS$_{m,t}$) from 0.80 to 0.85, for example, can expect to net itself an increase of 1,969 yen per capita (approximately $13 USD) in per capita transfers after the election. The increase is much smaller for municipalities in the middle of the ranking. A municipality that increases its Rank(Best LDP VS$_{m,t}$) from 0.55 to 0.6, for example, can expect to net itself an increase of 381 yen per capita (approximately $2.15 USD) in per capita transfers after the election. Among the relatively unsupportive municipalities, whose position in the ranking is 0.5 or lower, increases in rank are actually associated with slight increases in transfers. It is possible that municipalities at the bottom of the ranking, at least in support for LDP winner, are highly supportive of a winner from an opposition party. To the extent that the opposition winner

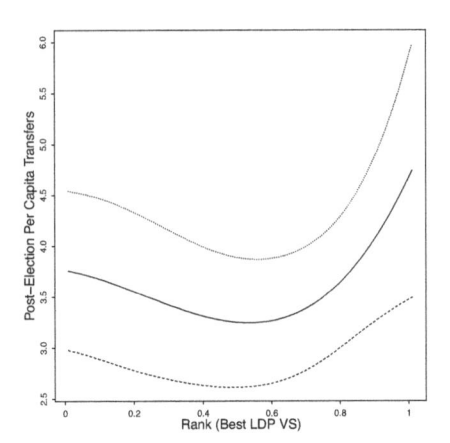

Figure 6.2 The relationship between rank and transfers is convex, 1980–1993. Predicted values (with 95% confidence intervals) from a regression of postelection per capita transfers received by municipalities (1980–1993) on a cubic specification of Rank(Best LDP VS$_{m,t}$), municipality-level controls, and district-year fixed effects.

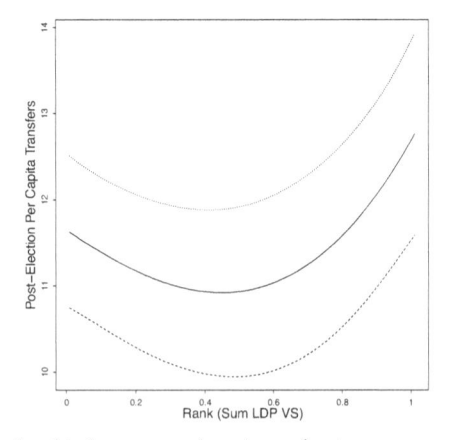

Figure 6.3 The relationship between rank and transfers is convex, 1996–2014. Predicted values (with 95% confidence intervals) from a regression of postelection per capita transfers received by municipalities (1996–2014) on a cubic specification of Rank(Best LDP VS$_{m,t}$), municipality-level controls, and district-year fixed effects.

is experienced, she may have some influence over the transfer process as well.

In the Appendix, I separate the sample into the pre- and post-1994 periods. Table A.5 presents the same two specifications in Table A.4, but on data from the pre-1994 period. Table A.3 presents the specification in Model 2 of Table A.4 (which uses Rank(Sum LDP VS$_{m,t}$)) with data from the post-1994 period. In all tests, the joint hypothesis test is statistically significant. Figure 6.2 displays predicted values and 95% confidence intervals from the regression in Model 1 of Table A.5. Figure 6.3 displays predicted values and 95% confidence intervals from the regression in Table A.6. The convex relationship is visible in both periods.

6.4 EVIDENCE OF THE THEORY'S MICROFOUNDATIONS

The above analyses established that patterns of resource allocations within electoral districts are consistent with LDP politicians pitting municipalities against each other in a competition for resources. Alternative specifications subjected other implications of the theory to rigorous empirical scrutiny and helped rule out alternative theories. We can help assuage any remaining concern that the relationship between support and resource allocations is explained by factors orthogonal to the theory by specifying the theory's underlying assumptions about LDP politicians and voters and presenting evidence of these.

6.4 Evidence of the Theory's Microfoundations

6.4.1 LDP Politicians Influence NTD Allocations

A core assumption is that LDP politicians are capable of influencing NTD allocations to municipalities. In Chapter 5, I described the process through which allocations are arrived at. It begins with central government ministries specifying categories of projects for which municipalities can apply for funding. Municipalities then put together applications for projects. Where possible, they send representatives to Tokyo to try to meet with the relevant decision-making bureau so that the application can be delivered and the case for the project be made in person. The LDP politicians are said to help municipal representatives secure meetings with the relevant decision-makers by providing introductions. They are also said to help representatives make the case for their project by accompanying them to the meetings. Eventually, bureaucrats decide which projects get funded.

In some countries, it is possible to request data on who central government bureaucrats are meeting with and when. In Japan, to the best of our knowledge, this is a black box: There is no publicly available data of this kind (Saito 2010). One study writes: "Exactly how representatives influence the distribution of government transfers is not well known" (Hirano 2011, 1086). In lieu of systematic evidence capturing politician–bureaucrat interactions, we can turn to less systematic evidence, which nevertheless makes a compelling case that LDP politicians can influence bureaucrat-determined resource allocations, and do so with an eye to the potential beneficiary's performance for them in elections.

The Japanese politics literature is replete with claims that LDP politicians can influence the allocation of central government resources.[27] Writing in the 1960s, one author describes LDP politicians as offering three main services to constituents: intercession with the government, support for community activities, and personal support for constituents (Thayer 1969, 94). Intercession with the government, in the author's words, consists of helping constituents secure central government funds for the construction of new facilities or the maintenance or repair of old ones. Road paving, bridge building, sewerage system improvement, and the building of gymnasiums and train stations are all mentioned as examples. LDP politicians secure these funds, the author explains, by putting pressure on "the appropriate government offices in Tokyo"

---

[27] The following studies all make this claim: Reed (2021); Christensen and Selway (2017); McMichael (2018); Naoi (2015); Reed, Scheiner and Thies (2012); Pempel (2010); Krauss and Pekkanen (2010); Saito (2010); Scheiner (2006); Bouissou (1999); Tani (1998); Ramseyer and Rosenbluth (1993); Hirose (1993); Sone and Kanazashi (1989); Curtis (1971); and Thayer (1969).

(Thayer 1969, 94). The author describes how a secretary of one LDP politician boasted about the politician's "high batting average" with construction ministry bureaucrats. In a drive around the politician's electoral district, the secretary even showed the author facilities that the politician had worked to secure the funding for.

Thirty years on, studies describe LDP politicians in strikingly similar ways. The LDP politicians are described as transferring "extensive wealth" from the national treasury to their home districts (Ramseyer and Rosenbluth 1993), using state resources to "build up their own locally-based, personal clientelistic networks" (Reed, Scheiner and Thies 2012, 359), and engaging in a "perennial scramble for pork from the national treasury" (Fukui and Fukai 1996, 278). They are "constantly visited at their Tokyo offices by delegations of politicians from back home, and spend a great deal of time trying to arrange appointments for them with bureaucrats in key ministries and agencies" (Fukui and Fukai 1996, 278). Knowing that "politicians affiliated with a party that controls the bureaucracy can redistribute extensive wealth from the national treasury to their home districts," potentially bringing in "highways, schools, airports, and cash," local government representatives prioritize soliciting help from their LDP-affiliated Diet Member(s) (Ramseyer and Rosenbluth 1993, 122). The projects LDP politicians reportedly secured for their constituents included indoor gyms, track and baseball fields, industrial parks, bridges over rivers, aquariums, technopolises, international universities, theme parks, ski slopes, waterfronts, and other tourist facilities (Fukui and Fukai 1996; Scheiner 2006).

Scholarship is unequivocal that the purpose of all this pork-barreling is to win LDP politicians votes. Fukui and Fukai (1996, 269) write that "for much of the postwar period," "the performance of Diet members in pork barrel politics made or broke their political careers," with the amount of money a politician was able to bring home determining their "worth to constituents" and "chances of reelection" (Fukui and Fukai 1996, 276). Japanese voters were described as preferring "a candidate who can deliver a bigger share of the benefits being distributed to one who represents them on the issues of the day" (Reed 1986, 35) and weighing a candidate's ability to bring "tangible benefits" back to her constituents more heavily than any "ideology and policy orientation" (Kohno and Nishizawa 1990, 159). As a result, candidates "routinely swear to help their constituents get more attention and help from Tokyo" in the form of "pork from the national treasury" (Fukui and Fukai 1996, 278). A case study of a former LDP Prime Minister known for his pork-barreling acumen, Tanaka Kakuei, observed that the projects Tanaka helped secure for his constituents were often "grandiose" and designed

6.4 Evidence of the Theory's Microfoundations

to "astound the locals." Tanaka, the author notes, even went so far as to keep "shabby" prior structures in place, right next to the new structures, "to serve as an ever-present reminder of the magnitude of improvement" (Schlesinger 1997, 103).

Scholars emphasize that money for geographically defined groups of voters was part of a broader electoral strategy of using the LDP's access to government resources to court select groups of voters, who could be relied on to turn out and vote for LDP candidates. According to Estevez-Abe (2008, 119), hikes in compensation for war veterans and survivors, fees for physicians, and even regulatory advantages over postal products "were all benefits purchased by loyal support for the ruling Liberal Democratic Party." In addition to special postmasters, physicians, and veterans and their families, other beneficiaries of favorable LDP-designed public policies, who return the favor with electoral support, are farmers, religious organizations, proprietors of small and medium-sized businesses, and declining industries and sectors (Maclachlan and Shimizu 2022; Reed 2021; Gentry 2021; Naoi 2015; Maclachlan 2006; Davis 2003). What binds these voters to the LDP, Pempel (2010, 234) explains, is less any shared ideology or commitment to the programmatic elements of the party's platform, and more the party's "not-too-subtle predisposition to divvy up the spoils of office." This author goes as far as to say that "numerous Japanese regions, economic sectors, and individual corporations were transformed into semi-permanent wards of the Japanese treasury with their LDP parliamentarians serving as welfare officers. The reciprocation came in the form of large blocs of pro-LDP votes delivered in return" (Pempel 2010).

Several studies delve into the question of how such exchange relationships materialize and are sustained. Sone and Kanazashi (1989) present an in-depth look at the electoral strategy of the aforementioned Tanaka Kakuei. Like other LDP politicians, Tanaka built an extensive personal support organization (a koenkai) in his district. Shaped like a pyramid, the organization had a headquarters at the top, liaison councils below that (organized at the level of the city or borough), and branches below that (317 in total, organized at the level of the "old towns and villages," meaning those that existed prior to amalgamations that took place in the 1950s). According to the authors, a key feature of Tanaka's organization was an "intertwining" of the functions of vote-gathering and constituent requests. Constituents who wanted things done in the district were encouraged to present their demands at the local branch of Tanaka's organization, which was staffed by a local politician loyal to Tanaka. The local politician would encourage the petitioner to "join" Tanaka's support organization, which meant leaving their name and address and agreeing to be contacted in advance of elections. The local politician would then relay the request upward to the liaison council, which would then relay it upward to the headquarters.

After elections, the headquarters would "work out the vote share for Tanaka in the different areas (branches), and make them compete against each other" (Sone and Kanazashi 1989, 110). While Tanaka ostensibly had a formula to determine how much public works spending and other subsidies areas would receive, people also knew that "how well" each area did for Tanaka, in terms of votes supplied, also factored into this calculation. The authors likened the relationship between voters, local politicians, and Tanaka himself to a "business exchange in which votes are traded for benefits for the community." A feature of Japan's governance institutions that greased the wheels of this exchange was the fact that municipalities were so dependent on funds from the central government (Scheiner 2006). The fact that local politicians had to cozy up to their LDP Diet Member(s) if they wanted money for their community left the branches of Tanaka's support organization with "no choice but to get out the vote for Tanaka" (Sone and Kanazashi 1989, 111).

The pyramid structure of campaign organization is when politicians divide up their electoral district into distinct geographic units and assign the responsibility of gathering votes in each unit to a single campaign manager, who then appoints staffers below her. Critically, pyramids are said to be a hallmark of LDP politicians' campaign organizations, but not of *non*-LDP politicians' organizations (Bouissou 1999; Tani 1998; Curtis 1971; Thayer 1969). Curtis (1971) studied the election campaign of LDP politician Sato Bunsei in the 1967 Lower House election. He writes:

> Sato's campaign organizations in the district's rural cities, towns, and villages followed a general pattern. His support, as is typical of the traditional organizational structure employed by conservative politicians, was organized on a *chiiki* or geographical basis.[28] Each city, town, and village has a campaign organization that deals directly with the candidate and his headquarters and is independent of the organizations in the other cities, towns, and villages. This is the so-called vertical approach to campaign organization – the creating of independent support groups in each administrative area. It is in contrast with the organization of Socialist party politicians who, because of the support of labor unions, are seen as using a "horizontal" approach. The labor unions which are used as the candidate' campaign organization have a membership which fans out over the district and cuts across *chiiki* lines. (Curtis 1971, 53)[29]

---

[28] *Chiiki* is "place."
[29] Curtis (1971) explains that Sato did not establish a branch in the smallest municipality in his district, the island village of Himeshima, on the grounds that nearly

6.4 Evidence of the Theory's Microfoundations

In a setting in which votes are tallied at the level of the municipality, structuring one's campaign organization in this manner creates clear lines of accountability, in which a politician can determine how hard her campaign managers are working on her behalf. By this logic, however, it would have made sense for *non*-LDP politicians to have structured their campaigns this way. The GBC theory helps us see that what sets LDP politicians apart from their non-LDP peers is their *access to government resources* that can be funneled to units in exchange for votes. It is possible that not having access to such resources meant that non-LDP politicians could not realize the same gains from a divide-and-conquer strategy.

Tanaka contested his last Lower House election in 1986; Sato, in 1990. What evidence do we have from recent years that LDP politicians can influence NTD allocations? In Chapter 4, I explained why democratically elected politicians are unlikely to make direct statements to the effect that they are tying the amount of government resources voters receive to their performance in elections. Nevertheless, we can find instances in which LDP politicians did make these statements. In January 2019, LDP Secretary General Nikai Toshihiro visited Tokushima prefecture in advance of an Upper House election. To a hotel room full of people employed in land improvement, Nikai said "It is natural that we would allocate more of the budget to places that tried hard for us in the election." He went on to say that the party would "take a break" from directing resources toward places that had not "worked with it," and even said that if the LDP did not do that, "there would be no value in its existence" (Tokushima Shimbun 2019).

Immediately after the 2017 Lower House election, an LDP candidate who lost his district in Niigata prefecture but managed to win a PR seat wrote on his blog that because four of the six districts in Niigata had been won by non-LDP politicians, the "current situation, in which money (yosan) is not coming to Niigata" would continue. In response, the opposition-aligned Governor held a press conference, in which he called the comments "proof that the LDP was administering unfairly." He said that the comments were equivalent to declaring "if you want money (yosan), you have to help elect LDP politicians" (Asahi Shimbun 2017). He then reassured his audience that he had consulted the amount of NTD (referring to the fund by name) that Niigata prefecture had received the previous fiscal year, and it was not, in fact, lower

---

every voter on the island voted for another LDP politician. In the 1967 election, 95% of votes cast in Himeshima went to this other LDP politician, leaving 5% to be divided among the remaining four candidates (Curtis 1971, 52–53). The author's fieldwork revealed that the mayor of Himeshima displayed plaques lauding the village's "high voting rate" (98% in the previous election) on the wall of his office.

than the amounts received by other prefectures. Another statement comes from the 2003 Lower House election.[30] Two days before the election, the Governor of Aichi prefecture visited the Minister of Internal Affairs and Communications LDP politician Aso Taro, to petition him on a project. In the meeting, Aso reportedly admonished the Governor, saying that he was in no position to present the petition given the poor showing for the party's candidates in recent elections (Asahi Shimbun 2003). This led to a local chapter of the opposition DPJ complaining that "Aichi prefecture is not the LDP's private property."[31]

Campaign manifestos prepared by LDP candidates and delivered to voters in advance of Lower House elections contain many statements alluding to their ability to influence central government resources, with a minority of LDP candidates actually *advertising* the amounts of money they had secured. Catalinac (2016) analyzed election manifestos written by 7,497 candidates contesting the eight Lower House elections held between 1986 and 2009.[32] In earlier years, LDP candidates promised to improve transportation systems and sewerage facilities, construct new subway lines, improve connections between their local area and the nearest bullet train station, help the local fishing industry by investing in fish grounds and fish farming, implement structural improvement projects for the local textile, glass, and lacquer ware industries, realize new financial measures to support small-and-medium-sized businesses, develop local harbors, improve the network of prefectural roads, farm roads, and forest roads, improve rivers, and develop public facilities in the realms of housing, schools, hospitals, nursery schools, sports facilities, and parks.[33] They also promised to invest in industries "distinctive to the area," naming fruit tree or livestock farming as examples, support local commercial and industrial associations, develop "successor training projects," beautify streets, parks, and recreational facilities, build facilities for the elderly and other cultural and leisure facilities, and invest in urban rivers, suburban agriculture, and public housing, respectively.[34]

---

[30] This was first referenced in Scheiner (2006).
[31] Other examples appear in Scheiner (2006: 110–111).
[32] In advance of Lower House elections in Japan, candidates draw up personal manifestos outlining their stances on issues, policy promises, areas of expertise, name, party affiliation, background, and anything else they want voters to know about them. The manifestos (senkyo koho) are distributed to all registered voters in the district just prior to the election.
[33] See, for example, the manifestos of LDP candidates Okonogi Hikosaburo, Makino Takamori, Eto Takami, and Miike Makoto in the 1980 election.
[34] See, for example, the manifestos of LDP candidates Mori Kiyoshi, Kano Masaru, Kato Koichi, Tamura Hajime, Sekiya Tsutsugu, Chikaoka Riichiro, Uetake Shigeo, and Aizawa Hideyuki in the 1990 election.

6.4 Evidence of the Theory's Microfoundations

In later years, LDP candidates promised tunnel roads, underground malls, parking lots, elevated railway lines and traffic interchanges, revitalization measures for shopping streets, the burying of power lines, the development of fishing ports, the construction of history museums, land readjustment projects, adjustments to make towns friendlier to those with disabilities, roads for runners and cyclists, policies to enhance the area's attractiveness to international tourists, improvements to waste management systems, projects for river renovation, and funds to ensure the area could "maintain high-quality ambulances and fire trucks with ladders."[35] They also emphasized that public works projects contributed to the local economy. One LDP candidate told his constituents that "without public works there can be no economy or employment," and promised to "strive for the efficient allocation of reserve funds and supplementary budgets for public works projects."[36] After the Fukushima earthquake and nuclear reactor disaster in 2011, LDP candidates began pledging funds for reconstruction and disaster prevention measures. They also promised to improve agricultural infrastructure, increase funds for wildlife damage control, implement measures to boost farmers' income and cultivate more farmers, maintain farmland, and reverse cuts implemented by the DPJ government (2009–2012).[37] While campaign promises are not direct evidence that LDP politicians can influence bureaucrat-determined allocations, it is hard to imagine why they would make these promises, and promises that appear *tailored* to the needs of their constituents, if they were unable to do so.

Let me anticipate three further questions. First, readers familiar with the Japanese politics literature may be thinking: "But hasn't Japanese politics changed? Haven't we been told that pork-barrelling is a thing of the past?" These readers are likely drawing on studies of the effects of Japan's 1994 electoral reform, which found that it reduced particularism and created more cohesive, hierarchical parties (Goplerud and Smith 2023; Catalinac 2018, 2015; Reed, Scheiner and Thies 2012; Rosenbluth and Thies 2010; Krauss and Pekkanen 2010). My answer is that Japanese politics has changed, but the theory in this book helps us see that change may have been concentrated in places where the (newly drawn) post-1994 electoral district *ruled out* the possibility of a tournament. In Chapter 5, I explained that Japan's 1994 electoral reform created new electoral districts, many of which were tournament-impossible. Whereas

---

[35] See, for example, the manifestos of LDP candidates Totsuka Shinya, Oita Seishiro, Yasuoka Okiharu, and Ioku Sadao in the 2000 election.
[36] See the manifesto of LDP candidate Oita Seishiro in the 2000 election.
[37] See, for example, the manifestos of LDP candidates Suzuki Shunichi and Komatsu Yutaka in 2012.

tournaments used to be impossible in only about 9% of districts prior to 1994, they became impossible in 27% of districts between 1994 and 2003, 38% of districts in 2005, and about 50% of districts thereafter. The theory leads us to expect that the increase in share of tournament-impossible districts would have created a more pronounced *bifurcation* in LDP politicians' electoral strategies, with LDP politicians in tournament-*possible* districts hewing to a tournament (and perhaps even finding tournaments easier to run now they are the sole LDP representative) and their counterparts in tournament-*impossible* districts embracing new electoral strategies.

Needless to say, there is considerable evidence of this bifurcation in the literature. Koellner (2009) explains how old-fashioned "vote mobilization" techniques, in which LDP politicians cultivate personal support organizations and treat them as vote banks, hiring staff to make phone calls to lists of members during campaigns and telling those members what the politician has done for the community, exist alongside modern "vote chasing" strategies, which involve using the LDP's brand, its programmatic policies, and the face of its leader to attract independent voters. His data show that membership in personal support organizations, for example, declined in the 1990s "but not on a massive scale" (Koellner 2009, 133). Membership declines in the industry and other organizations LDP politicians rely on for vote-gathering have also been documented (Reed 2021; Maclachlan 2014). Similarly, Catalinac (2016)'s analyses revealed that discussion of pork-barreling in the average LDP candidate election manifesto declined significantly after 1994 but still constituted roughly one-third of discussion through the 2009 election (the last one for which she has data). In that book, pork-barreling was defined as promises concerning a relatively narrow group of voters, and in practice, constituted promises to secure money for constituents. The case studies in Chapter 3 of Krauss and Pekkanen (2010) and all chapters in Otake (1998) also provide ample evidence that change occurred, but perhaps not on the scale expected by theories of electoral systems.

Merging the data collected for Catalinac (2016) to my data classifying electoral districts as tournament-possible or not provides systematic evidence that LDP candidate strategies are bifurcated along this dimension, and this is related to the type of electoral district they are in. For that book, I gathered the universe of 7,497 candidate election manifestos used in eight Lower House elections (1986–2009) and used unsupervised learning techniques to code the proportion of discussion devoted to pork-barreling and programmatic policies, respectively. These topic proportions offer a means of examining whether LDP candidates in tournament-possible districts adopt different electoral strategies than

6.4 Evidence of the Theory's Microfoundations

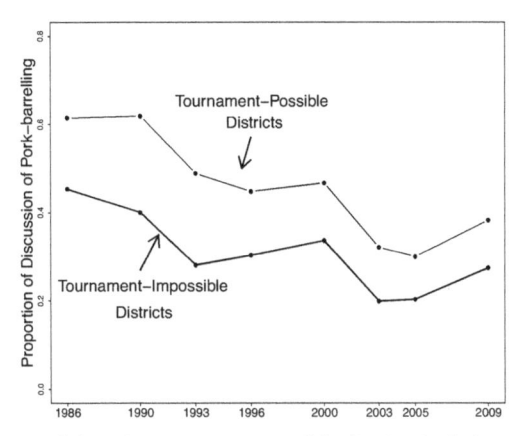

Figure 6.4 LDP candidates in tournament-possible districts include more discussion of pork-barreling in their manifestos, 1986–2009.
The dotted line plots the mean discussion of pork-barreling, drawn from topic modeling in prior work, in the manifestos of LDP candidates contesting tournament-possible districts. The solid line plots the mean discussion of pork-barreling for LDP candidates contesting tournament-impossible districts.

their counterparts in tournament-impossible districts. If the former set of LDP candidates are conducting tournaments, we can expect that their manifestos will reflect this, with a larger share of discussion devoted to pork-barreling.

I found a statistically significant difference in campaign strategy in exactly this direction: In every one of these Lower House elections, LDP candidates in tournament-possible districts devoted systematically more space in their manifestos to pork-barreling than their counterparts in tournament-impossible districts. Figure 6.4 plots mean discussion of pork-barreling in the manifestos of LDP candidates running in tournament-possible and tournament-impossible districts, respectively, in each election in the sample. These difference in means are statistically significant in all years, and hold up in regression analyses with pork-barreling discussion as a function of tournament-possible district, with controls for election year, district magnitude, and number of candidates running.

This is compelling evidence, from data gathered for a completely different purpose, that tournaments impact electoral competition. Electoral competition is qualitatively different in electoral districts in which tournaments are possible versus electoral districts where they are not. The fact that LDP candidates in tournament-possible districts devote more discussion to pork than their counterparts in tournament-impossible districts should also assuage any remaining concerns that the pattern of resource allocations uncovered in Section 6.2 are not the product of

LDP politicians' own actions. If LDP politicians were *not* the driving force behind these allocations, and they were coming from the actions of another actor, such as bureaucrats, we would be unlikely to observe a qualitatively different emphasis on pork-barreling in the campaign strategies of LDP politicians, depending on type of district.

Second, is it plausible that rank-and-file LDP politicians have the connections to bureaucrats that enable them to lobby on behalf of constituents? My answer is: "yes."[38] Let me offer two reasons, one connected to the *characteristics* of people who become LDP politicians and the other connected to *internal party organization*. One, the Japanese politics literature has established that the most common backgrounds of LDP politicians are former bureaucrat, former local politician, and second-generation politician, respectively (Horiuchi, Smith and Yamamoto 2020). According to data from Bergman et al. (2022), 26% of LDP politicians were former bureaucrats in 1980, and by 2000, this was still 25.5%. By definition, junior LDP politicians who had careers in the bureaucracy before entering politics have solved the problem of needing connections to the bureaucracy (Ramseyer and Rosenbluth 1993). Evidence of this comes from their campaign material: Bureaucrat-turned LDP candidates tell voters about their backgrounds and explain that it helps them get things for their constituents. In 1990, for example, a first-time LDP candidate told voters that he had worked for the Ministry of Labor for twenty-two years, and the experience and connections gleaned from participating in the formulation of national policies, budgets, and laws "will be useful to everyone as a liaison between Toyama and national politics."[39] Another veteran LDP politician described his goals as being to "make use of the 30 years I spent working at the Ministry of Finance," and "act as a liaison between the central government and local area, and secure funds from the central government for public works and other investment."[40]

Rank-and-file LDP politicians who are former local politicians have experience in a related domain: identifying projects that their community wants, building a consensus around those projects, and lobbying their LDP politician for assistance. For some of these local-politician-turned-LDP-politicians, that experience would have involved meeting with central government bureaucrats in Tokyo. While such meetings may not have led to deep bonds or sustained interactions, it would have given

---

[38] Other studies answering in the affirmative include Scheiner (2005, 2006); Saito (2010); Horiuchi and Saito (2003); Hirano (2006); Reed and Thies (2001); Hirose (1993); Yonehara (1986); and Ishihara (1986).
[39] Manifesto of Nagase Jinen.
[40] See manifesto of Aizawa Hideyuki.

6.4 Evidence of the Theory's Microfoundations

this subset of LDP politicians a modicum of experience with the bureaucracy, potentially laying the groundwork for a deeper relationship to be built after an election victory. Finally, Smith (2018a)'s data shows that the LDP is the most dynastic of all major parties in the twelve democracies he surveyed, with 39% of LDP-affiliated Diet Members in the 1996–2012 period claiming dynastic status. While the focus of research on dynastic politicians has been on the *electoral* advantages of inheriting a name and support base, it is also possible that these politicians inherit their family members' *connections to the bureaucracy*.

Aside from personal characteristics, a feature of the LDP's internal organization that provides rank-and-file LDP politicians with introductions to bureaucrats is its factions. Since its formation in 1955, the LDP has been a factionalized party, under which almost all LDP politicians affiliate with one of five (or six) factions (Krauss and Pekkanen 2010). The main purpose of an LDP faction is to muster the votes necessary for the faction leader (or the faction's preferred candidate) to win the party's presidential election.[41] Because of the party's Lower House majority, a victory in this election meant the person became Prime Minister (Tsurutani 1980). In order to secure those votes, faction leaders sought to make themselves indispensable to members, plying them with all manner of electoral support, which ran the gamut from campaign funds to introductions to high-ranking bureaucrats and interest groups. Masumi (1995) writes:

Rank-and-file Diet members obtained more than mere assistance in political funding from the faction "boss." They were able to exploit the influence of the boss and fellow faction members in channeling subsidies and other rewards of the pork barrel apparatus to their constituencies. The factions turned into a kind of mutual aid society for Diet members, who needed to satisfy the localized interests of their respective constituencies.

Ramseyer and Rosenbluth (1993, 59) agree with this assessment, calling LDP factions "non-ideological conduits of particularism." While research alluding to the role of faction leaders in helping rank-and-file members meet bureaucrats is older, the possibility remains that faction leaders still perform this function today.[42]

---

[41] While the electoral system the party uses to select its leaders has varied, in the vast majority of elections held since 1955, each LDP-affiliated Diet member had one vote and those votes carried the bulk of voting weight (Sasada 2010).

[42] Note that an implicit assumption here is that the LDP does not have a bureau that coordinates or screens LDP politicians' requests of bureaucrats. In an interview, I asked an LDP politician if his requests "had to go through the party" and he said "no" (Interview, LDP House of Councillors Member, Tokyo, Japan December 14, 2023). This assumption is shared by Hirano (2011, 1086), who writes: "The influence appears to be through a Diet member's informal connections which

6.4.2 Voters Are Aware of This Strategy

The theory assumes that there is at least some awareness among voters that the amount of resources one's community receives is a function of how it votes. A number of sources provide indirect evidence of this, but the theory expects that direct evidence will be hard to come by. Why? The threat to democratic integrity inherent in a tournament gives LDP politicians incentives to avoid statements that make it clear that voters are competing against each other. While LDP politicians may be more frank about the competitive nature of resource distribution when dealing with the local politicians and others they rely on for vote mobilization, this frankness is unlikely to extend to their everyday dealings with constituents. While future research could design an experiment to try to pick up on this implicitness and measure the extent of voters' understanding (and how this might compare to vote mobilizers' understanding), the best we can do in these pages is provide the following pieces of indirect evidence.

First, the campaign manifestos I referenced above are distributed to all registered voters in Japan and broad swaths of them pay attention to them during election campaigns. After every Lower House election, Japan's Association for the Promotion of Clean Elections conducts a survey on a representative sample of approximately 3,000 Japanese voters. One of the questions asks respondents to name any and all campaign material they "saw, listened to, or were persuaded by" during the course of the campaign. In the period 1972–2005, which covers the first twenty-five years of my study, an average of 42% of respondents named the manifesto when answering this question (Catalinac 2016, 67). Two reasons manifestos assume such prominence is because Lower House election campaigns are very short (only two weeks) and candidates face severe restrictions on their use of other media, such as TV, radio, or the internet, respectively (McElwain 2008). Given that LDP candidates devote large chunks of space in their manifesto to promises of projects for their community, we can conclude that many voters are aware that their LDP politicians plan to do this.

Second, indirect evidence of awareness that money for those projects is connected to how people vote comes from an unlikely place: a comic

---

help guide her constituents' applications for central government subsidies through the budgetary process." All available evidence points to lobbying being a relatively *decentralized* activity, in which LDP politicians largely rely on their own connections to bureaucrats, or connections provided by membership in an informal institution such as a party faction, while also leaning heavily on their status as members of the ruling party.

6.4 Evidence of the Theory's Microfoundations

book. Referenced in Saito (2010), in 1990 a comic book called *The Tractor for the Vote Fields* was published (Nabeshima and Maekawa 1989). This depicts the life of an LDP Lower House member, who carries around a piece of paper upon which the names of the municipalities in his electoral district appear, with their vote totals in the last election printed underneath. In one scene, the politician receives mayors in his office one by one, who visit to solicit his assistance with projects each wants funded in his municipality. The politician consults the sheet of paper and decides what should happen to each municipality's budget in response to its request. To one mayor, the politician declares that because his votes decreased in the mayor's municipality, there is "no point" in cooperating with him. Instead, the municipality's budget would be "cut in half!" To another mayor, he exclaims "you tried so hard for me in the last election!" The mayor replies "I risked my life and managed to double your vote share," to which the LDP lawmaker replies "The riverbed plan for Sango Town? Done! I'll also build you a new community hall."

While we cannot rule out the possibility that these scenes are entirely made up, they could indicate a modicum of awareness in the electorate that voters have to perform to get money. Interviews and case studies show that LDP politicians do carry around lists of municipalities, with their vote tallies listed. In an interview, a local politician told me that when he served on the staff of an LDP-affiliated Diet Member, "we calculated the vote share he got in every municipality in the district. Even if the municipality had a tiny number of people in it, I always had it in my head what proportion of them voted for him."[43] In a case study of an LDP Lower House member elected in Kagawa prefecture, Krauss and Pekkanen (2010, 72) wrote that the Member carried a laminated sheet with the election results for the past several elections, broken down by location, in the pocket behind the driver's seat of his campaign car. The authors observed that the Member noticed when his votes went down in a particular locale and "feels and acts as though he is chasing every vote."

Third, survey data suggests that geographically targetable spending of the type LDP politicians provide is of interest to Japanese voters. In 1977, the Cabinet Office carried out a one-time Survey of Public Works.[44] Targeting a representative sample of 10,000 Japanese voters, it asked whether respondents thought more public works was necessary for their community. About 65.2% of respondents replied in the affirmative, while 22.3% said no. As to the type of public works deemed necessary, 71.2% of respondents chose "public works that improves our quality of life, such

---

[43] Interview, Sendai, Japan, June 2018.
[44] To my knowledge, the survey has not been repeated. It can be found at: https://survey.gov-online.go.jp/s51/S52-02-51-20.html.

as housing, parks, sewerage systems, and roads we use every day" over other public works to ensure safety in the face of natural disasters or public works to facilitate economic development. When asked whether local public works had improved their quality of life, 46.9% said yes, 37.1% said not much, and only 3.2% said not at all. More recently, a 2012 poll conducted by a large newspaper, the Asahi Shimbun, showed that 38% of respondents still chose "increase" when asked whether they wanted the new government to increase or decrease public works projects.[45]

Fourth, a central implication of the theory is that in electoral districts where tournaments occur, voters in highly performing municipalities are less likely to vote on policy grounds. By making it clear that the amount of money municipalities receive is a function of electoral loyalty, with amounts increasing with loyalty in a convex fashion, the incumbent is able to engineer a situation in which it is very costly for voters in highly supportive municipalities to vote for anyone other than them. Because a handful of votes in these municipalities could mean the difference between first and second in loyalty, which could mean the difference between the money for a needed project versus not, the theory expects that voters in supportive municipalities will reason that, given the incumbent is likely to remain in power regardless of how they personally vote, it is better to forgo the opportunity to use their vote to communicate dissatisfaction with the party or its policies, and instead use it to make sure their community remains a priority when it comes to resource allocations. This means that in a tournament, large numbers of voters may *dislike* the incumbent and/or their policies but have few incentives to translate that dissatisfaction into their actual voting behavior.

For evidence of this, we can turn to the University of Tokyo-Asahi Shimbun Public Opinion Survey (Taniguchi and Asahi Shimbun 2019).[46] Conducted on a representative sample of 3,000 voters after every Lower House election since 2003, the surveys include an indicator for the electoral district in which respondents live. This enables us to examine whether responses differ by whether the respondent's district is tournament-possible or not. Whereas a better test would compare the responses of voters in highly supportive municipalities in tournament-possible districts with everyone else, the survey does not include indicators for municipality, so this will have to be left to future research.[47]

---

[45] This poll is available at www.asahi.com/special/08003/TKY201212110879.html.
[46] See www.masaki.j.u-tokyo.ac.jp/utas/utasindex_en.html for more information.
[47] Other public opinion surveys in Japan consulted for this project do not include codes for either electoral district or municipality.

6.4 Evidence of the Theory's Microfoundations

In the 2012 survey, which had a response rate of 63.3%, respondents were asked which policy areas were most important to them.[48] Fifteen areas were listed, including diplomacy and national security, pensions and medical care, education and parenting, political and administrative reform, industrial policy, agriculture, forestry, and fisheries, among others. Then, respondents were asked to evaluate each party's positions on the policy areas they had deemed most important.[49] Answers respondents could select were "positively," "somewhat positively," "not sure," "somewhat negatively," or "negatively."[50] A third question asked which party's candidate the respondent voted for in their electoral district (SSD). We can use these questions to examine whether the relationship between positive evaluations of the LDP's policies and voting for the LDP candidate differs for respondents in tournament-possible and tournament-impossible districts, respectively.[51]

In Table 6.10, I present the results of three regression models. The dependent variable in all models is Voted for the LDP Candidate, which takes a "1" for respondents who reported voting for the LDP candidate in the electoral district and "0" otherwise.[52] In Model 1, I examine the relationship between residing in a tournament-possible district and voting for the LDP candidate.[53] In Chapter 5, I used data on election outcomes to show that LDP candidates win at higher rates in these districts, so I expect the coefficient on Tournament-Possible District to be positive and statistically significant. This is indeed what we find: Controlling for the gender and age of respondent, survey respondents in a tournament-possible district are more likely to cast their votes for LDP candidates, relative to survey respondents in tournament-impossible districts.[54]

In Model 2, I examine the relationship between evaluating the LDP's policy positions positively and voting for the LDP candidate. The independent variable of interest, Likes LDP Policies, takes a "1" if the

---

[48] The question was "Which of the following policies is most important to you in this election? What is your second and third most important policy?"
[49] The question was "How do you evaluate the pledges of the Liberal Democratic Party on the policies you answered 'most important' in Q6?," adapted for each party.
[50] Respondents could also choose "do not know" or "no answer."
[51] Altogether, the 2012 survey furnishes 908 valid responses from 112 tournament-possible districts and 992 valid responses from 129 tournament-impossible districts.
[52] These are linear probability models.
[53] I drop respondents who selected "no answer" ($n = 10$).
[54] Gender is coded 1 for women and 0 for men.

Table 6.10 *Respondents in tournament-possible districts (Model 1) are more likely to vote for LDP candidates (Model 1), and respondents who like LDP policies are also more likely to vote for LDP candidates (Model 2) (2012 election). The coefficient on the interaction of the two is in the expected direction (negative), but it is not statistically significant.*

	Dependent variable: Voted for LDP		
	(Model 1)	(Model 2)	(Model 3)
Tournament-Possible District	0.078***		0.102***
	(0.022)		(0.029)
Likes LDP Policies		0.420***	0.446***
		(0.026)	(0.036)
Likes LDP Policies × Tournament-Possible District			−0.047
			(0.051)
Age	0.033***	0.003	0.002
	(0.007)	(0.008)	(0.008)
Gender	−0.042	0.025	0.026
	(0.022)	(0.024)	(0.024)
Constant	0.202***	0.283***	0.234***
	(0.032)	(0.036)	(0.039)
Observations	1,890	1,464	1,464
R^2	0.021	0.153	0.162

***$p < 0.001$.

respondent answered that they evaluated the LDP's policy positions "positively" or "somewhat positively," and "0" otherwise.[55] The coefficient on Likes LDP Policies is positive and statistically significant, controlling for the gender and age of respondent. This is evidence of broad congruence in the electorate between policy preferences and vote choice: Respondents who like LDP policies tend to vote for LDP candidates.

In Model 3, I examine the interaction of Tournament-Possible District and Likes LDP Policies. The theory expects that the relationship between liking LDP policies and voting for the LDP will be weaker in tournament-possible districts, on account of the fact that a portion of voters in these districts (in highly supportive municipalities) are prioritizing their municipality's *resource allocation* when casting their votes, not their policy preferences. The interaction is negative, but not statistically significant, while Tournament-Possible District and Likes LDP Policies remain positive and statistically significant. Thus, liking LDP policies is associated with voting for the LDP in both types of districts, and being in

[55] The sample size is smaller than in Model 1 as I drop respondents who selected "no answer" ($n = 28$) and respondents coded "not applicable" because they did not vote ($n = 401$).

6.4 Evidence of the Theory's Microfoundations

Table 6.11 *Among people who voted for the LDP, being in a tournament-possible district is negatively associated with liking LDP policies, relative to being in a tournament-impossible district.*

	Dependent variable: Likes LDP Policies	
	(Model 1)	(Model 2)
Tournament-Possible District	−0.097*	−0.095*
	(0.039)	(0.039)
Age		0.048***
		(0.012)
Gender		−0.155***
		(0.039)
Constant	0.572***	0.445***
	(0.029)	(0.059)
Observations	642	642
R^2	0.009	0.052

*$p < 0.05$; ***$p < 0.001$.

a tournament-possible district is associated with voting for the LDP, both for respondents who do and do not like the party's policies. However, while the sign on the interaction is in the expected (negative) direction, it is statistically insignificant, meaning that we do not have strong evidence that relationship between liking LDP policies and voting for the LDP is different in tournament-possible districts.[56] However, this could be because the respondents in the tournament-possible districts in the sample happen to reside in the *less* supportive municipalities, where the returns for prioritizing one's municipality's resource allocation when voting are lower, leaving more room for policy-based voting. If our respondents in tournament-possible districts resided in the less supportive municipalities, the distinction between them and respondents in tournaments-impossible districts would not be as stark.

In Table 6.11, I limit the sample to respondents who voted for the LDP's candidate in the SSD ($n = 642$). In both models, the dependent variable is Likes LDP Policies and the independent variable of interest is Tournament-Possible District. If the theory is correct and voters in tournament-possible districts are less likely to vote on policy grounds, then we would expect a negative, statistically significant coefficient on

---

[56] If the interaction was statistically significant, the impact of liking LDP policies on voting for the LDP in tournament-impossible districts would have been 0.446, while the impact of liking LDP policies on voting for the LDP in tournament-possible districts would have been 0.399, which is lower (the calculation is 0.446 + (−0.047*1)).

Tournament-Possible District. This would indicate that, among respondents who voted for LDP candidates in their districts, those residing in tournament-possible districts were significantly less likely to report liking LDP policies relative to their counterparts in tournament-impossible districts. This is exactly what we find. In Model 1, the coefficient on Tournament-Possible District is negative and statistically significant, and this holds after we add controls for age and gender of the respondent in Model 3.

In sum, there is evidence that voters voting for the LDP in tournament-possible districts are engaging in a different calculus than their counterparts voting for the party in a tournament-impossible district. This is also further evidence, from completely different data, of the bifurcated electoral competition described above: Voters appear to be using different heuristics to decide who to vote for in tournament-possible versus tournament-impossible districts.

6.5 WHERE PRIOR RESEARCH WENT WRONG

My results in this chapter have revealed a powerful relationship between electoral support and transfers within electoral districts, the direction and shape of which are consistent with expectations from the tournament theory. It also supplied a wealth of qualitative evidence that should assuage concerns that this relationship could be due to anything other than the deliberate actions of LDP politicians trying to stay in power. Given the wealth of qualitative evidence documented above, it may come as a surprise for readers to learn that no prior study uncovered this relationship, even when it looked at voting and transfer data similar to that which I examine.[57] On this basis, Hirano (2011) concluded that LDP politicians were not pipelines between the national treasury and their districts and had "limited personal influence over the amount of government transfers directed to their constituents" (Hirano 2011, 1082).

---

[57] The prior studies most relevant to analyses in this chapter are Saito (2010) and Hirano (2011), both of which examine the relationship between money and votes at the municipality level. Chapter 7 surveys research that examines the relationship between votes and money to electoral districts and prefectures, respectively. Note that Horiuchi and Saito (2003) also examine transfers to municipalities, but they do not examine the impact of electoral support for the LDP at the *municipality* level. Electoral support for the LDP, conceptualized as the share of a district's seats occupied by LDP politicians, is measured at the district level. In Chapter 7, I explain that their results show that this variable is negative and statistically significant for elections prior to 1994. This means that, controlling for other differences across municipalities, including in the number of Diet Members representing them, municipalities in districts where a larger share of those Diet Members were LDP-affiliated received *fewer* transfers.

6.5 Where Prior Research Went Wrong

Because a second goal of this book is to make substantive contributions to Japanese politics, this section explains why prior studies did not find persuasive evidence that resource allocations in Japan are driven by a reward-the-supporter logic.

One, the tournament theory holds that politicians can garner high levels of support by making municipalities compete against each other for prizes. Within districts, the observable implication of this is that prizes *follow* support, as I have shown in this chapter. But another implication of the theory, examined systematically in Chapter 7, is that the relative sizes of the municipalities in a given electoral district impacts the total amount of money politicians have to make available for prizes. As I explained in Chapter 4, when there is greater asymmetry in municipality size, politicians have to offer more money for the same level of support relative to when there is less asymmetry in municipality size. This means that the most supportive municipality in a district consisting of relatively *evenly* sized municipalities could receive a *smaller* prize, all else equal, than the least supportive municipality in a district consisting of unevenly sized municipalities.

The analyses in this chapter used district-year fixed effects to control for differences across electoral districts. As I explained, the use of district-year fixed effects enabled me to look *within* district-years. When I did that, I found that money increases with electoral support. By extension, however, any analysis that does *not* control for the fact that the size of the prize differs systematically according to the degree of asymmetry in municipality size may not find any evidence of a relationship between support and transfers. Such analyses may, in fact, find evidence of the *opposite* relationship: That municipalities with high levels of support receive *fewer* transfers. How? If the majority of electoral districts consist of relatively *evenly* sized municipalities, and the municipalities in those districts are receiving, on average, *less* money for a given level of support than municipalities in districts consisting of unevenly sized municipalities, then it is easy to see how, absent any controls for district-level asymmetry, higher levels of support could appear to correlate with fewer transfers.

This helps to explain why Saito (2010)'s empirical analyses yielded little evidence that municipalities with high levels of support received more transfers. Saito (2010) offered an argument that is very similar to ours: Drawing on Stokes (2005)'s notion of perverse accountability (gyaku setsumei sekinin in Japanese), he argued that the lack of a robust opposition in Japan enabled LDP politicians to convey to their supporters that because they are the ruling party, they will continue to be the ruling party. This created conditions under which LDP politicians could have supporters serve *their* interests (getting reelected), rather than the other way around, *them* serving their *constituents'* interests. The author argued that they did this by making their supporters compete in a "vote-gathering competition" (shuhyou gassen), in which they had to demonstrate their fealty to the party, election after election, in order to continue receiving government money.

While his argument is very much in keeping with the argument of this book, the results of his empirical tests were not entirely consistent with those claims. He found that municipalities supplying vote shares for the LDP that were higher than the *average* vote share supplied by a municipality in the same district tended to receive per capita transfer allocations that were larger than the average allocation received by a municipality in the same district (Models 1 and 2) (Saito 2010, 123). However, when the *absolute* amount of per capita transfer allocation was used, municipalities returning higher-than-average LDP vote shares were found to have received *smaller* per capita transfer allocations (Model 3). Once controls were added (also expressed in terms of deviation from the district average), a municipality's LDP vote share was found to have *no relationship* to its transfer allocation (Model 4).[58]

In Saito (2010)'s analysis, district-year fixed effects do not appear to have been used. As a consequence, it is not surprising that his results showed no relationship between support and transfers in one model and a statistically significant, *negative* relationship in another. I conducted supplementary analyses to check whether my interpretation of the dissonance between his results and mine is the correct one. In Model 1 of Table A.7, I examine the effect of my first measure of support, Best LDP VS$_{m,t}$, on per capita transfers after elections for municipalities in Lower House elections, 1980–2014 (excluding 2009). The sample and specification is identical to that in Model 1 of Table 6.1, except I use *year* fixed effects, not district-year fixed effects. In this regression, no district-level differences are controlled for. The coefficient on Best LDP VS$_{m,t}$ is negative and statistically significant. In Model 2 of Table A.7, I examine the effect of my second measure of support, Sum LDP VS$_{m,t}$. Again, the sample and specification is identical to that in Model 3 of Table 6.1, with the only difference being the use of year fixed effects instead of district-year fixed effects. The coefficient on Sum LDP VS$_{m,t}$ is negative and statistically significant. The results of these models serve as a stark

---

[58] Note that his dependent variable was the sum of the formula-based (LAT) and discretionary (NTD) transfer received by municipalities in the periods following the Lower House elections between 1977 and 1990, where "period following" are the years until the next election (Saito 2010, 116). In Chapter 5, I explained that there is little evidence that allocations of the former transfer are susceptible to influence by LDP politicians.

6.5 Where Prior Research Went Wrong

reminder that district-level differences matter greatly when it comes to determining a municipality's transfer allocation, and analyses that do not take these district-level differences into account risk mischaracterizing the relationship between support and transfers at the municipality level.

Hirano (2011) leveraged the sudden deaths of 67 Lower House Members between 1977 to 1992 to investigate whether the (NTD) transfers received by municipalities in those Members' bailiwicks declined in the wake of their deaths. Of these Members, 47 were LDP politicians and municipalities were treated as being part of a politician's bailiwick if they returned a vote share of 30% or higher for the politician. In a specification that compared the amount of transfers received during a given legislative session by municipalities that were and were not in bailiwicks of the newly deceased Member, he found that municipalities in the bailiwicks of someone who died experienced no noticeable reduction in transfers. His specification did not include district-year fixed effects, meaning that it did not explicitly compare municipalities that were supportive of a given Member who died with municipalities in the *same* district that were less supportive. This could explain his lack of results.[59]

A second reason prior work did not unearth the relationship between support and transfers that we uncovered above is because it relies on a different operationalization of electoral support altogether. To my knowledge, all prior work on the politics of transfers in Japan has used votes cast for all LDP candidates to construct a measure of electoral support. Almost always, it is votes cast for all LDP candidates, including losing ones, divided by the number of valid votes cast. In contrast, the tournament theory holds that it is only LDP politicians who *win* the election who will reward the municipalities that put them there with more government money after the election. The results thus far have borne this out: Tables 6.4 and 6.7 showed that increases in electoral support for losing LDP candidates were associated with *less* money after elections. Thus, the tournament theory holds that the appropriate numerator is votes cast for LDP *winners*, not votes cast for all LDP candidates. Moreover, because LDP politicians seek to maximize the number of votes cast for them out of

---

[59] In a second analyses, Hirano (2011) compared the amount of transfers received by municipalities in the bailiwicks of LDP candidates who narrowly won the last seat in their district with municipalities in the bailiwicks of LDP candidates who narrowly lost the last seat. His research question here was whether municipalities in the bailiwicks of the LDP politicians who narrowly won receive more transfers, on average, than municipalities in the bailiwicks of LDP politicians who narrowly lost. Notwithstanding differences across electoral districts, which are not fully controlled for, he finds evidence that they do. This is in keeping with my finding that municipalities returning high support for *losing* LDP candidates do not receive transfer allocations commensurate with their effort the way municipalities returning high support for winning LDP candidates do.

all available votes in the municipality, and not the share of votes cast, the appropriate denominator is not valid votes cast, but number of eligible voters in the municipality.

In Model 3 of Table A.7, I show how different the results look when electoral support is measured the way it has been previously. I examine the effect of an alternative measure of support, which matches how other studies have operationalized it. All LDP VS$_{m,t}$ is the number of votes cast for all LDP candidates competing in municipality m, divided by the total number of valid votes cast in municipality m.[60] In this model, the sample (municipalities in Lower House elections between 1980 and 2014, excluding 2009) and specification (year fixed effects instead of district-year fixed effects) is identical to that in Model 1 of the same table. The coefficient on All LDP VS$_{m,t}$ is negative and statistically significant.

In sum, Table A.7 bolsters this interpretation of why my results differ from results reported in previous work. The results in this table, when compared with those presented earlier in this chapter, also offer powerful evidence that district-level differences matter enormously. This implies that two municipalities could rank first in support, each returning a Best LDP VS$_{m,t}$ score of 0.8, for example, yet receive systematically different amounts of money, based on the type of district they are in. The theory has clear expectations about which district-level characteristic is likely to drive differences in amount of money received. Evaluating these predictions is the subject of Chapter 7.

---

[60] As noted in Chapter 5, this is sotai tokuhyouritsu in Japanese.

7

Which Electoral Districts Get More Money

The Japanese politics literature exhibits a puzzle. Time and again, we are told that Liberal Democratic Party (LDP) politicians use geographically targeted spending to cultivate loyal groups of supporters, who can be relied on to turn out and vote for them on election day.[1] Some studies go further and argue that it is these politicians' access to geographically targetable resources, as well as to other areas of government policy that can be parlayed into benefits for nationally organized groups of voters, that constitutes the most compelling explanation for the LDP's ability to vanquish its opponents, election after election, regardless of trends in its popularity, the state of the economy, or the electoral system. Yet whenever scholars have subjected this claim to empirical scrutiny, by collecting and analyzing data on votes and money, they have come up short. By this, I mean they have not furnished compelling evidence that spending is, in fact, channeled toward the party's supporters.[2] The lack of evidence for a claim that occupies a central place in scholarship on the party is curious and demands further investigation. If it is the product of restricting one's gaze to a handful of bad apples, who distort government resources in ways that might be troubling but are not generalizable to the broader pool of LDP politicians, then we should be looking elsewhere for explanations of the party's longevity at the reigns of power.

In this book, I offer a theory for how incumbents operating under a certain configuration of political institutions can use government resources to stay in power. The theory holds that whenever incumbents can discern

---

[1] Studies that make this claim include Reed (2021); Christensen and Selway (2017); McMichael (2018); Naoi (2015); Reed, Scheiner and Thies (2012); Saito (2010); Krauss and Pekkanen (2010); Pempel (2010); Estevez-Abe (2008); Hirano (2006); Scheiner (2006); Bouissou (1999); Tani (1998); Ramseyer and Rosenbluth (1993); Sone and Kanazashi (1989); Curtis (1971); and Thayer (1969).
[2] This is also a point made by McMichael (2018).

their electoral support at a disaggregated unit within their electoral district and influence allocations of central government resources to those same units, they will have the tools to conduct what I call "group-based clientelism" (GBC). By this, I mean they will have the ability to *tie* the amount of government resources each unit (group) receives to its voting behavior. Moreover, when there is a dominant party, I explain that politicians in that party can elicit the most support by pitting groups against each other in a *competition* for resources. By promising the most resources to the group that ranks first in electoral loyalty, the second-most resources to the group that ranks second, and so on, and making sure that the difference in amounts received by the first and second place-getter are larger than the difference in amounts received by the second and third place-getter, and so on, politicians in the dominant party can maximize the number of votes won, conditional upon resources delivered. In this competition, a "tournament," the amount of money groups receive is a function of how their level of electoral support stacks up against that of other groups in the same district. The group ranking first in electoral loyalty receives the most money (the largest prize), with the amount of money groups receive declining in rank in a *convex* (rather than linear) fashion.

In Chapter 5, I explained that the institutional context in which the majority of LDP politicians found themselves in for the better part of the postwar period met the conditions under which they would have been able to implement tournaments. More specifically, these politicians competed in electoral districts consisting of groups of voters (municipalities), at which vote tallies were observable and government resources (national treasury disbursements [NTD]) deliverable. Beginning in the mid 1990s, I explained how the combination of electoral reform (1994), municipal mergers (2001–2005), and urbanization reduced the share of electoral districts in which tournaments are possible to approximately half of all districts. In Chapter 6, I examined whether LDP politicians use tournaments in tournament-possible districts. I explained how I gathered data on the voting behavior, resource allocations, and other fiscal and demographic characteristics of the universe of Japanese municipalities in existence from 1980 until 2014. Using regression specifications designed to minimize the influence of confounders, weigh up evidence for rival theories, and take advantage of distinctive features of the two electoral systems Japan used during this time, I presented evidence consistent with tournaments being used by many LDP politicians. My findings show that the amount of money Japanese municipalities received in the years following Lower House elections has been a function of how their support stacked up against that of their competitors in the tournament (other municipalities in the same district). Moreover, the amount of money municipalities received in the years following these elections declined with rank in exactly the (convex) manner predicted by the theory.

In contrast to prior work, then, I was able to unearth a powerful connection between money and votes, and unmistakable evidence that money flows to the party's core supporters. Putting it like this, however, risks misconstruing the rule under which resources were allocated. Resources are not *targeted* at core supporters (or municipalities with higher concentrations of core supporters) on account of the fact that these voters are core supporters (or are inhabited by core supporters) and the party is making a concerted effort to buy votes from core supporters. Rather, resources are used as a *reward* for the high level of support they received and are allocated without regard to the *type* of voters in each group. In this way, core supporters are given no special advantages over other types of voters. They can expect to receive disproportionately large government outlays only if they continue to return disproportionately high levels of electoral support. This was clear when I zeroed in on municipalities that exhibited the highest or second-highest level of support for their district's LDP winner(s) (Table 6.5). I found that when those municipalities slipped in rank, they suffered declines in size of their resource allocation.

In this chapter, I change the focus from money flows *within* electoral districts to money flows *across* electoral districts. As I explained in Chapter 4, a vast scholarly literature has been interested in the question of why voters in certain electoral districts receive larger allocations of (discretionary) government resources than voters in other districts, even after controlling for a host of other (nonpolitical) determinants of resource allocations.[3] Various theories have been offered. Most boil down to the idea that variation in resource allocations across districts is a function of the *type* of voters residing in each. Whenever resource allocations across electoral districts are found to be *positively* correlated with district-level vote shares for the ruling party, then the ruling party is presumed to be favoring core supporters (e.g., Cox and McCubbins 1986). Theoretical models offer cogent arguments for why it makes sense to target core supporters. Whenever resource allocations across districts are found to be *negatively* correlated with vote shares for the ruling party, meaning that districts where the party received less support got more money, then the

---

[3] Studies that have been interested in this question include Rickard (2018); Zarazaga (2016); Tavits (2009); Cox (2009); Stokes (2005); Dahlberg and Johansson (2002); Dixit and Londregan (1996); Lindbeck and Weibull (1987); and Cox and McCubbins (1986).

ruling party is presumed to be favoring swing voters (e.g., Stokes 2005). A different set of formal theories provide the theoretical intuitions for this claim.

The tournament theory offers a different explanation for why resource allocations can vary so substantially across electoral districts, which moves scholarship in this area beyond the core-versus-swing dichotomy (Smith, Bueno de Mesquita and LaGatta, 2017; Smith and Bueno de Mesquita, 2012, 2019). To the extent that resource allocations vary across electoral districts, the theory holds that this will have little to do with the type of voter in each. Instead, it will be a function of the *ease* with which tournaments can be administered. Ease, Chapter 4 explains, is a function of the relative sizes of the groups of voters in each district. Why does relative size matter? To recap, tournaments work by creating an alternative dimension upon which voters can pivotal. When incumbents structure prizes so that they become exponentially larger at higher ranks, then provided that those prizes are sufficiently valuable, this encourages voters in municipalities with a chance of attaining a high rank to set aside whatever true feelings they may hold about the incumbent or her policies and turn out and support her in elections. As voters in all supportive municipalities come to this realization, turnout and electoral support increases, such that there is now little difference in support between the most supportive municipalities. This creates a situation where a very small number of votes in a supportive municipality can effect a change in rank, which can have big implications for a municipality's resource allocation. Critically, voters in supportive municipalities know that their votes will not matter to the *outcome* of the election but have been made to matter enormously for their municipality's *resource allocation*.

For a tournament to be an effective means of increasing support, however, voters have to be made *aware* that the incumbent plans to compare the performance of their municipality with that of other municipalities in the same district. But incumbents cannot make this explicit. As Chapter 4 explains, in a democracy politicians are supposed to vie for the support of voters, not make *voters* compete for *politicians'* time, attention, and resources. Because tournaments are antithetical to democracy (and indeed, threaten it), the incumbent's intention to rank groups based on electoral support and allocate resources on the basis of rank will all be implicit. This implicitness causes more problems when groups are asymmetrically sized than when groups are similarly sized. This is because there are different ways of comparing groups, and when groups are asymmetrically sized, those different ways of comparing groups can produce radically different results. Because different metrics lead to different results, and incumbents cannot easily *clarify* which metric they plan to use, voters in districts characterized by asymmetrically sized groups will have a great deal more trouble calibrating the degree of influence their vote holds over their municipality's ranking (and thus, its resource allocation). When voters have trouble calibrating the degree of influence their vote holds over their group's ranking (and hence, its resource allocation), they will be less inclined to turn out and support the incumbent.

As a result, the theory expects that incumbents in districts consisting of asymmetrically sized groups will have to offer *larger* prizes to convince the voters in their districts to use their votes to compete with other groups. This is Hypothesis 3. However, because incumbents will also prefer to minimize the amount of government money that has to be diverted to prizes, it is unlikely that they will deliver prizes large enough to totally offset the reduced propensity to turn out and vote for them among voters in these districts. The implication is that districts consisting of asymmetrically sized groups are likely to exhibit *lower* levels of electoral support, even as they receive *larger* prizes. This is Hypothesis 4. Looking across districts, then, the theory expects that resource allocations will be negatively correlated with electoral support. While resource allocations will be positively correlated *within* districts (due to the tournament), they will be negatively correlated *across* districts (due to variation in the ease with which tournaments can be administered). In other words, districts with less support for the LDP incumbent will receive more transfers.

Critically, this pattern will make it look like the LDP is *rewarding* districts for lower levels of support and *penalizing* districts for higher levels of support. Extant theories might attribute this to the party reasoning that, because core supporters are going to vote for it anyway, it would be prudent to direct geographically targeted resources toward swing voters. The tournament theory helps us see that this would be the *wrong* inference to draw about the determinants of allocations across districts, at least when politicians are using tournaments. The correct inference is that in districts in which groups vary greatly in size, voters require larger prizes to be drawn into a competition. This is not due to any intrinsic feature of those voters; rather, it is due to the relative sizes of the groups into which they are arranged. LDP politicians in these districts have to offer more resources than their counterparts in other districts. Because providing more resources is costly in terms of the politician's time and detracts from other policy goals, we can expect that politicians will settle for less support in these districts. But even this lower level of support will cost significantly more than a similarly low level of support in a district consisting of evenly sized groups.

This macrolevel expectation of the tournament theory provides a new explanation for why prior studies of the political determinants of transfers in Japan did not furnish compelling evidence that within electoral districts, money flowed to core supporters. The fact that districts can vary so significantly in the amount of money needed to entice voters to compete with each other means that two otherwise-similar municipalities could be offering the *same* level of support but be receiving qualitatively *different* amounts of postelection transfers. This situation would arise if the two municipalities were in districts where the degree of asymmetry in municipality size varied. Because prior work did not have the tournament theory from which to draw, it did not appreciate that the relative sizes of the groups into which voters are arranged exerts an independent effect on transfers. Thus, when scholars examined whether municipalities that were more supportive of their LDP incumbent received more transfers, they did not always restrict their comparison to municipalities *in the same district*. They adopted specifications that effectively asked whether, generally speaking, municipalities with higher levels of support received more transfers, and they found that the answer to this question was "no." In Chapter 6, I showed that once the comparison is limited to municipalities *in the same district*, accomplished with a regression specification that includes district-year fixed effects, municipalities with higher levels of electoral support *do* receive more transfers.

This chapter is devoted to empirically examining whether the degree of asymmetry in municipality size exerts an independent effect on the amount of transfers received by municipalities in the district, in the direction predicted by the theory. If, controlling for other differences across electoral districts, the total amount of money each district receives is found to be a function of the degree of asymmetry in sizes of its constituent municipalities, then this is further evidence that LDP politicians are using tournaments to get elected. This piece of evidence helps us discriminate between what Chapter 4 called contest-based compensation (a tournament), in which money is allocated on the basis of rank, and "output-calibrated compensation," in which money is awarded to groups in proportion to the group's contribution to the politician's total vote share in the district. If LDP politicians are using output-calibrated compensation, then we would still observe the positive relationship between electoral support and transfers *within* districts (documented in Chapter 6), but there would be no reason for the total amount of transfers awarded to districts to vary systematically with the relative size of constituent municipalities. Evidence of this is further evidence of contest-based compensation (a tournament).

7.1 EMPIRICAL STRATEGY

Chapter 4 fleshed out the theoretical underpinnings of the hypotheses this book tests. For ease of access, here are the two examined in this chapter.

- **Hypothesis 3**: Across electoral districts with LDP winners, resource allocations are a function of the degree of asymmetry in municipality size. All else equal, districts characterized by greater asymmetry in municipality size receive larger resource allocations.
- **Hypothesis 4**: Across electoral districts, support for the LDP is a function of the degree of asymmetry in size of municipalities therein. All else equal, electoral districts characterized by greater asymmetry in municipality size exhibit less support for the LDP.

7.1.1 Variables

In Chapter 5, I classified electoral districts used in Japan's Lower House elections as tournament-possible or tournament-impossible. Tournament-possible districts are divisible into more than one municipality, at which electoral support is discernible and to which resources are deliverable. It is in these districts in which LDP politicians can conduct tournaments. Because tournament-impossible districts consist of a single municipality, have sizeable shares of their voters residing in a municipality whose area is not fully contained in the district, or municipalities to which central government resources are not easily deliverable, they do not meet these conditions. Because LDP politicians cannot conduct tournaments in tournament-*impossible* districts, tournament-*possible* districts are the focus of my analyses in these empirical chapters.

As I explained in Chapter 6, my data consist of yearly observations (where t indicates the year) of electoral districts (d), municipalities (m), and candidates (c). Because tournament-possible districts are comprised of multiple self-contained municipalities, the creation of district-level variables capturing the level of support offered the LDP, the amount of money (NTD) received after elections, and other demographic and fiscal characteristics with the data I collected is relatively straightforward and simply requires the aggregation of these municipality-level variables. Below, I provide more detail.

First, I created Winning LDP $VS_{d,t}$, a variable capturing the level of support electoral district d offered its LDP winners.[4] Let $v_{c,m,t}$ represent the number of votes obtained by candidate c in municipality m in district d at time t. This is available for $t \in E = \{e_1, e_2, \ldots\} =$

---

[4] Where possible, I use the variable operationalizations in Catalinac, Bueno de Mesquita and Smith (2020).

{1980, 1983,...}, the years in which Lower House elections were held. Let $p_{m,t}$ represent the voting population in municipality m in district d at time t (the number of eligible voters). Several indicator functions can also be defined: let $w_{c,t}$ indicate whether candidate c won a seat in district d at time t, and $LDP_{c,t}$ indicate whether candidate c was a member of the LDP at time t. Because municipality m belongs to a single district d, I calculated, for each district d:

$$\text{Winning LDP VS}_{d,t} = \frac{\sum_{m \in d} \sum_{c \in m} \{LDP_{c,t} w_{c,t} v_{c,m,t}\}}{\sum_{m \in d} p_{m,t}}. \quad (7.1)$$

Colloquially, Winning LDP VS$_{d,t}$ captures the proportion of eligible voters in district d at time t who voted for a winning LDP candidate. Put differently, it is the share of available votes in district d at time t that was captured by winning LDP candidates. Note that this operationalization differs from alternative operationalizations in that the numerator is votes cast for *winning* LDP candidates (not all LDP candidates), while the denominator is number of *electors* (not votes cast).

Second, to capture my main independent variable, the degree of asymmetry in municipality size in district d at time t, I constructed a standardized Herfindahl Index, what I call HI$_{d,t}$. Let $n_{d,t}$ represent the number of municipalities in each district d at time t. Let $p_{d,t}$ represent the voting population of district d at time t. For each municipality m in district d at time t, I take its voting population ($p_{m,t}$) and divide this by the voting population of its district ($p_{d,t}$) to calculate the fraction of the district's population that lives in municipality m. For all municipalities in the same district, I square each of these fractions and take the sum of these squares. This first step creates an index that runs from 0 to 1, with 1 capturing a district in which every voter lives in a single municipality (the district's voters are concentrated in a single municipality) and lower numbers capturing districts in which voters are divided amongst the municipalities in the district.

Next, I standardize the index so that regardless of the number of municipalities in each district, HI$_{d,t} = 1$ captures a district in which the voting population is concentrated in a single municipality and HI$_{d,t} = 0$ captures a district in which the voting population is evenly divided amongst the municipalities in the district.[5] To do this, we take the sum of these squares minus 1 divided by the number of municipalities in

---

[5] Without standardizing the index by number of municipalities in a district, a district consisting of four municipalities in which the voting population was perfectly divided among each would have a higher score on the index (0.25) than a district consisting of five municipalities in which the voting population was perfectly divided among each (0.20). After standardizing the index by number of municipalities in the district, both of these hypothetical districts would have 0 on the index.

7.1 Empirical Strategy

the district, and divide this result by $1 - 1$ divided by the number of municipalities in the district. Concretely:

$$\text{HI}_{d,t} = \frac{\sum_{m \in d} \left(\frac{p_{m,t}}{p_{d,t}}\right)^2 - 1/n_{d,t}}{1 - 1/n_{d,t}}. \tag{7.2}$$

Colloquially, $\text{HI}_{d,t}$, uses variation in the populations of municipalities in district d to capture the degree to which a district's population is concentrated in a single municipality ($\text{HI}_{d,t} = 1$) or spread out evenly across multiple municipalities ($\text{HI}_{d,t} = 0$).

Third, I created Postelection Transfers$_{d,t}$, a variable capturing the logarithm of the per capita allocation of NTD received by districts in the fiscal years following Lower House elections. To do this, I took all municipalities in district d and summed the amounts of NTD received by them in the fiscal years following each Lower House election. This is the total amount of NTD received by district d in the year following an election held at t. I calculated the district's population analogously, by summing up the populations of the municipalities located within district d. Dividing the total amount of transfers received by district d in the year after the election by the population of district d generates a per capita measure, which I then take the logarithm of.

Fourth, I constructed district-level versions of the six control variables included in Chapter 6's analyses of transfers to municipalities. Population in district d at time t was calculated by summing the populations of municipalities in district d. Population density was calculated by dividing the district's population by its geographic area (in kilometers squared), captured by summing up the geographic area of all municipalities located within it. The fiscal strength of district d at time t was calculated by multiplying each municipality's value on the fiscal strength index by the fraction of the district's population constituted by that municipality, and then summing those for all municipalities in district d. The proportion of residents employed in primary industries; the proportion of residents aged fifteen and under and sixty-five and over; and per capita income at the district-level were created the same way (each municipalities' values were multiplied by the fraction of the district's population constituted by that municipality, and the resulting values were summed for municipalities in the same district).

7.1.2 Potential Confounders

My goal is to examine whether resource allocations across electoral districts vary systematically with the degree of asymmetry in municipality size. Prior work on resource allocations to larger entities – namely, electoral districts and prefectures – in Japan have identified other variables thought to influence the amount of money received by these larger entities. Any analyses attempting to establish the importance of a new variable such as district-level asymmetry should control for the potentially confounding effects of these variables. They are malapportionment; the share of a district's seats held by LDP politicians; the fiscal strength of the entity (the degree to which it can finance the cost of services itself or must rely on the central government); the number of municipalities in the district; and whether the district counts a senior LDP politician among its Lower House representatives, respectively. Here, I recount the claims scholars have made about why each of these variables matter and summarize what their empirical analyses showed. I conclude my discussion of each variable by explaining how I operationalize it with my data.

First, Horiuchi and Saito (2003) make the case that malapportionment – inequality in representation – affects the amount of central government transfers received by voters in different electoral districts. Malapportionment captures a situation in which some districts have more Diet Members per voter than others. When a system is malapportioned, the weight of an individual vote is not the same across districts: In some districts, more votes are required to elect a Diet Member than in others. How does malapportionment come about? While electoral districts may have been allotted the "correct" number of Diet members relative to population when their boundaries were first drawn up and the number of seats (their district magnitude) was decided upon, the combination of out- and in-migration over time usually necessitates corrections, either to the number of Diet Members elected in each district or to district boundaries themselves. Seats will need to be added to districts experiencing in-migration (urban districts) and subtracted from districts experiencing out-migration. If such corrections are not carried out, then malapportionment is the result.

In Japan, despite being required to use the results of censuses conducted at five-year intervals to prevent malapportionment from becoming too severe, successive LDP governments were very slow to correct vote-seat disparities (Horiuchi and Saito 2003; Meyer and Naka 1999). Despite malapportionment increasing in every Lower House election held under the party's watch, it managed to conduct "minor reapportionments" only four times between 1955 and 1994, when Japan's electoral reform necessitated a complete redrawing of district boundaries (which dramatically reduced malapportionment). It was not until 1986 and 1993, respectively, that the LDP government actually managed to take seats *away* from certain (rural) districts. Horiuchi and Saito (2003) posited that municipalities in overrepresented districts (those

7.1 Empirical Strategy

with more Diet representatives per voter) would receive more central government transfers. Regression analyses of the determinants of the amount of per capita transfers (the sum of both the formula-based [LAT] and discretionary [NTD] transfer described in Chapter 6) received by Japanese municipalities showed that district-level malapportionment (namely, the number of seats available in the district, divided by the district's population, in logs), had a positive, statistically significant effect on transfers, after controlling for other differences across municipalities. I constructed People Per Seat$_{d,t}$, which is the district's population divided by the number of seats available.[6]

Second, a variable that was controlled for in the cross-sectional analyses in Horiuchi and Saito (2003), conducted on separate years before and after Japan's electoral reform, was share of a district's seats occupied by LDP-affiliated politicians. Put simply, this is the share of a district's representatives who are LDP-affiliated. Their results showed that this exercised a statistically significant, *negative* impact on the amount of transfers received by Japanese municipalities in the years 1991 through 1993. In the years 1994 through 1998, the coefficient on this variable remained negative but ceased to be statistically significant. Viewed together, their results suggest that Japanese municipalities receive more transfers when their district has more Diet representatives per voter, but *fewer* transfers when more of those representatives are LDP-affiliated.

Other studies found similarly negative or null effects of indicators of electoral support for the LDP at the district-level. McMichael (2018) studied the determinants of the amount of per capita transfers (the sum of LAT and NTD) received by Japanese prefectures in the period 1958–1993. He tallies up the number of Lower House Members elected in each prefecture (electoral districts are perfectly contained within prefectures) and calculates the share of those Diet members who are LDP-affiliated. Various regression specifications, with logged and nonlogged dependent variables, with the full sample and a truncated sample, revealed that the share of a prefecture's Diet seats occupied by LDP politicians exercised either a statistically significant, *negative* impact on the amount of transfers received, or no effect. Saito (2010, Chapter 5) also studied the determinants of transfers to Japan's electoral districts over the period 1977–1990. Controlling for many other differences across electoral districts, he found that both the share of a district's seats held by LDP politicians and the size of the LDP's vote share at the district level had no effect on the amount of per capita transfers (the sum of LAT and

---

[6] Following Catalinac, Bueno de Mesquita and Smith (2020), I scaled it so that the value represents the number of people, in 100,000s, per available seat in the district.

NTD) received. In his regression models, the coefficients on these district-level indicators of the LDP's strength were always negative. In addition to Winning LDP VS$_{d,t}$, described above, I calculated LDP Seats$_{d,t}$, which captures the proportion of seats in district d that were won by LDP candidates.[7]

Third, Scheiner (2005, 2006) argued that fiscal centralization in Japan created a situation in which regions of the country that were prosperous and had less of a need for government transfers were less tethered to the ruling party than regions that were less prosperous and had a greater need for government transfers. By and large, the less-prosperous regions, characterized by lower incomes and weaker tax bases, were rural areas. There, he observed that local politicians tended to affiliate with the ruling LDP and use their ability to mobilize votes for LDP-affiliated Diet members to make sure those Diet Member favored their regions when deciding on allocations of central government transfers. Every year, the Japanese government makes data on the "fiscal strength" of each prefecture and municipality available. Put simply, this is an index created by dividing the prefecture or municipality's revenue by its needs.[8] Higher scores indicate greater autonomy from the central government, while lower scores indicate less autonomy. Regression analyses of the proportion of prefectural assembly members affiliated with an opposition party in Japan's forty-seven prefectures between 1971 and 1991 as a function of the prefecture's score on this index revealed that prefectures with greater autonomy from the central government (higher scores on the index) had larger shares of opposition-affiliated politicians than prefectures with less autonomy (lower scores on the index). My controls thus include variables capturing the fiscal strength of the district, as well as the proportion of district's population employed in agriculture.

Fourth, Saito (2010, Chapter 5) made the case that, in addition to malapportionment, the number of municipalities in electoral district d exercises an independent effect on the amount of transfers received by electoral district d. He argued that electoral districts consisting of multiple municipalities received larger transfer allocations than districts consisting of fewer municipalities. Why? His rationale was that electoral districts divided into more municipalities would have more local politicians. Because municipalities depend on the central government for transfers, most local politicians tend to affiliate with the LDP and mobilize votes

---

[7] In McMichael (2018)'s analysis of transfers to prefectures, he finds that prefectures in which the party lost a seat in the previous election tended to received more transfers. Below, I include specifications that control for this possibility using LDP Seats$_{d,t}$.

[8] For more information on this index, see McMichael (2017).

7.1 Empirical Strategy

for LDP-affiliated Diet Members in Lower House elections. Thus, electoral districts with more local politicians would have larger cadres of vote mobilizers for the LDP. Another feature of electoral districts consisting of multiple municipalities is that each municipality tends to be smaller. In smaller municipalities, he reasoned that those cadres of vote mobilizers would be better positioned to pressure residents to vote LDP. As a result, he posited that electoral districts with more municipalities would produce higher vote shares for the LDP. Regression analyses of the determinants of per capita transfers (the sum of both the formula-based and discretionary transfer) to Japan's electoral districts in the period 1977 through 1990 showed that the number of municipalities in district d was found to exercise a positive, statistically significant effect on the transfers it received, controlling for other differences across districts. I constructed Log(Number of Municipalities$_{d,t}$), which is the logarithm of the number of municipalities in each district.

Fifth (and finally), scholars have suggested that the seniority of the LDP politicians in the district might influence the amount of transfers received (McMichael 2018; Reed 2001; Meyer and Naka 1998, 1999). Their reasoning is that politicians with more terms in office would have built stronger connections to the bureaucracy, and given that bureaucrats decide on transfer allocations, stronger connections would translate into more projects approved for their municipalities. Reed (2001, 120) knits together the occurrence of large-scale corruption scandals implicating senior LDP politicians, the fact that a good number of those scandals involved the construction industry, the "massive" amounts spent on construction by the government each year, and the regular surfacing of anecdotes in the media alleging political influence over grant allocation as evidence corroborating this possibility. He writes: "In no country have so many prime ministers been investigated, tried, and even convicted on corruption charges before becoming prime minister ... and in no country have so many election campaigns focused on corruption scandals" (Reed 2001, 113–114).

To examine the impact of seniority on grant allocation, he compared annual amounts spent on construction in two electoral districts represented by *powerful* LDP politicians to annual amounts spent on construction in seven similar districts represented by *ordinary* LDP politicians. His research design had the advantage of selecting districts that spanned the entire prefecture. The two powerful politicians he selected were successive leaders of the faction headed by Tanaka Kakuei, who remains the most corrupt Prime Minister in Japan's history. The former (Takeshita Noboru) served as Prime Minister and the latter (Kanemaru Shin), who preferred to control things behind the scenes, had to step down after becoming embroiled in a massive scandal implicating the construction industry. Reed (2001) writes: "If Takeshita and Kanemaru proved unable to influence the allocation of public funds for their home prefectures, we can rest assured that no politician (with the possible exception of Tanaka himself) could do so."

Ultimately, his analysis revealed no differences in spending across the two sets of electoral districts. On this basis, he concluded that powerful LDP politicians do not influence the allocation of subsidies to local governments and "many of the anecdotes alleging political influence are simply false" (Reed 2001, 125). Echoing this, McMichael (2018) found that a variable capturing the number of terms served by all a prefecture's LDP politicians had no statistically significant relationship with transfers to that prefecture. I constructed Senior LDP Politician$_{d,t}$, which is a dummy variable coded "1" if one of the LDP winners in district d at time t had served at least five terms.[9]

7.2 ASYMMETRIC ELECTORAL DISTRICTS RECEIVE MORE MONEY

Having elucidated the electoral district-specific characteristics others suggest matter, let me return to the theory. The theory expects that the total amount of money LDP politicians will deliver to the groups of voters in their electoral district will be a function of the ease with which tournaments can be administered. Ease, in turn, is a function of the relative sizes of the groups in which voters reside. When groups are *similarly sized*, there will be less ambiguity over how the performance of groups will be compared to each other, so LDP politicians will be able to use relatively *small* prizes to entice groups to compete. When groups are *asymmetrically sized*, in contrast, there will be greater ambiguity over how groups will be compared to each other, so LDP politicians will have to proffer *larger* prizes in order to convince voters to turn out and vote for them. This is Hypothesis 3.

To examine this conjecture, I constructed HI$_{d,t}$, an index capturing, for every electoral district d at time t, the degree to which its population is concentrated in a single municipality (HI$_{d,t}$ = 1) or spread out evenly across multiple municipalities (HI$_{d,t}$ = 0). This is the main independent variable of interest in the analyses that follow. First, let us verify that we have variation in HI$_{d,t}$ across our periods of study. My sample in the analyses in this chapter is electoral districts in which LDP politicians are

---

[9] As McMichael (2018) and Krauss and Pekkanen (2010) argue, LDP politicians advance to leadership positions in the party, the Diet, or the Cabinet in their fifth term.

7.2 Asymmetric Districts Receive More Money

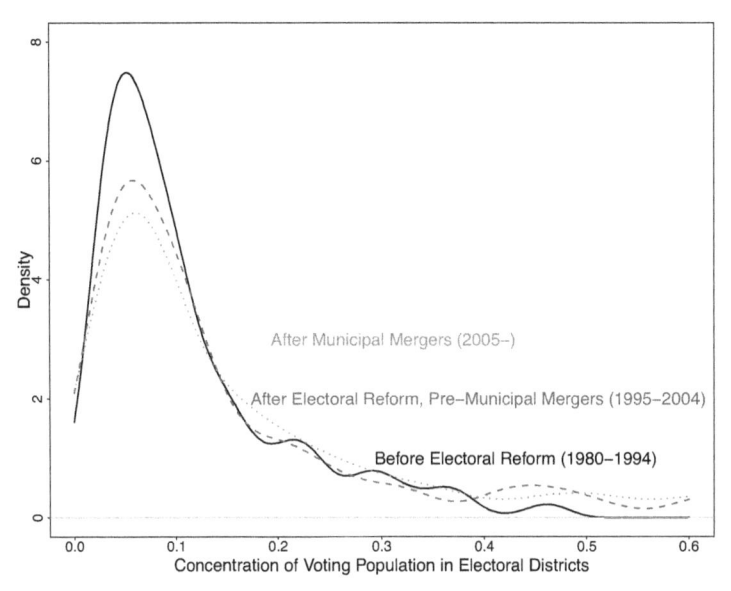

Figure 7.1 A plot of the concentration of voting population per electoral district for tournament-possible districts with LDP winners, 1980–2014.
Higher (lower) values indicate districts where the voting population is more (less) concentrated in a single municipality. The shape of the distribution is similar in all three periods.

conducting tournaments: thus, tournament-possible districts with LDP winners in all Lower House elections, 1980–2014.[10]

Figure 7.1 plots the distribution of voting concentration ($HI_{d,t}$) across this sample of electoral districts in three distinct periods. The black solid line plots the distribution in the 130 (and 129) multiseat districts used in Lower House elections from 1980 until 1993. The dark gray dotted line plots the distribution in the 300 single-seat districts (SSDs) used in the 1996, 2000, and 2003 Lower House elections. For the most part, these elections occurred prior to a large-scale reduction in number of municipalities, which took place over the 2001–2005 period. Finally, the light gray dotted line plots the distribution in the 300 SSDs used in the 2005, 2009, 2012, and 2014 Lower House elections. These elections occurred after many municipalities merged, which led to a substantial reduction in number of municipalities per district. In all three periods, the shape of the distribution is similar: There are fewer districts in which voters are concentrated in a single municipality (higher values of $HI_{d,t}$), and more districts in which voters are spread out across municipalities of relatively

---

[10] The empirical tests in this chapter were inspired by those in Catalinac, Bueno de Mesquita and Smith (2020).

similar sizes (lower values of $HI_{d,t}$). Importantly for my purpose, districts with both high and low voting concentration exist in all three periods.

7.2.1 Comparing Electoral Districts in the Same Election

To examine the effects of $HI_{d,t}$, I conduct regressions in which observations are electoral districts, not municipalities. Descriptive statistics pertaining to the district-level variables used in these regressions appear in Table A.8. Table 7.1 presents fixed effect regression models for the logarithm of per capita transfers received by electoral districts in the years following the Lower House elections held between 1980 and 2014 as a function of the concentration of the district's voting population ($HI_{d,t}$), year fixed effects, and other district-level controls. Because Chapter 6 established that tournaments are conducted by winning LDP politicians, observations are limited to districts that are tournament-possible and produced at least a single LDP winner.

In both models, year fixed effects mean that I am leveraging variation in the amounts of transfers received by districts with LDP winners in the same election. Both models also include district-level versions of the six municipality-level controls used in Chapter 6's analysis of transfers to municipalities within districts. One of these is fiscal strength, which prior work suggests will negatively influence transfer amounts. Other controls are operationalizations of the variables found in prior work to influence transfers to districts: malapportionment, number of municipalities in the district, share of seats occupied by LDP politicians, and whether a senior LDP politician represents the district (a dummy variable coded 1 and 0). I report robust standard errors clustered on electoral district.[11]

In Model 1, the coefficient on $HI_{d,t}$ is positive and statistically significant, indicating that in the period 1980–2014, districts characterized by greater asymmetry in municipality size received larger per capita transfer allocations after the election, controlling for other differences across districts, as well as features of a given election that might influence amounts of transfers received by all districts. Substantively, Model 1 tells us that a one standard deviation increase in $HI_{d,t}$ can be expected to net a district an extra 11.5% increase in per capita transfers after the election. Given that the mean per capita transfer to districts for these fiscal years was 30,576 yen, this amounts to a per capita increase of 3,517 yen. The mean district in this sample contained more than 500,000 voters; thus, a

---

[11] In this and all subsequent regressions in this chapter, I use district-level identifiers that change when a district's boundaries change. I rely on the identifiers in Reed and Smith (2015).

7.2 Asymmetric Districts Receive More Money

Table 7.1 *Across districts with at least one LDP winner, greater asymmetry in municipality size ($HI_{d,t}$) is associated with larger per capita transfer allocations after Lower House elections, 1980–2014.*

	Dependent variable: Postelection Transfers (log)	
	All electoral districts	Excludes prefectural capitals
	(Model 1)	(Model 2)
$HI_{d,t}$	0.712***	0.620***
	(0.128)	(0.147)
Fiscal Strength$_{d,t}$	−0.263*	−0.276*
	(0.107)	(0.118)
Dependent Population$_{d,t}$	4.409***	4.041***
	(0.537)	(0.553)
Farming Population$_{d,t}$	3.563***	3.351***
	(0.878)	(0.925)
Log(Population$_{d,t}$)	0.017	−0.048
	(0.107)	(0.120)
Log(Per Capita Income$_{d,t}$)	0.450***	0.405*
	(0.124)	(0.159)
Population Density$_{d,t}$	0.030*	0.028*
	(0.012)	(0.013)
Log(Number of Municipalities$_{d,t}$)	0.176***	0.153***
	(0.044)	(0.046)
People Per Seat$_{d,t}$	−0.078	−0.041
	(0.040)	(0.042)
Winning LDP VS$_{d,t}$	−0.311	−0.170
	(0.179)	(0.193)
LDP Senior Politician$_{d,t}$	−0.042	−0.037
	(0.028)	(0.029)
Observations	1,414	1,151
Year FE	Y	Y
R^2	0.407	0.391

Model 1 uses the full sample of districts, while Model 2 excludes districts in which prefecture capitals are located.

Robust standard errors clustered on electoral district in parentheses.
*$p < 0.05$, ***$p < 0.001$.
Regression models estimated with R's plm() package.

per capita increase of 3,517 yen translates into an increase of more than 1.841 billion yen, or almost $12 million in USD in today's exchange rate.

As I explained in Chapter 5, the upper tier of local government in Japan is the prefecture, of which Japan has forty-seven. Each prefecture has a capital city, in which the Governor and prefectural assembly sit. For the purpose of Lower House elections, each prefecture is divided into a varied number of electoral districts, one of which houses the prefecture's capital. Electoral districts in which prefectural capitals are located typically consist not only of the large (capital) city but also of the much-smaller towns and villages in the adjacent area. Because prefectural capitals are disproportionately large, these districts may have disproportionately high values of $HI_{d,t}$. This could be a concern if prefectural capitals receive more central government transfers for other reasons, such as enhanced lobbying capacity or closer connections to their LDP-affiliated Diet Members.

Across the twelve elections, I found that the average electoral district in which a prefectural capital is located contained twenty-seven municipalities and had an $HI_{d,t}$ of 0.22. The average electoral district *outside* the prefectural capital contained seventeen municipalities and had a lower $HI_{d,t}$ of 0.13. These differences in means are statistically significant. Thus, electoral districts hosting prefectural capitals *do* tend to be more asymmetric than districts not hosting prefectural capitals. In Model 2 of Table 7.1, I run the same model as in Model 1 but exclude districts in which prefectural capitals are located. The coefficient on $HI_{d,t}$ remains positive and statistically significant. This means that the results are not driven by the inclusion of districts that are characterized by greater asymmetry in municipality size and might receive additional transfers for other reasons. Substantively, according to Model 2, in districts outside the prefecture capital, a one-standard-deviation increase in $HI_{d,t}$ can be expected to net a district an extra 8.9% increase in per capita transfers. The mean per capita transfer to districts in this sample was 31,097 yen, so this amounts to a per capita increase of 2,776 yen.

In both models in Table 7.1, I controlled for Winning LDP $VS_{d,t}$, the share of eligible voters in the district who voted for winning LDP candidates. In both models, its coefficient is negative and not statistically significant. This means that, comparing districts with LDP winners in the same election, the strength of electoral support districts give their LDP winner(s) has no effect on transfers, at least when we are controlling for district-level asymmetry. In the Appendix, we present two additional tables. Table A.9 presents the same two models with LDP Seats$_{d,t}$ (the share of seats in a district won by LDP candidates) and LDP $VS_{d,t}$ (which includes votes for losing LDP candidates in the numerator), respectively.[12] Regardless of how we measure support for the LDP, $HI_{d,t}$ is found to

---

[12] Note that because we limit observations to electoral districts with LDP winners, LDP Seats$_{d,t}$ ranges from 0.2 to 1 in elections prior to 1994 and is limited to 1 after reform.

7.2 Asymmetric Districts Receive More Money

exercise a positive, statistically significant impact on postelection transfers. Table A.10 presents the same specifications in Table 7.1, but without any controls for strength of LDP support at the district-level. We do this because the theory *expects* the relationship between $HI_{d,t}$ and support for the LDP to be endogenous: Increases in $HI_{d,t}$ are expected to increase transfers because they lower the propensity to turn out and vote for the LDP. Thus, including both $HI_{d,t}$ and Winning LDP $VS_{d,t}$ could introduce posttreatment bias. In this model, the coefficients on $HI_{d,t}$ remain positive and statistically significant. Thus, it is unlikely that the coefficients on $HI_{d,t}$ in Table 7.1 are merely capturing the effects of support for the LDP.

7.2.2 Comparing Electoral Districts over Time

As I explained in Chapter 5, the introduction of a new electoral system consisting of SSDs in one tier and closed-list proportional representation (CLPR) in another tier in 1994 necessitated the redrawing of the boundaries of Japan's multiseat districts. 130 multiseat districts became 300 SSDs. Only eight of the new districts had the same borders as districts under the old electoral system, leaving 292 districts that were entirely new creations (Reed 1995, 1077).[13] This means that for the most part, electoral districts before and after 1994 are not comparable. The sample of districts in Table 7.1, which spans all Lower House elections held between 1980 and 2014, thus includes a set of districts in the five Lower House elections prior to reform (1980–1993) and then a totally different set of districts in the seven Lower House elections after reform (1996–2014). My use of year fixed effects in those models enabled me to leverage variation in $HI_{d,t}$ across districts within the same election.

I conducted separate sets of analyses that focus on districts in the five elections prior to reform and districts in the seven elections after reform, respectively. I do this for two reasons. One is to exploit the fact that I have stable district boundaries within the first period, which enables me to leverage variation in within-district $HI_{d,t}$ over time. If I find that district-level asymmetry exercises a positive, statistically significant impact on transfers when I leverage variation in district-level asymmetry across districts in the same election (above) *and* within the same district over time (below), this will provide even greater confidence in the results. The second reason I conduct separate analyses on both periods is to see if the

---

[13] Districts used in the CLPR tier are much larger. There are eleven in total, and these are drawn around the borders of Japan's 47 prefectures. These are not the subject of our analyses in this book.

positive relationship between $HI_{d,t}$ and transfers observed in Table 7.1 is observable under both electoral systems. The sample in Table 7.1 includes more observations from the post-1994 period than from the pre-1994 period, owing to the fact that the reform increased the number of districts, and also to the fact that my sample includes more elections under the new system. Because other scholars have demonstrated that Japan's electoral reform changed the allocation of transfers, both within and between districts (Hirano 2006; Horiuchi and Saito 2003), it would further increase confidence in my results if we observed the same relationship between district-level asymmetry and transfers, under both electoral systems.

Table 7.2 presents fixed effect regression models for the logarithm of per capita transfers received by electoral districts in the years following the five Lower House elections held between 1980 and 1993 as a function of the concentration of the district's voting population ($HI_{d,t}$), year fixed effects, and other controls. In Model 1, the specification is the same as Model 1 of 7.1 (year fixed effects and district-level controls), with observations restricted to the five elections prior to reform. The coefficient on $HI_{d,t}$ is positive and statistically significant, showing that, looking across districts in the same election, districts characterized by greater asymmetry in municipality size received more transfers. Substantively, Model 1 tells us that a one-standard-deviation increase in $HI_{d,t}$ can be expected to net a district an extra 13.7% in per capita transfers after the election. Given that the mean per capita transfer to districts in these fiscal years was 25,426 yen, this amounts to a per capita increase of 3,487 yen.

In Model 2, I add district fixed effects to the specification in Model 1. District fixed effects control for time-invariant features of districts that might be influencing the amount of transfers they receive after elections. As such, they help guard against the possibility that underlying characteristics of an electoral district, such as the voters who live therein, are driving any observed effect of $HI_{d,t}$ on postelection resource allocations. As I explained in Chapter 6, however, if there is little variation in the independent variable of interest within the same unit over time, then any effects of this variable will be subsumed by the unit fixed effect. In other words, the model will not be able to estimate its effect separately from the district fixed effect. We can expect that within-district change in $HI_{d,t}$ will be relatively slow-moving, as districts have to undergo quite-sizeable compositional shifts in population to effect meaningful changes in their scores. I illustrate this below in a discussion of municipalities in Nara prefecture, but suffice to say, this biases us against finding any effect of $HI_{d,t}$ in a specification with district fixed effects, unless we can observe the same district over many elections. The coefficient on $HI_{d,t}$ in Model 2 is nevertheless statistically significant. This is evidence that as districts

7.2 Asymmetric Districts Receive More Money

Table 7.2 Across electoral districts with at least one LDP winner, greater heterogeneity in municipality size (HI) is associated with receiving more per capita transfers after Lower House elections, 1980–1993.

	\multicolumn{4}{c|}{Dependent variable: Postelection Transfers (log)}			
	All electoral districts		Excludes prefectural capitals	
	(Model 1)	(Model 2)	(Model 3)	(Model 4)
$HI_{d,t}$	1.275***	2.336***	1.215**	3.242***
	(0.276)	(0.635)	(0.425)	(0.949)
Fiscal Strength$_{d,t}$	−0.233	−0.350*	−0.175	−0.212
	(0.203)	(0.136)	(0.199)	(0.188)
Dependent Population$_{d,t}$	6.881***	0.145	3.963*	−1.055
	(1.611)	(1.044)	(1.731)	(1.298)
Farming Population$_{d,t}$	3.575**	−1.016	2.342*	−2.655
	(1.313)	(1.177)	(1.004)	(1.439)
Log(Population$_{d,t}$)	0.100	−0.645***	−0.057	−0.988***
	(0.157)	(0.152)	(0.159)	(0.257)
Log(Per Capita Income$_{d,t}$)	0.338	0.459***	−0.117	0.117
	(0.218)	(0.114)	(0.235)	(0.148)
Population Density$_{d,t}$	0.045	−0.053*	0.041	−0.038
	(0.030)	(0.021)	(0.028)	(0.046)
Log(Number of Municipalities$_{d,t}$)	0.211	0.973**	0.173	0.489
	(0.111)	(0.304)	(0.128)	(0.407)
People Per Seat$_{d,t}$	−0.106	−0.020	−0.007	−0.010
	(0.065)	(0.028)	(0.056)	(0.032)
Winning LDP VS$_{d,t}$	−0.379	0.016	−0.062	0.054
	(0.222)	(0.049)	(0.221)	(0.054)
Senior LDP Politician$_{d,t}$	−0.112**	−0.004	−0.120**	0.0004
	(0.038)	(0.011)	(0.045)	(0.013)
Observations	578	578	382	382
Year FE	Y	Y	Y	Y
District FE	N	Y	N	Y
R^2	0.470	0.278	0.438	0.267

Models 1 and 2 use all districts, while Models 3 and 4 exclude districts in which prefecture capitals are located. Models 2 and 4 add district fixed effects.
Robust standard errors clustered on electoral district in parentheses.
*$p < 0.05$, **$p < 0.01$, ***$p < 0.001$.
Regression models estimated with R's plm() package.

become more asymmetric, they receive more transfers, controlling for changes in other district-level characteristics.[14]

In Models 3 and 4 of Table 7.2, I continue the focus on elections under the old electoral system (1980–1993) but restrict observations to districts outside prefecture capitals. Model 3 is the same as Model 2 in Table 7.1 (year fixed effects and district-level controls), but with the sample limited to districts outside prefectural capitals in elections prior to reform. The coefficient on $HI_{d,t}$ is positive and statistically significant. Model 4 adds district fixed effects to the specification in Model 3. The coefficient on $HI_{d,t}$ remains positive and statistically significant. In sum, these specifications provide evidence that in elections prior to electoral reform, among LDP-won, tournament-possible districts, district-level asymmetry exercises an independent effect on transfers.

In the models in Table 7.2, I controlled for Winning LDP $VS_{d,t}$. Its coefficient is not significant in any model. Its sign is negative with year fixed effects (Models 1 and 3) and positive with year and district fixed effects (Models 2 and 4). In Models 2 and 4, the coefficient on Winning LDP $VS_{d,t}$ captures the effect of within-district change in strength of support for the LDP. Thus, in contrast to what McMichael (2018) found at the prefecture level, a waning of support for the party within districts does not appear to have triggered an influx of transfers. In Tables A.11 and A.12, I present the same four models, replacing Winning LDP $VS_{d,t}$ with LDP Seats$_{d,t}$ and LDP $VS_{d,t}$, respectively. Results are strikingly similar to those in Table 7.2: $HI_{d,t}$ is always found to exercise a positive, statistically significant impact on transfers after the election in all models. Thus, no matter how electoral support for the LDP is measured, $HI_{d,t}$ is found to exercise a positive, statistically significant impact on transfers after the election in elections prior to reform.

Next, I run similar models on observations from the seven elections following reform. Table 7.3 presents fixed effect regression models for the logarithm of per capita transfers received by electoral districts in the years following the seven Lower House elections post-reform, as a function of the concentration of the district's voting population ($HI_{d,t}$), year

---

[14] In regression models with the full sample (districts from all twelve elections in Table 7.1), the addition of a district fixed effect renders $HI_{d,t}$ positive but not statistically significant. In this sample, half the observations are districts prior to electoral reform (which exhibit meaningful variation), but the other half are districts in the postreform period. I discuss this further below, but many districts created in 1994 underwent dramatic changes to their boundaries and municipal composition right in the middle of the post-electoral reform period. The lack of statistical significance in a specification with district fixed effects with the full sample could reflect the fact that many districts in the postreform era were not around long enough to estimate their effect separately from the district fixed effect.

7.2 Asymmetric Districts Receive More Money

Table 7.3 Across districts with at least one LDP winner, greater heterogeneity in municipality size (HI) is associated with receiving more per capita transfers after Lower House elections, 1996–2014.

	Dependent variable: Postelection Transfers (log)	
	All electoral districts	Excludes prefectural capitals
	(Model 1)	(Model 2)
$HI_{d,t}$	0.510***	0.525**
	(0.147)	(0.162)
Fiscal Strength$_{d,t}$	−0.473***	−0.570***
	(0.131)	(0.155)
Dependent Population$_{d,t}$	4.174***	3.775***
	(0.620)	(0.646)
Farming Population$_{d,t}$	3.692**	3.825**
	(1.318)	(1.325)
Log(Population$_{d,t}$)	0.185	0.045
	(0.250)	(0.272)
Log(Per Capita Income$_{d,t}$)	0.634***	0.708***
	(0.131)	(0.139)
Population Density$_{d,t}$	0.029*	0.025*
	(0.012)	(0.012)
Log(Number of Municipalities$_{d,t}$)	0.099	0.091
	(0.051)	(0.055)
People Per Seat$_{d,t}$	−0.126	−0.073
	(0.080)	(0.087)
Winning LDP VS$_{d,t}$	−0.380	−0.133
	(0.355)	(0.370)
Senior LDP Politician$_{d,t}$	0.006	0.014
	(0.035)	(0.034)
Observations	836	769
Year FE	Y	Y
R^2	0.414	0.437

Model 1 uses all districts, while Model 2 excludes districts in which prefecture capitals are located.
Robust standard errors clustered on electoral district in parentheses.
*$p < 0.05$, **$p < 0.01$, ***$p < 0.001$.
Regression models estimated with R's plm() package.

fixed effects, and other time-varying controls. In Model 1, the coefficient on $HI_{d,t}$ is positive and statistically significant, showing that, controlling for idiosyncratic features of any given election that could influence the amount of transfers received by all districts in that election, districts characterized by greater asymmetry in municipality size received more transfers. Substantively, Model 1 tells us that a one-standard-deviation increase in $HI_{d,t}$ can be expected to net a district an extra 9.5% in per capita transfers after the election. Given that the mean per capita transfer to districts in these fiscal years was 34,733 yen, this amounts to a per capita increase of 3,284 yen. In Model 2, we run the same model as in Model 1, but on a sample of districts that excludes prefectural capitals. The coefficient on $HI_{d,t}$ remains positive and statistically significant.

In my analysis of the 1980–1993 period (Table 7.2), I used district fixed effects to control for the possibility that time-invariant features of electoral districts could be driving the observed relationship between asymmetry and transfers. The postelectoral reform period, however, does not offer us a similarly large set of electoral districts whose boundaries and internal composition are constant across consecutive elections. As I explained in Chapter 5, 91% of all electoral districts were tournament-possible under the old electoral system and almost all of them had at least one LDP winner. Moreover, we observe this set of districts across five elections. After electoral reform, the share of tournament-possible districts dropped to 73% and then kept dropping, reaching about 50%. In addition, two sets of redistricting occurred (in 2003 and 2014), in which districts were eliminated in some prefectures and created in others (The Japan Times 2002; Pekkanen, Reed and Smith 2016). For districts affected by the 2003 redistricting, then, we have two observations until 2003, in 1996 and 2000, respectively. For districts created in 2003, we have a maximum of four observations (in 2005, 2009, 2012, and 2014, respectively), unless they were also affected by the 2014 redistricting, in which case we have fewer. While this leaves a set of tournament-possible districts unaffected by redistricting, many of these districts saw their internal composition change decisively due to mergers of municipalities located within them. Thus, while a district's borders (and official code) can be the same across two elections, the district may have undergone a major change in the arrangement of voters into municipalities. In short, features of the post-1994 era suggests we should be cautious about using district fixed effects.

The models in Table 7.3 included Winning LDP $VS_{d,t}$ as a control. Its coefficient is negative and statistically insignificant in both models. Thus, comparing districts in the same election with LDP winners, the strength of support voters offered this winner is found to have no relationship with the amount of transfers it receives.[15] In sum, district-level asymmetry is found to exercise a positive, statistically significant impact

---

[15] There is no need to examine alternative operationalizations of support for the LDP because the fact that the postreform era uses SSDs and I limit observations

7.2 Asymmetric Districts Receive More Money

on the amount of transfers received by districts in the years following Lower House elections, both before and after electoral reform.

7.2.3 Japan's 1994 Electoral Reform as a Quasiexperiment

Japan's 1994 electoral reform entailed the drawing up of 300 new districts. Thus, districts before and after 1994 are not comparable. For Japan's 3,300+ municipalities, the redrawing of district boundaries meant being placed in an entirely new district, consisting of a different mix of municipalities. Because the new districts were *smaller* than the old districts, many new districts were composed of a subset of municipalities from the older, larger district. Thus, in the vast majority of cases, municipalities did not find themselves facing an entirely new set of competitors in the tournament but a set they were already familiar with. Nevertheless, the creation of a new district from a subset of municipalities in the old district means that, for most municipalities, my variable of interest – the degree of asymmetry in municipality size – decisively changed.

Let me illustrate this with two municipalities, Nara City (population 359,604 in 1996) and Tsukigase Village (population 2,028 in 1996), both in Nara prefecture. In the five elections held between 1980 and 1993, these municipalities were in the old Nara First District. Comprised of forty-seven municipalities, this district included ten cities (with populations ranging from approximately 350,000 to 36,000), twenty towns (populations from 28,000 to 5,000), and seventeen villages (populations from 6,000 to 700). This large district sent five representatives to the Lower House. In 1980, its $HI_{d,t}$ was 0.067, right at the median for electoral districts in this period. Over time, it became slightly more asymmetrical, as the populations of its cities increased and the populations of its smaller municipalities declined. By 1993, its $HI_{d,t}$ score was 0.074, which amounts to small increase of 0.007.

The 1994 reform broke up the old district, like it did all districts. Nara City and Tsukigase Village were the only municipalities placed in the new Nara First. Nine municipalities went into Nara Second District, twelve municipalities went into Nara Third, and twenty four municipalities went into Nara Fourth. The asymmetry in size between Nara City and Tsukigase Village, with the former's population being 175 times the latter, meant that the new Nara First had the largest $HI_{d,t}$ of any district in 1996: 0.977. Thus, after having experienced little change in $HI_{d,t}$ between 1980 and 1993, Nara City and Tsukigase Village both experienced dramatic increases in $HI_{d,t}$ between the 1993 and 1996 election, going from $HI_{d,t} =$

to districts with LDP winners mean that LDP Seats$_{d,t}$ has the value of 1 for all observations and LDP VS$_{d,t}$ is identical to Winning LDP VS$_{d,t}$.

0.074 to 0.977. The nine municipalities that went into Nara Second also experienced increases in $HI_{d,t}$ (going from 0.074 in 1993 to 0.10 in 1996) and so did the twenty-four municipalities going into Nara Fourth (going from 0.074 to 0.137). In contrast, the twelve municipalities that went into Nara Third experienced a decrease (going from 0.074 to 0.036).

This experience, of very little change in $HI_{d,t}$ in the thirteen years between 1980 and 1993 and then an abrupt change in $HI_{d,t}$ between 1993 and 1996, is reflective of the broader population of Japanese municipalities. For every municipality in my data, I took their $HI_{d,t}$ scores in the five elections between 1980 and 1993 and calculated the standard deviation in these scores. The average standard deviation provides an indicator of the degree of change in $HI_{d,t}$ experienced by the average Japanese municipality over these thirteen years. It is 0.006. I then did the same for every municipality in the 1993 and 1996 elections (took their two $HI_{d,t}$ scores, calculated the standard deviation in these, and then took the mean). This showed that the average municipality experienced a change in $HI_{d,t}$ of 0.030 between 1993 and 1996, five times larger than the change experienced over the preceding thirteen years.

The reason municipalities experienced little change in $HI_{d,t}$ between 1980 and 1993 is because district boundaries were stable. While there were "minor reapportionments" in 1986 and 1993, neither involved the redrawing of district boundaries. Each merely entailed the adding of seats to some districts and the subtracting of seats from others (Horiuchi and Saito 2003, 672). This means that virtually all municipalities squared off against the *same* set of competitors at every election.[16] In this setting, changes in district-level asymmetry were driven by changes in the *populations* of the municipalities comprising the district. Most commonly, residents of smaller municipalities relocated to larger ones, either in the same electoral district or in another one. In the former case, this pattern of migration would lead to an increase in district-level asymmetry. In the latter case, it would likely result in changes to the degree of asymmetry in *both* districts, depending on the relative sizes of the municipalities from which and to which they moved, relative to other municipalities in the district. Critically, however, population shifts along these lines do not have the same impact on $HI_{d,t}$ as being plucked from one district, with one set of competitors, and placed in another, with a different set of competitors.

I can take advantage of these abrupt changes in $HI_{d,t}$ to conduct another test of Hypothesis 3. Specifically, I can examine the effect of changes in district-level asymmetry between the 1993 and 1996 elections on change in the per capita transfers received in the years following

---

[16] I say "virtually all" because there were a small number of *municipalities* whose borders changed during this time.

7.2 Asymmetric Districts Receive More Money

these two elections for all municipalities present in both years. If my hypothesis about the effects of district-level asymmetry is correct, municipalities that experienced greater increases in district-level asymmetry between the two elections will have received a greater increase in their transfer allocation (over and above what they received the year after the previous election) than municipalities that experienced smaller increases in district-level asymmetry.

To do this, I took the universe of municipalities in tournament-possible districts present in the 1996 election and calculated ΔPostelection Transfers$_{m,t}$ for each. This is the logarithm of the per capita transfers received in the year after the 1996 election, minus the logarithm of the per capita transfers received in the year after the 1993 election. This is the dependent variable in the following regressions. My main independent variable is ΔHI$_{d,t}$, which is the municipality's HI$_{d,t}$ score in the 1996 election, minus its HI$_{d,t}$ score in 1993. To control for the possibility that changes in other municipality-level attributes could be driving any observed effect of ΔHI$_{d,t}$, I constructed analogous Δ scores for my six municipality-level control variables, by taking each municipality's value in 1996 and subtracting from this its value in 1993. I also constructed ΔSum LDP VS$_{m,t}$ analogously, by taking a municipality's value on Sum LDP VS$_{m,t}$ in the 1996 election and subtracting its value in the 1993 election. Developed in Chapter 6, Sum LDP VS$_{m,t}$ is my preferred indicator of electoral support at the municipality level. It captures the share of available votes in municipality m that were cast for the district's LDP winner(s).

In Table 7.4, Model 1 presents linear regressions of ΔPostelection Transfers$_{m,t}$ as a function of ΔHI$_{d,t}$, prior transfers, support for the LDP winner in the 1996 election, changes in other municipality-level attributes, and fixed effects for the municipality's district in 1996. Chapter 6's municipality-level analyses showed that the main determinants of transfer allocations after elections are a municipality's relative level of support for the LDP and the transfers it received the year of the election, respectively. Thus, the model includes both: a municipality's Sum LDP VS$_{m,t}$ measured in 1996 and the logarithm of the municipality's per capita transfer allocation the year of the election (1996). My use of district fixed effects enables me to control for features of the municipality's district in 1996 that could have consequences for the amounts of transfers received by all municipalities in the same district. As I mentioned, these could include district-level versions of the same municipality-level variables, such as fiscal strength, as well as malapportionment, number of municipalities in the district, share of seats occupied by LDP politicians, and characteristics of those LDP politicians.

Table 7.4 *Increases in district-level asymmetry between 1993 and 1996 are associated with increases in postelection transfer allocations, controlling for prior transfers, change in support for the LDP winner and other municipality-level attributes, change in district-level attributes, and features of their electoral districts in 1996.*

	Dependent variable: ΔPostelection Transfers$_{m,t}$	
	(Model 1)	(Model 2)
Δ HI$_{d,t}$	0.550*	1.106*
	(0.238)	(0.433)
Sum LDP VS$_{m,t}$	−0.129	−0.130
	(0.136)	(0.137)
Δ Sum LDP VS$_{m,t}$	−0.197	−0.192
	(0.144)	(0.151)
Log(Transfers$_{m,t}$)	0.039	0.038
	(0.022)	(0.022)
Δ Fiscal Strength$_{m,t}$	−0.174	−0.182
	(0.193)	(0.193)
Δ Dependent Population$_{m,t}$	2.700	2.816
	(9.326)	(9.353)
Δ Farming Population$_{m,t}$	1.472	1.738
	(5.755)	(5.798)
Δ Log(Population$_{m,t}$)	1.089	1.137
	(3.394)	(3.400)
Δ Log(Per Capita Income$_{m,t}$)	−0.275	−0.306
	(0.250)	(0.251)
Δ Population Density$_{m,t}$	−0.537	−0.542
	(0.645)	(0.646)
Δ Log(Number of Municipalities$_{d,t}$)		0.285
		(0.233)
Δ People Per Seat$_{d,t}$		−0.043
		(0.110)
Δ Senior LDP Politician$_{d,t}$		−0.107
		(0.105)
Δ LDP Seats$_{d,t}$		0.360
		(0.345)
Constant	−0.016	0.115
	(0.157)	(0.347)
Observations	2,108	2,108
Fixed Effects for 1996 District	Y	Y
R^2	0.090	0.092

*$p < 0.05$.

7.2 Asymmetric Districts Receive More Money

Importantly, if all municipalities in the same 1996 district had come from the *same* 1993 district, all would have identical values of $\Delta HI_{d,t}$, which means I would not be able to estimate its effect separately from that of the 1996 district fixed effect. My inclusion of both $\Delta HI_{d,t}$ and a district fixed effect is possible because some districts in 1996 consist of municipalities that originated from *different* 1993 districts. While these municipalities all ended up in the same district in 1996, the fact that some came from one 1993 district and others came from another 1993 district means that they have *distinct* $\Delta HI_{d,t}$ scores. The presence of this "mixing" in my set of 1996 districts is what enables me to estimate the effects of different degrees of change in district-level asymmetry between the two elections in a specification that includes a fixed effect for the municipality's district in 1996. In this specification, then, the coefficient on $\Delta HI_{d,t}$ will tell us whether, of the set of municipalities that ended up in the same district in 1996, those whose $\Delta HI_{d,t}$ scores are larger, meaning they experienced a greater increase in district-level asymmetry when they moved into the new district, also experienced a greater increase in their postelection transfer allocation.

The coefficient on $\Delta HI_{d,t}$ in Model 1 of Table 7.4 is positive and statistically significant. This means that municipalities that experienced a greater increase in district-level asymmetry between the 1993 and 1996 election than their same-district counterparts saw a greater increase in their postelection transfer allocation, controlling for changes in other municipality-level attributes, as well as the absolute level of support the municipality offered the LDP in 1996 and the amount of transfers it received in 1996. My inclusion of ΔSum LDP VS$_{m,t}$ as a control variable means that my results are telling us that regardless of whether a municipality's support for the LDP went up or down between the two elections, municipalities shifted into a district characterized by greater asymmetry than their old district experienced a bigger increase in their postelection transfer allocation.

The coefficient on the amount of transfers the municipality received the year of the election is positive and statistically insignificant. This means that receiving more transfers in the 1996 fiscal year is not associated with experiencing a larger change in transfers between 1994 and 1997, respectively. Similarly, neither the absolute *level* of support the municipality offered the LDP in 1996, nor the degree of *change* in its support between the two elections, is found to be significantly related to change in its postelection transfer allocation. This suggests that the main determinant of change in a municipality's postelection transfer allocation is not electoral support or change in other time-varying municipality-level attributes, but change in district-level asymmetry. This is powerful evidence that municipalities in districts characterized by greater asymmetry in municipality size receive more transfers.

In Model 1 of Table 7.4, my use of a fixed effect for the municipality's 1996 district means that I am leveraging variation in $\Delta \text{HI}_{d,t}$ across municipalities in the same 1996 district. Having come from different 1993 districts, however, these municipalities will also vary in the degree of change they experienced in *other* district-level features. Model 1 controls for changes in *municipality*-level attributes between the two elections, but not in *district*-level attributes. For example, while most municipalities would have experienced a reduction in the degree to which their district was malapportioned between 1993 and 1996, there could be variation across municipalities in the same 1996 district as to the extent to which malapportionment had been reduced, relative to their old district. Horiuchi and Saito (2003)'s findings suggest that municipalities that experienced greater reductions in malapportionment between the two elections experienced a larger drop in their transfer allocation. Similarly, because the 1996 districts are smaller than the 1993 districts, most municipalities would have also experienced a reduction in the number of municipalities in their district (and correspondingly, in the number of local politicians in their district). But there could be variation across municipalities in the same 1996 district as to the extent to which they experienced a reduction in the number of municipalities. Saito (2010) gives us reason to believe that municipalities experiencing greater declines in number of municipalities in their district will experience larger declines in their transfer allocation.

In Model 2 of Table 7.4, I add controls for change in five district-level features between 1993 and 1996 that could also have consequences for change in municipality *m*'s postelection transfer allocation. I keep everything else about the specification identical to that in Model 1. The inclusion of these variables helps me verify that the effects of $\Delta \text{HI}_{d,t}$ in Model 1 are not simply capturing the effects of change in *other* district-level attributes between 1993 and 1996 that could also have consequences for change in a municipality's transfer allocation. Specifically, for each municipality present in 1996, I constructed Δ People Per Seat$_{d,t}$, Δ log(Number of Municipalities$_{d,t}$), Δ LDP Seats$_{d,t}$, Δ District Magnitude$_{d,t}$, and Δ LDP Senior Politician$_{d,t}$. This involves taking the municipality's value on each variable in 1996 and subtracting its value in 1993. We find that the coefficient on $\Delta \text{HI}_{d,t}$ remains positive and statistically significant and is larger than in Model 1.[17] This reduces

---

[17] Δ District Magnitude$_{d,t}$ is not estimated separately in this regression, which means that when a 1996 district has municipalities from different 1993 districts, those

any concern that the effects of $\Delta \text{HI}_{d,t}$ are driven by changes in other district-level characteristics.

In sum, the analyses in this section constitute powerful evidence for Hypothesis 3. Controlling for other differences across electoral districts, including in support for LDP winner(s), and differences across elections, districts characterized by greater asymmetry in municipality size are found to have received more money than districts characterized by less asymmetry in municipality size (Tables 7.1–7.3). Moreover, we found that as districts become more asymmetric, they receive more money, controlling for other changes, including in strength of support for their LDP winner(s) (Table 7.2, Model 2). This means that district-level asymmetry exercises an independent effect on the amount of money Japanese municipalities receive. We saw this even more clearly when we studied what happened when municipalities were plucked from one district in 1993 and placed into a different district in 1996: Municipalities shifted into districts characterized by greater asymmetry in municipality size than their old district experienced an increase in transfers, controlling for changes in a host of other variables, including in support for the LDP (Table 7.4). This is powerful evidence that the same municipality receives more money for a given level of support when its district is characterized by greater asymmetry in municipality size.

7.3 ASYMMETRIC ELECTORAL DISTRICTS EXHIBIT LESS SUPPORT

Section 7.2 established that districts characterized by greater asymmetry in municipality size receive more money. As I explained above, the tournament theory would explain this with the following logic: In a tournament, incumbents structure prizes such that they become exponentially larger at higher ranks. This creates neck-and-neck competition for these higher ranks, which increases the amount of influence wielded by a single vote. Whereas a single vote is never likely to influence who wins the election, it could influence where one's group ends up in the ranking. If increases in rank translate into exponentially larger increases in rewards, then this means that individual votes can wield considerable weight over how much money one's group receives.

However, all of this hinges on voters realizing that the incumbent plans to compare the performance of their group with the performance of other groups in the same district. Incumbents have difficulty making this explicit without drawing attention to the fact that tournaments

different 1993 districts had identical district magnitudes (and were captured by the 1996 district fixed effect).

turn the accountability relationship central to the democratic process on its head. As Chapter 4 explains, it turns out that when groups are asymmetrically sized, an incumbent who ranks groups on the basis of *number* of votes received could end up with a qualitatively different ranking than an incumbent who ranks groups on the basis of the *share* of voters who voted for them. Because different metrics of comparison lead to different rankings, and because incumbents have difficulty clarifying which metric they intend to use, voters in districts characterized by asymmetrically sized groups will find it more difficult to calibrate the degree of influence their vote holds over the size of their group's prize. Being unable to calibrate this influence translates into a lower propensity to turn out and support the incumbent. Anticipating this, incumbents have incentives to increase the size of the prize delivered to groups in districts characterized by greater asymmetry, to encourage them to turn out in spite of the murkiness surrounding how groups will be compared. This is Hypothesis 3.

What are the implications for electoral support? The theory expects that district-level asymmetry will exercise such a pernicious impact on voter willingness to turn out and support the incumbent that even though the incumbent will try to offset this reduced propensity to turn out and support her with larger prizes, it is unlikely she will be able to offer a prize large enough to completely offset this. This is because incumbents also prefer to minimize the amount of government resources (not to mention time devoted to lobbying) that must be diverted to the generation of prizes. Thus, while incumbents in asymmetric districts *could* deliver a prize large enough to increase the level of support they receive to the level enjoyed by their counterparts in less asymmetric districts, they will also be cognizant of the hefty commitment of resources (and time) that this entails. Thus, another implication of the theory is that incumbents in districts characterized by greater asymmetry in municipality size will be delivering more money (Hypothesis 3) but, in spite of this, will still receive lower levels of electoral support (Hypothesis 4).

In this way, the tournament theory provides an explanation for why, across districts, electoral support for the LDP is often found to be *negatively* correlated with the amount of transfers received. It explains this puzzle in the following way: Incumbents find it harder to get support in districts characterized by greater asymmetry in municipality size. Thus, in these districts, they have to offer more (in terms of money) but will get less (in terms of support). Across districts, then, it will look like politicians are engaging in the curious activity of *rewarding* districts for lower levels of electoral support and *penalizing* districts for high levels of electoral support. Or it may look like they are using resources to court relatively

7.3 Asymmetric Districts Exhibit Less Support

unsupportive voters. But they are doing no such thing. Instead, a previously *unnoticed* characteristic of the electoral district (asymmetry in municipality size) is exercising an *independent* effect on electoral support. It is lowering support in some districts and increasing it in others. Politicians, for their part, are *anticipating* the effects of this variable. They know that in highly asymmetric districts, they have to deliver more, while in less asymmetric districts, they can deliver less. This leads to a pattern of spending across districts that is the *inverse* of the pattern of spending within districts: Across districts, politicians deliver the most money to districts where they got the least support and the least money to districts where they get the most support.

To examine Hypothesis 4, I turn to analyses with electoral support for the LDP as the dependent variable (not transfers) and district-level asymmetry ($HI_{d,t}$) as the independent variable. Whereas Tables 7.1–7.3 showed that district-level asymmetry increases transfers, my question here is "Does it also depress levels of electoral support for the LDP?"

Table 7.5 presents fixed effect regression models of electoral support for the LDP in Lower House elections from 1980 until 2014 as a function of the concentration of the district's voting population ($HI_{d,t}$), year fixed effects, and other time-varying district-level controls. Whereas the sample in the analyses of transfers above was limited to tournament-possible districts with LDP winners, here we broaden the sample to include all tournament-possible districts. My three dependent variables are Winning LDP $VS_{d,t}$, a variable capturing the amount of support the district offered its LDP winner(s) (Model 1), LDP $VS_{d,t}$, a variable capturing the amount of support the district offered all LDP candidate(s) (Model 2), and LDP Seats$_{d,t}$, the share of seats available in the district that were captured by LDP winners (Model 3). Year fixed effects mean that I am leveraging variation in the degree of asymmetry in municipality size across districts in the same election. In addition to district-level versions of the six demographic controls used throughout this book, I also control for district magnitude, malapportionment, the number of municipalities in the district, whether there is a senior LDP politician in the district, and the number of LDP candidates running in the district. I report robust standard errors clustered on electoral district.

I add the latter control, for the number of LDP candidates, because of the well-known observation that under Japan's old electoral system, when more LDP candidates ran in a district, LDP supporters risked spreading their votes too thinly amongst those candidates, which on occasion resulted in fewer of them getting elected than if voters had concentrated their votes on a select few LDP candidates. This situation arose because Japan's electoral system conferred a single, nontransferable vote

Table 7.5 *Across districts, greater heterogeneity in municipality size (HI) is associated with lower levels of electoral support for the LDP in Lower House elections, 1980–2014.*

	Dependent variables		
	Winning LDP VS$_{d,t}$	LDP VS$_{d,t}$	LDP Seats$_{d,t}$
	(Model 1)	(Model 2)	(Model 3)
HI$_{d,t}$	−0.073*	−0.043*	−0.204*
	(0.030)	(0.017)	(0.084)
Fiscal Strength$_{d,t}$	−0.051**	−0.043***	−0.187***
	(0.017)	(0.012)	(0.053)
Dependent Population$_{d,t}$	−0.022	0.065	−0.259
	(0.080)	(0.045)	(0.229)
Farming Population$_{d,t}$	0.438*	0.250	0.350
	(0.203)	(0.137)	(0.535)
Log(Population$_{d,t}$)	0.037	0.015	0.281*
	(0.056)	(0.039)	(0.139)
Log(Per Capita Income$_{d,t}$)	0.039***	0.033***	0.109**
	(0.011)	(0.008)	(0.036)
Population Density$_{d,t}$	−0.008***	−0.007***	−0.025***
	(0.002)	(0.001)	(0.006)
Total Seats$_{d,t}$	−0.063***	−0.082***	−0.215***
	(0.016)	(0.012)	(0.038)
Log(Number of Municipalities$_{d,t}$)	0.00002	0.002	−0.032
	(0.011)	(0.006)	(0.031)
People Per Seat$_{d,t}$	−0.029	−0.018	−0.091
	(0.019)	(0.012)	(0.051)
Senior LDP Politician$_{d,t}$	0.105***	0.046***	0.263***
	(0.007)	(0.004)	(0.019)
Number LDP Candidates$_{d,t}$	0.080***	0.130***	0.194***
	(0.007)	(0.007)	(0.017)
Observations	1,877	1,877	1,877
Year FE	Y	Y	Y
R^2	0.332	0.618	0.211

Robust standard errors clustered on electoral district in parentheses.
*$p < 0.05$, **$p < 0.01$, ***$p < 0.001$.
Regression models estimated with R's plm() package.

on voters, but more than one candidate was elected in each district. This meant that votes could not be transferred to another candidate of the same party should a voter have voted for a candidate who secured enough votes to win. In such a system, parties can suffer from running too many candidates (Cox and Niou 1994). Thus, districts with more LDP candidates may have cast more *votes* for LDP candidates, but if more of

7.3 Asymmetric Districts Exhibit Less Support

those votes went to LDP candidates who *lost* the election, then those districts might have arbitrarily smaller Winning LDP VS$_{d,t}$ and LDP Seats$_{d,t}$ scores, respectively. Controlling for the number of LDP candidates in a district ensures that errors of this type are not confounding my ability to estimate the effect of district-level asymmetry on support for the party.

In all three models, the coefficient on HI$_{d,t}$ is negative and statistically significant. This means that districts characterized by greater asymmetry in municipality size exhibit *less* support for the LDP, controlling for other differences across districts and features specific to a given election. Substantively, Model 1 tells us that a one-standard-deviation increase in HI$_{d,t}$ is expected to lower the district's level of electoral support for LDP winners by 1.24%. The sample mean of Winning LDP VS$_{d,t}$ was 0.25, meaning that 25% of eligible voters in the average district cast their ballots for winning LDP candidates. Model 2 tells us that a one-standard-deviation increase in HI$_{d,t}$ is expected to lower the district's level of support for LDP candidates by 0.73%. The sample mean of LDP VS$_{d,t}$ was 0.31, meaning that 31% of eligible voters in the average district cast their ballots for LDP candidates. Model 3 tells us that a one-standard-deviation increase in HI$_{d,t}$ is expected to lower the share of a district's seats won by the LDP by 3.5%. The sample mean of LDP Seats$_{d,t}$ was 0.62, meaning that on average, 62% of the seats available in a district were won by LDP candidates. This is evidence for Hypothesis 4: District-level asymmetry depresses support for the LDP.

Dividing up the sample into preelectoral and postelectoral reform reveals that the negative, statistically significant coefficient on HI$_{d,t}$ in the models in Table 7.5 is a feature of elections under the *new* electoral system, but not under the old. If we confine observations to districts under the old electoral system (1980–1993) and run the same models, we find that districts characterized by greater asymmetry in municipality size do *not* exhibit systematically lower levels of support for the LDP, whether support is measured in share of voters who voted for LDP winners, share of voters who voted for LDP candidates, or share of seats won by the LDP. The coefficient on HI$_{d,t}$ is negative but not statistically significant in any model (see Table A.13). However, running the same models on districts from the seven elections in the postelectoral reform period produces coefficients on HI$_{d,t}$ that are negative and statistically significant (see Table A.14). Thus, district-level asymmetry leads to noticeably lower support rates for the LDP in elections after reform, but not in elections before reform.[18]

---

[18] Let me add the caveat that, if we conduct regressions with *municipalities* as observations, not electoral districts, then we observe HI$_{d,t}$ exercising a negative, statistically

Which Electoral Districts Get More Money

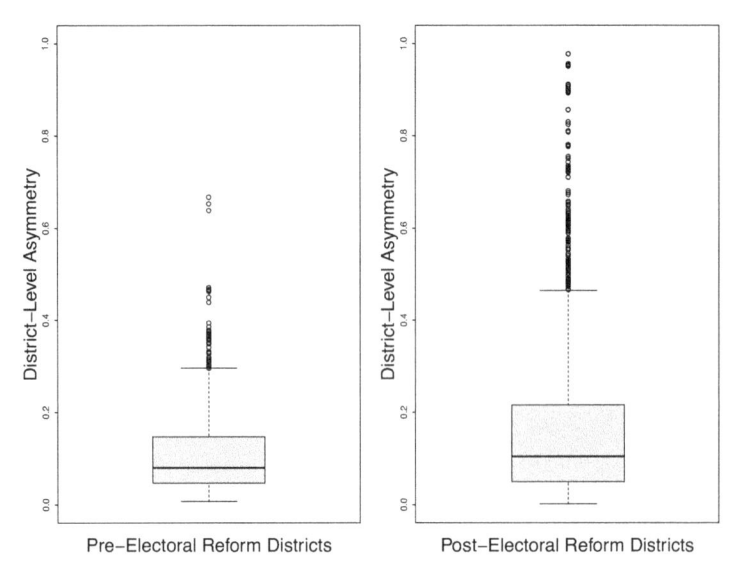

Figure 7.2 This plots the concentration of voting population ($HI_{d,t}$) in districts prior to Japan's electoral reform in 1993 (on the left) and in districts after reform (on the right). Higher (lower) values indicate districts where the voting population is more (less) concentrated in a single municipality.

To understand what could account for this difference, recall that the theory expects that we would not observe districts characterized by greater asymmetry in municipality size exhibiting less support for the LDP if the LDP politicians competing in them had delivered prizes large enough to offset voters' reduced propensity to turn out and support them. The fact that we do not observe a statistically significant, negative correlation between district-level asymmetry and support for the LDP in the prereform period could reflect the fact that LDP politicians were delivering enough money to these districts to increase their support to a level indistinguishable to those of their counterparts in other districts. The fact that we observe a statistically significant, negative correlation between district-level asymmetry and support for the LDP in the postreform period could indicate that LDP politicians in this period were less able to deliver the sums necessary to raise their level of support.

A possible reason for this could be that the redrawing of electoral districts in 1994 had the effect of *increasing* district-level asymmetry. Figure 7.2 plots the distribution of $HI_{d,t}$ across tournament-possible districts in the 1980–1993 elections ($n = 586$ districts) and in the 1996–2014 elections ($n = 1,291$ districts), respectively. A Kolmogorov–Smirnov test confirms that the distributions are significantly different

significant effect on all measures of support for the LDP in both periods, controlling for many other district- and municipality-level characteristics.

(p>0.001). Before electoral reform, mean $HI_{d,t}$ across districts was 0.11, only one-quarter of districts had values of 0.15 or higher, and the most asymmetric district was at 0.67. In contrast, after electoral reform, mean $HI_{d,t}$ was 0.18, one-quarter of districts had values of 0.22 or higher, and the most asymmetric district was at 0.98. In 1993, the most asymmetric district was Ehime First District ($HI_{d,t}$ = 0.67). It was made up of ten municipalities, which included one large city (Matsuyama City, population = 452,057), one smaller city (Hojo City, population = 29,315), five towns (with populations ranging from approximately 20,000 to 4,000), and three villages (populations ranging from 3,000 to 1,000). In contrast, the most asymmetric district in 1996 was Nara First ($HI_{d,t}$ = 0.98), which I discussed above.

Why does this matter? The increase in district-level asymmetry that accompanied Japan's 1994 electoral reform, which redrew the boundaries of almost every single district, would have increased the amounts of money that needed to be delivered to convince voters to use their votes to compete with other municipalities. If certain LDP politicians were not delivering these larger sums, perhaps because they lacked the ability to do so, this would account for the more pronounced negative impact of $HI_{d,t}$ on support in the post-1994 period.

7.4 RECONCILING PUZZLES IN PRIOR WORK

Earlier in this chapter, we presented evidence that districts characterized by greater asymmetry in municipality size received more transfers than districts characterized by less asymmetry in municipality size. Then, we showed that despite receiving more transfers, districts characterized by greater asymmetry in municipality size exhibit systematically *lower* levels of support for the LDP, with the negative relationship between district-level asymmetry and electoral support being especially pronounced in the post-1994 era. This provides a compelling explanation for a central puzzle in Japanese politics: Why money has been found to flow to relatively *unsupportive* electoral districts, where the share of voters voting for the LDP is lower than other electoral districts. The reason this pattern of spending is puzzling is because it is at odds with the near-universal assessment of the LDP as a party that is adept at using its monopoly access to government resources to create and nurture loyal groups of supporters, who can be relied on to turn out and vote for LDP politicians, election after election.

Until now, scholars noticing this pattern have suggested that it may be attributable to a concerted effort to use government resources to buy the votes of swing voters (Horiuchi and Saito 2003). Under this argument, party leaders, who want to increase their party's seat share, funnel resources toward electoral districts in which the party does poorly, presumably with the intent of increasing support. However, a swing voter-based argument runs into difficulties on both theoretical and empirical grounds. Theoretically, any electoral strategy that relies on channeling benefits toward voters who do not support the party risks depleting support among all types of voters. Under this allocation rule, voters in so-called core districts would realize that feigning a lack of support for the incumbent represented their best chance of receiving more government transfers, while voters in so-called swing districts would realize that they could receive an even larger allocation if they lowered their support further. Thus, it is not difficult to see how an incumbent pursuing this strategy risks failing to capture enough votes and losing the election, which would be the worst possible outcome. Empirically, too, an electoral strategy of diverting resources to swing districts requires that party leaders have the tools to shield the transfer system from the actions of their members representing core districts, who will presumably also be agitating for more funds. There is little evidence, in either the preelectoral or postelectoral reform period, that LDP leaders wielded this kind of control.

This chapter has offered a different explanation for why money flows to districts in which LDP vote shares are lower. Importantly, this explanation does not require us to revise our understanding of the LDP as a party that funnels benefits to core supporters. In a nutshell, this pattern of resource allocations across districts is perfectly consistent with a pattern of resource allocations within districts in which government money is funneled to core supporters – not blithely, but according to a tournament in which the most supportive groups get the most money, and money declines as a function of electoral support. The reason why this allocation rule within districts leads to the opposite relationship between support and transfers across districts is because the relative sizes of the groups into which voters in a district are arranged exercises an *independent* effect on the amount of resources incumbents have to offer voters to entice them to compete against one another. In districts characterized by greater asymmetry in group size, more money is required. Thus, in these districts, incumbents offer more (money) but are also likely to settle for less (support). This produces the negative correlation between support and transfers across districts that has perplexed scholars.

For voters in Japan, the book thus far has identified two variables that impact the amount of discretionary transfers their municipalities receive. One is their municipality's position in a rank ordering of municipalities in the district constructed on the basis of electoral support. The battery

7.4 Reconciling Puzzles in Prior Work

of tests conducted in Chapter 6 show that within districts, municipalities that attain high positions in this ranking receive more transfers after the election than their counterparts attaining lower positions. The second variable is the degree of asymmetry in size of the municipalities in their district. The tests in this chapter show that municipalities in districts characterized by greater asymmetry in municipality size receive more money for a given level of support. Importantly, this could give rise to a situation in which a municipality placing first in one district receives *less* than a municipality placing last in another district. This would occur if the first municipality's district consisted of evenly sized municipalities and the latter municipality's district consisted of asymmetrically sized municipalities.

8

How Tournaments Impact Decisions to Vote

Thus far, this book has offered evidence that LDP politicians use tournaments to get elected. Before election campaigns, they dangle the promise of central government resources over the heads of voters in their electoral districts. After votes are counted, they calculate how much support they received from each of the municipalities therein. Then, via pressure exerted on central government bureaucrats, they engineer a situation in which the largest prize goes to the most supportive municipality, the second-largest prize goes to the second-most supportive municipality, and so on. Making the difference in amounts received by the most supportive and second-most supportive municipalities larger than the difference in amounts received by the second-most and third-most supportive, which is in turn larger than the difference in amounts received by the third-most and fourth-most supportive, and so on, creates a situation where a handful of votes in a highly supportive municipality can be enough to bring about meaningful change in a municipality's resource allocation. This gives voters in those municipalities reason to set aside whatever personal feelings they harbor toward the incumbent and reason that, given she will very likely be reelected, they may as well use their vote to make sure their municipality continues to be prioritized when it comes to resource allocations. For the incumbent, the competition this engenders among voters in supportive municipalities is a convenient way of amassing enough votes to win.

In Chapters 6 and 7, I looked for evidence of tournaments in postelection allocations of national treasury disbursements (NTD). Headline findings were threefold. One, within electoral districts, the amount of NTD municipalities receive in the years following Lower House elections was found to be a function of its position in a rank order of municipalities, constructed on the basis of support for the LDP incumbent. More specifically, municipalities at higher ranks (exhibiting greater support for their LDP incumbent) received larger postelection resource allocations

(Hypothesis 1). Two, also within districts, the amount of NTD municipalities receive was found to increase with their position in this ranking, but not in a linear fashion, in a *convex* fashion. By this, I mean that the returns to increases in rank increase at an increasing rate as a municipality climbs the ranks. A municipality that increases its rank from second to first place can expect a much larger increase in its NTD allocation than a municipality that experiences an equivalent one-rank increase at a lower position in the ranking (such as from six to five). This is evidence that LDP incumbents deliberately make the amounts available for municipalities to fight over larger at higher ranks (Hypothesis 2).

Three, across electoral districts, the total amount of NTD received by a district's voters is found to vary according to the relative size of the municipalities therein. The more similarly sized the municipalities in a given electoral district are, the less (money) is needed to motivate them to compete against each other. Thus, when the amount of NTD received by all municipalities in each district is tallied up, the total amount of money electoral districts receive is found to increase with the degree of asymmetry in municipality size (Hypothesis 3). Even though districts with asymmetrically sized municipalities receive more money, my analyses also reveal that they tend to deliver less support for the LDP (Hypothesis 4).

In this chapter, I look for evidence of a tournament in voter decisions to turn out and vote. The theory expects that decisions to vote will hinge on *where* in the ranking a municipality is expected to place. Why? Making a municipality's resource allocation contingent upon its rank, and designing rewards so that they increase with rank at an increasing rate creates a situation in which highly supportive municipalities will all vie for first place. This creates a situation in which a handful of votes could be enough to change a municipality's ranking and hence bring about a sizeable increase in its resource allocation. Thus, in municipalities projected to place well in the tournament, a single vote wields considerable influence over the amount of resources a municipality receives. All else equal, then, we can expect that voters will be systematically more motivated to go to the polls in municipalities projected to place highly in the tournament, which are in the running for a very large prize. In these municipalities, voters might realize that their vote is immaterial to the *outcome* of the election (after all, the incumbent is likely to win), but material to the amount of money their municipality receives after the election. Voters turn out to avoid being the reason their municipality misses out on a large prize, which would be the outcome if it failed to main the high ranking it attained last time or missed out on boosting its ranking this time.

The situation is different in municipalities not projected to place highly. These municipalities may not regularly deliver large shares of their voting population to the LDP incumbent and may have pockets of support for *non*-LDP candidates. Amongst these relatively unsupportive municipalities, increases in rank will still bring about increases in resources, but any increase in resources that comes from an increase in rank at the middle-to-lower end of the ranking will be smaller. Because of this, neck-and-neck competition at the middle-to-lower end of the ranking will be much less likely to materialize. Amongst supportive municipalities, it is the *anticipation* of a large increase in resources that galvanizes voters to make the effort to go to the polls, regardless of how they feel about the incumbent and regardless of whether they think their vote will affect the election's outcome. As more and more voters use their vote this way, neck-and-neck competition for rank increases materializes, which further increases the influence of a single vote. Among less supportive municipalities, the situation is different: knowing that increases in rank are unlikely to yield anything short of a modest increase in resources, more voters will calculate that they may as well stay home on election day, given that the resources their municipality stands to win will hardly be affected by whether or not they personally vote. As more and more voters make this calculation, turnout will decrease, which in turn means that more votes become necessary to change the municipality's ranking.

In this chapter, I devise three sets of tests that examine whether the motivation to vote differs according to a municipality's projected position in the ranking. To conduct these, I operationalize new variables that capture the degree to which a municipality concentrates its votes on a single LDP winner.[1] Using these variables, I first examine whether, within electoral districts in the same election, turnout increases as municipalities concentrate larger shares of valid votes cast on a single LDP winner. This is Hypothesis 5. Next, I continue to restrict the comparison to municipalities in the same district in the same election and examine whether, if I rank municipalities in terms of the degree to which votes are concentrated on a single LDP winner, increases in vote concentration at the top of the ranking, amongst municipalities that are already concentrating many votes on a single LDP winner, bring about larger increases in turnout than increases in vote concentration at the middle or bottom of the ranking. This is Hypothesis 6. As with the tests in Chapters 6 and 7, all these tests take confounders seriously, pit the predictions of the tournament theory against those of rival theories, and are sensitive to the specifics of the electoral system under which incumbents are competing.

---

[1] The support variables operationalized in Chapter 6 are not used for these tests because the denominator in those support variables (voting population) is the same as in turnout (voting population).

8.1 Empirical Strategy

By comparing turnout rates between municipalities in the same district-year, these first sets of tests hold constant the effect of all variables influencing turnout that operate at the level of the district-year. A factor influencing turnout at this level, which we know exercises a decisive influence on voter decisions to go to the polls, is the *competitiveness* of the race. A vast literature in political science has established that when a race is projected to be competitive, more voters will go to the polls. When a race is not projected to be competitive, in contrast, more voters decide to sit the election out. By definition, competitive elections mean narrow margins of victory, and narrow margins of victory increase the probability that one's vote might *matter*, in the sense of helping to determine who wins.

My third test leverages variation across electoral districts in the degree to which races are projected to be competitive to conduct an additional test of Hypothesis 5. To ascertain whether the motivation to vote differs systematically according to *where* in the ranking a voter's municipality is likely to end up, I examine whether projections of increased competitiveness have a *smaller* impact on turnout rates in municipalities projected to place highly in the ranking. In municipalities projected to place highly, the theory expects that motivations to vote will be driven primarily by voters' desire to realize a larger resource allocation. Thus, turnout in highly supportive municipalities should be *less* affected by situational elements of a given election, such as closeness. It is likely to remain high even when an election is not projected to be close. In contrast, in municipalities not projected to place highly, turnout is more likely to be affected by situational elements, such as competitiveness.[2] Thus, we can expect that turnout in the less supportive municipalities within a given electoral district will be more sensitive to projections of closeness. Like my other tests, the tests crafted in this section consider whether my results are better explained by rival theories, particularly one positing that turnout in Japanese elections is a function of a conditional relationship between district-level competitiveness and population density (Cox, Rosenbluth and Thies 1998).

8.1 EMPIRICAL STRATEGY

Chapter 4 fleshed out the theoretical underpinnings of the hypotheses this book tests. For ease of access, here are the two examined in this chapter:

- **Hypothesis 5**: Within electoral districts, turnout rates are a function of a municipality's position in a rank ordering of municipalities,

---

[2] I use competitiveness and closeness interchangeably here.

constructed on the basis of support for the LDP winner in the most recent election.
- **Hypothesis 6**: Within electoral districts, the impact of increases in rank on turnout in a municipality increases as municipalities climb the ranks.

8.1.1 Variables

As I explained in Chapter 6, my data consist of yearly observations (where t indicates the year) of electoral districts (d), municipalities (m), and candidates (c). Let $n_{d,t}$ capture the number of municipalities in district d in year t.[3] First, I created variables that capture the degree to which municipality m favored a single LDP winner in an election held in year t. Let $v_{m,t}$ represent the number of valid votes cast in municipality m at time t. This is available for $t \in E = \{e_1, e_2, ...\} = \{1980, 1983, ...\}$, the years in which Lower House elections were held. Let $v_{c,m,t}$ represent the number of votes cast for candidate c in municipality m at time t. Let $LDP_{c,t}$ indicate whether candidate c was a member of the LDP at time t and $w_{c,t}$ indicate whether candidate c won a seat in district d at time t. I calculated:

$$\text{Single LDP Winner VS}_{m,t} = \frac{max_{c \in m}\{LDP_{c,t} w_{c,t} v_{c,m,t}\}}{v_{m,t}} \quad (8.1)$$

In words, this takes the number of votes received by all LDP winners in municipality m at time t, identifies the LDP winner who won the largest number of votes, and divides the number of votes won by this LDP winner by the number of valid votes cast in the municipality.[4] To obtain a high value on Single LDP Winner VS$_{m,t}$, municipalities have to cast more of their votes, however many are cast, for a single LDP winner. Note that municipalities in electoral districts without a single LDP winner all receive 0 on Single LDP Winner VS$_{m,t}$.

In the preelectoral reform period (1980–1993), candidates in Lower House elections competed in multimember districts (MMDs). In the postelectoral reform period, they competed in single-member districts. Thus, the number of winning candidates (and hence, the number of LDP winners) varies across district-years. A municipality that manages to send

---

[3] As with the analyses in Chapter 6, municipalities straddling more than one electoral district are excluded from the creation of these variables.
[4] The number of valid votes cast is calculated by taking the sum of the number of valid votes cast for all candidates who ran in the district-year.

8.1 Empirical Strategy

40% of votes cast to a single LDP winner in a district that produces four LDP winners could be said to have more strongly identified with that winner than a municipality that sent the same 40% of votes cast to a single LDP winner in a district with only one LDP winner. To make sure that district-level differences in the number of winners (district magnitude) are not producing systematic differences in Single LDP Winner VS$_{m,t}$ that could have consequences for my results, I also constructed a ranked version of this variable, which is comparable across municipalities with different numbers of LDP winners.

Concretely, for the n municipalities located in district-year dt, I ranked them by values on Single LDP Winner VS$_{m,t}$ and then standardized the ranking so that the municipality with the smallest Single LDP Winner VS$_{m,t}$ (the lowest degree of identification with a single LDP winner) always receives 0 on Rank(Single LDP Winner VS$_{m,t}$) and the municipality with the largest Single LDP Winner VS$_{m,t}$ (highest degree of identification with a single LDP winner) always receives 1 on Rank(Single LDP Winner VS$_{m,t}$).[5] Note that as municipalities in districts without LDP winners all have 0 on Single LDP Winner VS$_{m,t}$, they cannot be ranked.[6]

Given that the variables operationalized in Chapter 6 were explicitly designed to capture the municipality's position in the ranking, which is also what I want to capture here, why can I not use these variables here? Using these support variables (Best LDP VS$_{m,t}$ and Sum LDP VS$_{m,t}$ and their corresponding ranked versions) would not produce compelling tests of my hypotheses on account of the fact that the denominator in all four support variables is the number of eligible voters in municipality m, which is also the denominator in turnout (as I explain below). Thus, by construction, municipalities with higher values on the four support variables used in Chapter 6 will have higher values on turnout. In contrast, a high value on the variable operationalized above, Single LDP Winner VS$_{m,t}$, simply means that municipality m sent most votes cast to a single LDP winner; it is agnostic about whether the number of votes cast was high

---

[5] To do this, I first ranked municipalities so that the lowest-ranked municipality receives 0 and the highest-ranked municipality receives one less than the number of municipalities in the district ($n_{d,t} - 1$). Then, dividing each municipality's value on this ranking by the total number of municipalities in its district-year minus 1 ($n_{d,t} - 1$) standardizes the index so that in each district-year, the municipality with the lowest degree of identification with a single LDP winner receives 0 and the municipality with the highest degree of identification with a single LDP winner receives 1.

[6] These municipalities receive NA on Rank(Single LDP Winner VS$_{m,t}$).

or low, relative to voting population. This variable is better suited to discerning whether increases in the degree to which votes are concentrated on a single LDP winner are associated with more voters making the decision to turn out.

Next, let $p_{m,t}$ represent the number of eligible voters in municipality m at time t (the voting population). My dependent variable, turnout in municipality m, is calculated by taking the number of valid votes cast in the municipality and dividing this by the number of eligible voters. More formally:

$$\text{Turnout}_{m,t} = \frac{v_{m,t}}{p_{m,t}}. \qquad (8.2)$$

Finally, as a measure of the competitiveness of the race in a given electoral district in a given year, I compute $\text{Margin}_{d,t}$. This is the number of votes cast for the last winner in district d at the election at t, minus the number of votes cast for the first loser, divided by the total number of valid votes cast in district dt. Analyses of races with a single winner routinely use the difference in number of votes won between the winner and the first loser (or first runner up), divided by votes cast, as an indicator of the competitiveness of a district. Studies of Japanese politics have shown that the same operationalization, but between the "last" winner and the first loser, is appropriate when there is more than one winner (e.g., Ariga 2015). When there are four winners, then, $\text{Margin}_{d,t}$ is the difference between the number of votes won by the fourth-placed candidate (the last winner) and the number of votes won by the fifth-placed candidate (the first loser). Generally speaking, larger values of $\text{Margin}_{d,t}$ mean a larger gap in votes received by the last winner and the first loser, which indicates a *less* competitive race.

8.1.2 Potential Confounders

My goal is to ascertain whether a municipality's projected position in a rank order of municipalities in its district, constructed on the basis of support for the LDP incumbent, exercises an independent effect on voter decisions to turn out. More specifically, I want to know if increases in position in the ranking bring about increases in turnout, and if those increases bring about even larger increases in turnout when municipalities are at the top of the ranking than when they are at the middle or bottom. To conduct compelling tests of this hypothesis, I must be mindful of alternative variables that could influence the relationship between vote concentration and turnout, and I must control for these variables.

8.1 Empirical Strategy

The political science literature on the drivers of turnout is vast.[7] Studies of turnout in Japanese elections have established the influence of the following six variables: the projected closeness of the race (Jou 2009; Cox, Rosenbluth and Thies 1998), the electoral system (Smith 2018b), changes in electoral rules (Kohno 1997b), the number of seats available in the district (district magnitude) (Muraoka and Barceló 2019), the number of representatives elected in the district per voter (Fujimura 2020; Horiuchi 2005), and urbanness (Cox, Rosenbluth and Thies 1998; Richardson 1973), respectively. Let us briefly review the findings on each.

First, a vast literature establishes that when elections are projected to be *close*, meaning the margin of victory between the winner and loser is expected to be narrow, more voters make the effort to go to the polls (e.g., Blais 2000; Endersby, Galatas and Rackaway 2002; Jou 2010).[8] One explanation for this is rooted in voter psychology and specifically, in the desire for one's vote to matter. This explanation holds that the closer an election is projected to be, the higher the chance that a single vote could decide the outcome. Because going to the polls is costly and takes time away from other activities, voters will be more willing to incur these costs when they believe their vote might influence the outcome. Another explanation is rooted in the calculations of political elites (e.g., Key 1949; Cox and Munger 1989). This locates the impetus of decisions to turn out in the behavior of elites and argues that elites try harder to mobilize votes for their preferred candidates when elections are expected to be close, and this increased mobilization drives the positive relationship between closeness and turnout.

In the Japanese context, at least two studies have found evidence that district-level competitiveness influences turnout. Jou (2010) was interested in whether, under Japan's mixed-member majoritarian (MMM)

---

[7] In their meta-analysis of this literature, Cancela and Geys (2016) note three classes of explanatory variables that scholars have invoked to account for differences in turnout rates across geographically defined units. One is socioeconomic variables such as population, population density, or ethnic homogeneity; another is political variables such as closeness or political fragmentation; and the third is institutional variables such as electoral system, voter registration, or the presence of concurrent elections (see also Kostelka et al. 2023). Importantly, institutional variables are found to have an impact up to four times' as great as socioeconomic or political variables.

[8] After Downs (1957)'s observation that it is not rational for anyone to vote because the costs of voting vastly outweigh the likelihood that a single vote will ever be pivotal, Riker and Ordeshook (1968) argued that people vote for other reasons, such as to affirm their commitment to the democratic process or fulfil what they perceive as a social obligation. Dowding (2005) offers a summary. Despite the fact that a single vote is hardly ever pivotal, a large literature has nevertheless found that turnout increases in close elections. Thus, the desire to influence the outcome of elections appears to exercise at least some sway over individual decisions to turn out.

electoral system, the addition of the proportional representation (PR) tier attenuated the relationship between competitiveness at the level of the single-seat district (SSD) and turnout. His reasoning was that in a mixed system like Japan's, voters who support parties with little chance of placing first in the SSD can influence those parties' seat tallies by turning out and casting a PR ballot for them. Because voters cast ballots for the SSD race and the PR race during the same trip to a polling station, the influence of the PR ballot could attenuate any relationship between SSD-level competitiveness and turnout. Notwithstanding this logic, his analyses of the 2005 and 2009 Lower House elections revealed that SSD-level competitiveness "emerges as having the most substantial impact on turnout among all socio-demographic and political variables tested" (Jou 2010, 1055).

Another study examined whether district-level competitiveness influenced turnout in Japanese elections during the period prior to electoral reform, when MMDs were used (Cox, Rosenbluth and Thies 1998). While the authors found evidence of this, they further hypothesized that the impact of district-level competitiveness depended on the density of social ties within districts. Their reasoning was that close elections produce higher turnout via the actions of elites, who engage in calculations as to whether or not efforts to mobilize votes will bear fruit. In districts with dense social ties ("high social capital"), they reasoned that elites understood that every additional voter contacted and urged to vote would have a larger number of friends and acquaintances to whom this message would be passed on. Thus, close elections would produce more intense elite mobilization, and hence, higher turnout, in districts with dense social ties. In support of this, they studied turnout at the district level in Lower House elections between 1967 and 1993. Controlling for differences between election years, they showed that less competitive elections (larger margins separating the last winner from the first loser) have lower turnout, but less competitive elections have even lower turnout in districts where social ties are dense (sparsely populated districts and districts with more women and children under fifteen). In urban districts, where social ties are the least dense, the effect of closeness on turnout was found to be "almost nil" (Cox, Rosenbluth and Thies 1998, 468).

Second, another strand of literature holds that turnout is decisively influenced by *electoral system*. Specifically, elections under PR have been shown to have higher turnout rates than elections under majoritarian systems. Why? As I alluded to in my discussion of Jou (2010), under PR, seats accrue to parties in proportion to their vote share; thus, there are few wasted votes. In a majoritarian system, in contrast, votes cast for losing candidates are wasted, as are votes cast for district winners in excess

8.1 Empirical Strategy

of the number needed to win. The larger number of wasted votes in a majoritarian system is thought to depress turnout. Cox, Fiva and Smith (2016), however, caution against blanket statements that turnout will be higher under PR. They point out that the winner-take-all nature of elections under majoritarian rules means that close races are likely to produce turnout levels that exceed those in a PR system, but uncompetitive races will not. Thus, the question of whether turnout is higher under PR or majoritarian rules boils down to inquiring as to the share of races in the majoritarian system that are competitive. If there are few competitive races, then aggregate turnout will be low and will increase if the system switches to PR. If there are many competitive races, in contrast, aggregate turnout is likely to be high and may suffer a decline if the system is switched to PR. In a comparison of turnout in the last three elections held under SNTV-MMD and the first three under MMM, Smith (2018b) finds that turnout is lower under the new system.

Third, Kohno (1997b) studied the impact of *electoral reforms* on turnout. His analyses showed that turnout declined in the first election held under Japan's new mixed-member system (in 1996) and also fell in the first election held under SNTV-MMD (in 1947). He argues that these declines can be attributed to the complexity and/or newness of the system, and/or the fact that the redrawing of district boundaries meant that many voters faced entirely new slates of candidates, with which it was costly to familiarize oneself.

Fourth, turnout is also thought to be decisively influenced by *district magnitude* (the number of representatives elected in a district). Canonical models of electoral systems compare majoritarian systems, assumed to have a district magnitude of 1, with PR systems, assumed to have a district magnitude much greater than 1 (and sometimes, in the hundreds). But electoral systems qualifying as majoritarian can have district magnitudes greater than 1, while electoral systems qualifying as proportional can have smaller district magnitudes. Thus, more recent work seeks to isolate the independent effect of district magnitude itself. On the one hand, larger district magnitudes are thought to produce higher turnout on the grounds that an increase in the number of candidates running means that more voters would find a candidate aligned with their preferences. On the other hand, when district magnitudes are very large, the large number of candidates competing places a large cognitive burden on voters, who must acquire the information needed to adjudicate between them (Taagepera, Selb, and Grofman 2014). This is particularly the case when candidates rely on personal characteristics, as opposed to party labels, to distinguish themselves from co-partisans (Muraoka and Barceló 2019). As a result, district magnitudes over four are typically thought to produce lower turnout. Muraoka and Barceló (2019) study this in Japan. They leverage the fact that until 2011, district magnitudes in municipal assembly elections increased discontinuously at certain population thresholds and was strictly applied (municipalities whose populations fell below a threshold had to call for new elections).[9] Among municipalities in their sample, whose district magnitudes ranged from 6 to 46, they found that increases in district magnitude was associated with a decline in turnout.

Fifth, the *number of representatives per voter* (electorate size) is also thought to influence turnout. In smaller electorates, representatives are elected with a smaller number of votes, which means that votes count more. Horiuchi (2005) conducts a cross-national study of this hypothesis, which includes extensive analyses with data from Japan. He finds that turnout is higher in municipal assembly elections than in national elections in Japan, and he argues that this is primarily (although, not only) due to the smaller electorate size. Across municipalities, he also finds that turnout in assembly elections is higher in smaller municipalities than in larger ones. Due to the way numbers of assembly members are assigned, smaller municipalities have a larger number of elected representatives per capita than larger municipalities. In his analyses of turnout in the 2005 and 2009 Lower House elections in Japan, Jou (2010) includes a control for electorate size. He explains that while Japan's 1994 electoral reform reduced the disparity across districts in terms of number of votes needed to elect a representative, it did not eliminate it. He counts several districts that have more than twice as many voters as the smallest district. Nevertheless, he found that this variable had no systematic relationship with turnout in the elections he examined. In contrast, a study of turnout in Upper House elections found that electorate size is negatively correlated with turnout (Fujimura 2020).

Sixth, early work on turnout in Japanese elections found that it was almost always higher in *rural communities* than in urban ones (Richardson 1973). The main reason for this, alluded to above when I discussed Cox, Rosenbluth and Thies (1998), is thought to be that voters in rural areas are more likely to be longstanding residents and therefore better integrated into networks and associations that could be harnessed by candidates for the purpose of vote mobilization. While candidates benefit from being able to tap into communities with well-established social networks everywhere, Japan's use of SNTV-MMD prior to 1994 made these networks of particular value to LDP candidates. Under this system, LDP candidates were campaigning against each other and had

---

[9] The Local Autonomy Law stipulated that if the number of municipal residents was less than or equal to 50,000, for example, the maximum number of council members could be 26.

no party organization upon which to draw. They contested elections by emphasizing their personal characteristics, background, and connections, as well as what they planned to get done in the district. Between elections, they cultivated personal support organizations, called koenkai, by plying voters with all manner of favors, including assistance with requests, parties, and trips to the hot springs. It was koenkai members who did the bulk of the vote mobilization during the relatively short campaign period (McElwain 2008). If it is easier to mobilize votes in rural areas due to higher density of social ties, then we are likely to observe more vigorous vote mobilization by LDP candidates in those areas, and thus, higher turnout.[10]

The good news is that my research design controls for all these variables except the last. By including district-year fixed effects in the main tests of Hypotheses 5 and 6, I am able to hold constant the effects of all variables operating at this level. While these variables could be creating vast disparities in turnout rates across electoral districts, driving up turnout in some districts and driving it down in others, my use of district-year fixed effects enables me to look *within* district-years, to see if a municipality's projected position in the ranking exercises an independent effect on turnout, notwithstanding these other differences. Of the six variables, one operating at the level of the municipality, which I need to control for, is urbanness (or more broadly, density of social ties). I operationalize this with population density, proportion of the population employed in farming, and the proportion of population aged fifteen and under and sixty-five and older, respectively. Later in the chapter, I exclude district-year fixed effects from the specification, which enables me to leverage variation across districts in competitiveness to conduct an additional test of Hypothesis 5.

8.2 CONCENTRATING VOTES ON A SINGLE LDP WINNER INCREASES TURNOUT

First, across municipalities in the same electoral district in the same election, is the share of voters who bother to turn out and vote higher in municipalities that more strongly identify with a single LDP winner? To answer this question, Table 8.1 presents the results of two-way fixed effect

---

[10] Notwithstanding this logic, the analyses in Cox, Rosenbluth and Thies (1998) found that the relationship between ruralness and turnout at the district level in Lower House elections under SNTV-MMD is mediated by closeness, to the extent that there was almost no difference in turnout between rural and urban areas when races are uncompetitive. On the new system, there is some evidence that urban–rural differences in turnout have reduced (Jou 2010).

Table 8.1 *Municipalities that concentrate more votes on a single LDP winner have higher turnout in Lower House elections, 1980–2014.*

	Dependent variable: Turnout$_{m,t}$			
	(Model 1)	(Model 2)	(Model 3)	(Model 4)
Single LDP Winner VS$_{m,t}$	0.026***	0.019***		
	(0.002)	(0.003)		
Rank(Single LDP) Winner VS$_{m,t}$)			0.006***	0.004***
			(0.001)	(0.001)
Turnout$_{m,t-1}$	0.727***	0.241***	0.732***	0.224***
	(0.008)	(0.011)	(0.008)	(0.012)
Fiscal Strength$_{m,t}$	−0.008***	0.009**	−0.008***	0.012***
	(0.001)	(0.003)	(0.001)	(0.003)
Dependent Population$_{m,t}$	0.136***	0.185***	0.144***	0.186***
	(0.010)	(0.015)	(0.010)	(0.017)
Farming Population$_{m,t}$	0.026***	0.051**	0.030***	0.045*
	(0.005)	(0.019)	(0.005)	(0.022)
Log(Population$_{m,t}$)	−0.008***	−0.055***	−0.008***	−0.065***
	(0.0003)	(0.004)	(0.0003)	(0.005)
Log(Per Capita Income$_{m,t}$)	0.006***	0.015***	0.005**	0.015***
	(0.002)	(0.004)	(0.002)	(0.004)
Population Density$_{m,t}$	0.00004	0.022***	−0.00004	0.027***
	(0.0003)	(0.005)	(0.0003)	(0.005)
Observations	24,936	24,936	20,885	20,885
District-Year FE	Y	Y	Y	Y
Municipality FE	N	Y	N	Y
R^2	0.775	0.158	0.778	0.162

Robust standard errors clustered on municipality in parentheses.
*$p < 0.05$, **$p < 0.01$, ***$p < 0.001$.
Regression models estimated with R's plm() package.

regression models of Turnout$_{m,t}$ in the twelve Lower House elections held between 1980 and 2014 as a function of Single LDP Winner VS$_{m,t}$ (Models 1 and 2) and Rank(Single LDP Winner VS$_{m,t}$) (Models 3 and 4).[11] My sample is nonsplit municipalities in tournament-possible districts. All specifications control for turnout in the previous Lower House election, as well as six time-varying features of Japanese municipalities that could influence the relationship between vote concentration and turnout: population (log), per capita income (log), fiscal strength, population density, the proportion of the population employed in primary industries, and the proportion of the population aged fifteen and under

[11] Descriptive statistics pertaining to the variables used in these analyses appear in Table A.15.

8.2 Concentrating Votes Increases Turnout

and sixty-five and over, respectively.[12] These are the same municipality-level variables controlled for in the analysis of transfers. My discussion above identified the latter three variables as potentially important confounders. I report robust standard errors clustered on municipality.

All specifications include district-year fixed effects, which control for features of district d at time t that could be increasing or decreasing turnout in all the municipalities therein. As I explained, a time-varying characteristic of a district-year thought to exert a positive impact on turnout is competitiveness: If a race is projected to be more competitive than usual, perhaps because of the entry of new candidates or a scandal involving an incumbent, voters may calculate that their vote has more of a chance of influencing the election's outcome, and thus, will be more likely to turn out. In addition to closeness, the above discussion identified electoral system, district magnitude, and number of representatives per voter as other district-specific variables that could influence turnout. By controlling for all features of district d at time t that could influence turnout, district-year fixed effects enables us to look *within* district-years. Thus, the coefficients on Single LDP Winner VS$_{m,t}$ and Rank(Single LDP Winner VS$_{m,t}$) will tell us whether municipalities that identified more strongly with a single LDP winner relative to other municipalities in the same district-year had higher turnout. In each specification, I report robust standard errors clustered on municipality.[13]

In Models 1 and 3, coefficients on my measures of vote concentration are positive and statistically significant. This indicates that within district-years, controlling for time-varying features of municipalities that matter for turnout, municipalities that concentrate more of the votes cast on a single LDP winner have higher turnout. Substantively, Model 1 of Table 8.1 tells us that a one-standard-deviation increase in Single LDP Winner VS$_{m,t}$ can be expected to increase turnout by 0.62%. As I explained in Chapter 6, this is the *average* effect of a one-standard-deviation increase, no matter where it takes place in the ranking. The theory expects that increases in voting concentration will exert a much larger impact on turnout when they occur at the top of the ranking than when they occur at the middle or bottom. The sample mean of Turnout$_{m,t}$ in these elections was 0.73, meaning that on average, 73% of eligible voters in a municipality turned out to vote. The coefficient on prior turnout is also positive and statistically significant. If voting patterns are persistent,

---

[12] Note that population density captures the number of thousands of people per square kilometer.

[13] The number of observations is smaller in Models 3 and 4 because municipalities are not ranked in terms of Single LDP Winner VS$_{m,t}$ when there are no LDP winners in a district.

then prior turnout would have been influenced by prior vote concentration, which could account for the positive relationship between turnout in the previous election and turnout in this election. The persistence of voting patterns tends to diminish the size of our estimates of the effect of vote concentration. If I exclude prior turnout from Model 1, for example, the coefficient on Single LDP Winner VS$_{m,t}$ is more than three times' larger.

In Models 2 and 4, I add municipality fixed effects to the specifications in Models 1 and 3. A municipality fixed effect controls for time-invariant features of a municipality that could be influencing turnout, such as geographic features that influence the accessibility of polling stations. A municipality fixed effect takes care of the possibility that underlying differences of this nature between the municipalities in a district-year could be driving any observed relationship between vote concentration and turnout. Even after adding municipality fixed effects, I find that the coefficients on my vote concentration variables remain positive and statistically significant. This reduces concern that underlying differences between the municipalities are responsible for the observed effects of Single LDP Winner VS$_{m,t}$ and Rank(Single LDP Winner VS$_{m,t}$) in Models 1 and 3. What Models 2 and 4 tell us is that when the *same* municipality concentrates more of the votes cast on a single LDP winner, it has higher turnout than when it concentrates fewer votes.

It is likely that the lagged dependent variable (all models) and the municipality fixed effect (Models 2 and 4) are absorbing some of the effects of my control variables, particularly when they exhibit minimal variation over time. Nevertheless, controlling for other differences between municipalities, my results suggest that increases in fiscal strength, per capita income, the proportion of the population who are dependent, the proportion of the population employed in agriculture, and population density are all associated with higher turnout. On the other hand, increases in population per se is associated with lower turnout.

In sum, in Chapter 6 I found that within district-years, exhibiting high levels of support for a single LDP winner is associated with receiving more government resources after the election. Here, I have shown that within district-years, concentrating more votes on a single LDP winner is also associated with higher voter turnout. This is consistent with the idea that as municipalities become more and more devoted to the election of a single LDP winner, their chance of winning the largest prize increases, which motivates more voters in the municipality to turn out to vote. The fact that variation in turnout is a function of the degree to which a municipality identifies with a single LDP winner is further evidence that LDP politicians win elections by engaging in group-based clientelism (GBC).

8.2 Concentrating Votes Increases Turnout

8.2.1 Before Electoral Reform, 1980–1993

Next, I divide up the time period, which enables me to accomplish two goals. One is to examine whether turnout is a function of vote concentration under *both* electoral systems Japan has used in the 1980–2014 period. My analyses of resource allocations in Chapter 6 revealed that LDP politicians used tournaments in both periods, so I expect that turnout will also be a function of vote concentration in both periods. The second reason I divide up the time period is to leverage features of each period to craft nuanced tests that further help to distinguish between my claim and those of rival theories.

First, I conduct two types of tests to examine whether a similar relationship between vote concentration and turnout is apparent when analyses are limited to the five Lower House elections held between 1980 and 1993. To recap, in these elections, Japan was divided into between 129 and 130 multimember electoral districts, voters cast a single vote for a candidate, and the top n vote-getters in each district won a seat, where n ranged from two to six. Table 8.2 presents the same four specifications presented in Table 8.1, with the same set of controls but limits observations to elections in the 1980–1993 period. The coefficients on the indicators of voting concentration are positive and statistically significant in all specifications. Models 1 and 3, which use district-year fixed effects, tell us that municipalities that concentrated more votes on a single LDP winner have higher turnout than their same-district counterparts that concentrated fewer votes on a single LDP winner. Models 2 and 4, which use both district-year fixed effects and municipality fixed effects, tell us that when the same municipality concentrated more votes on a single LDP winner, its turnout rate was higher than when it concentrated fewer votes on a single LDP winner. Substantively, the coefficient on Single LDP Winner VS$_{m,t}$ in Model 1 tells us that on average, a one-standard-deviation increase in voting concentration is expected to translate into an 0.35% increase in turnout (mean turnout in this period was higher, at 79%).

Second, as I explained in Chapter 6, the 1980–1993 period was characterized by a very high degree of stability in municipality and electoral district boundaries. This means that Japanese municipalities faced the same set of competitors in the tournament, election after election. I can take advantage of this by conducting a first difference regression, which is an alternative means of estimating the effects of within-municipality changes in vote concentration. If, controlling for changes in other time-varying municipality-level features with consequences for turnout (such as population density), as well as features of a municipality's district-year

Table 8.2 *Municipalities that concentrate more votes on a single LDP winner have higher turnout in Lower House elections, 1980–1993.*

	Dependent variable: Turnout$_{m,t}$			
	(Model 1)	(Model 2)	(Model 3)	(Model 4)
Single LDP Winner VS$_{m,t}$	0.024***	0.020***		
	(0.002)	(0.003)		
Rank(Single LDP) Winner VS$_{m,t}$			0.007***	0.004***
			(0.001)	(0.001)
Turnout$_{m,t-1}$	0.720***	−0.109***	0.724***	−0.112***
	(0.009)	(0.013)	(0.009)	(0.013)
Fiscal Strength$_{m,t}$	−0.008***	0.015***	−0.008***	0.015***
	(0.002)	(0.004)	(0.002)	(0.004)
Dependent Population$_{m,t}$	0.110***	0.052*	0.110***	0.057**
	(0.012)	(0.022)	(0.012)	(0.022)
Farming Population$_{m,t}$	0.033***	−0.050*	0.035***	−0.048
	(0.005)	(0.025)	(0.005)	(0.025)
Log(Population$_{m,t}$)	−0.008***	−0.085***	−0.007***	−0.086***
	(0.0004)	(0.011)	(0.0004)	(0.011)
Log(Per Capita Income$_{m,t}$)	−0.001	0.008	−0.001	0.007
	(0.002)	(0.005)	(0.002)	(0.005)
Population Density$_{m,t}$	−0.001***	0.021**	−0.001**	0.022**
	(0.0004)	(0.007)	(0.0004)	(0.007)
Observations	12,398	12,398	12,288	12,288
District-Year FE	Y	Y	Y	Y
Municipality FE	N	Y	N	Y
R^2	0.770	0.059	0.768	0.057

Robust standard errors clustered on municipality in parentheses.
*$p < 0.05$, **$p < 0.01$, ***$p < 0.001$.
Regression models estimated with R's plm() package.

that could influence turnout in all the municipalities therein, I find that increases in the degree to which a municipality concentrates votes on a single LDP winner are correlated with higher turnout, this will further bolster confidence in the theory.

Table 8.3 examines the effect of changes in vote concentration between two consecutive Lower House elections on change in turnout in those same elections for municipalities in the Lower House elections held between 1983 and 1993. Because my data begins in 1980, the 1983 election is the first election for which I can compute change variables (I call these Δ variables). In both specifications, the dependent variable is ΔTurnout$_{m,t}$, which is the municipality's turnout rate in the Lower House election held at *t*, minus its turnout in the previous Lower

8.2 Concentrating Votes Increases Turnout

Table 8.3 *Increases in voting concentration between two consecutive elections in the same municipality are associated with increases in turnout, 1980–1993.*

	Dependent variable: $\Delta \text{Turnout}_{m,t}$	
	(Model 1)	(Model 2)
Δ Single LDP Winner VS$_{m,t}$	0.017***	
	(0.003)	
Δ Rank(Single LDP Winner VS$_{m,t}$)		0.003***
		(0.001)
Δ Fiscal Strength$_{m,t}$	0.012**	0.012**
	(0.004)	(0.004)
Δ Dependent Population$_{m,t}$	0.007	0.001
	(0.029)	(0.029)
Δ Farming Population$_{m,t}$	−0.033	−0.031
	(0.026)	(0.026)
Δ Log(Population$_{m,t}$)	−0.154***	−0.153***
	(0.032)	(0.033)
Δ Log(Per Capita Income$_{m,t}$)	0.018***	0.019***
	(0.005)	(0.005)
Δ Population Density$_{m,t}$	0.021	0.019
	(0.013)	(0.014)
Observations	12,393	12,224
District-Year FE	Y	Y
Municipality FE	Y	Y
R^2	0.019	0.017

Robust standard errors clustered on municipality in parentheses.
**$p < 0.01$, ***$p < 0.001$.
Regression models estimated with R's plm() package.

House election. Positive values on $\Delta \text{Turnout}_{m,t}$ mean that municipality m increased its turnout between the two elections. In Model 1, I examine the effect of ΔSingle LDP Winner VS$_{m,t}$, which is the municipality's value on Single LDP Winner VS$_{m,t}$ in the Lower House election, minus its value on Single LDP Winner VS$_{m,t}$ in the previous Lower House election. Positive values on ΔSingle LDP Winner VS$_{m,t}$ mean that municipality m had higher values on Single LDP Winner VS$_{m,t}$ in the second election. In Model 2, I examine the effect of Δ Rank(Single LDP Winner VS$_{m,t}$), which is constructed analogously.

In both specifications, I control for changes in my six municipality-level variables, constructing analogous Δ variables for each. Both specifications also use municipality fixed effects, which control for time-invariant features of municipality *m* that could plausibly be correlated with both changes in voting concentration and changes in turnout. Both specifications also use district-year fixed effects, which control for the possibility that systematic differences between districts in the second election could influence the degree to which voting concentration and turnout changed for all municipalities in that district. Because almost all municipalities are located in the same electoral district in the period, any changes to district-level features with consequences for turnout, such as the entry of new candidates projected to shake up the race, will act on all municipalities in that district simultaneously. This means that they are accounted for with the district-year fixed effect.

The coefficients on Δ Single LDP Winner VS$_{m,t}$ and Δ Rank(SingleLDP Winner VS$_{m,t}$) are positive and statistically significant. Thus, increases in the degree to which the same municipality concentrated votes on a single LDP winner were associated with higher turnout in the municipality, even controlling for changes in other features of the municipality or its electoral district that might matter for turnout.

8.2.2 Competing Explanations and Placebo Tests

As I explained, in the 1980–1993 period, candidates competed in MMDs. In almost every district, the LDP ran more than one candidate, and in the vast majority of districts, at least two of those LDP candidates were successful. I can leverage these features of the period to design four placebo tests.

To recap, the theory expects that within district-years, the relationship between concentrating votes on a single LDP winner and turnout in Japanese municipalities will be positive. The mechanism thought to produce this relationship is the large prize that municipalities become eligible for as more and more of their voters cast their votes for the same LDP winner. As a municipality becomes more dedicated to the election of a single LDP winner, voters will become more motivated to set aside their true feelings about the incumbent (and ignore the fact that their vote is unlikely to make a difference to the outcome of the election) and make the effort to vote. In doing so, they are trying to avoid being the reason their municipality misses out on a large prize. If this is the case, then it follows that within district-years, municipalities that concentrate larger shares of votes cast on a *single* LDP winner will have higher turnout (as I show above), but municipalities that concentrate larger shares of votes on the LDP per se, whether this means delivering more votes to LDP winners (plural) or to LDP candidates (both winners and losers), will not necessarily have higher turnout. Put differently, a municipality that delivers more

8.2 Concentrating Votes Increases Turnout

votes to the LDP *could* have higher turnout, but only if those votes are *concentrated* on a single LDP winner.[14]

To examine these observable implications of the theory, I constructed:

$$\text{All LDP Winners VS}_{m,t} = \frac{\sum_{c \in m}\{LDP_{c,t} w_{c,t} v_{c,m,t}\}}{v_{m,t}}. \quad (8.3)$$

In words, this takes the number of votes received by all LDP winners in municipality m at time t, takes the sum of these, and divides this by the total number of valid votes cast in the municipality. To obtain a high value on All LDP Winners $VS_{m,t}$, municipalities must send more of the votes cast to LDP winners; however the distribution of votes among those LDP winners is arranged. In addition, I constructed:

$$\text{All LDP Candidates VS}_{m,t} = \frac{\sum_{c \in m}\{LDP_{c,t} v_{c,m,t}\}}{v_{m,t}}. \quad (8.4)$$

In words, this takes the number of votes received by all LDP candidates in municipality m at time t, takes the sum of these, and divides this by the total number of valid votes cast in the municipality. To obtain a high value on All LDP Candidates $VS_{m,t}$, municipalities must cast more votes for LDP candidates, regardless of whether those candidates win or lose and however the distribution of votes among them is arranged.

Table 8.4 presents two-way fixed effect regression models of Turnout$_{m,t}$ in the five Lower House elections held between 1980 and 1993. All specifications control for time-varying municipality-level characteristics that might matter for turnout, including turnout in the previous election, as well as district-year and municipality fixed effects. In Model 1, the independent variable of interest is All LDP Winners $VS_{m,t}$. Its coefficient is positive but not statistically significant. Thus, there is no evidence that municipalities delivering larger shares of votes cast to LDP winners per se had higher turnout than municipalities delivering smaller shares of votes cast to these winners. Whereas Table 8.2 showed that concentrating votes on a single LDP winner produces higher turnout, Model 1 in Table 8.4 shows that sending more votes to LDP winners, *plural*, is not associated with higher turnout.

In Model 2, I examine the effect of All LDP Candidates $VS_{m,t}$. Its coefficient is negative and not statistically significant. Thus, municipalities

---

[14] In Chapter 6, my analyses relied on variables capturing levels of electoral support delivered to both a single LDP winner and all LDP winners. Both variables were found to have a positive, statistically significant relationship with postelection transfers. If most Japanese municipalities concentrate votes on a single LDP winner, as they are incentivized to do under the tournament, their values on the two support variables might not be sufficiently different to pick up differences in transfers, especially since transfers are not solely the prerogative of LDP politicians (they also involve bureaucrats).

Table 8.4 *Municipalities delivering more votes to the LDP per se, whether to all LDP winners (Model 1) or to all LDP candidates, winning and losing (Model 2), do not have higher turnout in Lower House elections, 1980–1993. Similarly, municipalities that concentrate more votes on a single LDP loser (Model 3) and municipalities that concentrate more votes on a non-LDP winner (Model 4) do not have higher turnout.*

	Dependent variable: Turnout$_{m,t}$			
	(Model 1)	(Model 2)	(Model 3)	(Model 4)
All LDP Winners VS$_{m,t}$	0.005			
	(0.003)			
All LDP Candidates VS$_{m,t}$		−0.001		
		(0.004)		
Single LDP Loser VS$_{m,t}$			−0.009**	
			(0.003)	
Single Non-LDP+ Winner VS$_{m,t}$				−0.006
				(0.004)
Turnout$_{m,t-1}$	−0.106***	−0.105***	−0.103***	−0.105***
	(0.013)	(0.013)	(0.013)	(0.013)
Fiscal Strength$_{m,t}$	0.014***	0.014***	0.014***	0.014***
	(0.004)	(0.004)	(0.004)	(0.004)
Dependent Population$_{m,t}$	0.052*	0.051*	0.051*	0.052*
	(0.022)	(0.022)	(0.022)	(0.022)
Farming Population$_{m,t}$	−0.051*	−0.053*	−0.051*	−0.054*
	(0.025)	(0.025)	(0.025)	(0.025)
Log(Population$_{m,t}$)	−0.086***	−0.086***	−0.086***	−0.087***
	(0.011)	(0.011)	(0.011)	(0.011)
Log(Per Capita Income$_{m,t}$)	0.008	0.007	0.008	0.008
	(0.005)	(0.005)	(0.005)	(0.005)
Population Density$_{m,t}$	0.021**	0.022***	0.021**	0.022***
	(0.007)	(0.007)	(0.007)	(0.007)
Observations	12,398	12,398	12,398	12,398
District-Year FE	Y	Y	Y	Y
Municipality FE	Y	Y	Y	Y
R^2	0.053	0.053	0.054	0.053

Robust standard errors clustered on municipality in parentheses.
*$p < 0.05$, **$p < 0.01$, ***$p < 0.001$.
Regression models estimated with R's plm() package.

that delivered larger shares of votes cast to LDP candidates, both winning and losing, do not have systematically higher turnout than municipalities in the same district-year that delivered smaller shares of votes cast to LDP candidates. This is line with my expectations and provides further support

8.2 Concentrating Votes Increases Turnout

for my claim that it is support for a single LDP winner, not support for the LDP per se.

Next, the theory leads us to expect that municipalities that concentrate larger shares of votes on a single LDP *winner* will have higher turnout (as I have shown), but municipalities that concentrate larger shares of votes on a single LDP candidate who *loses* the election are unlikely to exhibit higher turnout. Why? To realize the kind of intense competition between municipalities over which will emerge as the most supportive, which is what encourages more and more voters in highly supportive municipalities to turn out, a candidate must be able to make her promises to influence central government bureaucrats credible. Any question mark over her ability to win the election reduces the credibility of those promises, which harms her ability to create this competition. In support of this, the analyses in Chapter 6 revealed that NTD allocations were not a function of how much municipalities supported their LDP candidate when those candidates lost the election.

To examine whether it is LDP candidates who win the election who are able to transform voting into a competition, and not those who lose, I constructed:

$$\text{Single LDP Loser VS}_{m,t} = \frac{max_{c \in m}\{LDP_{c,t}(1 - w_{c,t})v_{c,m,t}\}}{v_{m,t}}. \quad (8.5)$$

This takes the number of votes received by losing LDP candidates in the municipality at time t, identifies the losing LDP candidate who won the largest number of votes in the municipality, and divides the number of votes won by this candidate by the total number of votes cast in the municipality. To obtain a high value on Single LDP Loser VS$_{m,t}$, municipalities have to cast more of their votes, however many are cast, for a single LDP loser.

In Table 8.4's Model 3, I examine the effect of Single LDP Loser VS$_{m,t}$. Its coefficient is negative and statistically significant, in line with my expectations. This means that municipalities that concentrate larger shares of votes on a single LDP loser tend to have systematically *lower* turnout than same-district municipalities that concentrate smaller shares of votes on a single LDP loser. This is evidence that LDP candidates who lose the election are unable to create the kind of competition among supportive municipalities that translates into higher turnout. Indeed, the fact that municipalities concentrating larger shares of votes on a single LDP loser appear to have *lower* turnout makes sense because municipalities concentrating smaller shares of votes on an LDP candidate who loses are likely concentrating larger shares of votes on an LDP candidate who wins, and I expect that those municipalities experience higher turnout.

Finally, the evidence thus far suggests that tournaments are the preserve of LDP winners, not winners from the opposition parties. Chapter 6 confirmed that opposition winners do not seem able to direct money to supportive municipalities, even when they constituted the government after the 2009 election. Thus, we are unlikely to observe municipalities concentrating larger shares of votes cast on *non*-LDP winners exhibiting systematically higher turnout. However, I need to also be mindful of the finding in Chapter 6 that LDP-aligned *independent* winners, who were admitted into the LDP after the election, were granted access to central government resources after their victory and engaged in GBC in the exact same manner as ordinary LDP winners (who had gained the party's nomination prior to the election). In that chapter, I constructed LDP+$_{c,t}$ to indicate whether candidate c was either a member of the LDP at the time of the election or a conservative-aligned independent who joined the LDP after the election. Using this same variable, I constructed:

$$\text{Single Non-LDP+ Winner VS}_{m,t} = \frac{max_{c \in m}\{(1 - LDP+_{c,t})w_{c,t}v_{c,m,t}\}}{v_{m,t}}.$$
(8.6)

This takes the number of votes received by candidates who were *neither* an LDP winner *nor* an independent winner admitted into the LDP after the election in the municipality at time t, identifies the (non-LDP+) winner who won the largest number of votes, and divides the number of votes won by this candidate by the total number of votes cast in the municipality. To obtain a high value on Single Non-LDP+ Winner VS$_{m,t}$, municipalities have to cast more of their votes, however many are cast, for a single non-LDP (or LDP-aligned independent) winner.

In Table 8.4's Model 4, I examine the effect of Single Non-LDP+ Winner VS$_{m,t}$. Its coefficient is negative and not statistically significant. Thus, in line with my expectations, municipalities concentrating larger shares of votes on a non-LDP winner did not have higher turnout. This is further evidence that opposition winners do not engage in GBC.

8.2.3 After Electoral Reform, 1996–2014

Next, I turn to the 1996–2014 period. In this period (and since), Japan has been using a MMM system, in which a portion of candidates are elected via first-past-the-post in single-seat districts and another portion are elected from party lists in regional blocs via closed-list proportional representation. As Chapter 5 explains, whereas 91% of electoral districts were tournament-possible under the preelectoral reform period, this dropped to around 73% in the 1996, 2000, and 2003 elections,

8.2 Concentrating Votes Increases Turnout

around 62% in the 2005 election, and then around 50% in the 2009, 2012, and 2014 elections. Thus, the analyses in this section pertains to a smaller share of electoral districts.

As I explained in Chapter 6, the post-1994 period was characterized by instability in the boundaries of both municipalities and electoral districts. By 2005, 61% of the municipalities in existence in 2000 had undergone an amalgamation that had resulted in profound changes to its borders. In addition, two redistricting plans, one carried out prior to the 2003 election and the other carried out prior to the 2014 election, resulted in a redrawing of the boundaries of numerous electoral districts. Thus, in addition to changes to their *own* borders, many municipalities found themselves in one electoral district in one election, with one set of competitors, and then in a different electoral district in the next election, with a different set of competitors. Even in the absence of changes to the borders of one's own electoral district, if some of the municipalities in that district had merged between two elections, the arrangement of voters into municipalities would have changed. Chapter 4 explained why this variable – the degree of asymmetry in municipality size – is expected to matter enormously for both the overall support an LDP incumbent can hope to muster in a district and the amount of resources needed to muster it. This was corroborated with the analyses in Chapter 7.

For my purpose, these boundary changes mean that in contrast to the 1980–1993 period, I do not have a set of municipalities whose borders remained the same and whose competitors in the tournament also remained the same for a period of consecutive elections. For this reason, I implement the same regressions as above but rely on the lagged dependent variable to control for the possibility that underlying differences between municipalities could be driving my results, not municipality fixed effects. Table 8.5 presents the results of fixed effect regressions of Turnout$_{m,t}$ in the seven Lower House elections held between 1996 and 2014 as a function of Single LDP Winner VS$_{m,t}$ (Model 1) and Rank(Single LDP Winner VS$_{m,t}$) (Model 3), respectively. In both specifications, I control for turnout in the previous Lower House election and same six time-varying municipality-level characteristics that may matter for vote concentration and turnout. I include district-year fixed effects and report robust standard errors clustered on municipality.

The coefficients on both indicators of vote concentration are positive and statistically significant. Thus, controlling for other features of municipalities with consequences for turnout, including turnout in the previous election, I find that municipalities that concentrated larger shares of votes

Table 8.5 *Municipalities that concentrate more votes on a single LDP winner have higher turnout in Lower House elections, 1996–2014.*

	Dependent variable: Turnout$_{m,t}$	
	(1)	(2)
Single LDP Winner VS$_{m,t}$	0.033***	
	(0.005)	
Rank(Single LDP Winner VS$_{m,t}$)		0.005***
		(0.001)
Turnout$_{m,t-1}$	0.728***	0.733***
	(0.011)	(0.012)
Fiscal Strength$_{m,t}$	−0.008***	−0.008***
	(0.002)	(0.002)
Dependent Population$_{m,t}$	0.189***	0.213***
	(0.015)	(0.015)
Farming Population$_{m,t}$	0.004	0.009
	(0.007)	(0.008)
Log(Population$_{m,t}$)	−0.008***	−0.009***
	(0.0004)	(0.001)
Log(Per Capita Income$_{m,t}$)	0.024***	0.025***
	(0.003)	(0.003)
Population Density$_{m,t}$	0.001***	0.002***
	(0.0003)	(0.0004)
Observations	12,538	8,597
District-Year FE	Y	Y
R^2	0.781	0.791

Robust standard errors clustered on municipality in parentheses.
***$p < 0.001$.
Regression models estimated with R's plm() package.

on a single LDP winner tended to have higher turnout than their same-district counterparts that concentrated smaller shares of votes on a single LDP winner. Substantively, the coefficient on Single LDP Winner VS$_{m,t}$ in Model 1 tells us that a one-standard-deviation increase in voting concentration is expected to translate into a 1% increase in turnout. The sample mean of Turnout$_{m,t}$ in this period was 0.66, meaning that on average, 66% of eligible voters in a municipality turned out to vote. Again, this is the *average* effect of increases in voting concentration; I expect increases in voting concentration to produce even larger increases in turnout among municipalities already concentrating many votes on LDP winners (examined below).

8.2 Concentrating Votes Increases Turnout

8.2.4 Competing Explanations and Placebo Tests

As I explained above, the theory expects that LDP candidates who win the election would have been able to create the perception that resource allocations, at least among highly supportive municipalities, are poised on a knife edge. It is this *perception*, that one's vote could determine whether one's municipality wins a large prize or has to settle for a smaller one, that drives up turnout. It is much less likely, in contrast, that LDP candidates who lose the election and winning candidates from other parties would have been able to create a similar perception. In support of this, my analyses in Chapter 6 found that winning LDP candidates were able to lean on central government bureaucrats in ways that translated into resources being a function of support, but neither their losing LDP counterparts nor their winning non-LDP counterparts were able to do so. Thus, the theory expects that within electoral districts, municipalities concentrating more votes on a single LDP winner will have higher turnout (as I have shown), but there will be no such relationship between concentrating votes on losing LDP candidates and concentrating votes on non-LDP winners, respectively, and turnout.

In Table 8.6, I present fixed effect regression models of Turnout$_{m,t}$ in the seven Lower House elections held between 1996 and 2014. In all specifications, I control for turnout in the previous Lower House election and same six time-varying municipality-level characteristics that I think might matter for both vote concentration and turnout. I include district-year fixed effects and report robust standard errors clustered on municipality. In Model 1, I limit observations to municipalities in the 458 district-years without LDP winners (defined as districts in which the LDP candidate did not place first). My variable of interest is Single LDP Loser VS$_{m,t}$, which is the number of votes cast for the losing LDP candidate, divided by the total number of valid votes cast in the municipality. This variable captures the degree to which municipalities concentrated their votes on the district's losing LDP candidate. Its coefficient is negative and not statistically significant. Thus, concentrating votes on an LDP candidate who loses the election is not associated with higher turnout.

In Model 2, I limit observations to municipalities in the 145 district-years in which the LDP candidate lost the electoral district but managed to enter parliament via PR. As I explained in Chapter 6, this set of LDP candidates lost the election by relatively narrow margins. Of all losing LDP candidates, these candidates were the ones who came closest to winning their districts. My analyses in Chapter 6 suggested that in these districts, postelection resource allocations were not a function of electoral support. Consistent with this, the coefficient on Single LDP Loser VS$_{m,t}$ in

Table 8.6 *Municipalities concentrating more votes on losing LDP candidates (Models 1 and 2) and DPJ winners (Model 3) do not have higher turnout in Lower House elections, 1996–2014.*

	Dependent variable: Turnout$_{m,t}$		
	(Model 1) (LDP Candidate Loses SSD)	(Model 2) (LDP Candidate Loses SSD, Wins PR Seat)	(Model 3) (DPJ Candidate Wins SSD)
Single LDP Loser VS$_{m,t}$	−0.014 (0.009)	−0.008 (0.014)	
Single DPJ Winner VS$_{m,t}$			0.004 (0.011)
Turnout$_{m,t-1}$	0.724*** (0.020)	0.683*** (0.044)	0.722*** (0.025)
Fiscal Strength$_{m,t}$	−0.007** (0.002)	−0.009 (0.005)	−0.002 (0.003)
Dependent Population$_{m,t}$	0.141*** (0.028)	0.172*** (0.052)	0.078* (0.030)
Farming Population$_{m,t}$	0.004 (0.013)	0.008 (0.021)	0.009 (0.015)
Log(Population$_{m,t}$)	−0.008*** (0.001)	−0.009*** (0.002)	−0.005*** (0.001)
Log(Per Capita Income$_{m,t}$)	0.021*** (0.006)	0.018* (0.009)	0.015* (0.008)
Population Density$_{m,t}$	0.001* (0.0004)	0.001* (0.001)	−0.0003 (0.0003)
Observations	3,941	1,199	2,091
District-Year FE	Y	Y	Y
R^2	0.756	0.768	0.785

Robust standard errors clustered on municipality in parentheses.
*$p < 0.05$, **$p < 0.01$, ***$p < 0.001$.
Regression models estimated with R's plm() package.

Model 2 is similarly negative and not statistically significant. The absence of a relationship between vote concentration and turnout in municipalities in these districts is consistent with the theory's expectation that losing LDP candidates find it difficult to create the perception in supportive municipalities that every vote counts, due to its potential to bring about a sizeable increase in its resource allocation.

In Model 3, I limit observations to municipalities in the 280 district-years with Democratic Party of Japan (DPJ) winners (defined as districts

8.3 Relationship between Vote Concentration & Turnout

in which the DPJ candidate placed first). Let $DPJ_{c,t}$ indicate whether candidate c was a member of DPJ at time t. Using a similar equation as above, I constructed:

$$\text{Single DPJ Winner VS}_{m,t} = \frac{max_{c \in m}\{DPJ_{c,t} w_{c,t} v_{c,m,t}\}}{v_{m,t}}. \quad (8.7)$$

In words, this takes the number of votes received by the DPJ winner in municipality m at time t, and divides this by the number of valid votes cast in the municipality. This variable captures the degree to which municipalities concentrated their votes on the district's winning DPJ candidate. Its coefficient is positive but not statistically significant. This is further evidence that winning DPJ candidates did not contest elections by dangling the promise of ever-larger resource allocations over the heads of voters in supportive municipalities, which is the mechanism that produces the positive relationship between concentrating votes on district winners and turnout in LDP-won districts.

8.3 A CONVEX RELATIONSHIP BETWEEN VOTE CONCENTRATION AND TURNOUT

Next, we move to Hypothesis 6. Here, I am interested in whether, within electoral districts, the relationship between concentrating votes on a single LDP winner and turnout is *convex*, rather than linear. The theory holds that LDP politicians can amass enough votes to win by pitting municipalities against each other in a competition for resources. By offering the largest prize to the most supportive municipality, the second-largest prize to the second-most supportive municipality, and so on, and making the difference in amounts received larger at higher ranks, politicians can create a situation where handfuls of votes in relatively supportive municipalities can mean the difference between a large prize and a much smaller one. This gives voters in those municipalities incentives to set aside their personal feelings about the incumbent and think primarily about the degree of influence their vote wields over the size of their municipality's prize.

In Chapter 6, I found that the distribution of postelection resource allocations within electoral districts exhibited this pattern: Namely, further increases in electoral support among municipalities that were already very supportive yielded much a larger increase in postelection resource allocations than a similar increase in electoral support among municipalities that were less supportive. I expect to observe a similar relationship between electoral support and turnout: Namely, I expect that turnout will rise at an increasing rate as municipalities concentrate more and more

How Tournaments Impact Decisions to Vote

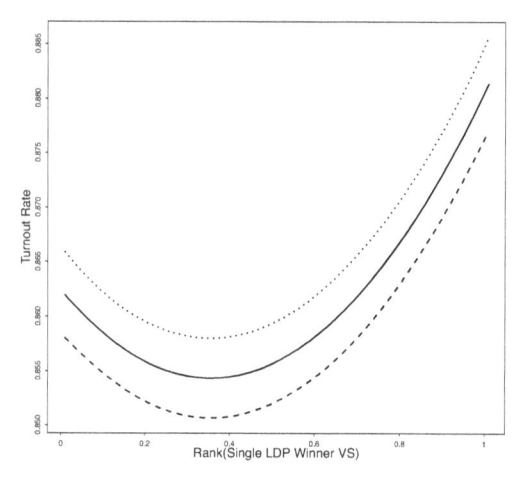

Figure 8.1 The relationship between rank and turnout is convex, 1980–2014. Predicted values (with 95% confidence intervals) from a regression of turnout in Japanese municipalities in the twelve Lower House elections held between 1980 and 2014 on a cubic specification of Rank(Single LDP Winner VS$_{m,t}$), municipality-level controls, and district-year fixed effects.

votes on a single LDP winner. Put differently, a municipality experiencing a one-unit increase in vote concentration at the top of the ranking will experience a larger increase in turnout than a municipality experiencing the same one-unit increase in vote concentration at the middle or bottom of the ranking. This would be evidence that decisions to vote are being influenced by the size of the prize one's group stands to win.

In Table A.16, I present the result of a fixed effect regression of Turnout$_{m,t}$ as a function of Rank(Single LDP Winner VS$_{m,t}$), as well as its quadratic and cubic transformations, for all municipalities in the twelve Lower House elections held between 1980 and 2014. As I explained in Chapter 6, a joint hypothesis test can tell us whether the coefficients on my measure of vote concentration, as well as its quadratic and cubic transformations, are jointly significant. The model controls for time-varying municipality-level characteristics that matter for turnout, as well as district-year fixed effects. I report robust standard errors clustered on municipality.

The joint hypothesis test is statistically significant. This is evidence that the relationship between concentrating votes on a single LDP winner and turnout is not linear. To visually depict the convexity, Figure 8.1 plots predicted values and 95% confidence intervals from the regression model in Table A.16. The figure shows that once a municipality is at the median or above in terms of vote concentration (0.5–1 on the *x*-axis), the effects of further increases in rank (vote concentration) increase at an increasing rate. For municipalities at the very top of the ranking, the

8.4 Competitiveness Depends on Vote Concentration

returns to further increases in vote concentration are the largest. Substantively, a municipality that increases its Rank(Single LDP Winner VS$_{m,t}$) from 0.95 to 1, for example, can expect an increase in turnout of 0.40%. The same increase in rank translates into smaller increases in turnout among municipalities at lower ranks. A municipality that increases its Rank(Single LDP Winner VS$_{m,t}$) from 0.8 to 0.85 can expect an increase in turnout of 0.30%, while a municipality that increases its Rank(Single LDP Winner VS$_{m,t}$) from 0.5 to 0.55 can only expect an increase in turnout of 0.11%.[15]

8.4 IMPACT OF COMPETITIVENESS DEPENDS ON VOTE CONCENTRATION

While the above tests held all variables operating at the level of the district-year constant and examined the relationship between support for a single LDP winner and turnout among municipalities in the same district-year, we can also harness the variation at this level to devise further tests of Hypothesis 5.

As I mentioned above, a large literature has established that more voters go the polls when a race is projected to be close. One reason for this is that when a race is close, a single voter stands more of a chance of influencing who wins. For incumbents seeking reelection, the fact that many voters lack a compelling reason to make the effort to turn out unless they expect the race to be close presents a problem, the severity of which only worsens as incumbents gain in experience and electoral security. The problem facing incumbents is: How can they motivate enough people to turn out and vote for them, election after election, even with the knowledge that their vote wields little-to-no influence over who wins? GBC more generally, and the form it takes with a dominant party, a tournament, presents a solution to this problem. By making the allocation of government resources a function of electoral support and calibrating the amounts received such that the most supportive municipalities stand to receive significantly more money with only a few more votes, incumbents are able to increase the amount of influence wielded by a single vote. Individual votes continue to wield little-to-no influence over *who wins the election*, but individual votes in supportive municipalities now wield an extraordinary degree of influence on another dimension: the amount of *resources* one's municipality receives.

---

[15] The same convex relationship is visible when observations are limited to the preelectoral and postelectoral reform periods.

This leads to the expectation that, across electoral districts, turnout will be higher in races projected to be competitive. But within electoral districts, the tournament theory leads us to expect that projections of competitiveness will have a *heterogeneous* impact on turnout rates, depending on where in the ranking a given municipality is likely to end up. In municipalities that are highly supportive of the incumbent, the competition for resources has magnified the influence of a single vote and decisions to turn out are primarily motivated by attempts to influence the size of the municipality's prize. As such, projections of increased competitiveness are expected to exert a smaller impact on turnout. In municipalities that are less-supportive of the incumbent, in contrast, the influence of a single vote has not been magnified in the same way. In these municipalities, decisions to turn out will be less motivated by the desire to influence the amount of resources received by one's municipality. As such, projections of closeness are likely to exert a larger impact on turnout.

To examine this, it would be ideal to have measures of district-level competitiveness derived in advance of elections, which reflected perceptions in the electorate to how competitive the upcoming race was going to be. I could then see whether, in electoral districts where races were projected to be competitive, turnout increased *less* in municipalities that are highly supportive of the incumbent than in municipalities that are less supportive. In lieu of an independently derived measure, I compute the variable $\text{Margin}_{d,t}$. As I explained above, this is the margin of victory of the "last" winner in a district-year.[16] Critically, I use $\text{Margin}_{d,t}$ as a proxy for how competitive voters *anticipated* that the race would be in their district. Thus, if a district has a large $\text{Margin}_{d,t}$ (indicating a *less* competitive election), I assume that voters knew the race would be less competitive when they made their decisions to vote. Similarly, if a district has a small $\text{Margin}_{d,t}$ (indicating a *more* competitive election), I assume that voters knew the race would be competitive when they made their decisions to vote.[17]

In Table 8.7, I present the results of two-way fixed effect regressions of Japanese municipalities in the twelve Lower House elections held between 1980 and 2014. In both models, the dependent variable is turnout in municipality m ($\text{Turnout}_{m,t}$). In Model 1, my independent variable of interest is $\text{Margin}_{d,t}$, which is measured at the level of the district-year and is therefore identical for all municipalities in a given district-year.

[16] In an SSD, this is the difference in votes received by the winner and loser; in a multi-seat district, it is the difference in votes received by the nth-placed candidate and the $n + 1$-placed candidate, where n is district magnitude.
[17] Because $\text{Margin}_{d,t}$ is measured after votes have been cast, it is possible that voters anticipated a close election, but the outcome was not one, or vice versa. A stronger test of this hypotheses would use survey or other data to derive this measure.

8.4 Competitiveness Depends on Vote Concentration

Higher values of Margin$_{d,t}$ indicate *less* competitive elections. In Model 2, I am interested in the effect of Margin$_{d,t}$, Rank(Single LDP Winner VS$_{m,t}$) (the independent variable from above), and their interaction. Both models control for the same time-varying municipality-level characteristics that might influence the relationship between vote concentration and turnout, including turnout in the previous Lower House election. Both models also use municipality fixed effects to control for the possibility that time-invariant features of municipalities could be driving any relationship I find, and year fixed effects to control for systematic features of a given election year that could influence turnout in all municipalities.

Importantly, the models in Table 8.7 are different from those presented earlier in this chapter in that they do not use district-year fixed effects. Above, I was interested in comparing municipalities in the same district-year. A district-year fixed effect enabled me to control for all the ways district-years differ from each other. Here, I am interested in leveraging variation that occurs at the level of the district-year (the competitiveness of the race). I want to compare municipalities in competitive races with otherwise-similar municipalities in less competitive races. My first question of interest is whether, controlling for other differences between municipalities, decreases in competitiveness (increases in margin) decrease turnout (Model 1). My second question of interest is whether, controlling for other differences between municipalities, decreases in competitiveness (increases in margin) decrease turnout *less* in highly supportive municipalities (Model 2).

Because I am not using district-year fixed effects, I need to control for other features of district-years that might exert a systematic effect on competitiveness, vote concentration, and turnout. In addition to year fixed effects, which also control for the fact that two different electoral systems were used during this time, I control for population per seat (the degree to which the district is malapportioned), the number of seats available (district magnitude), the number of candidates running in the district, and the number of LDP candidates running in the district. I also control for the degree of asymmetry in municipality size, which the previous chapter showed matters for the overall level of support LDP winners can hope to muster in a district.[18] I report robust standard errors clustered on the municipality.

In Model 1, the coefficient on Margin$_{d,t}$ is negative and statistically significant. This means that, controlling for time-invariant and time-varying features of municipalities, time-varying features of a municipality's district, and differences across elections, municipalities in districts in which

---

[18] District-level variables were described in Chapter 7.

Table 8.7 *Increases in competitiveness impact turnout differently, depending on how supportive a municipality is for its LDP winner, 1980–2014.*

	Dependent variable: Turnout$_{m,t}$	
	(Model 1)	(Model 2)
Margin$_{d,t}$	−0.123***	−0.155***
	(0.003)	(0.005)
Rank(Single LDP Winner VS$_{m,t}$)		−0.002
		(0.001)
Margin$_{d,t}$:Rank(Single LDP Winner VS$_{m,t}$)		0.057***
		(0.008)
Turnout$_{m,t-1}$	0.271***	0.221***
	(0.009)	(0.010)
Fiscal Strength$_{m,t}$	0.005	0.005
	(0.004)	(0.004)
Dependent Population$_{m,t}$	0.296***	0.293***
	(0.017)	(0.019)
Farming Population$_{m,t}$	0.053*	0.046
	(0.022)	(0.025)
Log(Population$_{m,t}$)	−0.021***	−0.034***
	(0.005)	(0.006)
Log(Per Capita Income$_{m,t}$)	0.019***	0.016**
	(0.005)	(0.005)
Population Density$_{m,t}$	0.039***	0.050***
	(0.006)	(0.007)
HI$_{d,t}$	0.011*	0.012
	(0.005)	(0.007)
Log(Number of Municipalities$_{d,t}$)	−0.004*	−0.005*
	(0.002)	(0.002)
People Per Seat$_{d,t}$	−0.002***	−0.004***
	(0.001)	(0.001)
Number LDP Candidates$_{d,t}$	0.008***	0.008***
	(0.001)	(0.001)
Number of Candidates$_{d,t}$	0.004***	0.005***
	(0.0003)	(0.0003)
Total Seats$_{d,t}$	−0.005***	−0.007***
	(0.001)	(0.001)
Observations	24,936	20,885
Municipality Fixed Effects	Y	Y
Year Fixed Effects	Y	Y
R^2	0.276	0.272

Increases in margin separating winner from loser (*decreases* in competitiveness) have a negative impact on turnout in municipalities in Lower House elections, 1980–2014 (Model 1). However, they have a *smaller* negative impact in municipalities positioned to do well in the tournament (those concentrating larger shares of the vote on a single LDP winner) (Model 2).

Robust standard errors clustered on municipality in parentheses.
*$p < 0.05$, **$p < 0.01$, ***$p < 0.001$.
Regression models estimated with R's plm() package.

8.4 Competitiveness Depends on Vote Concentration

the margin separating the last winner and first loser is larger – indicating a *less* competitive election – have *lower* turnout. My use of municipality fixed effects means that I can interpret this as the effect of increases in margin (decreases in district-level competitiveness) within the same municipality over time. The negative, statistically significant coefficient on Margin$_{d,t}$ means that when the same municipality is in a district with a larger margin separating last winner from first loser (a *safer* district), its turnout rate is lower than when it is in a district with a smaller margin (a *competitive* district). Substantively, the coefficient on Margin$_{d,t}$ in Model 1 tells us that a one-standard-deviation increase in Margin$_{d,t}$ is expected to depress turnout by 1.80%. Thus, the competitiveness of races in Japan systematically affects turnout, as it does elsewhere.

In Model 2, I am interested in whether Margin$_{d,t}$ exerts a systematically *different* effect on turnout, depending on whether the municipality concentrates a large share of votes on a single LDP winner, which puts it in the running for a large prize after the election, or concentrates a small share of votes on a single LDP winner, which would put it out of contention for a large prize. The coefficient on Margin$_{d,t}$ remains negative and statistically significant, while the coefficient on Margin$_{d,t}$ * Rank(Single LDP Winner VS$_{m,t}$) is positive and statistically significant. This means that the effect of district-level competitiveness is, in fact, different, depending on the degree to which a municipality concentrates votes on a single LDP winner.

For municipalities whose Rank(Single LDP Winner VS$_{m,t}$) is 0, meaning they ranked last in their district in terms of identifying with a single LDP winner, the effect of a one-unit increase in Margin$_{d,t}$ on turnout is −0.155.[19] Substantively, for the least supportive municipality in the district, a one-standard-deviation increase in Margin$_{d,t}$ (a decrease in competitiveness) is expected to lower turnout by 2.33%. In contrast, for municipalities whose Rank(Single LDP Winner VS$_{m,t}$) is 1, meaning they ranked first in terms of identifying with a single LDP winner, the effect of a one-unit increase in Margin$_{d,t}$ on turnout is −0.098.[20] Substantively, for municipalities at the highest rank, a one-standard-deviation increase in Margin$_{d,t}$ (a decrease in competitiveness) is expected to lower turnout by 1.47%. Thus, while decreases in competitiveness have a negative effect on turnout in all municipalities, decreases in competitiveness have a *larger* negative effect on turnout in municipalities not slated to do well in the tournament.

Figure 8.2 plots the average marginal effect of Margin$_{d,t}$, with 95% confidence intervals, at different levels of Rank(Single LDP

---

[19] $-0.155 + (0.057 * 0) = -0.155$.
[20] $-0.155 + (0.057 * 1) = -0.098$.

How Tournaments Impact Decisions to Vote

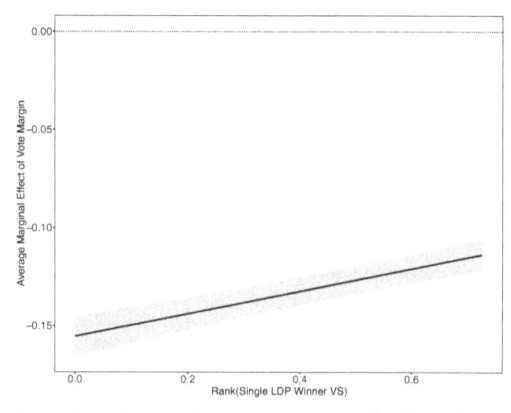

Figure 8.2 The black line depicts the average marginal effect of Margin$_{d,t}$, with 95% confidence intervals, at different levels of Rank(Single LDP Winner VS$_{m,t}$). Estimates are from Model 2 of Table 8.7.

Winner VS$_{m,t}$). Among the relatively unsupportive municipalities (lower values of Rank(Single LDP Winner VS$_{m,t}$)), the effect of increases in Margin$_{d,t}$ (decreases in competitiveness) on turnout is more negative than among the relatively supportive municipalities (higher values of Rank(Single LDP Winner VS$_{m,t}$)).[21]

It is worth pointing out that, for the most part, the direction and effects of the district-level controls is consistent with the existing literature. The coefficient on People Per Seat is negative and statistically significant. This indicates that, controlling for other differences between municipalities, both in their own characteristics and in characteristics of their districts, municipalities in districts with more people per representative (meaning larger electorate sizes) have lower turnout. The coefficient on Total Seats is also negative and statistically significant. This means that on average, municipalities in districts with larger district magnitude have lower turnout. The coefficients on Number of Candidates and Number of LDP Candidates are both positive and statistically significant, indicating that on average, municipalities in districts with more candidates running and districts with more LDP candidates running, respectively, have higher turnout. District-level asymmetry, my variable of interest in Chapter 7, is positively related to turnout in Model 1, but not in Model 2. In Chapter 7, we found that district-level asymmetry lowers support for the LDP. If this is the case, then these districts may produce more competitive races. To the extent they do so, any effects of this variable may be captured by Margin$_{d,t}$.

---

[21] The same relationship between variables is present when observations are limited to the preelectoral and postelectoral reform periods.

8.4 Competitiveness Depends on Vote Concentration

8.4.1 Competing Explanations

In line with the theory, the above analyses demonstrated that the impact of district-level competitiveness on turnout is different at different levels of voting concentration. An intriguing finding about elections in Japan, at least under the old electoral system, is that competitiveness exerts a larger impact on turnout in rural areas, where social ties are denser (Cox, Rosenbluth and Thies 1998). The authors studied this in a regression with electoral districts as observations and interacted the competitiveness of the race in each district with measures of the electoral district's ruralness. This represents a confounder that I ought to take seriously: Could my finding that the impact of competitiveness is different at different levels of identification with a single LDP winner be explained by the fact that the impact of competitiveness is also different at different levels of ruralness?

In Table 8.8, I present the results of two-way fixed effect regression models of Japanese municipalities in the twelve Lower House elections held between 1980 and 2014. In both models, the dependent variable is Turnout$_{m,t}$. Both models control for the same time-varying municipality-level characteristics as above, including turnout in the previous election; the same time-varying district-level characteristics as above; and use year fixed effects and municipality fixed effects (also as above). I report robust standard errors clustered on the municipality.

In Model 1, I use an interaction between Margin$_{d,t}$ and Population Density to examine whether their findings hold in my data, in which observations are municipalities (not districts) in the entire period (not just prior to 1993). I find that the coefficient on Margin$_{d,t}$ is negative and statistically significant, while the coefficient on Margin$_{d,t}$*Population Density is positive and statistically significant. Thus, the impact of district-level competitiveness on turnout does appear to be *different*, depending on ruralness. Substantively, for the least dense municipality in my sample (with 1.3 people per square kilometer), a one-standard-deviation increase in Margin$_{d,t}$ (the district becomes less competitive) is estimated to decrease turnout by 1.88%. For the most dense municipality in my sample (19,275 people per square kilometer), the same one-standard-deviation increase in Margin$_{d,t}$ is estimated to decrease turnout by only 1.29%. Thus, while declines in competitiveness (increases in Margin$_{d,t}$ separating winner from loser) negatively impacts turnout everywhere, they have a larger negative effect in the most dense (rural) municipalities. This is what Cox, Rosenbluth and Thies (1998) found at district level.

In Model 2, I include both the interaction of interest from Table 8.7 (Model 1) which was Margin$_{d,t}$* Rank(Single LDP Winner VS$_{m,t}$),

Table 8.8 *Increases in margin separating winner from loser (decreases in competitiveness) have a larger negative impact on turnout in rural (less population dense) municipalities (Model 1). My finding that increases in margin have a smaller negative impact on turnout in municipalities slated to do well in the tournament is not explained by this (Model 2).*

	Dependent variable: Turnout$_{m,t}$	
	(Model 1)	(Model 2)
Margin$_{d,t}$	−0.129***	−0.166***
	(0.003)	(0.005)
Population Density$_{m,t}$	0.035***	0.044***
	(0.006)	(0.007)
Rank(Single LDP Winner VS$_{m,t}$)		−0.003*
		(0.001)
Margin$_{d,t}$:Population Density$_{m,t}$	0.011***	0.017***
	(0.002)	(0.004)
Margin$_{d,t}$:Rank(Single LDP Winner VS$_{m,t}$)		0.065***
		(0.008)
Turnout$_{m,t-1}$	0.271***	0.221***
	(0.009)	(0.010)
Fiscal Strength$_{m,t}$	0.006	0.007
	(0.004)	(0.004)
Dependent Population$_{m,t}$	0.293***	0.287***
	(0.016)	(0.019)
Farming Population$_{m,t}$	0.041	0.033
	(0.022)	(0.024)
Log(Population$_{m,t}$)	−0.023***	−0.037***
	(0.005)	(0.006)
Log(Per Capita Income$_{m,t}$)	0.021***	0.018***
	(0.005)	(0.005)
HI$_{d,t}$	0.011*	0.011
	(0.005)	(0.007)
Log(Number of Municipalities$_{d,t}$)	−0.004*	−0.004*
	(0.002)	(0.002)
People Per Seat$_{d,t}$	−0.002***	−0.004***
	(0.001)	(0.001)
Number LDP Candidates$_{d,t}$	0.008***	0.007***
	(0.001)	(0.001)
Number of Candidates$_{d,t}$	0.004***	0.005***
	(0.0003)	(0.0003)
Total Seats$_{d,t}$	−0.006***	−0.007***
	(0.001)	(0.001)
Observations	24,936	20,885
Municipality Fixed Effects	Y	Y
Year Fixed Effects	Y	Y
R^2	0.278	0.274

Robust standard errors clustered on municipality in parentheses.
**$p < 0.01$, ***$p < 0.001$.
Regression models estimated with R's plm() package.

8.5 Takeaways for Japanese Politics

and the interaction of interest from Table 8.8 (Model 1) which was Margin$_{d,t}$*Population Density. The coefficient on Margin$_{d,t}$ remains negative and statistically significant, while the coefficient on Margin$_{d,t}$* Rank(Single LDPWinner VS$_{m,t}$) remains positive and statistically significant. For a municipality at the mean of population density (559 people per square kilometer), these coefficients tell us that the effect of a one-standard-deviation increase in Margin$_{d,t}$ on turnout in the municipality concentrating the least votes on a single LDP winner is −2.35%. In contrast, the effect of the same one-standard-deviation increase in Margin$_{d,t}$ in a municipality concentrating the most votes on a single LDP winner is 1.37%. The bottom line is, even if we control for the fact that the impact of competitiveness is conditional upon population density, with competitiveness increasing turnout more in rural municipalities than in urban areas, we still find that the impact of competitiveness is conditional upon the share of votes concentrated on a single LDP winner in the municipality. Municipalities ranked highest in support for their LDP incumbent are the least affected by increases or decreases in the competitiveness of the race.

8.5 TAKEAWAYS FOR JAPANESE POLITICS

We have found that turnout in Japanese elections is decisively influenced by the degree to which a voter's municipality identifies with a single LDP winner. Within electoral districts, as municipalities concentrate more votes on a single LDP winner, their turnout increases, with further increases in vote concentration among municipalities already concentrating large shares of their votes on a single LDP winner translating into even larger increases in turnout. The same relationship is not observed when municipalities concentrate more votes on a single winner from another party. Nor is it observed when municipalities concentrate more votes on a losing LDP candidate. Nor is it observed when municipalities spread their votes out across several LDP winners (possible in multiseat districts prior to 1994). The positive relationship between vote concentration and turnout in electoral districts with LDP winners is consistent with the tournament's expectation that many Japanese voters make their decisions to turn out with an eye to the amount of resources their municipality is slated to receive after the election.

This means that a portion of voters in Japan are making the effort to vote in order to receive an allocation of government resources that they anticipate their municipality might not receive if they did not make the effort to turn out. Whereas political scientists tend to believe that high turnout is indicative of a healthy democracy with an engaged populace, the findings in this chapter imply that high turnout may not be an unalloyed good. In some instances, it may be driven by a decidedly undemocratic competition for resources, in which voters are turning out and voting for their LDP incumbent not because they are partial to her policies or believe she is competent, but because they are unwilling to put their community's access to needed resources on the line. If the extent to which voters can turn their back on these incentives without material ramification is a function of how needy their community is, then the tournament creates a situation in which voters in communities that stand to benefit the *most* from well-structured, growth-oriented government policies are the ones with the least amount of voice. The ability of these voters to use elections to transmit their preferences to elected officials and hold those officials accountable for their actions has been curtailed.

9

Conclusion

In this book, I have argued that whenever members of an incumbent party have the ability to observe their vote tallies at the level of a group of voters within their electoral district and target resources at the same level, they will be able to implement group-based clientelism (GBC). By this, I mean that they will be able to *tie* the amount of government resources these groups receive after elections to the level of support the group gave the politician in the election. While the precise manner in which they will do this is likely to vary according to contextual factors such as whether their party is dominant, the broader point is that when politicians contest elections under this set of political institutions, it makes more sense for them to attempt to form clientelistic exchanges with *groups of voters*, whose votes are observable, than with individual voters, whose votes are never, or hardly ever, observable. This is because being able to observe levels of support from groups allows politicians to form exchanges with those groups that are *enforceable*. It will be relatively easy for the politician to discern how a group's support for her stacks up against that of other groups or whether it met or exceeded a particular target she set. Being unable to observe how individuals vote makes it extraordinarily difficult – indeed, virtually impossible – for politicians to form enforceable exchanges with individual voters.

In making this claim, I am advocating that scholars of clientelism reconsider their focus on what the literature calls "individual-based clientelism" and make room, theoretically and empirically, for further investigation of the possibility that, in settings satisfying these conditions, politicians form clientelistic relationships with groups. The evidence in this book shows that GBC has been an integral component of the electoral strategies of many politicians in Japan's ruling Liberal Democratic Party (LDP) since at least 1980, the first year in which I have data. Because the conditions that enable LDP politicians to conduct GBC do not appear to be Japan specific, and are shared by other countries, the findings in this book suggest that there is likely much to be gained from making the conceptual leap from politicians and individuals to politicians and groups. Such a leap has the potential to significantly advance our understanding of how incumbent political parties use the resources they control by virtue of being in government to lay the groundwork for their success in future elections. Establishing that they do this will then allow political scientists to devote concerted attention to the question of what effects this laying of the groundwork has on the quality of competition and by extension, the form and functioning of democracy.

I can point to two concrete examples of how a shift in focus from individuals to groups could further our understanding of how politicians use the targeted distribution of benefits around the time of elections. Once we consider the possibility that politicians are cultivating clientelistic relationships with *groups*, we can see that a type of material good scholars thought lay *outside* the purview of clientelism – namely, largess bestowed on *groups* of voters, otherwise known as club goods, pork-barrel politics, or partisan bias – could be being used clientelistically, in a manner that keeps groups tethered to their incumbents and restricts the freedom of choice of their members to vote for whomever they please. If this is the case, the bad news is that allocations of these goods may be posing a larger threat to democratic integrity and specifically, to the capacity of elections to serve as transmission belts of voter preferences than we realized. The good news, on the other hand, is that the clientelistic-*like* behaviors that we observe politicians engaging in, in which individuals are given a bag of rice or a small amount of cash in the hope this leads to a vote, may be posing *less* of a threat. It is not that these efforts to buy the votes of individuals are harmless, as they lead to obvious advantages for politicians with access to such goods. But they do not *take away* the freedom of voters to vote for whoever they choose the way "real clientelism" does, as a voter will always be able to claim that *they* supplied one of the votes the politician received, and the secret ballot means that the politician will not know the difference.

To offer another example, once we consider the possibility that politicians might be cultivating clientelistic relationships with groups, we can see that the structure of the electoral districts in which they are competing determines their ability to pull groups into such exchanges. To the extent that there is a consensus in the clientelism literature that political institutions cannot explain the demand for clientelism and exercise very little sway over whether the politicians in a given country will choose clientelistic versus programmatic linkages with voters, the theory and empirics in this book break with this consensus. GBC is only possible under a given set of political institutions. This gives us a clear answer to the question of

Conclusion

how to eradicate clientelism. With the caveat that it is never that simple, the findings of this book nevertheless suggest that when electoral districts are *not* divisible into groups of voters, at which electoral support is discernible and resources targetable, politicians might have no choice but to embrace qualitatively different electoral strategies, in which distributive politics, at least as it is targeted at groups of voters, plays less of a role.

In Japan between 1980 and 2014, two processes led to fundamental change in the structure of electoral districts. One was top-down and deliberate, while the other was bottom-up and of natural causes. By "top-down and deliberate," I mean that Japan's electoral reform in 1994 and municipal amalgamations of the early-mid 2000s were actions taken by the governments in question, one of which was not LDP controlled, which ended up reducing the share of electoral districts in Lower House elections that satisfy the conditions for GBC. By "bottom-up and of natural causes," I mean that the decisions of Japanese voters to move to larger cities also played a role in reducing the share of electoral districts meeting these conditions. Urbanization means that large cities keep getting bigger. Over time, this has led to more electoral districts consisting of municipalities that are so large they spill out beyond the border of a single district into another district and sometimes into more than one. Other changes that reformers interested in undoing the institutional conditions that underpin GBC could consider, which may be more difficult to pull off, include reforming the rules governing the counting of votes, such that votes are counted at the level of the electoral district as a whole and not within the district; tinkering with subnational governance so that the lower-tier entities to which central government resources are deliverable cover a larger geographic area than any one electoral district or at least, are not neatly nested within a single district; or reduce the discretion exercised by central government bureaucrats over the allocation of funds to those lower-tier entities.

In addition to these general interest contributions to the study of distributive politics, clientelism, pork-barrel politics, and electoral strategies, respectively, this book has also offered substantive contributions to the field of Japanese politics. It has presented empirical evidence, encompassed in scores of regression tables as well as anecdotes, interviews, comic books, case studies, and other qualitative accounts, that politicians in Japan's LDP contest elections by making allocations of national treasury disbursements contingent on how much electoral support municipalities gave them in the most recent election. While the *claim* that LDP politicians use money to buy votes is not new, *evidence* for this claim, which explains *how* LDP politicians use *which* transfer to buy the votes of *whom*, has been lacking. This book drew on a theory that was introduced to political science recently, *after* most of the prior studies of money and votes in Japan were conducted (Smith, Bueno de Mesquita and LaGatta 2017; Smith and Bueno de Mesquita 2019, 2012). The theory holds that politicians in a dominant party like the LDP will be able to win the most votes, conditional on resources delivered, by conducting tournaments between the groups in their electoral districts. Catalinac, Bueno de Mesquita and Smith (2020) began the process of examining whether LDP politicians conduct tournaments. This book picks up where that article left off, subjecting more of the theory's implications to empirical testing, expanding the period studied to include Lower House elections after 2000, considering a wider range of evidence, and fleshing out the theory's implications for longstanding questions of interest in Japanese politics.

My book fleshes out the logic under which money is connected to votes in Japan. This enables me to provide corroborating evidence for a claim that has been part of the Japanese politics canon since at least the 1960s (McMichael 2018; Naoi 2015; Reed 2021; Reed, Scheiner and Thies 2012; Saito 2010; Scheiner 2006; Fukui and Fukai 1996; Ramseyer and Rosenbluth 1993; Pempel 1990; Curtis 1971; Thayer 1969). It also brings us much closer to answering what is perhaps *the* question in the study of Japanese politics: Why elections have been dominated by a single party for the near duration of that party's existence. Until now, the field has struggled to explain why electoral reforms, economic recessions, revelations of incompetence or corruption, and transformations to the party system, which are all variables associated with changes in government in other democracies, have had such a limited impact in Japan. My book suggests that while the impact of *those* variables may have been limited, the variable highlighted in my theory – the degree to which electoral districts are divisible into groups of voters, at which levels of support at discernible and resources targetable – has likely had a larger impact. My book shows that when electoral districts are reconfigured in ways that mean the conditions for tournaments are no longer satisfied, LDP politicians cannot implement them. They move away from distributive politics and toward competition on programmatic policies. Critically, they start doing *worse* in elections, relative to their peers still competing in tournament-possible districts. LDP candidates in tournament-impossible districts recoup lower vote shares and are more likely to lose the election.

Until 1994, more than ninety percent of the electoral districts used in Lower House elections met the conditions for a tournament. From this "high point," the processes that led to the reconfiguration of electoral districts impacted only a subset of them. As such, the impact of this reconfiguration on the party's aggregate electoral strategy has likely been obscured. That said, this book shows that as of 2014, about half of all voters in Japan reside in electoral districts that are structured in ways that make tournaments impossible. This is likely creating a bifurcated electorate and bifurcated ruling party. Half of all voters in Japan are subject to GBC and tournaments, while the other half are not. Half of all members of the ruling party are leveraging their dominant party status to pit the municipalities in their electoral districts against each other in a competition for resources. They are likely investing in a particular style of election campaigning, a particular set of relationships (with central government bureaucrats and local politicians), and a particular type of funding being a fixture of annual budgets. The other half are staking out positions on programmatic policies to win and likely have their ears to the ground in terms of what the median voter in their district wants. They may prefer to *reduce* the share of the government's budget devoted to public works and other projects useful for buying votes.

9.1 QUESTIONS FOR FUTURE WORK

My book puts new questions on the research agenda of scholars of comparative politics and political economy. Top of the list should be gathering the kind of information that would enable us to gauge the viability of GBC in other democracies around the world, both today and historically. As I explained in Chapter 3, determining whether electoral districts are divisible into groups of voters, at which electoral support is discernible and resources targetable, entails gathering information on how votes in elections are counted, how electoral districts are drawn up, and what the relationship between the central government and lower-tier entities looks like, fiscal and otherwise. Chapter 3 explained that while some of these facts are easy to come by, others are not. Specifically, determining the degree to which the level at which votes are counted overlaps with the lower-tier entities to which central government resources are deliverable, on the one hand, and are nested within larger electoral districts on the other, can require the kind of deep dive into a case that we did with Japan in Chapter 5. This chapter can serve as a blueprint for how political scientists should go about putting together information that would allow them to classify other countries.

Once we have identified the set of democracies in which GBC is or has been viable, we can tackle several sets of questions. One concerns whether politicians use GBC to get elected in these countries, and how, exactly, they seek to tie central government resources to electoral support. My focus on the puzzle of LDP dominance in Japan led me to the tournament as the form of GBC that dominant parties will find attractive. But other settings will make different forms of GBC attractive to politicians. These different forms should be fleshed out, using theory and empirics. Beyond identifying the precise allocation rule that politicians use, researchers should also investigate the nuts and bolts of how politicians actually implement GBC, including how they create the perception in the electorate that goods will be a function of votes, how they identify projects of interest to the groups of voters in their electoral districts, and how they get their hands on government resources to fund these projects. As I explain in Chapter 2, a prominent subgenre of clientelism research has studied brokers, who can be local politicians, business people, or other prominent community members. This research holds that brokers play important roles in helping politicians identify which individuals they should buy votes from and in monitoring whether these individuals vote for the politician on election day. Under GBC, how a given individual votes is less of a concern to politicians, so brokers are likely playing roles that are no less important, but qualitatively different.

Once we know the universe of cases in which GBC is viable, and we have made headway in fleshing out how it is conducted in different settings, a second set of questions researchers should tackle concern how politics in countries with GBC might differ from politics in countries without GBC. For example, it is possible that the clientelistic linkages political parties form with groups in countries with GBC are more robust than the programmatic linkages parties form with individuals. If so, then parties in GBC countries may be less vulnerable to the challenge posed by new parties touting populist or far-right rhetoric, which attempt to pull voters away from their attachment to established parties. Returning to distributive politics, it is also possible that it is the countries in which GBC is impossible that we observe concerted efforts by politicians to buy the votes of individuals. If so, then it is in these countries that we may observe politicians devoting energy to weighing up who to target with their vote buying and how much to offer them. It is also in these settings that we may observe clientelistic practices declining with economic development, as individual votes become too costly to buy and people tire of the impact these practices have on the wider broader political system. As I explain in Chapter 3, under GBC, there may be little relationship between clientelism and economic development.

A key contribution of this book has been to build on the work done in Catalinac, Bueno de Mesquita and Smith (2020) to show that tournaments can be used to motivate electoral support in a real-world setting: a wealthy industrialized democracy, nonetheless. There, politicians in the ruling party get elected by dangling the promise of an ever-larger prize over the heads of groups of voters in their electoral districts and

9.1 Questions for Future Work

creating the understanding that where groups rank in terms of how supportive they are for the politician determines the size of their prize. At the end of the day, politics is all about the distribution of valued goods, many of which are distributed in the absence of predefined sets of rules. Central governments have to decide which communities will get new libraries, sports stadiums, and other infrastructure. Prime ministers have to decide which of their party's members will be awarded Cabinet positions. International organizations have to decide which countries will receive development aid. Wealthy countries have to decide which of their less wealthy counterparts will receive preferential trade agreements. How are decisions about who gets what arrived at?

Despite large bodies of work on the allocation of such goods, the possibility that goods which actors have a certain degree of discretion over are being distributed on the basis of a *competition*, in which their potential recipients are being forced to compete to satisfy some *other* need of the actor in charge of distributing the good, and only receive the good if they emerge victorious in this competition, has not received adequate attention by political scientists. An exception is work in Chinese politics, which provides evidence that the central government uses competitions between local government officials to allocate promotions (Li and Zhou 2005). In that case, what local government officials have to do to win the tournament and secure the valued promotion is achieve economic growth in their locale. The evidence in this book should convince political scientists to devote further attention to the possibility that actors with largess to deliver in other realms of politics are leveraging tournaments between potential recipients. Considering this has the potential to shed new light on the allocation of these discretionary goods, on the one hand, and also on the sources of incumbency advantage, the influence of special interests, the determinants of bureaucratic promotion, leader selection, Cabinet portfolio allocation, and other areas.

The groups I have focused on in this book are geographically defined. However, there is nothing about the theory that suggests it is limited to geographically defined groups. Politicians will also be able to conduct GBC with *non*geographically focused groups, such as sectoral or religious associations, provided two conditions are held: one, those groups have ways of making their levels of support for the politician discernible at more than one location within the politician's electoral district, and two, those groups constitute entities to which central government resources can be delivered. For example, a group that wants to make the number of votes it has to deliver observable to politicians could decide to field candidates in elections to *other* tiers of government. Take a religious organization that decides to field candidates in local elections all over a country. After the election, the organization will be able to point to its candidates' vote tallies in each of the locations at which votes are counted as evidence of its vote-gathering prowess. If electoral districts in local elections map onto those used in national elections, politicians contesting elections at the national level will have the tools to discern how many votes the organization is capable of supplying her. This could provide fodder for the politician to form a clientelistic exchange with that group, in which she exchanges promises to push the group's interests in parliament for help with re-election.

In Japan, one way sectoral organizations make the number of votes they are capable of supplying the LDP observable is by fielding candidates in Upper House elections (Reed 2021; Maclachlan 2014; Estevez-Abe 2008). In one tier of the electoral system used to select Upper House members, a single electoral district that spans the whole country is used and the electoral system is open-list proportional representation. This means voters write down the name of a party or a candidate endorsed by one of those parties. Since the LDP's formation, a number of nationally organized sectoral groups have asked the LDP to put their candidates on the party's ticket. After elections, these groups can point to the number of voters who wrote down their candidate's name in the nationwide district as evidence of the number of votes their group is capable of marshaling for the party. Further, because vote tallies are reported in a disaggregated fashion in Japan, politicians contesting elections in the other (Lower) House will also be able to discern the number of votes the group is capable of marshalling in their electoral district. In this setting, too, politicians contesting Lower House elections will have the means of cultivating clientelistic relationships with these groups, in which the politician might offer tax, regulatory, or other advantages in return for votes delivered.[1] Future scholarship should examine whether the combination of different sets of political institutions and different electoral systems can make GBC with nongeographically-focused groups possible.

Another important question is how GBC interacts with competition on programmatic grounds. In many countries, parties adopt electoral strategies that combine the targeting of voters with discretionary material benefits with the targeting of voters with programmatic policies that

---

[1] In the two exchanges I have just sketched out, the number of votes supplied by the group will only be observable in the local or Upper House election (in the Lower House election, the votes supplied by the group will be mixed in with those supplied by other voters). Because the politician will not be able to monitor the group's performance as effectively in her own election, this raises the possibility that groups could shirk.

9.1 Questions for Future Work

promise benefits to broader swaths of voters (Kitschelt and Singer 2018; Magaloni, Diaz-Cayeros and Estévez 2007). This book shows that the LDP is one such party, and it makes the case that the reason the LDP is bifurcated along this dimension is not because of differences in the inherent characteristics of LDP politicians or the voters they represent, but because some LDP politicians are elected in tournament-possible districts, while others are elected in tournament-impossible districts. In this book, I have concentrated on establishing that tournaments are conducted in tournament-possible districts and that LDP politicians in tournament-impossible districts adopt qualitatively different electoral strategies. Future research should investigate how the electoral strategies LDP politicians adopt in one sphere impact those adopted in the other sphere, and vice versa. For example, the fact that half the party's members are getting elected via distributive politics may be setting limits on the nature and ideological slant of the programmatic policies the other half of the party is able to offer voters. Investigating these and other questions will contribute to a deeper understanding of the dynamics of policymaking in Japan and what could spell the end of the LDP's nearly seventy-year stranglehold on Japanese politics.

Appendix A

A.1 SUPPLEMENTARY TABLES FOR CHAPTER 2

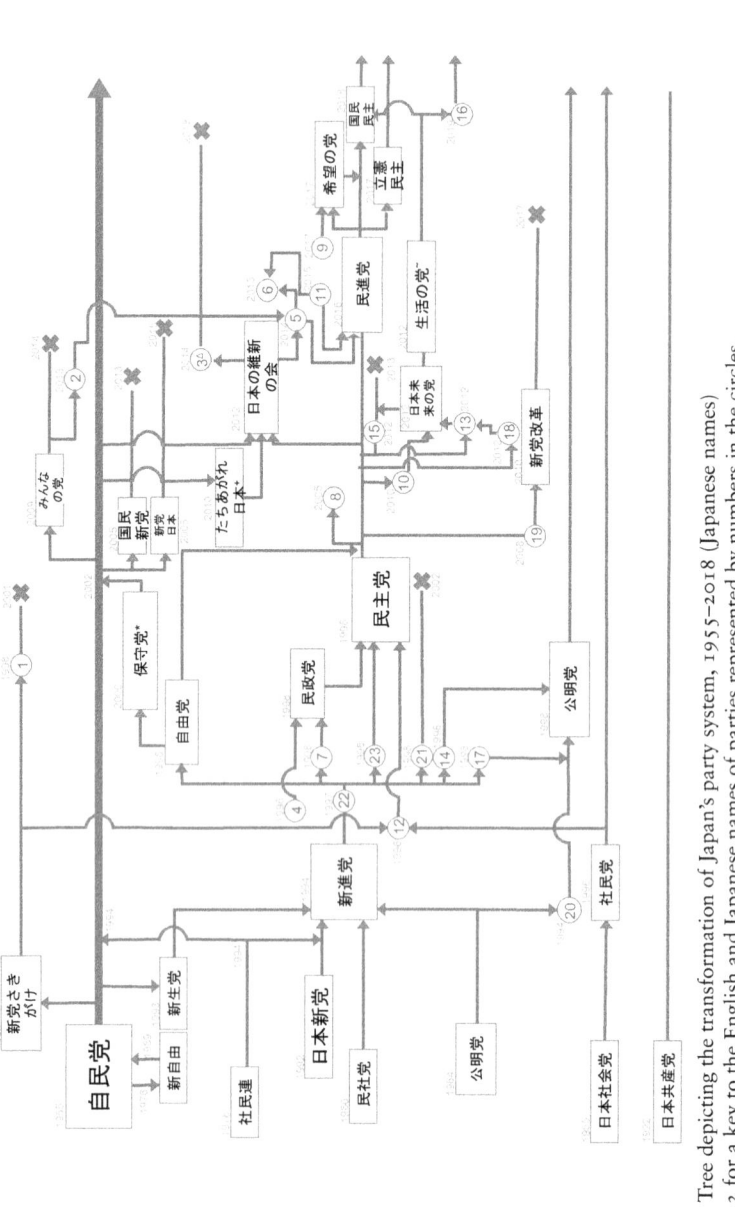

Figure A.1 Tree depicting the transformation of Japan's party system, 1955–2018 (Japanese names)
See Figure A.2 for a key to the English and Japanese names of parties represented by numbers in the circles.

1. Sakigake/ さきがけ
2. Unity Party/ 結いの党
3. Party for Future Generations/ 次世代の党
4. Sun Party/ 太陽党
5. Japan Innovation Party/ 維新の党
6. Initiatives for Osaka/ 大阪の維新の党
7. Voice of the People/ 国民の声
8. New Party Daichi/ 新党大地
9. Tomin First no Kai/ 都民ファースト
10. Genzei Nippon/ 減税日本
11. Vision of Reform/ 改革結集の会
12. Democratic Party of Japan/ 民主党
19. Japan Renaissance Party/ 改革クラブ
20. Komei/ 公明
21. Japan Renaissance Party/ 改革クラブ
22. Kaito/ 解党
23. New Fraternity Party/ 新党友愛
13. People's Life First/ 国民の生活が第一
14. New Party Peace/ 新党平和

15. Green Wind/ みどりの風
16. Reiwa Shinsengumi/ れいわ新選組
17. Dawn Party/ 黎明クラブ
18. Kizuna Part/ 新党きづな

*The Conservative Party changed its name to New Conservative Party (保守党 → 保守新党) 太陽の党

+The Sunrise Party of Japan changed its name to the Sunrise Party (たちあがれ日本 → 太陽の党)

ΔThe Party for Future Generations changed its name to the Party for Japanese Kokoro (次世代の党 → 日本のこころを大切にする党)

~ The People's Life Party changed its name to People's Life Party & Taro Yamamoto and Friends
(生活の党 → 生活の党と山本太郎と仲間達)

Figure A.2 Key to the English and Japanese names of parties represented by numbers in Figures 2.1 and A.1.

Appendix A

A.2 NOTES ON DATA COLLECTION, CHAPTERS 6–8

To examine the hypotheses offered in Chapter 4, I put together a comprehensive new dataset on the universe of Japanese municipalities that existed in any form between 1980 and 2014. This data is an expanded, cleaned-up version of data collected for Catalinac, Bueno de Mesquita and Smith (2020). Putting it together entailed extracting data from three data sources, cleaning the data, compiling it into a single dataset, and constructing variables to test my hypothesis. This was a difficult undertaking for several reasons, one of which was the thousands of changes to the borders of municipalities and electoral districts that took place during this period, which were all dealt with differently across the data sources. I strove to create a dataset that accounted for every single one of these changes with unique municipality and district codes, which would facilitate the use of state-of-the-art regression specifications to test my hypotheses. Below, I explain how the dataset was made.

The first step was to compile voting data. For data on voting behavior in the twelve Lower House elections held between 1980 and 2014, I relied on the municipality-level election results compiled by Mizusaki (2014). Known as the JED-M Sosenkyo data, this is not a compiled dataset, but a series of text files, each of which pertains to a single electoral district in a single election. Electoral districts were multimember prior to 1994, electing between three and five candidates, and single member after 1994. Each file contains district-specific information, including the number of seats available, the number of municipalities in the district, the voting population, the number of votes cast, the number of valid votes cast, the number of candidates running, and the names of those candidates and their party affiliations. Each file also contains a list of the municipalities in the district and records, for each municipality, the voting population, number of votes cast, number of valid votes cast, and number of valid votes cast for each candidate. A feature of this dataset that proved difficult is that municipalities (and electoral districts, for that matter) are identified by the *name* they had at the time of the election, not by any government-issued code. Files for elections held after 1994 attach a suffix onto the names of municipalities spanning more than one district, but files for elections held prior to 1994 do not. In these elections, I identified this small number of municipalities by extracting municipalities whose names appeared in more than one file and were located in contiguous electoral districts.[1]

---

[1] Note that the fourteen municipalities located on the Amami Islands, which constituted an electoral district until the 1993 election, when they were merged into Kagoshima 1, were excluded from the data.

A.2 Notes on Data Collection, Chapters 6–8

After extracting the municipality-level voting data, I used the Reed and Smith (2015) dataset to attach pertinent information about the identity of the candidates who ran in each electoral district in each election. Of particular interest was whether the candidate was an incumbent, the number of terms the candidate had served in the Lower House (if any), and whether the candidate had run as an independent, only to join the LDP after the election. Under Japan's old electoral system, a good number of the independents running in any given election were those who had failed to win the LDP's official endorsement prior to the election but had every intention of joining the party after the election, should they emerge victorious. Sometimes these candidates had even been fielded by an LDP faction intent on enlarging its numbers. Faction leaders would seek out districts in which the party's incumbents were all affiliated with other factions. Should there be another candidate aspiring to run there, the faction would throw its resources behind this candidate, with the idea that if she was victorious, she could join the party (and faction) after the election (Reed 2009). Japanese politics researchers regularly find that these LDP-aligned independents behave like regular LDP candidates (e.g., Ariga 2015). I also relied on the Reed and Smith (2015) data for its unique electoral district identifiers, which denote changes to district boundaries. Most of these changes occurred with the electoral reform in 1994 and with the redistricting that occurred between 2000 and 2003 and 2012 and 2014, respectively.

For NTD allocations, as well as other fiscal and demographic variables, I turned to the Nikkei Economic Electronic Databank System (or "Nikkei NEEDs" for short). Nikkei NEEDs provided data on the following municipality-level variables for the 1980–2012 period: total NTD allocation, total taxable income, population, fiscal strength, number of residents employed in primary industries, number of residents aged fifteen and below, number of residents aged sixty-five and above, and area size. I used these variables to construct the dependent variable (the per capita NTD allocation received by a municipality in the year after Lower House elections), as well as lags of the dependent variable and indicators of need in each municipality, which are standard controls in work on the political determinants of transfers in Japan. For each of the eight variables, NEEDs supplied a spreadsheet of data compiled from various government reports.[2] For NTD allocations and fiscal strength, NEEDs uses municipalities' "general account settlements," which are released after the fiscal year is over (April 1 until March 31) and municipalities have settled their

---

[2] A description of the data is available at https://needs.nikkei.co.jp/. I used NEEDs data from 2015.

Appendix A

accounts (April to May).[3] For total taxable income, NEEDs relies on annual reports published by the Ministry of Internal Affairs and Communications.[4] For population, it relies on annual reports published by the Japan Geographic Data Center.[5] For residents in primary industries and aged fifteen and below and sixty-five and above, it uses data from censuses carried out every five years.[6] Finally, for area size (measured in kilometers squared), it relies on data from Japan's Geospatial Information Authority.[7]

The NEEDs spreadsheets contain data pertaining to all municipalities that existed in the post-2000 period. For this set of municipalities, data was typically available from 1980 until either 2012 or the fiscal year prior to the municipality ceasing to exist (due to a municipal merger). This data structure posed significant challenges. To explain, consider Municipality A, which ceased to exist in 2005 due to a merger with a neighboring municipality. The new (merged) entity is called Municipality B. In the NEEDs data, both municipalities are included and are distinguished by name and official municipality code.[8] For Municipality A, data is populated from 1980 until fiscal year 2004. For Municipality B, however, some variables are populated from 2005 onward (which corresponds to the years it exists), while other variables are populated from 1980 until 2012. Because Municipality B did not exist until fiscal year 2005, the

---

[3] For towns and villages, it uses the government's "Shichoson Betsu Kessan Jyokyo Shirabe." For cities and special wards, it uses data collated by the Nikkei Shimbun. Reports from the 2002 fiscal year onward are available at www.soumu.go.jp/iken/kessan_jokyo_2.html. The "fiscal strength" of a municipality is an index that reflects the proportion of the cost of services that a municipality is able to finance with its own tax revenue.

[4] The "Shicho Son Zei Kazei Jyoukyou Nado no Shirabe" report.

[5] The "Jyuumin Kihon Daichou Jinkou Youran" report.

[6] For the off-years, we took the value in the census year closest to the off-year.

[7] The "Zenkoku Todoufuken Shikuchouson Betsu Menseki Shirabe" report. This data was only available from 1998. I assigned municipalities with identical names and government codes in previous years to the area size they had in 1998.

[8] A merit of the NEEDs data is that information about earlier and later border changes can be incorporated into municipality names and codes. In my final dataset, for municipalities that experience a boundary change in 2005, for example, the municipality's name in the years prior to 2005 includes a suffix that describes, in parentheses, what happens in 2005. When it comes to the code, NEEDs assigns new codes every time a new entity is created but uses coding conventions to indicate whether a municipality is an earlier version of another municipality. For example, when a larger municipality absorbs other, smaller municipalities, the larger municipality might have the same name before and after the merger (with the suffix attached in earlier years, explaining what happens in later years) and the same code, distinguished by a decimal suffix. For example, let us say Municipality A exists until 2005, after which it absorbs a few municipalities on its border. Its name is Municipality A before and after 2005 (with the suffix attached to the name in earlier years), and its code is 100.1 before 2005 and 100 thereafter.

A.2 Notes on Data Collection, Chapters 6–8

variables populated from 1980 until 2004 are imputed. Using a comprehensive list of the 2,198 municipal mergers that have occurred since 2000, scripts were written to keep data for the years in which municipalities actually existed and delete data for the years in which they did not. This left me with fiscal and demographic information for almost all the Japanese municipalities that existed in any form between 1980 and 2012.[9] In the dataset, variables are populated only for the years in which a municipality existed.

After creating the dataset of fiscal and demographic variables, the next task was to merge this with the voting data. This posed another significant challenge: The voting data is compiled soon after each Lower House election and identifies municipalities by the names they had *at the time*. The NEEDs data, in contrast, was published in 2015 and identifies municipalities by name and official municipality code, but both the name and code reflect the ones used by the municipality *in the post-2000 period*. The name a municipality used in 2001, for example, can be slightly different to the name it had in 1991, not because of any changes to its border, but because it changed its name, has a name for which slightly different renderings in Japanese are possible, or experienced a population change that resulted in a change in its designation (as a city, town, or village).[10] Similarly, the official code a municipality used in 2001 can be different from the code it used in 1991, even though its borders are identical. These problems meant that I had municipality-years in the voting data that did not match municipality-years in the carefully pruned fiscal and demographic data.

To remedy this, I used a comprehensive dataset compiled by Kuniaki Nemoto, in which the municipality-years in the JED-M voting data had been matched by hand to the official codes these municipalities had at the time. Using his data, I investigated all unmatched observations (municipalities in the voting data that had not been matched to municipalities in the fiscal/demographic data). I found that the vast majority of observations had not been matched due to tiny differences in the rendering of municipality names. I also found that 158 unmatched observations pertained to municipalities that had existed in the 2003 and 2005 Lower House elections (and thus, had voting data) but had ceased to exist later

---

[9] We say "almost all" because NEEDs does not report data for the handful of municipalities that disappeared prior to 2000. Because these municipalities did not exist in the post-2000 period, NEEDs does not make data available for them.

[10] In Japanese, designations as cities (shi), towns (chou), and villages (son) appear as suffixes attached to municipality name. Moreover, municipalities sometimes change their names; for example, to differentiate themselves from another municipality in Japan with the same name.

Appendix A

that same fiscal year due to a municipal merger (fiscal/demographic variables are not reported for municipalities in fiscal years in which they cease to exist). Through this, I was able to match almost all municipality-years for which I had voting data to municipality-years for which fiscal and demographic data existed.

The final step in the data collection was adding fiscal and demographic variables for the 2013, 2014, and 2015 fiscal years, which were not included in the NEEDs data. Fortunately, data for these years was available in the Japanese government's online statistics portal. I downloaded data on my variables of interest and merged them into the master dataset. Compared to earlier years, adding data for more recent years is straightforward due to the smaller number of municipalities, smaller number of name changes, and fewer changes to the borders of municipalities. It only required taking into account a handful of changes to municipality names and codes. The final master data contains variables pertaining to 105,353 municipality-years.

A.3 SUPPLEMENTARY MATERIAL FOR CHAPTER 6

Table A.1 *Descriptive statistics for the variables used in Chapter 6's analysis of transfer allocations to municipalities within districts, 1980–2014.*

Statistic	N	Mean	St. Dev.	Min	Max
Postelection Transfers (log)	29,088	−3.483	0.781	−6.526	1.448
Log(Transfers$_{m,t}$)	29,913	−3.469	0.770	−7.922	1.954
Best LDP VS$_{m,t}$	30,270	0.262	0.168	0.000	0.918
Rank (Best LDP VS$_{m,t}$)	25,653	0.500	0.306	0.000	1.000
Sum LDP VS$_{m,t}$	30,270	0.338	0.200	0.000	0.918
Rank (Sum LDP VS$_{m,t}$)	25,653	0.500	0.306	0.000	1.000
High LDP VS$_{m,t}$	30,270	0.230	0.171	0.000	0.918
Best LDP+ VS$_{m,t}$	30,270	0.272	0.165	0.000	0.918
Best Senior LDP VS$_{m,t}$	30,270	0.127	0.167	0.000	0.918
Best Non-LDP VS$_{m,t}$	30,270	0.131	0.133	0.000	0.818
Best Losing LDP VS$_{m,t}$	30,270	0.059	0.110	0.000	0.940
District Winner VS$_{m,t}$	30,270	0.281	0.144	0.001	0.918
Fiscal Strength$_{m,t}$	29,748	0.422	0.279	0.000	3.030
Dependent Population$_{m,t}$	29,021	0.364	0.047	0.025	0.642
Farming Population$_{m,t}$	29,020	0.091	0.072	0.000	0.625
Log(Population$_{m,t}$)	30,241	9.570	1.256	5.215	13.638
Log(Per Capita Income$_{m,t}$)	29,913	−0.145	0.403	−2.148	2.008
Population Density$_{m,t}$	30,241	0.734	1.796	0.001	21.237

A.3 Supplementary Material for Chapter 6

Table A.2 *The same specifications in Table 6.2 are presented here, with a control for the municipality-level vote share captured by the LDP's highest vote-getter in the district. The results are not explained by this rival theory.*

	Dependent variable: Postelection Transfers (log)			
	(Model 1)	(Model 2)	(Model 3)	(Model 4)
Best LDP VS$_{m,t}$	0.150**			
	(0.055)			
Rank (Best LDP VS$_{m,t}$)		0.036*		
		(0.017)		
Sum LDP VS$_{m,t}$			0.152**	
			(0.050)	
Rank (Sum LDP VS$_{m,t}$)				0.051**
				(0.018)
Log(Transfers$_{m,t}$)	0.435***	0.436***	0.435***	0.436***
	(0.012)	(0.012)	(0.012)	(0.012)
High LDP VS$_{m,t}$	0.020	0.036	0.022	0.025
	(0.040)	(0.039)	(0.039)	(0.039)
Fiscal Strength$_{m,t}$	−0.011	−0.020	−0.012	−0.020
	(0.075)	(0.076)	(0.075)	(0.076)
Dependent Population$_{m,t}$	0.686*	0.588	0.694*	0.589
	(0.334)	(0.331)	(0.334)	(0.331)
Farming Population$_{m,t}$	−0.567	−0.617	−0.556	−0.614
	(0.328)	(0.329)	(0.326)	(0.328)
Log(Population$_{m,t}$)	−0.515***	−0.520***	−0.512***	−0.517***
	(0.116)	(0.116)	(0.116)	(0.116)
Log(Per Capita Income$_{m,t}$)	0.028	0.025	0.030	0.028
	(0.071)	(0.072)	(0.071)	(0.071)
Population Density$_{m,t}$	0.026	0.032	0.025	0.032
	(0.075)	(0.077)	(0.075)	(0.077)
Observations	15,526	15,416	15,526	15,416
District-Year FE	Y	Y	Y	Y
Municipality FE	Y	Y	Y	Y
R^2	0.205	0.205	0.205	0.206

Robust standard errors clustered on municipality in parentheses.
*$p < 0.05$, **$p < 0.01$, ***$p < 0.001$.
Regression models estimated with R's plm() package.

Appendix A

Table A.3 *The same specifications in Table 6.4, with alternative specifications of electoral support.*

	Dependent variable: Postelection Transfers			
	(Model 1)	(Model 2)	(Model 3)	(Model 4)
Sum LDP VS$_{m,t}$	0.153**			
	(0.048)			
Sum Senior LDP VS$_{m,t}$	0.028			
	(0.048)			
Sum LDP+ VS$_{m,t}$		0.180***		
		(0.049)		
Sum Non-LDP VS$_{m,t}$			0.048	
			(0.060)	
Sum Losing LDP VS$_{m,t}$				−0.251***
				(0.061)
Log(Transfers$_{m,t}$)	0.435***	0.435***	0.436***	0.436***
	(0.012)	(0.012)	(0.012)	(0.012)
Fiscal Strength$_{m,t}$	−0.012	−0.012	−0.014	−0.012
	(0.075)	(0.075)	(0.075)	(0.075)
Dependent Population$_{m,t}$	0.695*	0.689*	0.691*	0.699*
	(0.334)	(0.334)	(0.333)	(0.333)
Farming Population$_{m,t}$	−0.558	−0.556	−0.589	−0.567
	(0.326)	(0.326)	(0.327)	(0.326)
Log(Population$_{m,t}$)	−0.512***	−0.510***	−0.526***	−0.529***
	(0.116)	(0.116)	(0.116)	(0.116)
Log(Per Capita Income$_{m,t}$)	0.030	0.032	0.020	0.026
	(0.071)	(0.071)	(0.071)	(0.071)
Population Density$_{m,t}$	0.025	0.025	0.028	0.028
	(0.074)	(0.074)	(0.075)	(0.074)
Observations	15,526	15,526	15,526	15,526
District-Year FE	Y	Y	Y	Y
Municipality FE	Y	Y	Y	Y
R^2	0.205	0.205	0.205	0.206

Robust standard errors clustered on municipality in parentheses.
*$p < 0.05$, **$p < 0.01$, ***$p < 0.001$.
Regression models estimated with R's plm() package.

A.3 Supplementary Material for Chapter 6

Table A.4 *A municipality's per capita transfers in the year following Lower House elections as a cubic function of its position in a ranking constructed on the basis of electoral support, 1980–2014.*

	Dependent variable: Postelection Transfers	
	(Model 1)	(Model 2)
Rank (Best LDP VS$_{m,t}$)	−2.060*	
	(1.009)	
Rank (Best LDP VS$_{m,t}$)^2	−0.264	
	(3.235)	
Rank (Best LDP VS$_{m,t}$)^3	3.150	
	(2.586)	
Rank (Sum LDP VS$_{m,t}$)		−2.100*
		(0.970)
Rank (Sum LDP VS$_{m,t}$)^2		0.016
		(2.823)
Rank (Sum LDP VS$_{m,t}$)^3		2.837
		(2.211)
Fiscal Strength$_{m,t}$	2.395***	2.402***
	(0.612)	(0.613)
Dependent Population$_{m,t}$	21.733***	22.170***
	(4.102)	(4.109)
Farming Population$_{m,t}$	0.220	0.121
	(2.326)	(2.337)
Log(Population$_{m,t}$)	−1.295***	−1.277***
	(0.264)	(0.261)
Log(Per Capita Income$_{m,t}$)	2.014	2.002
	(1.134)	(1.134)
Population Density$_{m,t}$	0.325***	0.321***
	(0.076)	(0.076)
Observations	23,909	23,909
District-Year FE	Y	Y
R^2	0.047	0.046
Joint Hypothesis Test	0.000	0.000

Robust standard errors clustered on municipality in parentheses.
*$p < 0.05$, ***$p < 0.001$.
Regression models estimated with R's plm() package.

Appendix A

Table A.5 *A municipality's per capita transfers in the year following Lower House elections as a cubic function of its position in a ranking constructed on the basis of electoral support, 1980–1993.*

	Dependent variable: Postelection Transfers	
	(Model 1)	(Model 2)
Rank (Best LDP VS$_{m,t}$)	−0.653	
	(1.561)	
Rank (Best LDP VS$_{m,t}$)^2	−3.098	
	(5.323)	
Rank (Best LDP VS$_{m,t}$)^3	4.730	
	(4.345)	
Rank (Sum LDP VS$_{m,t}$)		−0.780
		(1.474)
Rank (Sum LDP VS$_{m,t}$)^2		−2.587
		(4.552)
Rank (Sum LDP VS$_{m,t}$)^3		4.157
		(3.643)
Fiscal Strength$_{m,t}$	1.272*	1.262*
	(0.522)	(0.524)
Dependent Population$_{m,t}$	23.603**	23.993**
	(8.275)	(8.384)
Farming Population$_{m,t}$	−2.207	−2.277
	(2.769)	(2.820)
Log(Population$_{m,t}$)	−1.331***	−1.308***
	(0.385)	(0.376)
Log(Per Capita Income$_{m,t}$)	1.716	1.674
	(1.199)	(1.198)
Population Density$_{m,t}$	0.415***	0.403**
	(0.125)	(0.124)
Observations	15,416	15,416
District-Year FE	Y	Y
R^2	0.039	0.038
Joint Hypothesis Test	0.000	0.000

Robust standard errors clustered on municipality in parentheses.
*$p < 0.05$, **$p < 0.01$, ***$p < 0.001$.
Regression models estimated with R's plm() package.

A.3 Supplementary Material for Chapter 6

Table A.6 *A municipality's per capita transfers in the year following Lower House elections as a cubic function of its position in a ranking constructed on the basis of electoral support, 1996–2014.*

	Dependent variable: Postelection Transfers
Rank (Sum LDP $VS_{m,t}$)	−2.788
	(1.553)
Rank (Sum LDP $VS_{m,t}$)^2	1.723
	(4.063)
Rank (Sum LDP $VS_{m,t}$)^3	2.196
	(2.917)
Fiscal Strength$_{m,t}$	5.010***
	(1.002)
Dependent Population$_{m,t}$	30.372***
	(6.029)
Farming Population$_{m,t}$	4.003
	(3.510)
Log(Population$_{m,t}$)	−1.092***
	(0.166)
Log(Per Capita Income$_{m,t}$)	3.722
	(2.149)
Population Density$_{m,t}$	0.248*
	(0.104)
Observations	8,493
District-Year FE	Y
Joint Hypothesis Test	0.000
R^2	0.084

Robust standard errors clustered on municipality in parentheses.
***$p < 0.001$.
Regression models estimated with R's plm() package.

Appendix A

Table A.7 *Without controlling for district-level differences thought to influence transfers, the relationship between electoral support and transfers becomes negative and statistically significant (Models 1 and 2), 1980–2014. Similarly, there is a negative relationship between support and transfers when votes for losing LDP candidates are included in the numerator (Model 3).*

	Dependent variable: Postelection Transfers		
	(Model 1)	(Model 2)	(Model 3)
Best LDP VS$_{m,t}$	−0.039*		
	(0.018)		
Sum LDP VS$_{m,t}$		−0.054**	
		(0.017)	
All LDP VS$_{m,t}$			−0.072***
			(0.016)
Log(Transfers$_{m,t}$)	0.788***	0.788***	0.788***
	(0.007)	(0.007)	(0.007)
Fiscal Strength$_{m,t}$	−0.018	−0.018	−0.016
	(0.024)	(0.024)	(0.024)
Dependent Population$_{m,t}$	0.369***	0.370***	0.360***
	(0.106)	(0.105)	(0.105)
Farming Population$_{m,t}$	−0.021	−0.014	−0.008
	(0.071)	(0.071)	(0.071)
Log(Population$_{m,t}$)	−0.004	−0.004	−0.004
	(0.004)	(0.004)	(0.004)
Log(Per Capita Income$_{m,t}$)	−0.166***	−0.166***	−0.171***
	(0.020)	(0.020)	(0.020)
Population Density$_{m,t}$	0.008***	0.008***	0.007***
	(0.002)	(0.002)	(0.002)
Observations	27,225	27,225	27,225
Year FE	Y	Y	Y
R^2	0.681	0.681	0.681

Robust standard errors clustered on municipality in parentheses.
*$p < 0.05$, **$p < 0.01$, ***$p < 0.001$.
Regression models estimated with R's plm() package.

A.4 SUPPLEMENTARY MATERIAL FOR CHAPTER 7

Table A.8 *Descriptive statistics for the variables used in Chapter 7's analysis of transfer allocations to electoral districts. Observations are tournament-possible electoral districts with LDP winners in Lower House elections, 1980–2014.*

Statistic	N	Mean	St. Dev.	Min	Max
Postelection Transfers (log)	1,414	−3.488	0.597	−7.071	−0.407
Fiscal Strength$_{d,t}$	1,414	0.598	0.250	0.000	1.414
Farming Population$_{d,t}$	1,414	0.043	0.034	0.0002	0.195
Dependent Population$_{d,t}$	1,414	0.334	0.060	0.007	0.483
Population Density$_{d,t}$	1,414	1.415	2.952	0.020	18.278
Log(Population$_{d,t}$)	1,414	13.168	0.498	10.950	14.630
Log(Per Capita Income$_{d,t}$)	1,414	0.038	0.413	−2.204	1.585
HI$_{d,t}$	1,414	0.145	0.153	0.002	0.978
Total Seats$_{d,t}$	1,414	2.203	1.558	1	6
People Per Seat$_{d,t}$	1,414	3.249	1.172	0.570	5.897
Log(Number of Municipalities$_{d,t}$)	1,414	2.615	0.867	0.693	4.159
LDP VS$_{d,t}$	1,414	0.342	0.102	0.090	0.677
Winning LDP VS$_{d,t}$	1,414	0.325	0.100	0.074	0.657
LDP Seats$_{d,t}$	1,414	0.819	0.252	0.200	1.000
Senior LDP Politician$_{d,t}$	1,414	0.474	0.499	0	1
Number LDP Candidates$_{d,t}$	1,414	1.629	0.922	1	5

Appendix A

Table A.9 *The same models in Table 7.1, but with alternative indicators for strength of LDP support in the district. Models 1 and 3 use LDP Seats$_{d,t}$, while Models 2 and 4 use LDP VS$_{d,t}$.*

	Dependent variable: Postelection Transfers (log)			
	All electoral districts		Excludes prefectural capitals	
	(Model 1)	(Model 2)	(Model 3)	(Model 4)
HI$_{d,t}$	0.720***	0.716***	0.620***	0.619***
	(0.129)	(0.128)	(0.147)	(0.148)
Fiscal Strength$_{d,t}$	−0.253*	−0.263*	−0.264*	−0.278*
	(0.106)	(0.106)	(0.117)	(0.118)
Dependent Population$_{d,t}$	4.368***	4.405***	4.008***	4.033***
	(0.537)	(0.537)	(0.551)	(0.552)
Farming Population$_{d,t}$	3.547***	3.487***	3.391***	3.268***
	(0.867)	(0.881)	(0.918)	(0.921)
Log(Population$_{d,t}$)	−0.008	0.022	−0.080	−0.040
	(0.109)	(0.109)	(0.125)	(0.121)
Log(Per Capita Income$_{d,t}$)	0.444***	0.447***	0.400*	0.403*
	(0.123)	(0.124)	(0.158)	(0.159)
Population Density$_{d,t}$	0.031*	0.031*	0.028*	0.028*
	(0.012)	(0.012)	(0.013)	(0.013)
Log(Number of Municipalities$_{d,t}$)	0.174***	0.175***	0.152***	0.151**
	(0.043)	(0.044)	(0.046)	(0.046)
People Per Seat$_{d,t}$	−0.067	−0.077	−0.031	−0.040
	(0.040)	(0.040)	(0.042)	(0.042)
LDP Seats$_{d,t}$	−0.220		−0.183	
	(0.127)		(0.143)	
LDP VS$_{d,t}$		−0.188		−0.056
		(0.196)		(0.209)
Senior LDP Politician$_{d,t}$	−0.046	−0.047	−0.037	−0.041
	(0.029)	(0.029)	(0.030)	(0.029)
Observations	1,414	1,414	1,151	1,151
Year FE	Y	Y	Y	Y
R^2	0.407	0.405	0.392	0.391

Robust standard errors clustered on electoral district in parentheses.
*$p < 0.05$, **$p < 0.01$, ***$p < 0.001$.
Regression models estimated with R's plm() package.

A.4 Supplementary Material for Chapter 7

Table A.10 *The models in Table 7.1 with no controls for the strength of support for the LDP.*

	Dependent variable: Postelection Transfers (log)	
	All electoral districts	Excludes prefectural capitals
	(Model 1)	(Model 2)
$HI_{d,t}$	0.715***	0.614***
	(0.129)	(0.146)
Fiscal Strength$_{d,t}$	−0.260*	−0.272*
	(0.104)	(0.117)
Dependent Population$_{d,t}$	4.407***	4.036***
	(0.536)	(0.550)
Farming Population$_{d,t}$	3.267***	3.177***
	(0.880)	(0.932)
Log(Population$_{d,t}$)	0.037	−0.033
	(0.107)	(0.120)
Log(Per Capita Income$_{d,t}$)	0.436***	0.397*
	(0.124)	(0.160)
Population Density$_{d,t}$	0.033**	0.029*
	(0.012)	(0.013)
Log(Number of Municipalities$_{d,t}$)	0.171***	0.150**
	(0.043)	(0.046)
People Per Seat$_{d,t}$	−0.078	−0.043
	(0.040)	(0.042)
Observations	1,414	1,151
Year FE	Y	Y
R^2	0.402	0.389

Robust standard errors clustered on electoral district in parentheses.
*$p < 0.05$, **$p < 0.01$, ***$p < 0.001$.
Regression models estimated with R's plm() package.

Appendix A

Table A.11 *The models in Table 7.2 with an alternative control for strength of LDP support in the district (LDP Seats$_{d,t}$ instead of Winning LDP VS$_{d,t}$).*

	Dependent variable: Postelection Transfers (log)			
	All electoral districts		Excludes prefectural capitals	
	(Model 1)	(Model 2)	(Model 3)	(Model 4)
HI$_{d,t}$	1.280***	2.340***	1.206**	3.240***
	(0.272)	(0.636)	(0.423)	(0.948)
Fiscal Strength$_{d,t}$	−0.238	−0.352**	−0.174	−0.212
	(0.207)	(0.136)	(0.199)	(0.188)
Dependent Population$_{d,t}$	6.820***	0.145	3.980*	−1.028
	(1.617)	(1.046)	(1.734)	(1.303)
Farming Population$_{d,t}$	3.602**	−0.998	2.359*	−2.586
	(1.305)	(1.185)	(1.009)	(1.448)
Log(Population$_{d,t}$)	0.068	−0.644***	−0.066	−0.985***
	(0.156)	(0.152)	(0.162)	(0.258)
Log(Per Capita Income$_{d,t}$)	0.343	0.460***	−0.112	0.124
	(0.218)	(0.113)	(0.234)	(0.147)
Population Density$_{d,t}$	0.045	−0.053*	0.041	−0.037
	(0.031)	(0.021)	(0.028)	(0.046)
Log(Number of Municipalities$_{d,t}$)	0.212	0.975**	0.173	0.494
	(0.111)	(0.304)	(0.128)	(0.408)
People Per Seat$_{d,t}$	−0.092	−0.020	−0.006	−0.013
	(0.061)	(0.028)	(0.053)	(0.032)
LDP Seats$_{d,t}$	−0.293*	0.003	−0.070	0.021
	(0.136)	(0.026)	(0.128)	(0.029)
Senior LDP Politician$_{d,t}$	−0.111**	−0.004	−0.118*	0.001
	(0.038)	(0.011)	(0.046)	(0.013)
Observations	578	578	382	382
Year FE	Y	Y	Y	Y
District FE	N	Y	N	Y
R^2	0.474	0.278	0.439	0.267

Robust standard errors clustered on electoral district in parentheses.
*$p < 0.05$, **$p < 0.01$, ***$p < 0.001$.
Regression models estimated with R's plm() package.

A.4 Supplementary Material for Chapter 7

Table A.12 *Table 7.2 with an alternative control for strength of LDP support in the district (LDP VS$_{d,t}$ instead of Winning LDP VS$_{d,t}$).*

	Dependent variable: Postelection Transfers (log)			
	All electoral districts		Excludes prefectural capitals	
	(Model 1)	(Model 2)	(Model 3)	(Model 4)
HI$_{d,t}$	1.292***	2.326***	1.229**	3.218***
	(0.277)	(0.635)	(0.426)	(0.944)
Fiscal Strength$_{d,t}$	−0.233	−0.354**	−0.181	−0.225
	(0.204)	(0.136)	(0.200)	(0.192)
Dependent Population$_{d,t}$	6.970***	0.124	3.928*	−1.132
	(1.619)	(1.042)	(1.731)	(1.318)
Farming Population$_{d,t}$	3.585**	−1.049	2.268*	−2.762
	(1.311)	(1.181)	(1.000)	(1.478)
Log(Population$_{d,t}$)	0.101	−0.646***	−0.048	−0.995***
	(0.158)	(0.152)	(0.161)	(0.259)
Log(Per Capita Income$_{d,t}$)	0.335	0.460***	−0.123	0.125
	(0.219)	(0.113)	(0.235)	(0.148)
Population Density$_{d,t}$	0.046	−0.053*	0.042	−0.040
	(0.030)	(0.021)	(0.028)	(0.047)
Log(Number of Municipalities$_{d,t}$)	0.211	0.966**	0.172	0.480
	(0.112)	(0.304)	(0.128)	(0.405)
People Per Seat$_{d,t}$	−0.102	−0.020	−0.0004	−0.010
	(0.066)	(0.028)	(0.057)	(0.032)
LDP VS$_{d,t}$	−0.306	0.035	0.065	0.092
	(0.253)	(0.076)	(0.235)	(0.085)
Senior LDP Politician$_{d,t}$	−0.119**	−0.004	−0.125**	−0.00000
	(0.039)	(0.011)	(0.046)	(0.013)
Observations	578	578	382	382
Year FE	Y	Y	Y	Y
District FE	N	Y	N	Y
R^2	0.467	0.278	0.438	0.269

Robust standard errors clustered on electoral district in parentheses.
*$p < 0.05$, **$p < 0.01$, ***$p < 0.001$.
Regression models estimated with R's plm() package.

Appendix A

Table A.13 *Table 7.5 on the sample of electoral districts from the preelectoral reform period, 1980–1993*

	Dependent variables:		
	Winning LDP VS$_{d,t}$	LDP VS$_{d,t}$	LDP Seats$_{d,t}$
	(Model 1)	(Model 2)	(Model 3)
HI$_{d,t}$	−0.087	−0.044	−0.137
	(0.062)	(0.042)	(0.096)
Fiscal Strength$_{d,t}$	0.020	0.017	−0.022
	(0.026)	(0.022)	(0.043)
Dependent Population$_{d,t}$	−0.110	0.186	−0.410
	(0.248)	(0.194)	(0.392)
Farming Population$_{d,t}$	0.160	0.139	0.090
	(0.221)	(0.172)	(0.289)
Log(Population$_{d,t}$)	−0.083	−0.130	−0.031
	(0.116)	(0.075)	(0.171)
Log(Per Capita Income$_{d,t}$)	−0.003	−0.011	0.013
	(0.016)	(0.014)	(0.027)
Population Density$_{d,t}$	−0.005	−0.004	−0.009
	(0.004)	(0.003)	(0.005)
Total Seats$_{d,t}$	−0.021	−0.028	−0.102*
	(0.029)	(0.020)	(0.041)
Log(Number of Municipalities$_{d,t}$)	0.0002	−0.008	−0.011
	(0.018)	(0.014)	(0.024)
People Per Seat$_{d,t}$	−0.021	0.010	−0.035
	(0.044)	(0.028)	(0.068)
Senior LDP Politician$_{d,t}$	0.038***	0.020***	0.060***
	(0.009)	(0.006)	(0.015)
Number LDP Candidates$_{d,t}$	0.063***	0.102***	0.143***
	(0.007)	(0.006)	(0.012)
Observations	586	586	586
Year FE	Y	Y	Y
R^2	0.585	0.827	0.583

Robust standard errors clustered on electoral district in parentheses.
*$p < 0.05$, ***$p < 0.001$.
Regression models estimated with R's plm() package.

A.4 Supplementary Material for Chapter 7

Table A.14 *Table 7.5 on the sample of electoral districts from the postelectoral reform period, 1996–2014.*

	Dependent variables:		
	Winning LDP VS$_{d,t}$	LDP VS$_{d,t}$	LDP Seats$_{d,t}$
	(Model 1)	(Model 2)	(Model 3)
HI$_{d,t}$	−0.074*	−0.047*	−0.196*
	(0.033)	(0.022)	(0.094)
Fiscal Strength$_{d,t}$	−0.043	−0.049**	−0.122
	(0.027)	(0.019)	(0.077)
Dependent Population$_{d,t}$	−0.031	0.061	−0.277
	(0.093)	(0.061)	(0.270)
Farming Population$_{d,t}$	0.606	0.289	1.042
	(0.334)	(0.212)	(0.969)
Log(Population$_{d,t}$)	0.170*	0.164**	0.243
	(0.078)	(0.054)	(0.237)
Log(Per Capita Income$_{d,t}$)	0.052**	0.057***	0.123*
	(0.016)	(0.017)	(0.054)
Population Density$_{d,t}$	−0.009***	−0.009***	−0.027**
	(0.002)	(0.002)	(0.008)
Log(Number of Municipalities$_{d,t}$)	−0.002	0.001	−0.029
	(0.014)	(0.009)	(0.039)
People Per Seat$_{d,t}$	−0.062**	−0.058***	−0.081
	(0.024)	(0.016)	(0.073)
Senior LDP Politician$_{d,t}$	0.148***	0.067***	0.393***
	(0.010)	(0.006)	(0.025)
Observations	1,291	1,291	1,291
Year FE	Y	Y	Y
R^2	0.268	0.292	0.188

Robust standard errors clustered on electoral district in parentheses.
*$p < 0.05$, **$p < 0.01$, ***$p < 0.001$.
Regression models estimated with R's plm() package.

Appendix A

A.5 SUPPLEMENTARY MATERIAL FOR CHAPTER 8

Table A.15 *Descriptive statistics pertaining to the variables used in Chapter 8's analyses of turnout in Japanese municipalities in Lower House elections, 1980–2014.*

Statistic	N	Mean	St. Dev.	Min	Max
Turnout$_{m,t}$	30,270	0.729	0.105	0.364	0.981
Turnout$_{m,t-1}$	26,588	0.742	0.099	0.399	0.981
Single LDP Winner VS$_{m,t}$	30,270	0.362	0.233	0.000	0.970
Rank(Single LDP Winner VS$_{m,t}$)	25,653	0.500	0.306	0.000	1.000
All LDP Winners VS$_{m,t}$	30,270	0.458	0.255	0.000	0.974
All LDP Candidates VS$_{m,t}$	30,270	0.540	0.186	0.000	0.974
Single LDP Loser VS$_{m,t}$	30,270	0.081	0.149	0.000	0.968
Single Non-LDP+ Winner VS$_{m,t}$	30,270	0.161	0.174	0.000	0.958
Single DPJ Winner VS$_{m,t}$	30,270	0.039	0.136	0.000	0.906
Margin$_{d,t}$	30,270	0.111	0.143	0.0001	0.906
Fiscal Strength$_{m,t}$	29,748	0.422	0.279	0.000	3.030
Dependent Population$_{m,t}$	29,021	0.364	0.047	0.025	0.642
Farming Population$_{m,t}$	29,020	0.091	0.072	0.000	0.625
Log(Population$_{m,t}$)	30,241	9.570	1.256	5.215	13.638
Log(Per Capita Income$_{m,t}$)	29,913	−0.145	0.403	−2.148	2.008
Population Density$_{m,t}$	30,241	0.734	1.796	0.001	21.237

A.5 Supplementary Material for Chapter 8

Table A.16 *Turnout rates as a cubic function of the degree to which a municipality concentrated votes on a single LDP winner relative to other municipalities in its district-year, for all Japanese municipalities, 1980–2014.*

	Dependent variable: Turnout$_{m,t}$
Rank(Single LDP Winner VS$_{m,t}$)	−0.044***
	(0.009)
Rank(Single LDP Winner VS$_{m,t}$)^2	0.064**
	(0.022)
Rank(Single LDP Winner VS$_{m,t}$)^3	−0.0004
	(0.015)
Fiscal Strength$_{m,t}$	−0.032***
	(0.004)
Dependent Population$_{m,t}$	0.432***
	(0.022)
Farming Population$_{m,t}$	0.066***
	(0.012)
Log(Population$_{m,t}$)	−0.022***
	(0.001)
Log(Per Capita Income$_{m,t}$)	0.034***
	(0.004)
Population Density$_{m,t}$	−0.003***
	(0.001)
Observations	24,320
District-Year FE	Y
Joint Hypothesis Test	0.000
R^2	0.520

Robust standard errors clustered on municipality in parentheses.
**$p < 0.01$, ***$p < 0.001$.
Regression models estimated with R's plm() package.

References

ACE: The Electoral Knowledge Network. 2013. "The ACE Encyclopaedia: Parties and Candidates." http://aceproject.org/ace-en/topics/pc/pca/pca02/pca02b.

Akizuki, Kengo. 1995. Institutionalizing the Local System: The Ministry of Home Affairs and Intergovernmental Relations in Japan. In *The Japanese Civil Service and Economic Development: Catalysts of Change*, ed. Hyung-Ki Kim, Michio Muramatsu, T. J. Pempel and Kozo Yamamura. Oxford: Oxford University Press pp. 337–366.

Albertus, Michael. 2019. "Theory and Methods in the Study of Distributive Politics." *Political Science Research and Methods* 7(3):629–639.

Allen, Oliver E. 1993. *The Tiger: The Rise and Fall of Tammany Hall*. Reading, MA: Addison-Wesley.

Amano, Kenya and Saori N. Katada. N.D. "Economic Policy Trilemma and Longevity of a Political Party: A Study of Japan's Liberal Democratic Party in a Comparative Perspective." Paper Presented at the American Political Science Association Meeting, Los Angele, CA, September 2023.

Arase, David. 2010. "Japan in 2009: A Historic Election Year." *Asian Survey* 50(1):40–55.

Ariga, Kenichi. 2015. "Incumbency Disadvantage under Electoral Rules with Intraparty Competition: Evidence from Japan." *The Journal of Politics* 77(3):874–887.

Asahi Shimbun. 2003. "Jimin Otosu Aichi 'Chinjyo Hodo Hodo Ni' Soumusho Yatsu Atari? Nagoya." *Asahi Shimbun* p. 2. November 18.

Asahi Shimbun. 2017. "Jimin: Ishizaki Shi 'Kuni Yosan, Niigata Ni Oritekonai' 'Mousou wo Motomeru,' Jimin Ga Hihan, Niigata Ken." *Asahi Shimbun* pp. Niigata Edition, p. 25. November 9.

Asahi Shimbun. 2021. "Jimin Daburu Rakusen. Kita Kyushu, Hajimete Jimoto Yoto Daigishi ga Fuzai ni." *Asahi Shimbun* p. 2. November 5.

Aspinall, Edward, Meredith L. Weiss, Allen Hicken and Paul D. Hutchcroft. 2022. *Mobilizing for Elections: Patronage and Political Machines in Southeast Asia*. New York, NY: Cambridge University Press.

Baldwin, Kate. 2013. "Why Vote with the Chief? Political Connections and Public Goods Provision in Zambia." *American Journal of Political Science* 57(4): 794–809.

Banful, Afua Branoah. 2011. "Do Formula-Based Intergovernmental Transfer Mechanisms Eliminate Politically Motivated Targeting? Evidence from Ghana." *Journal of Development Economics* 96(2):380–390.

References

Bawn, Kathleen and Michael Thies. 2003. "A Comparative Theory of Electoral Incentives: Representing the Unorganized under PR, Plurality and Mixed-Member Electoral Systems." *Journal of Theoretical Politics* 5(1):5–32.

Bergman, Matthew E., Cory L. Struthers, Matthew S. Shugart, Robert J. Pekkanen and Ellis S. Krauss. 2022. "The Party Personnel Datasets: Advancing Comparative Research in Party Behavior and Legislative Organization across Electoral Systems." *Legislative Studies Quarterly* 47(3):741–759.

Bessho, Shunichiro. 2016. Case Study of Central and Local Government Finance in Japan. ADBI Working Paper Series 599 Asian Development Bank Institute.

Blais, André. 2000. *To Vote or Not to Vote?: The Merits and Limits of Rational Choice Theory*. Pittsburgh, PA: University of Pittsburgh Press.

Blattman, Christopher, Mathilde Emeriau and Nathan Fiala. 2018. "Do Anti-Poverty Programs Sway Voters? Experimental Evidence from Uganda." *The Review of Economics and Statistics* 100(5):891–905.

Bouissou, Jean-Marie. 1999. Organizing One's Support Base under SNTV: The Case of the Japanese Koenkai. In *Elections in Japan, Korea, and Taiwan under the Single Non-Transferable Vote*, ed. Bernard Grofman, Sung-Chull Lee, Edwin Winckler and Brian Woodall. Ann Arbor, MI: Michigan University Press pp. 87–120.

Brierley, Sarah and Noah L. Nathan. 2021. "The Connections of Party Brokers: Which Brokers Do Parties Select?" *The Journal of Politics* 83(3):884–901.

Brun, Diego Abente and Larry Diamond. 2014. *Clientelism, Social Policy, and the Quality of Democracy*. Baltimore, MD: JHU Press.

Brusco, Valeria, Marcelo Nazareno and Susan C. Stokes. 2004. "Vote Buying in Argentina." *Latin American Research Review* 39(2):66–88.

Bussell, Jennifer. 2019. *Clients and Constituents: Political Responsiveness in Patronage Democracies*. New York, NY: Oxford University Press.

Calvo, Ernesto and Maria Victoria Murillo. 2004. "Who Delivers? Partisan Clients in the Argentine Electoral Market." *American Journal of Political Science* 48(4):742–757.

Cammett, Melani and Sukriti Issar. 2010. "Bricks and Mortar Clientelism: Sectarianism and the Logics of Welfare Allocation in Lebanon." *World Politics* 62(3):381–421.

Camp, Edwin, Avinash Dixit and Susan Stokes. 2014. "Catalyst or Cause? Legislation and the Demise of Machine Politics in Britain and the United States." *Legislative Studies Quarterly* 39(4):559–592.

Cancela, João and Benny Geys. 2016. "Explaining Voter Turnout: A Meta-Analysis of National and Subnational Elections." *Electoral Studies* 42: 264–275.

Carey, John and Matthew Shugart. 1995. "Incentives to Cultivate a Personal Vote: A Rank Ordering of Electoral Formulas." *Electoral Studies* 14:417–439.

Carlson, Matthew and Steven R. Reed. 2018a. *Political Corruption and Scandals in Japan*. Ithaca and London: Cornell University Press.

Carlson, Matthew and Steven R. Reed. 2018b. Scandals during the Abe Administrations. In *Japan Decides 2017: The Japanese General Election*, ed. Robert J. Pekkanen, Steven R. Reed, Ethan Scheiner and Daniel Smith. London: Palgrave MacMillan pp. 109–112.

Caselli, Mauro and Paolo Falco. 2019. Your Vote Is (No) Secret! How Low Voter Density Harms Voter Anonymity and Biases Elections in Italy. EconPol

References

Working Paper 26 Leibniz Institute for Economic Research at the University of Munich.

Catalinac, Amy. 2015. "From Pork to Policy: The Rise of Programmatic Campaigning in Japanese Elections." *Journal of Politics* 78(1).

Catalinac, Amy. 2016. *Electoral Reform and National Security in Japan: From Pork to Foreign Policy.* New York, NY: Cambridge University Press.

Catalinac, Amy. 2018. "Positioning under Alternative Electoral Systems: Evidence from Japanese Candidate Election Manifestos." *American Political Science Review* 112(1):31–48.

Catalinac, Amy, Bruce Bueno de Mesquita and Alastair Smith. 2020. "A Tournament Theory of Pork Barrel Politics: The Case of Japan." *Comparative Political Studies* 53(10–11):1619–1655.

Catalinac, Amy and Lucia Motolinia. 2021*a*. "Geographically-Targeted Spending in Mixed-Member Majoritarian Electoral Systems." *World Politics* 73(4): 668–771.

Catalinac, Amy and Lucia Motolinia. 2021*b*. "Why Geographically-Targeted Spending Under Closed-List Proportional Representation Favors Marginal Districts." *Electoral Studies* 71:102329.

Chandra, Kanchan. 2007. *Why Ethnic Parties Succeed: Patronage and Ethnic Head Counts in India.* New York, NY: Cambridge University Press.

Christensen, Ray. 2006. "An Analysis of the 2005 Japanese General Election: Will Koizumi's Political Reforms Endure?" *Asian Survey* 46(4):497–516.

Christensen, Ray and Joel Sawat Selway. 2017. "Pork-Barrel Politics and Electoral Reform: Explaining the Curious Differences in the Experiences of Thailand and Japan." *The Journal of Asian Studies* 76(2):283–310.

Christensen, Ray and Kyle Colvin. 2009. Stealing Elections: A Comparison of Election Night Corruption in Japan, Canada, and the United States. In *Political Change in Japan: Electoral Behavior, Party Realignment, and the Koizumi Reforms*, ed. Kay Shimizu, Steven R. Reed and Kenneth McElwain. Stanford University: Walter H. Shorenstein Asia-Pacific Research Center pp. 199–218.

Chubb, Judith. 1982. *Patronage, Power and Poverty in Southern Italy: A Tale of Two Cities.* Cambridge University Press.

Conover, Emily, Román A. Zárate, Adriana Camacho and Javier E. Baez. 2020. "Cash and Ballots: Conditional Transfers, Political Participation, and Voting Behavior." *Economic Development and Cultural Change* 68(2):541–566.

Cooperman, Alicia Dailey. 2024. "Bloc Voting for Electoral Accountability." *American Political Science Review* 118(3):1222–1239.

Correa, Diego Sanches and Jose Antonio Cheibub. 2016. "The Anti-Incumbent Effects of Conditional Cash Transfer Programs." *Latin American Politics and Society* 58(1):49–71.

Cox, Gary W. 1990. "Centripetal and Centrifugal Incentives in Electoral Systems." *American Journal of Political Science* 34(4):903–935.

Cox, Gary W. 1997. *Making Votes Count: Strategic Coordination in the World's Electoral Systems.* Cambridge: Cambridge University Press.

Cox, Gary W. 2009. "Swing Voters, Core Voters, and Distributive Politics." In *Political Representation*, ed. Ian Shapiro, Sue C. Stokes, Elisabeth Jean Wood, and Alexander S. Kirshner. New York, NY: Cambridge University Press pp. 342–357.

References

Cox, Gary W. and Emerson Niou. 1994. "Seat Bonuses under the Single Non-transferable Vote System: Evidence from Japan and Taiwan." *Comparative Politics* 26(2):221–236.

Cox, Gary W., Frances M. Rosenbluth and Michael F. Thies. 1998. "Mobilization, Social Networks, and Turnout: Evidence from Japan." *World Politics* 50(3):447–474.

Cox, Gary W. and Frances Rosenbluth. 1995. "Anatomy of a Split: The Liberal Democrats of Japan." *Electoral Studies* 14(4):355–76.

Cox, Gary W., Jon H. Fiva and Daniel M. Smith. 2016. "The Contraction Effect: How Proportional Representation Affects Mobilization and Turnout." *The Journal of Politics* 78(4):1249–1263.

Cox, Gary W. and Matthew D. McCubbins. 1986. "Electoral Politics as a Redistributive Game." *Journal of Politics* 48(2):370–389.

Cox, Gary W. and Michael C. Munger. 1989. "Closeness, Expenditures, and Turnout in the 1982 US House Elections." *American Political Science Review* 83(1):217–231.

Cox, Karen E. and Leonard Schoppa. 2002. "Interaction Effects in Mixed Member Electoral Systems: Theory and Evidence from Germany, Japan, and Italy." *Comparative Politics* 35(9):1027–1053.

Crisp, Brian F., Benjamin Schneider, Amy Catalinac and Taishi Muraoka. 2021. "Capturing Vote-Seeking Incentives and the Cultivation of a Personal and Party Vote." *Electoral Studies* 72:102369.

Cruz, Cesi. 2019. "Social Networks and the Targeting of Vote Buying." *Comparative Political Studies* 52(3):382–411.

Curtis, Gerald. 1971. *Election Campaigning, Japanese Style*. New York: Columbia University Press.

Curtis, Gerald. 1999. *The Logic of Japanese Politics: Leaders, Institutions, and the Limits of Political Change*. New York, NY: Columbia University Press.

Dahlberg, Matz and Eva Johansson. 2002. "On the Vote-Purchasing Behavior of Incumbent Governments." *American Political Science Review* 96(1):27–40.

Daily Yomiuri. 2009. "DPJ Grabs Tokyo Poll Spoils. Becomes Largest Party in Assembly; LDP Left Licking Wounds." *Daily Yomiuri*. July 13.

Davis, Christina L. 2003. *Food Fights over Free Trade: How International Institutions Promote Agricultural Trade Liberalization*. Princeton, NJ: Princeton University Press.

Davis, Christina L. and Jennifer Oh. 2007. "Repeal of the Rice Laws in Japan: The Role of International Pressure to Overcome Vested Interests." *Comparative Politics* 40(1):21–40.

de Kadt, Daniel and Evan S. Lieberman. 2020. "Nuanced Accountability: Voter Responses to Service Delivery in Southern Africa." *British Journal of Political Science* 50(1):185–215.

De La O., Ana Lorena. 2015. *Crafting Policies to End Poverty in Latin America: The Quiet Transformation*. New York, NY: Cambridge University Press.

Dellmuth, Lisa Maria and Michael F. Stoffel. 2012. "Distributive Politics and Intergovernmental Transfers: The Local Allocation of European Union Structural Funds." *European Union Politics* 13(3):413–433.

Denemark, David. 2000. "Partisan Pork Barrel in Parliamentary Systems: Australian Constituency-Level Grants." *Journal of Politics* 62(3):896–915.

References

Desposato, Scott and Ethan Scheiner. 2008. "Governmental Centralization and Party Affiliation: Legislator Strategies in Brazil and Japan." *The American Political Science Review* 102(4):509–524.

DeWit, Andrew. 2002. "Dry Rot: The Corruption of General Subsidies in Japan." *Journal of the Asia Pacific Economy* 7(3):355–378.

Diaz-Cayeros, Alberto, Federico Estévez and Beatriz Magaloni. 2016. *The Political Logic of Poverty Relief: Electoral Strategies and Social Policy in Mexico.* New York, NY: Cambridge University Press.

Dixit, Avinash and John Londregan. 1996. "The Determinants of Success of Special Interests in Redistributive Politics." *Journal of Politics* 58:1132–1155.

Dowding, Keith. 2005. "Is It Rational to Vote? Five Types of Answer and a Suggestion." *The British Journal of Politics and International Relations* 7(3):442–459.

Downs, Anthony. 1957. *An Economic Theory of Democracy.* New York, NY: Harper and Row.

Duverger, Maurice. 1963. *Political Parties: Their Organization and Activity in the Modern State.* New York, NY: John Wiley.

Endersby, James W., Steven E. Galatas and Chapman B. Rackaway. 2002. "Closeness Counts in Canada: Voter Participation in the 1993 and 1997 Federal Elections." *Journal of Politics* 64(2):610–631.

Endo, Masahisa, Robert J. Pekkanen and Steven R. Reed. 2013. The LDP's Path Back to Power. In *Japan Decides 2012: The Japanese General Election*, ed. Robert J. Pekkanen, Steven R. Reed and Ethan Scheiner. London: Palgrave Macmillan UK pp. 49–64.

Eshima, Shusei, Yusaku Horiuchi, Shiro Kuriwaki and Daniel M. Smith. N.D. "Winning Elections with Unpopular Policies: Valence Advantage and Single-Party Dominance in Japan." Unpublished https://papers.ssrn.com/sol3/papers.cfm?abstract_id=4371978

Estevez-Abe, Margarita. 2008. *Welfare and Capitalism in Postwar Japan.* New York, NY: Cambridge University Press.

Fedderson, Timothy J. 2004. "Rational Choice Theory and the Paradox of Not Voting." *Journal of Economic Perspectives* 18(1):99–112.

Finan, Federico and Laura Schechter. 2012. "Vote Buying and Reciprocity." *Econometrica* 80(2):863–881.

Fouirnaies, Alexander and Hande Mutlu-Eren. 2015. "English Bacon: Copartisan Bias in Intergovernmental Grant Allocation in England." *The Journal of Politics* 77(3):805–817.

Fujimura, Naofumi. 2020. "Effect of Malapportionment on Voter Turnout: Evidence from Japan's Upper House Elections." *Election Law Journal: Rules, Politics, and Policy* 19(4):542–551.

Fukui, Haruhiro and Shigeko N. Fukai. 1999. Campaigning for the Japanese Diet. In *Elections in Japan, Korea, and Taiwan under the Single Non-Transferable Vote*, ed. B. Grofman, S. C. Lee, E. A. Winckler and B. Woodall. Ann Arbor, MI: Michigan University Press pp. 121–152.

Fukui, Haruhiro and Shigeko N. Fukai. 1996. "Pork Barrel Politics, Networks, and Local Economic Development in Contemporary Japan." *Asian Survey* 36(3):268–286.

References

Fukumoto, Kentaro, Yusaku Horiuchi and Shoichiro Tanaka. 2020. "Treated Politicians, Treated Voters: A Natural Experiment on Political Budget Cycles." *Electoral Studies* 67:102206.

Funk, Patricia and Christina Gathmann. 2013. "How Do Electoral Systems Affect Fiscal Policy? Evidence from Cantonal Parliaments, 1890–2000." *Journal of the European Economic Association* 11(5):1178–1203.

Galanter, Marc and Thomas Palay. 1991. *Tournament of Lawyers: The Transformation of the Big Law Firm*. Chicago, IL: University of Chicago Press.

Gallagher, Michael. 1991. "Proportionality, Disproportionality and Electoral Systems." *Electoral Studies* 10(1):33–51.

Gans-Morse, Jordan, Sebastián Mazzuca and Simeon Nichter. 2014. "Varieties of Clientelism: Machine Politics during Elections." *American Journal of Political Science* 58(2):415–432.

Gentry, Hope Dewell. 2021. "The Political Strategy of Appealing to Religious Nationalism: Examining Motivations to Join Religious Organizations by Japanese LDP Politicians." *Politics and Religion* 14(4):691–711.

Geys, Benny 2006. "Rational Theories of Voter Turnout: A Review." *Political Studies Review* 4(1):16–35.

Golden, Miriam A. and Eugenia Nazrullaeva. 2023. *The Puzzle of Clientelism: Political Discretion and Elections around the World*. Elements in Political Economy. Cambridge University Press. www.cambridge.org/core/elements/puzzle-of-clientelism/88A948968E0C25B29A31BCDEB2DCE4DF

Golden, Miriam A. and Lucio Picci. 2008. "Pork-Barrel Politics in Postwar Italy, 1953–94." *American Journal of Political Science* 52(2):268–289.

Golden, Miriam A. and Brian Min. 2013. "Distributive Politics around the World." *Annual Review of Political Science* 16(1):73–99.

Goplerud, Max and Daniel M. Smith. 2023. "Who Answers for the Government? Bureaucrats, Ministers, and Responsible Parties." *American Journal of Political Science* 67(4):963–978.

Gottlieb, Jessica, Guy Grossman, Horacio Larreguy and Benjamin Marx. 2019. "A Signaling Theory of Distributive Policy Choice: Evidence from Senegal." *The Journal of Politics* 81(2):631–647.

Gottlieb, Jessica and Horacio Larreguy. 2020. "An Informational Theory of Electoral Targeting in Young Clientelistic Democracies: Evidence from Senegal." *Quarterly Journal of Political Science* 15(1):73–104.

Harris, J. Andrew and Daniel N. Posner. 2019. "(Under What Conditions) Do Politicians Reward Their Supporters? Evidence from Kenya's Constituencies Development Fund." *American Political Science Review* 113(1): 123–139.

Hayashida, Kazuhiro. 1967. "Development of Election Law in Japan." *Hosei Kenkyu* 34(1):51–104.

Hicken, Allen. 2007. How Do Rules and Institutions Encourage Vote Buying? In *Elections for Sale: The Causes and Consequences of Vote Buying*, ed. Frederic Charles Schaffer. Lynne Rienner Boulder, CO pp. 47–60.

Hicken, Allen. 2011. "Clientelism." *Annual Review of Political Science* 14(1):289–310.

Hicken, Allen and Noah L. Nathan. 2020. "Clientelism's Red Herrings: Dead Ends and New Directions in the Study of Nonprogrammatic Politics." *Annual Review of Political Science* 23(1):277–294.

References

Higashijima, Masaaki and Hidekuni Washida. 2024. "Varieties of Clientelism across Political Parties: New Measures of Patron–Client Relationships." *European Political Science Review* 16(2):260–280.

Hirano, Shigeo. 2006. "Electoral Institutions, Hometowns, and Favored Minorities: Evidence from Japanese Electoral Reforms." *World Politics* 58:51–82.

Hirano, Shigeo. 2011. "Do Individual Representatives Influence Government Transfers? Evidence from Japan." *Journal of Politics* 73(4):1081–1094.

Hirose, Michisada. 1993. *Hojokin to Seikento*. Tokyo: Asahi Shimbunsha.

Holland, Alisha C. and Brian Palmer-Rubin. 2015. "Beyond the Machine: Clientelist Brokers and Interest Organizations in Latin America." *Comparative Political Studies* 48(9):1186–1223.

Horiuchi, Yusaku. 2005. *Institutions, Incentives and Electoral Participation in Japan: Cross-level and Cross-national Perspectives*. London: Routledge Curzon.

Horiuchi, Yusaku, Daniel M. Smith and Teppei Yamamoto. 2018. "Measuring Voters' Multidimensional Policy Preferences with Conjoint Analysis: Application to Japan's 2014 Election." *Political Analysis* 26(2):190–209.

Horiuchi, Yusaku, Daniel M. Smith and Teppei Yamamoto. 2020. "Identifying Voter Preferences for Politicians' Personal Attributes: A Conjoint Experiment in Japan." *Political Science Research and Methods* 8(1):75–91.

Horiuchi, Yusaku and Jun Saito. 2003. "Reapportionment and Redistribution: Consequences of Electoral Reform in Japan." *American Journal of Political Science* 47(4):669–682.

Horiuchi, Yusaku, Jun Saito and Kyohei Yamada. 2015. "Removing Boundaries, Losing Connections: Electoral Consequences of Local Government Reform in Japan." *Journal of East Asian Studies* 15:99–125.

Hoshi, Takeo and Phillip Y. Lipscy, eds. 2021. "The Political Economy of the Abe Government." In *The Political Economy of the Abe Government and Abenomics Reforms*, ed. Takeo Hoshi and Phillip Y. Lipscy. Cambridge, UK: Cambridge University Press. pp. 3–40.

Huber, John D. and Michael M. Ting. 2013. "Redistribution, Pork, and Elections." *Journal of the European Economic Association* 11(6):1382–1403.

Hutchcroft, Paul D. et al. 2014. Linking Capital and Countryside: Patronage and Clientelism in Japan, Thailand, and the Philippines. In *Clientelism, Social Policy, and the Quality of Democracy*, ed. Diego Abente Brun and Larry Diamond. Baltimore, MD: Johns Hopkins University Press pp. 174–203.

Imai, Kosuke, Gary King and Carlos Velasco Rivera. 2019. "Do Nonpartisan Programmatic Policies Have Partisan Electoral Effects? Evidence from Two Large Scale Experiments." *Journal of Politics* 81(2):714–730.

Ishihara, Nobuo. 1986. The Local Public Finance System. In *Japan's Public Sector: How Government Is Financed*, ed. Tokue Shibata. Tokyo: University of Tokyo Press pp. 132–155.

Jensenius, Francesca R. and Pradeep Chhibber. 2023. "Privileging One's Own? Voting Patterns and Politicized Spending in India." *Comparative Political Studies* 56(4):503–529.

Jou, Willy. 2009. "Electoral Reform and Party System Development in Japan and Taiwan: A Comparative Study." *Asian Survey* 49(5):759–785.

Jou, Willy. 2010. "Voter Turnout in Japan: An Aggregate-Level Analysis of the 2005 and 2009 General Elections." *Asian Survey* 50(6):1032–1057.

References

Kabashima, Ikuo and Gill Steel. 2007. "How Junichiro Koizumi Seized the Leadership of Japan's Liberal Democratic Party." *Japanese Journal of Political Science* 8(1):95–114.

Kato, Junko. 1998. "When the Party Breaks Up: Exit and Voice among Japanese Legislators." *The American Political Science Review* 92(4):857–870.

Keefer, Philip and Stuti Khemani. 2009. "When Do Legislators Pass on Pork? The Role of Political Parties in Determining Legislator Effort." *American Political Science Review* 103(1):99–112.

Key, Valdimer O. 1949. *Southern Politics in State and Nation*. New York, NY: Knopf.

Kitschelt, Herbert. 2000. "Linkages between Citizens and Politicians in Democratic Polities." *Comparative Political Studies* 33(6–7):845–879.

Kitschelt, Herbert and Daniel M. Kselman. 2013. "Economic Development, Democratic Experience, and Political Parties' Linkage Strategies." *Comparative Political Studies* 46(11):1453–1484.

Kitschelt, Herbert and Matthew Singer. 2018. Linkage Strategies of Authoritarian Successor Parties. In *Life after Dictatorship: Authoritarian Successor Parties Worldwide*, ed. James Loxton and Scott Mainwaring. Cambridge: Cambridge University Press pp. 53–83.

Kitschelt, Herbert and Steven I. Wilkinson. 2007. Citizen–Politician Linkages: An Introduction. In *Patrons, Clients, and Policies*, ed. Herbert Kitschelt and Steven I. Wilkinson. New York, NY: Cambridge University Press pp. 1–49.

Kitschelt, Herbert et al. 2013. *Democratic Accountability and Linkages Project*. Durham, NC: Duke University.

Koellner, Patrick. 2009. "Japanese Lower House Campaigns in Transition: Manifest Changes or Fleeting Fads?" *Journal of East Asian Studies* 9(1):121–149.

Kohno, Masaru. 1997a. *The Creation of the Liberal Democratic Party in 1955*. Princeton NJ: Princeton University Press pp. 68–90.

Kohno, Masaru. 1997b. "Voter Turnout and Strategic Ticket-Splitting under Japan's New Electoral Rules." *Asian Survey* 37(5):429–440.

Kohno, Masaru and Yoshitaka Nishizawa. 1990. "A Study of the Electoral Business Cycle in Japan: Elections and Government Spending on Public Construction." *Comparative Politics* 22(2):151–66.

Konishi, Weston. 2009. "The Democratic Party of Japan: Its Foreign Policy Position and Implications for U.S. Interests." *Congressional Research Report for Congress*. August 17.

Kostelka, Filip, Eva Krejcova, Nicolas Sauger and Alexander Wuttke. 2023. "Election Frequency and Voter Turnout." *Comparative Political Studies* 56(14):2231–2268.

Kramon, Eric. 2017. *Money for Votes: The Causes and Consequences of Electoral Clientelism in Africa*. New York, NY: Cambridge University Press.

Krauss, Ellis S., Kuniaki Nemoto and Robert J. Pekkanen. 2012. "Reverse Contamination: Burning and Building Bridges in Mixed-Member Systems." *Comparative Political Studies* 45(6):747–773.

Krauss, Ellis S. and Robert J. Pekkanen. 2010. *The Rise and Fall of Japan's LDP. Political Party Organizations as Historical Institutions*. Ithaca, NY: Cornell University Press.

References

Krauss, Ellis S. and Robert J. Pekkanen. 2004. "Explaining Party Adaptation to Electoral Reform: The Discreet Charm of the LDP." *Journal of Japanese Studies* 30:1–34.

Krauss, Ellis S., Robert J. Pekkanen and Benjamin Nyblade. 2006. "Electoral Incentives in Mixed-Member Systems: Party, Posts, and Zombie Politicians in Japan." *American Political Science Review* 100(2):183–193.

Kuo, Didi. 2018. *Clientelism, Capitalism, and Democracy: The Rise of Programmatic Politics in the United States and Britain.* New York, NY: Cambridge University Press.

Kushida, Kenji E. and Phillip Y. Lipscy. 2013. The Rise and Fall of the Democratic Party of Japan. In *Japan under the DPJ: The Politics of Transition and Governance*, ed. Kenji E. Kushida and Phillip Y. Lipscy. Stanford, CA: The Walter H. Shorenstein Asia-Pacific Research Center, pp. 3–42.

Labonne, Julien. 2012. The Local Electoral Impacts of Conditional Cash Transfers: Evidence from a Field Experiment. CSAE Working Paper Series 2012–09 Centre for the Study of African Economies, University of Oxford.

Larreguy, Horacio, Cesar E. Montiel Olea and Pablo Querubin. 2017. "Political Brokers: Partisans or Agents? Evidence from the Mexican Teachers' Union." *American Journal of Political Science* 61(4):877–891.

Larreguy, Horacio, John Marshall and Pablo Querubín. 2016. "Parties, Brokers, and Voter Mobilization: How Turnout Buying Depends upon the Party's Capacity to Monitor Brokers." *American Political Science Review* 110(1):160–179.

Layton, Matthew L. and Amy Erica Smith. 2015. "Incorporating Marginal Citizens and Voters: The Conditional Electoral Effects of Targeted Social Assistance in Latin America." *Comparative Political Studies* 48(7):854–881.

Lazear, Edward P. and Sherwin Rosen. 1981. "Rank-Order Tournaments as Optimum Labor Contracts." *The Journal of Political Economy* 89(5):841–64.

Lee, Frances E. 2004. "Bicameralism and Geographic Politics: Allocating Funds in the House and Senate." *Legislative Studies Quarterly* 29(2):185–213.

Li, Hongbin and Li-An Zhou. 2005. "Political Turnover and Economic Performance: The Incentive Role of Personnel Control in China." *Journal of Public Economics* 89(9–10):1743–1762.

Liff, Adam P. 2021. "Japan in 2020: COVID-19 and the End of the Abe Era." *Asian Survey* 61(1):49–64.

Liff, Adam P. 2022. "Japan in 2021: COVID-19 (Again), the Olympics, and a New Administration." *Asian Survey* 62(1):29–42.

Liff, Adam P. and Ko Maeda. 2019. "Electoral Incentives, Policy Compromise, and Coalition Durability: Japan's LDP–Komeito Government in a Mixed Electoral System." *Japanese Journal of Political Science* 20(1):53–73.

Lindbeck, Assar and Jörgen W. Weibull. 1987. "Balanced-Budget Redistribution as the Outcome of Political Competition." *Public Choice* 52(3):273–297.

Lindberg, Staffan I. and Minion K. C. Morrison. 2008. "Are African Voters Really Ethnic or Clientelistic? Survey Evidence from Ghana." *Political Science Quarterly* 123(1):95–122.

Linos, Elizabeth. 2013. "Do Conditional Cash Transfers Shift Votes? Evidence from the Honduran PRAF." *Electoral Studies* 32(4):864–874.

References

Machidori, Satoshi. 2023. *Political Reform Reconsidered: The Trajectory of a Transformed Japanese State*. Springer Nature. https://link.springer.com/book/10.1007/978-981-19-9433-3

Maclachlan, Patricia L. 2004. "Post Office Politics in Modern Japan: The Postmasters, Iron Triangles, and the Limits of Reform." *Journal of Japanese Studies* 30(2):281–313.

Maclachlan, Patricia L. 2006. "Storming the Castle: The Battle for Postal Reform in Japan." *Social Science Japan Journal* 9(1):1–18.

Maclachlan, Patricia L. 2014. "The Electoral Power of Japanese Interest Groups: An Organizational Perspective." *Journal of East Asian Studies* 14(3):429–458.

Maclachlan, Patricia L. and Kay Shimizu. 2022. *Betting on the Farm: Institutional Change in Japanese Agriculture*. Ithaca, NY: Cornell University Press.

Maeda, Ko. 2023. The 2021 Election Results: Continuity and Change. In *Japan Decides 2021: The Japanese General Election*, ed. Robert J. Pekkanen, Steven R. Reed and Daniel M. Smith. Springer International Publishing pp. 23–39. eBook.

Maeda, Ko. 2010. "Factors behind the Historic Defeat of Japan's Liberal Democratic Party in 2009." *Asian Survey* 50(5):888–907.

Maeda, Ko. 2012. "An Irrational Party of Rational Members: The Collision of Legislators' Reelection Quest with Party Success in the Japan Socialist Party." *Comparative Political Studies* 45(3):341–365.

Maeda, Yukio. 2016. The Abe Cabinet and Public Opinion: How Abe Won Re-election by Narrowing Public Debate. In *Japan Decides 2014: The Japanese General Election*, ed. Robert J. Pekkanen, Steven R. Reed and Ethan Scheiner. London: Palgrave Macmillan UK pp. 89–102.

Magaloni, Beatriz. 2006. *Voting for Autocracy: Hegemonic Party Survival and Its Demise in Mexico*. Vol. 296 New York, NY: Cambridge University Press.

Magaloni, Beatriz, Alberto Diaz-Cayeros and Federico Estévez. 2007. Clientelism and Portfolio Diversification: A Model of Electoral Investment with Applications to Mexico. In *Patrons, Clients and Policies: Patterns of Democratic Accountability and Political Competition*, ed. Herbert Kitschelt and Steven I. Editors Wilkinson. Cambridge, UK: Cambridge University Press pp. 182–205.

Malik, Rabia. 2019. "(A) Political Constituency Development Funds: Evidence from Pakistan." *British Journal of Political Science* 51(3): 963–980.

Malik, Rabia. 2023. "Lesser of Two Evils: Allocating Resources to Opposition Districts in Pakistan." *Legislative Studies Quarterly* 48(2):241–271.

Mares, Isabela, 2015. *From Open Secrets to Secret Voting: Democratic Electoral Reforms and Voter Autonomy*. New York, NY: Cambridge University Press.

Mares, Isabela and Lauren E. Young. 2019. *Conditionality & Coercion: Electoral Clientelism in Eastern Europe*. Oxford: Oxford University Press.

Mares, Isabela and Lauren E. Young. 2016. "Buying, Expropriating, and Stealing Votes." *Annual Review of Political Science* 19:267–288.

Masumi, Junnosuke. 1995. *Contemporary Politics in Japan*. Berkeley: University of California Press. Trans. L. E. Carlisle.

Matsumoto, Tomoko, Kenneth Mori McElwain, Kensuke Okada, and Junko Kato. 2024. "Generational differences in economic perceptions", *Electoral Studies* 91, 102830.

McCubbins, Matthew D. and Frances Rosenbluth. 1995. Party Provision for Personal Politics. Dividing the Vote in Japan. In *Structure and Policy in Japan and*

References

the United States, ed. Peter F. Cowhey and Matthew D. McCubbins. New York, NY: Cambridge University Press pp. 35–55.

McElwain, Kenneth Mori. 2008. "Manipulating Electoral Rules to Manufacture Single-Party Dominance." *American Journal of Political Science* 52(1):32–47.

McElwain, Kenneth Mori. 2012. "The Nationalization of Japanese Elections." *Journal of East Asian Studies* 12(3):323–350.

McGillivray, Fiona. 2004. *Privileging Industry: The Comparative Politics of Trade and Industrial Policy*. Princeton, NJ: Princeton University Press.

McKean, Margaret and Ethan Scheiner. 2000. "Japan's New Electoral System: La Plus ça Change." *Electoral Studies* 19:447–77.

McMichael, Taylor C. 2017. "When Formulas Go Political: The Curious Case of Japan's Financial Index." *Japanese Journal of Political Science* 18(3):407–425.

McMichael, Taylor C. 2018. "Electoral Strategy and Intergovernmental Transfers in Postwar Japan." *Asian Survey* 58(5):847–873.

Medina, Luis Fernando and Susan Stokes. 2007. Monopoly and Monitoring: An Approach to Political Clientelism. In *Patrons, Clients, and Policies*, ed. Herbert Kitschelt and Steven Wilkinson. New York, NY: Cambridge University Press pp. 68–83.

Meyer, Stephen A. and Shigeto Naka. 1998. "Legislative Influences in Japanese Budgetary Politics." *Public Choice* 94:267–88.

Meyer, Stephen A. and Shigeto Naka. 1999. "The Determinants of Japanese Local Benefit-Seeking." *Contemporary Economic Policy* 17(1):87–96.

Mihaljek, Dubravko. 1997. Japan. In *Fiscal Federalism in Theory and Practice*. USA: International Monetary Fund. www.elibrary.imf.org/view/book/9781557756633/ch012.xml

Mizusaki, Tokifumi. 2014. *Sosenkyo Deta Besu. JED-M Deta*. Tokyo: LDB.

Mochida, Nobuki. 2001. Taxes and Transfers in Japan's Local Public Finance. In *Local Government Development in Post-War Japan*, ed. Michio Muramatsu, Ikuo Kume and Farrukh Iqbal. Oxford: Oxford University Press pp. 85–111.

Mochida, Nobuki. 2008. *Fiscal Decentralization and Local Public Finance in Japan*. London: Routledge.

Morton, Rebecca B. 1991. "Groups in Rational Turnout Models." *American Journal of Political Science* 35(3):758–776.

Motolinia, Lucia. 2021. "Electoral Accountability and Particularistic Legislation: Evidence from an Electoral Reform in Mexico." *American Political Science Review* 115(1):97–113.

Mueller, Wolfgang C. 2007. Political Institutions and Linkage Strategies. In *Patrons, Clients, and Policies*, ed. Herbert Kitschelt and Steven Wilkinson. New York, NY: Cambridge University Press pp. 251–275.

Muraközy, Balázs and Almos Telegdy. 2016. "Political Incentives and State Subsidy Allocation: Evidence from Hungarian Municipalities." *European Economic Review* 89:324–344.

Muraoka, Taishi and Joan Barceló. 2019. "The Effect of District Magnitude on Turnout: Quasiexperimental Evidence from Nonpartisan Elections under SNTV." *Party Politics* 25(4):632–639.

Myerson, Roger W. 1993. "Incentives to Cultivate Favored Minorities under Alternative Electoral Systems." *American Political Science Review* 87(4):856–869.

Nabeshima, Kenny and Tsukasa Maekawa. 1989. *Hyoden no Torakuta*. Tokyo: Shogakukan.

References

Nam, Koon Woo. 1977. "The Crisis of Japan's Liberal Democratic Party." *Asian Affairs* 4(6):356–370.

Naoi, Megumi. 2015. *Building Legislative Coalitions for Free Trade in Asia: Globalization as Legislation*. Cambridge, UK: Cambridge University Press.

Nemoto, Kuniaki, Ellis S. Krauss and Robert J. Pekkanen. 2008. "Policy Dissension and Party Discipline: The July 2005 Vote on Postal Privatization in Japan." *British Journal of Political Science* 38(3):499–525.

Nemoto, Kuniaki and Matthew S. Shugart. 2013. "Localism and Coordination under Three Different Electoral Systems: The National District of the Japanese House of Councillors." *Electoral Studies* 32(1):1–12.

Nichter, Simeon. 2008. "Vote Buying or Turnout Buying? Machine Politics and the Secret Ballot." *American Political Science Review* 102(1):19–31.

Nichter, Simeon. 2014. "Conceptualizing Vote Buying." *Electoral Studies* 35:315–327.

Nichter, Simeon. 2018. *Votes for Survival: Relational Clientelism in Latin America*. Cambridge Studies in Comparative Politics. New York, NY: Cambridge University Press.

Noble, Gregory W. 2010. "The Decline of Particularism in Japanese Politics." *Journal of East Asian Studies* 10:239–273.

Noble, Gregory W. 2016. Abenomics in the 2014 Election: Showing the Money (Supply) and Little Else. In *Japan Decides 2014: The Japanese General Election*, ed. Robert J. Pekkanen, Steven R. Reed and Ethan Scheiner. London: Palgrave Macmillan UK pp. 155–169.

Nyblade, Benjamin. 2013. Keeping It Together: Party Unity and the 2012 Election. In *Japan Decides 2012: The Japanese General Election*, ed. Robert J. Pekkanen, Steven R. Reed and Ethan Scheiner. London: Palgrave Macmillan UK pp. 20–33.

Nyblade, Benjamin and Steven R. Reed. 2008. "Who Cheats? Who Loots? Political Competition and Corruption in Japan, 1947–1993." *American Journal of Political Science* 52(4):926–941.

Otake, Hideo. 1996. "Forces for Political Reform: The Liberal Democratic Party's Young Reformers and Ozawa Ichiro." *Journal of Japanese Studies* 22(2):269–294.

Otake, Hideo. 1998. Overview. In *How Electoral Reform Boomeranged. Continuity in Japanese Campaigning Style*, ed. Hideo Otake. Tokyo: Japan Center for International Exchange pp. ix–xxxi.

Patterson, Dennis and Ko Maeda. 2007. "Prime Ministerial Popularity and the Changing Electoral Fortunes of Japan's Liberal Democratic Party." *Asian Survey* 47(3):415–433.

Pekkanen, Robert J. and Saadia M. Pekkanen. 2015. "Japan in 2014: All about Abe." *Asian Survey* 55(1):103–118.

Pekkanen, Robert J. and Steven R. Reed. 2016. From Third Force to Third Party: Duverger's Revenge? In *Japan Decides 2014: The Japanese General Election*, ed. Robert J. Pekkanen, Steven R. Reed and Ethan Scheiner. London: Palgrave Macmillan UK pp. 62–71.

Pekkanen, Robert J. and Steven R. Reed. 2023. Japanese Politics between 2017 and 2021. In *Japan Decides 2021: The Japanese General Election*, ed. Robert J. Pekkanen, Steven R. Reed and Daniel M. Smith. Springer International Publishing pp. 13–22. eBook.

References

Pekkanen, Robert J., Steven R. Reed and Daniel M. Smith. 2016. Japanese Politics between the 2012 and 2014 Elections. In *Japan Decides 2014: The Japanese General Election*, ed. Robert J. Pekkanen, Steven R. Reed and Ethan Scheiner. London: Palgrave Macmillan UK pp. 9–21.

Pekkanen, Robert J., Steven R. Reed and Ethan Scheiner. 2016. Introduction: Take a Second Look at the 2014 Election, It's Worth It. In *Japan Decides 2014: The Japanese General Election*, ed. Robert J. Pekkanen, Steven R. Reed and Ethan Scheiner. London: Palgrave Macmillan UK pp. 3–8.

Pekkanen, Robert J. and Steven R. Reed. 2013. Japanese Politics between the 2009 and 2012 Elections. In *Japan Decides 2012: The Japanese General Election*, ed. Robert J. Pekkanen, Steven R. Reed and Ethan Scheiner. London: Palgrave Macmillan UK pp. 8–19.

Pekkanen, Robert J. and Steven R. Reed. 2018. The Opposition: From Third Party Back to Third Force. In *Japan Decides 2017: The Japanese General Election*, ed. Robert J. Pekkanen, Steven R. Reed, Ethan Scheiner and Daniel Smith. London: Palgrave MacMillan pp. 77–92.

Pempel, T. J. 1990. *Introduction: Uncommon Democracies: The One-Party Dominant Regimes*. Ithaca, NY: Cornell University Press pp. 1–32.

Pempel, T. J. 1998. *Regime Shift: Comparative Dynamics of the Japanese Political Economy*. Ithaca, NY: Cornell University Press.

Pempel, T. J. 2010. "Between Pork and Productivity: The Collapse of the Liberal Democratic Party." *Journal of Japanese Studies* 36(2):227–254.

Piattoni, Simona et al. 2001. *Clientelism, Interests, and Democratic Representation: The European Experience in Historical and Comparative Perspective*. Cambridge, UK: Cambridge University Press.

Ramseyer, Mark and Frances Rosenbluth. 1993. *Japan's Political Marketplace*. Cambridge, MA: Harvard University Press.

Ravanilla, Nico, Dotan Haim and Allen Hicken. 2022. "Brokers, Social Networks, Reciprocity, and Clientelism." *American Journal of Political Science* 66(4):795–812.

Reed, Stephen R. 2009. "Party Strategy or Candidate Strategy? How Does the LDP Run the Right Number of Candidates in Japan's Multi-Member Districts?" *Party Politics* 15:295–314.

Reed, Stephen R. and Daniel M. Smith. 2015. "The Reed-Smith Japanese House of Representatives Elections Data Set." https://sites.google.com/site/danielmarkhamsmith/data

Reed, Steven R. 1986. *Japanese Prefectures and Policymaking*. Pittsburgh, PA: University of Pittsburgh Press.

Reed, Steven R. 1990. "Structure and Behaviour: Extending Duverger's Law to the Japanese Case." *British Journal of Political Science* 20(3):335–356.

Reed, Steven R. 1995. "The Nomination Process for Japan's Next General Election: Waiting for the *Heiritsu-sei*." *Asian Survey* 35(12):1075–1086.

Reed, Steven R. 2001. Impersonal Mechanisms and Personal Networks in the Distribution of Grants. In *Local Government Development in Post-war Japan*, ed. Michio Muramatsu, Ikuo Kume and Farrukh Iqbal. New York, NY: Oxford University Press pp. 112–131.

Reed, Steven R. 2007. "Duverger's Law Is Working in Japan." *Senkyo Kenkyu (Electoral Studies)* 22:96–106.

Reed, Steven R. 2021. "Patronage and Predominance: How the LDP Maintains Its Hold on Power." *Social Science Japan Journal* 25(1):83–100.

Reed, Steven R., Ethan Scheiner, Daniel M. Smith and Michael F. Thies. 2013. The 2012 Election Results: The LDP Wins Big by Default. In *Japan Decides 2012: The Japanese General Election*, ed. Robert J. Pekkanen, Steven R. Reed and Ethan Scheiner. London: Palgrave Macmillan UK pp. 34–46.

Reed, Steven R., Ethan Scheiner and Michael F. Thies. 2012. "The End of LDP Dominance and the Rise of Party-Oriented Politics in Japan." *Journal of Japanese Studies* 38(2):353–375.

Reed, Steven R. and Kay Shimizu. 2009. Avoiding a Two-Party System: The Liberal Democratic Party versus Duverger's Law. In *Political Change in Japan: Electoral Behavior, Party Realignment, and the Koizumi Reforms*, ed. Kay Shimizu, Steven R. Reed and Kenneth McElwain. Stanford: Walter H. Shorenstein Asia-Pacific Research Center, Stanford University pp. 29–46.

Reed, Steven R. and Michael Thies. 2001. The Causes of Electoral Reform in Japan. In *Mixed Member Electoral Systems: The Best of Both Worlds?*, ed. Matthew S. Shugart and Martin P. Wattenberg. New York, NY: Oxford University Press pp. 152–172.

Repeta, Lawrence. 2014. "Japan's 2013 State Secrecy Act – The Abe Administration's Threat to News Reporting 2013." *The Asia-Pacific Journal Japan Focus* 12(10). https://apjjf.org/2014/12/10/lawrence-repeta/4086/article

Richardson, Bradley M. 1973. "Urbanization and Political Participation: The Case of Japan." *American Political Science Review* 67(2):433–452.

Rickard, Stephanie J. 2018. *Spending to Win: Political Institutions, Economic Geography, and Government Subsidies*. New York, NY: Cambridge University Press.

Riker, William H. and Peter C. Ordeshook. 1968. "A Theory of the Calculus of Voting." *American Political Science Review* 62(1):25–42.

Rizzo, Tessalia. N.D. "When Clients Exit: Breaking the Clientelist Feedback Loop." www.dropbox.com/s/mg56bfukhqm15fr/Rizzo-WhenClientsExit_Draft_MostRecent.pdf?dl=0

Rosas, Guillermo, Noel P. Johnston and Kirk Hawkins. 2014. "Local Public Goods as Votepurchasing Devices? Persuasion and Mobilization in the Choice of Clientelist Payments." *Journal of Theoretical Politics* 26(4):573–598.

Rosenbluth, Frances and Michael Thies. 2010. *Japan Transformed. Political Change and Economic Restructuring*. Princeton, NJ: Princeton University Press.

Rueda, Miguel R. 2017. "Small Aggregates, Big Manipulation: Vote Buying Enforcement and Collective Monitoring." *American Journal of Political Science* 61(1):163–177.

Saito, Jun. 2010. *Jiminto Choki Seiken no Seiji Keizaigaku*. Tokyo: Keiso Shobo.

Sakaiya, Shiro. 2009. "Nihoin Seiji no Hoshuka to Senkyo Kyouso." *Senkyo Kenkyu* 25(2):5–17.

Sasada, Hironori. 2010. "The Electoral Origin of Japan's Nationalistic Leadership: Primaries in the LDP Presidential Election and the 'Pull Effect'." *Journal of East Asian Studies* 10:1–30.

Scheiner, Ethan. 2005. "Pipelines of Pork: A Model of Local Opposition Party Failure." *Comparative Political Studies* 38:799–823.

References

Scheiner, Ethan. 2006. *Democracy without Competition in Japan. Opposition Failure in a One-Party Dominant State*. New York, NY: Cambridge University Press.

Scheiner, Ethan. 2007. Clientelism in Japan: The Importance and Limits of Institutional Explanations. In *Patrons, Clients, and Policies*, ed. Herbert Kitschelt and Steven Wilkinson. New York, NY: Cambridge University Press pp. 276–297.

Scheiner, Ethan, Daniel M. Smith and Michael F. Thies. 2016. The 2014 Japanese Election Results: The Opposition Cooperates but Fails to Inspire. In *Japan Decides 2014: The Japanese General Election*, ed. Robert J. Pekkanen, Steven R. Reed and Ethan Scheiner. London: Palgrave Macmillan UK pp. 22–38.

Scheiner, Ethan, Daniel M. Smith and Michael F. Thies. 2018. The 2017 Election Results: An Earthquake, a Typhoon, and Another Landslide. In *Japan Decides 2017: The Japanese General Election*, ed. Robert J. Pekkanen, Steven R. Reed, Ethan Scheiner and Daniel M. Smith. Cham: Springer International Publishing pp. 29–50.

Schlesinger, Jacob M. 1997. *Shadow Shoguns. The Rise and Fall of Japan's Postwar Political Machine*. Stanford, CA: Stanford University Press.

Schwartz, Thomas. 1987. "Your Vote Counts on Account of the Way It Is Counted: An Institutional Solution to the Paradox of Not Voting." *Public Choice* 54:101–21.

Scott, James C. 1972. "Patron-Client Politics and Political Change in Southeast Asia." *American Political Science Review* 66(1):91–113.

Shefter, Martin. 1977. "Party and Patronage: Germany, England, and Italy." *Politics & Society* 7(4):403–451.

Shefter, Martin. 1994. *Political Parties and the State: The American Historical Experience*. Princeton, NJ: Princeton University Press.

Shirai, Sayuri. 2005. "Growing Problems in the Local Public Finance System of Japan." *Social Science Japan Journal* 8(2):213–238.

Smith, Alastair and Bruce Bueno de Mesquita. 2012. "Contingent Prize Allocation and Pivotal Voting." *British Journal of Political Science* 42:371–92.

Smith, Alastair and Bruce Bueno de Mesquita. 2019. "Motivating Political Support with Group-Based Rewards." *Journal of Theoretical Politics* 31(2):156–182.

Smith, Alastair, Bruce Bueno de Mesquita and Tom LaGatta. 2017. "Group Incentives and Rational Voting." *Journal of Theoretical Politics* 29(2):299–326.

Smith, Daniel M. 2016. Candidates in the 2014 Election: Better Coordination and Higher Candidate Quality. In *Japan Decides 2014: The Japanese General Election*, ed. Robert J. Pekkanen, Steven R. Reed and Ethan Scheiner. London: Palgrave Macmillan UK pp. 118–133.

Smith, Daniel M. 2018a. *Dynasties and Democracy: The Inherited Incumbency Advantage in Japan*. Stanford, CA: Stanford University Press.

Smith, Daniel M. 2018b. Electoral Systems and Voter Turnout. In *The Oxford Handbook of Electoral Systems*. New York, NY: Oxford University Press pp. 193–212.

Smith, Sheila. 2018c. Foreign Policy. In *Japan Decides 2017: The Japanese General Election*, ed. Robert J. Pekkanen, Steven R. Reed, Ethan Scheiner and Daniel Smith. London: Palgrave MacMillan pp. 329–345.

References

Sone, Yasunori and Masao Kanazashi, eds. 1989. *Bijual Zeminaaru: Nihon no Seiji [Visual Seminar: Politics in Japan]*. Tokyo: Nihon Keizai Shinbunsha.

Stokes, Susan C. 2005. "Perverse Accountability: A Formal Model of Machine Politics with Evidence from Argentina." *American Political Science Review* 99:315–25.

Stokes, Susan C. 2007. Political Clientelism. In *The Oxford Handbook of Comparative Politics*, ed. Carles Boix and Susan C. Stokes. Oxford: Oxford University Press pp. 604–627.

Stokes, Susan C., Thad Dunning, Marcelo Nazareno and Valeria Brusco. 2013. *Brokers, Voters, and Clientelism: The Puzzle of Distributive Politics*. New York, NY: Cambridge University Press.

Sugawara, Taku. 2002. Heiritsu Seika no Senkyo Undo. In *Senkyo Posuta no Kenkyuu*, ed. Todai Ho Kabashima Ikuo Zemi Hen. Tokyo: Bokutakusha chapter 7, pp. 197–211.

Sugiyama, Satoshi. 2020. "Japan's DPP Approves CDP Merger as Snap Poll Speculation Grows." *Japan Times* . August 19.

Suzuki, Y. and Y. Takahashi. 2015. "Kokkoshishutsukin no Kouzou Henka ni Tsuite Yubarishi no Jirei." *Ikoma Keizai Ronsou [Ikoma Journal of Economics]* 13(1):41–68.

Szwarcberg, Mariela. 2015. *Mobilizing Poor Voters: Machine Politics, Clientelism, and Social Networks in Argentina*. New York, NY: Cambridge University Press.

Taagepera, Rein, Peter Selb and Bernard Grofman. 2014. "How Turnout Depends on the Number of Parties: A Logical Model." *Journal of Elections, Public Opinion & Parties* 24(4):393–413.

Tani, Satomi. 1998. Political Realignment in Hyogo and Okayama. In *How Electoral Reform Boomeranged. Continuity in Japanese Campaigning Style*, ed. Hideo Otake. Tokyo: Japan Center for International Exchange pp. 59–96.

Taniguchi, Masaki and Asahi Shimbun. 2019. "The University of Tokyo-Asahi Survey." www.masaki.j.u-tokyo.ac.jp/utas/utasindex_en.html

Tatebayashi, Masahiko. 2004. *Giin Kodo no Seiji Keizaigaku. Jiminto Shihai no Seido Bunseki. [The Political Economy of Politician's Behavior]*. Tokyo: Yuhikaku.

Tavits, Margit. 2009. "Geographically Targeted Spending: Exploring the Electoral Strategies of Incumbent Governments." *European Political Science Review* 1(1):103–123.

Thayer, Nathaniel. 1969. *How the Conservatives Rule Japan*. Princeton, NJ: Princeton University Press.

The Japan Times. 2002. "Package of Redistricting Bills Approved by Lower House." *Japan Times*. July 19.

Thies, Michael F. and Yuki Yanai. 2013. Governance with a Twist: How Bicameralism Affects Japanese Lawmaking. In *Japan Decides 2012: The Japanese General Election*, ed. Robert J. Pekkanen, Steven R. Reed and Ethan Scheiner. London: Palgrave Macmillan UK pp. 225–244.

Tiberghien, Yves. 2013. Election Surprise: Abenomics and Central Bank Independence Trump Nationalism and Fukushima. In *Japan Decides 2012: The Japanese General Election*, ed. Robert J. Pekkanen, Steven R. Reed and Ethan Scheiner. London: Palgrave Macmillan UK pp. 195–200.

References

Tobias, Julia E., Sudarno Sumarto and Habib Moody. 2014. "Assessing the Political Impacts of a Conditional Cash Transfer: Evidence from a Randomized Policy Experiment in Indonesia." *The SMERU Research Institute*.

Tokushima Shimbun. 2019. "'Senkyo Ganbaru Chiho ni Yosan' Nikai Jiminto Kanjicho, Tokushima hi De Hatsugen." *Tokushima Shimbun*. June 30.

Tsurutani, Taketsugu. 1980. "The LDP in Transition? Mass Membership Participation in Party Leadership Selection." *Asian Survey* 20(8):844–859.

Uchiyama, Yu. 2010. *Koizumi and Japanese Politics: Reform Strategies and Leadership Style*. London: Routledge.

Wang, Chin-Shou and Charles Kurzman. 2007. The Logistics: How to Buy Votes. In *Elections for Sale: The Causes and Consequences of Vote Buying*, ed. Frederic Charles Schaffer. Boulder, CO: Lynne Rienner pp. 61–78.

Wantchekon, Leonard. 2003. "Clientelism and Voting Behavior: Evidence from a Field Experiment in Benin." *World Politics* pp. 399–422.

Ward, Hugh and Peter John. 1999. "Targeting Benefits for Electoral Gain: Constituency Marginality and the Distribution of Grants to English Local Authorities." *Political Studies* 47(1):32–52.

Ward, Robert E. 1966. "Recent Electoral Developments in Japan." *Asian Survey* pp. 547–567.

Weese, Eric. 2015. "Political Mergers as Coalition Formation: An Analysis of the Heisei Municipal Amalgamations." *Quantitative Economics* 6(2):257–307.

Weitz-Shapiro, Rebecca. 2012. "What Wins Votes: Why Some Politicians Opt Out of Clientelism." *American Journal of Political Science* 56(3):568–583.

Weitz-Shapiro, Rebecca. 2014. *Curbing Clientelism in Argentina: Politics, Poverty, and Social Policy*. New York, NY: Cambridge University Press.

Yamada, Kyohei. 2016. "Crucial Decisions by Small Towns and Villages: Why Did Some Municipalities Choose to Merge but Others Did Not during the Nationwide Wave of Municipal Mergers in Japan?" *International Journal of Public Administration* 39(6):480–491.

Yamada, Kyohei. 2018. "From a Majority to a Minority: How Municipal Mergers in Japan Changed the Distribution of Political Powers and the Allocation of Public Services within a Merged Municipality." *Urban Affairs Review* 54(3):560–592.

Yamada, Kyohei and Kiichiro Arai. 2021. "Do Boundary Consolidations Alter the Relationship between Politicians and Voters? The Case of Municipal Mergers in Japan." *Local Government Studies* 47(4):519–545.

Yıldırım, Kerem and Herbert Kitschelt. 2020. "Analytical Perspectives on Varieties of Clientelism." *Democratization* 27(1):20–43.

Yokomichi, Kiyotaka. 2007. "The Development of Municipal Mergers in Japan." *COSLOG Up-to-Date Documents on Local Autonomy in Japan* 1:1–22.

Yomiuri Shimbun. 2009. "Hirei ha Minshu 42 Pasento. Yusei Iji. Yomiuri Shimbun Seron Chosa." *Yomiuri Shimbun*. July 24.

Yonehara, Junshichiro. 1986. Financial Relations between National and Local Governments. In *Japan's Public Sector: How Government Is Financed*, ed. Tokue Shibata. Tokyo: University of Tokyo Press pp. 156–168.

Zarazaga, Rodrigo. 2016. "Party Machines and Voter-Customized Rewards Strategies." *Journal of Theoretical Politics* 28(4):678–701.

Zucco, Cesar. 2013. "When Payouts Pay Off: Conditional Cash Transfers and Voting Behavior in Brazil 2002–10." *American Journal of Political Science* 57(4):810–822.

Index

Abe Shinzo, 39, 46, 47, 49, 64, 203
Abenomics, 45
Allied Occupation of Japan, 140
Aso Taro, 39, 203, 216

campaign manifestos, 216–219, 222
clientelism
   brokers, 84, 86, 103, 104, 316
   collective action, 10
   definitions, 5, 77, 78, 83, 84, 86, 90, 107
   economic development, 105, 106, 316
   implications for democracy, 79, 107
   policy recommendations, 102, 313
   problem of contingency, 6, 81–83, 85
   target of exchange, 7, 85, 86, 88–91, 107, 133, 134
constitution, 28, 140
consumption tax, 46
corruption, 144, 245
COVID-19, 48

Ehime First District, 269
Election Management Commission, 142, 143
election manifestos, 62
elections
   House of Councilors (HOC)
      1998, 37
      2007, 39
      2010, 41
      2013, 45, 47
   House of Representatives (HOR)
      1993, 31
      1996, 34, 58
      2000, 38
      2003, 38
      2005, 38, 62, 63, 171
      2009, 39, 40, 171, 172, 203–206
      2012, 42, 58
      2014, 45, 64
      2017, 48, 64, 216
      2021, 49, 64
electoral districts
   boundaries of, 94, 140–142, 144–146, 258
   conditions for GBC, 8, 12, 21, 87, 163, 165–167, 169–172, 181, 218, 235, 239, 295, 313–315, 318
   ruralness, 34, 39, 40, 63, 66, 67, 97, 242–244
   vote counting within, 92–97
electoral systems
   and particularism. *See* particularism, reasons for
   Japan's 1994 electoral reform, 14, 22, 23, 32, 56, 63, 68, 71, 166, 171, 195, 218, 251, 257, 281
   mixed-member majoritarian (MMM), 32, 33, 57–61, 177
   open-list proportional representation (OLPR), 318
   single nontransferable vote in multimember districts (SNTV-MMD), 54–56, 61, 66, 140, 177, 267

Fiscal Investment and Loan Program (FILP), 156
Fukuda Yasuo, 39, 203

Hatoyama Yukio, 64, 203
House of Councilors (HOC), 29, 37, 39, 41, 140
   elections. *See* elections, House of Councilors (HOC)
House of Representatives (HOR), 29, 140, 144

Index

House of Representatives (HOR) (cont.)
  elections. *See* elections, House of Representatives (HOR)

Kanemaru Shin, 246
Kishida Fumio, 49
Koike Yuriko, 47
Koizumi Junichiro, 38, 63, 64, 161, 171

Law No. 43, 140
Local Autonomy Law, 141
Local Public Finance Law, 156

malapportionment, 242, 243
methods
  fixed effects, 175, 183, 186, 188, 196, 197, 254, 256, 303
  variables, 178–180, 183, 201, 239–241, 243–246, 276–278
Mihara Asahiko, 161
Ministry of Internal Affairs and Communication (MIC), 154, 157
municipalities
  categories of, 142, 177
  financing of, 66, 99, 147–150, 152, 153, 161, 244
  government outlays to, 68, 69, 147, 152
  local allocation tax (LAT), 152–155, 162, 243, 244
  national treasury disbursements (NTD), 152, 153, 155–162, 165, 178, 180, 216, 243, 244, 314
  lobbying, 159, 211
  mergers of, 146, 161, 167, 177, 197, 295
  ordinance-designated cities, 166
  responsibilities of, 142, 144, 150, 151
  ruralness, 150, 155, 195, 283, 307, 309
  split, 163, 165, 177, 178, 181, 313

Nara City, 257, 258
Nara First District, 257, 258, 269
Nikai Toshihiro, 215

Ozawa Ichiro, 37

paradox of voting, 113, 128
particularism
  electoral system, 67, 200
  lobbying for, 115, 212, 213
  reasons for, 56, 60, 68, 126, 128, 171
  to core supporters, 66, 68, 131–133, 136, 236, 237, 269, 270
  to swing voters, 130, 136, 236, 237, 270

type of goods, 66, 89, 97–99, 107, 128, 212, 216–219, 312, 318
party system
  transformation in, 51
political institutions, 8, 91, 93, 101, 102, 105, 313
political parties
  Conservative Party, 38
  Constitutional Democratic Party (CDP), 48, 49, 53
  Democratic Party (DP), 47, 48
  Democratic Party for the People (DPP), 48, 49
  Democratic Party of Japan (DPJ), 37, 38, 40–42, 46, 47, 53, 58, 64, 203, 204, 299
  Japan Communist Party (JCP), 29, 49
  Japan Innovation Party (JIP), 46–49
  Japan Restoration Party (JRP), 42, 46
  Japan Socialist Party (JSP), 29, 53
  Komeito, 38, 53, 60, 64
  Liberal Democratic Party (LDP)
    campaigning, 54–59, 61–63, 214, 215, 222
    diversified linkage party, 28, 72, 218, 319
    dual candidacy, 60, 200, 298
    factions, 67, 221
    formation of, 28
    former occupations, 220, 221
    LDP-aligned independents, 201
    loss of power, 23, 25, 31, 33, 39, 40, 54, 64, 203–206, 319
    presidential election, 67
    relationship with bureaucrats, 15, 160, 161, 211–213, 220, 221
    seniority, 245, 246
    support groups, 63, 213, 218, 318
    support rates, 51, 53
  Liberal Party (1997), 37, 38
  Liberal Party (2016), 47, 48
  New Frontier Party (NFP), 34, 37
  New Liberal Club, 31
  Nippon Ishin no Kai (JIP), 47
  Party for Future Generations (PFG), 46
  Party for Japanese Kokoro, 47
  Party of Hope, 47, 48
  Peoples' Life First (PLP), 42, 46
  Sakigake, 33, 34
  Social Democratic Party (SDP), 34
  Tokyoites First, 47
  Tomorrow Party of Japan, 42
  Your Party, 42, 46

Index

populism, 316
pork-barrel politics. *See* particularism
prefectural capitals, 250, 254
Public Office Election Law (POEL), 142, 143

Sato Bunsei, 214
Suga Yoshihide, 49

Takeshita Noboru, 246
Tanaka Kakuei, 213, 214
tournaments
    asymmetrically sized groups, 16, 17, 121–123, 125, 229, 232, 236–238, 246–248, 257, 258, 263–265
    collective action, 111
    conditions for, 114, 117, 120
    formal models, 109
    implications of, 11, 110, 111, 127, 129, 130, 136, 169, 170, 207, 208, 224, 317

implicitness, 121
labor economics, 112
law firms, 113, 120
pivotality, 114, 116–119
prizes and prize structure, 9, 10, 14, 115, 118, 120, 123–126, 130, 134–136, 207, 208, 234, 238
ranking methods, 9, 122, 123
turnout, 18, 117–119, 126, 170, 273–275, 299–301
Tractor for the Vote Fields, 223
turnout
    determinants of, 278–283, 301–303, 305–307, 309
    in a tournament. *See* tournaments, turnout

voter surveys, 15, 16, 21, 51, 53, 224, 225, 227, 228

Yamamoto Kozo, 161

www.ingramcontent.com/pod-product-compliance
Ingram Content Group UK Ltd.
Pitfield, Milton Keynes, MK11 3LW, UK
UKHW041855250225
455528UK00006B/47